Sweating Bullets

Notes about Inventing PowerPoint

Robert Gaskins

Vinland Books

San Francisco ● *London*

International Standard Book Number: 978-0-9851424-2-1 (paperback)
Library of Congress Control Number: 2012936438

THE POWERPOINT QUADRANSCENTENNIAL EDITION
First published 2012 by

Vinland Books
2443 Fillmore Street
San Francisco, CA 94115

Vinland Books
27, Old Gloucester Street
London WC1N 3XX

www.vinlandbooks.com

1 3 5 7 9 10 8 6 4 2

For Leanna

CONTENTS

CONTENTS

CONTENTS

PART I: INTRODUCTION TO POWERPOINT

1 Presenting PowerPoint

Any software that is even dimly remembered after twenty-five years cannot have been a failure. So there is no suspense here: the Power-Point saga ends well. We created something new and lots of people wanted to use it. And more than just being remembered, after twenty-five years, PowerPoint is used more widely than ever.

The PowerPoint group evaded great dangers twice, each time pulling out an improbable win. First we were a startup named Forethought; we nearly died many times, but we gained an investment from Apple (its first) and we managed to turn our concept into an acclaimed product. Second, now sought by many suitors, we were an acquisition by Microsoft (its first, also); here we contrived to become an independent business unit and to remain in Silicon Valley, so the product development continued under our control until success was assured.

Each of the early PowerPoint people played an important role in our success, and we were fortunate to have an exceptionally smart and resourceful group. If my telling of the story sometimes seems to read like I'm talking about the work of one person, that is only because I am selectively calling up my own perspective; PowerPoint was realized by the devoted effort of the whole number of us. It was a great honor and a delightful experience to be able to work alongside all these people.

It would be ideal to write what I remember about all the people—more than a hundred—who made major contributions to the formative years of PowerPoint, but I don't have space to describe everyone, even briefly. Faced with this problem, I've restricted myself to mentioning only the people who joined PowerPoint by the time of the acquisition by Microsoft. I remember a great deal about everyone else; my reason for not trying to describe what every single person accomplished is that the scope would be unmanageable.

(Perhaps it will be possible to gather narratives of favorite memories from most of the people who worked on PowerPoint in the early years, and to publish the whole collection together; if so, that compilation will provide a very interesting picture.)

Hence, I have focused here on my own personal experience, which came in four periods, each somewhat unconventional:

1. Before PowerPoint, I learned a number of things that I needed to know, but instead of a conventional path of increasing business responsibility, I spent my time in universities and research labs. I had no experience whatsoever in developing or managing any commercial software products.

2. Three years at a startup (Forethought), but instead of the conventional path of funding a new idea, I joined an existing failed startup investment to carry out a "restart." This meant that instead of having a perfectly clean slate, I needed to deal with a lot of pre-existing factors—some helpful, some not.

3. Five years at a larger company (Microsoft), but instead of the conventional path of being hired and promoted internally, I suddenly materialized as head of a distant acquisition. This meant that I was immediately in a senior position, with lots of access to Bill Gates and other top executives, and with great freedom, but without having any background of established credibility and without a network of internal friends and allies, though also with no lurking enemies.

4. Following that, I retired, and so avoided the conventional path consisting of a startup reprise that ends in ignominious failure.

During the two middle periods, my job resembled what Steve Jobs described when he was at NeXT:

> There needs to be someone who is sort of the keeper and re-iterator of the vision. ... it really helps if there is someone there saying "We are one step closer. The goal definitely exists. It isn't just a mirage out there." So in a thousand and one little and somewhat larger ways, the vision needs to be reiterated. I do that a lot. (Jobs 1985)
>
> *(This is from a video documenting Steve Jobs in the early days of NeXT Computer; at about 14:00 minutes the video shows Steve*

talking with overhead transparencies, sliding a sheet of opaque paper down his slide manually to get a "progressive disclosure" of one point at a time—an effect later automated in PowerPoint.)

It was often my job to be the "keeper and re-iterator of the vision" for PowerPoint, and I constantly worked on explaining that vision. I wrote endless versions of it and gave thousands of pitches about it. Most of what is included here is that vision along with how it was realized.

I think of PowerPoint as being finished at the end of 1992, because that is the time when I retired and left the group—at the moment when version 3.0 had just shipped on both Windows and Macintosh. The whole product framework was completed in that release, as far as I was concerned. The initial innovation that I could do was done then, and this account ends at that same point. The history of PowerPoint since 1992 is beyond my scope, except for a few final ruminations.

Edsger Dijkstra famously remarked in one of his early essays that " 'clarity' has pronounced quantitative aspects," and I have repeated his insight many times over the years (Dijkstra, Structured Programming (EWD249) 1969). Sadly, the length of this account is dismal evidence that, despite some effort, clarity has probably not been achieved.

2 *Contemporary Evidence*

All history, so far as it is not supported by contemporary evidence, is romance.
—Samuel Johnson, in Boswell's *Journal of a Tour to the Hebrides*

I have quoted at length from documents that I wrote at the time when I was working on PowerPoint. Most of these have not been available before, and until now I hadn't looked at them for twenty years or more. The words I wrote then have an authority which can't be matched by anyone's memory—certainly not by mine.

Some of my contemporaneous documents were written for other people to read and some were written only as my own notes. All of them were written for use at the time; I had no spare moments to write anything addressed to posterity or with an eye to its use in the future.

I have used: (1) all my pocket calendars in which I scheduled nearly every meeting and every trip; (2) my complete collection of bound lab notebooks (2,400 pages total) in which I documented nearly every meeting and conversation—often, I find, down to exact quotations within quote marks—along with decisions and major events; and (3) a series of more polished documents that I wrote from time to time addressed to our investors (and potential investors) and to my fellow managers. These include periodic business plans, forecasts and financial projections, product planning documents, and product schedules, along with several one-of-a-kind documents such as a complete short history of Forethought written in the weeks immediately after the shipment of PowerPoint 1.0 and before the Microsoft acquisition.

Nearly all the records I have from that era are on paper, not digital media. Apart from my personal calendars and lab notebooks, almost the only documents that I possess are from the early years of Power-Point as a startup, before Microsoft. When I retired from Microsoft, I purposely did not take with me any company documents or email from the period after the acquisition. Over the years, though, some of the reports I wrote or read then have surfaced in the various legal proceedings and have been made public on the Internet, so occasionally I've run across one that I can quote here.

Quotes attributed to individuals are so quoted in my contemporaneous notes. Extracts from old documents have citations to the reference list, and most previously unpublished documents are now on line. The References section following the text provides details on all sources, with links to online versions.

I have used the name "PowerPoint" throughout these memoirs, although the product was called "Presenter" during its whole initial development and was renamed at the very last moment before shipment. But in all direct quotations from original documents, I have not changed the name "Presenter."

3 The First Qualification of an Historian

I have tried to exclude from this account almost all material that I did not observe first-hand or document to myself at the time.

On a number of topics, the world knows much more now than I could have known back then—for instance, I gather that a lot of material has surfaced about the confusing struggle within Microsoft and IBM over Windows versus OS/2. I haven't tried even to find such material, much less to incorporate it here. On such topics I've just preserved from my own contemporaneous notes the conflicting news and advice that I received within Microsoft at the time, reflecting how bewildering it was for application developers.

The attempt to limit my account to what I observed and recorded at the time at least gives me what Johnson called "the first qualification of an historian":

> The writer of his own life has at least the first qualification of an historian, the knowledge of the truth; and though it may be plausibly objected that his temptations to disguise it are equal to his opportunities of knowing it, yet I cannot but think that impartiality may be expected with equal confidence from him that relates the passages of his own life, as from him that delivers the transactions of another.
>
> —Samuel Johnson, *The Idler*, No. 84, 24 November 1759

There is a lot about later PowerPoint that I don't know, so I can't speak about it. In the twenty years since my departure, the people who remained there when I left, followed by hundreds more, have managed to continually improve the product in ways that I didn't envision, to connect it to all the structure of the new world (such as the Internet), and to maintain it amidst rapid progress. Both Windows and Macintosh have completely changed (several times each, actually) requiring the repeated reimplementation of PowerPoint. Just as a satisfied user of PowerPoint, I can see that the group who have continued the work have done very well. If that weren't true, PowerPoint would now be as long-forgotten as most of the other products introduced twenty-five years ago into that very different world.

I only occasionally speculate about something that happened at Microsoft after I left. My sources for these speculations are usually general news reports. I retain great affection for all the people at Microsoft and for the company, but I've had virtually no contact with them after my retirement, mostly because I was out of the country. Any "insider knowledge" ends on the date of my leaving in late 1992.

4 *Powerful Emotions Recollected in Tranquility*

When the story of PowerPoint was being lived, it was as desperate struggle: a struggle to create a product that nobody much seemed to understand or appreciate, and also a struggle to accomplish that with barely adequate resources amidst constant distractions which could not be neglected.

I had hanging on the wall of my office a Japanese wood-block print triptych by the Meiji artist Yoshitoshi, the set of his prints known as "The Battle at Monjuro Gate, Kanei Temple, Mount Toei" (1874). It shows about a hundred people in confused groups on several levels of a red temple gate, fighting desperately with swords and lances amidst dead bodies—at night, in driving rain, with fires burning in every direction and heavy smoke from cannon. I used to tell people who asked that it was from Yoshitoshi's well-known series of prints entitled *One Hundred Views of the Software Business*.

Unfortunately, it's no longer possible to capture much of the spirit of those days. We look back now from a time when PowerPoint is done and has become known to almost everyone in the world.

Microsoft says that the Office product including PowerPoint is now installed on more than one billion computers, in every country worldwide. Just about every organization in the world uses it, not only companies large and small but entrepreneurs, artists, non-profits, students, governments, and religious leaders. Primary school children must pass exams in using PowerPoint, since their teachers believe that knowing it will be vital to their future success—at all levels of education and in their careers. Steven Pinker says that "these days scientists ... cannot lecture without PowerPoint." Sermons are delivered using PowerPoint in church buildings rebuilt to incorporate large screens for the purpose. The Secretary of State uses PowerPoint to address the United Nations on questions of war and peace. Newspapers and magazines and books mention PowerPoint casually with no explanation needed. Novelists write chapters of their books in PowerPoint. Rich Gold says that "within today's corporation, if you want to communicate an idea to your peers or to your boss or to your employees or to your customer or even to your enemy, you use PowerPoint."

Looking back, it seems that PowerPoint must always have been an obviously great idea. That isn't true at all; it took conviction and determination to pitch the idea repeatedly, hundreds of times, without getting much response, and to keep refining the idea in the face of prolonged skepticism. It's much different before the success comes.

While developing PowerPoint, we faced the very real prospect of liquidation at least every six months. For three Christmases in a row, we took off a week for the holidays only after carefully calculating that we had enough money in the bank to pay our payroll taxes, accrued wages and vacations, and minimal severances, since it seemed almost certain that we would have to liquidate early in the New Year. This made the holidays considerably less festive.

Tom McConnell, from our major investor New Enterprise Associates (NEA), spent a lot of his time then working with Forethought and attending our board meetings along with Dick Kramlich; he wrote me years later that "It's amazing to recall ... that you developed PowerPoint with meager resources ... ." "Meager" certainly captures the situation.

My descriptions of events recollected now sometimes seem coolly calculated, where at the time they were usually improvisations, based on intuition and wild hopes. If you knew ahead of time that your idea was going to have a billion customers, you'd know what to do and you'd have the resources to do it; when we were figuring out what to do, we were just one more unpromising startup, with a blotted history, barely scraping along from stratagem to stratagem.

5 *PowerPoint Has Many Fathers, Especially Three*

There's a saying about how "success has a thousand fathers, but failure is an orphan." The good thing about PowerPoint is that it has been successful enough to have a lot of fathers and mothers claiming it.

Every year or so, someone who played a role in the history of Power-Point, early or late, is interviewed for publication and ends up being represented as pretty much responsible for PowerPoint, and then I get mail complaining about what the interviewee has said. But I don't join in the complaints, because I can almost always see how what has been said is reasonable.

Any really successful major product really does acquire hundreds of fathers and mothers who are justified in taking credit for important parts of that success. Nothing could be more natural than that each of them should most clearly see his own contribution and should magnify its importance. And in addition, there are even more people close to the product who were enthusiastic and who wanted very much to make a vital contribution, even if they never actually were in a position to do so.

But for PowerPoint it's not hard to single out the three people who made the earliest and most critical contributions. First, it was my idea, and I started working on it in July of 1984, and worked alone for about three months, just on the most basic product definition, with many distractions. Second, Dennis Austin very soon joined me, in October

1984, and we then worked closely together for about a year and a half—a lifetime in startup years. Third, in May of 1986, we were joined by Tom Rudkin, and the three of us worked together for about another year—another good long time. At the end of that period, nearly three years altogether of intensive work, we shipped PowerPoint 1.0 for Mac, with the program files on the diskettes dated 20 April 1987.

The foundations of PowerPoint's success were contained in the early decisions made by Bob and Dennis and Tom during the three years leading up to PowerPoint 1.0. More than one billion personal computers today are running software reflecting those early decisions made by the three of us. But the foundations were not enough, and the success of PowerPoint was built also in the early phases when a few other people made vital contributions, as well as in later phases when scores and then hundreds of people were involved in working on it.

Left to right: Tom Rudkin (Wizard #3), Bob Gaskins (Wizard #1), and Dennis Austin (Wizard #2), reunited to collaborate again, this time on solving the problem of how to divide a cake into 200 equal portions. The photo was taken at a celebration held at the Microsoft Silicon Valley campus in Mountain View in the summer of 2007. The inscription reads "Happy 20th Year Anniversary Power Point!" [sic], showing that the proper formatting of the name "PowerPoint" had not even in twenty years yet become familiar to cake decorators. (Photo by Judea Eden, herself Wizard #17.)

6 *All the Wizards in Order of Appearance (Division I)*

We have a canonical list of "all the Graphics Business Unit (GBU) wizards, in order of appearance" which includes the first 119 employees who worked on PowerPoint. The group I knew included those who joined us by the time of the shipment of version 3.0 on Windows and Mac (Division I, 69 people, listed below in this section). After that there was a second group of those who joined prior to moving from the fabled offices on Sand Hill Road (Division II, 50 more people, in the next section).

All of the first group of people listed below can say that they worked on PowerPoint when it was still a real startup venture with unknown outcome, and when it still was managed by the people who began it. Chances of making a big contribution are high under these circumstances, and many of the people in this list were absolutely critical—as I well know, because I worked closely with all of them and remember them vividly.

The list is called "GBU Wizards" because it is the official list of employees of the Microsoft Graphics Business Unit, with Microsoft dates of service bridged back to date of hiring at Forethought. We called ourselves "the wizards of Menlo Park" since we were located in Menlo Park, California (and those of us who had read biographies of Edison knew that it was in memory of a wizard from a different Menlo Park).

Thus, Bob Gaskins was Wizard #1, Dennis Austin was Wizard #2, Tom Rudkin was Wizard #3, and so forth, as the earliest-hired of the Forethought employees to join the Microsoft GBU. (There were other employees of Forethought who didn't join the GBU at the acquisition; but a couple of them did re-join us, and I'll discuss them later.) As is typical of startups, the "order of appearance" was taken seriously in conferring informal status.

Notice the very small numbers: there are only six people on this list who worked on PowerPoint 1.0 for Mac: there's me, and there were the original architect and developer (Dennis Austin), the second architect and developer (Tom Rudkin), one program manager (Keith Sturdivant), one QA engineer (Robert Lotz), and one public-facing person handling reception, telephones, events, and much else (Kathi Baker). After the six of us, everyone else in the PowerPoint saga joined a company that already had a successful shipping product—a major watershed event.

We also used contract writers, contract print designers, and contract manufacturing companies, and we commissioned some code from consulting developers Tom Evslin of Solutions, Inc. and Tony Meadow and his colleagues at Bear River Associates. There were also essential people in Forethought doing sales and marketing and accounting and such for our other products, who added PowerPoint to their product lists.

After the first product shipment, we had Harris Meyers join us in development. We were lucky enough to have Aniko Somogyi join us at the very moment of the acquisition; she had previously worked at Microsoft in Redmond and had just moved to our area independently. Dennis Abbe, a critical development resource, actually signed on prior to the acquisition but didn't relocate and report in until after it happened. After those three more, everyone beginning with Wizard #10 joined a functioning Microsoft business unit, which, although still far from any real success, was obviously beyond the harshest uncertainties of a startup, since it was part of Microsoft.

A year later, when PowerPoint 2.0 for Mac shipped (a big step forward), the total headcount was still only 16. Two years after that, when PowerPoint 2.0 for Windows shipped (a truly major milestone), total headcount was still only 36. More people were added soon afterward so they could contribute to the huge following version, but after a further two years, when PowerPoint 3.0 had shipped on both platforms, headcount had less than doubled—still below 70 people hired, and actually fewer than that, since half a dozen people had moved on over the five years. By then it was obvious that PowerPoint really was a big success, and had a good chance of continuing that success in the future.

There were a total of 100 or so people in our building—we hosted a large crew from our vendor Publishing Power, who managed all the writing and print production, we had people from Genigraphics working on product components, and we had contract testers to supplement our own QA staff, but these people are not listed in the wizards list (apart from a few honorary members). This was the point at which I left the group, so these are the people that I knew very well.

There are two special cases of people on this list who appear out of logical order. Darrell Boyle, Wizard #35, had been the VP of Marketing at Forethought during its early phases, even slightly before my time, but had left soon after we started working on the PowerPoint idea. Three years after the acquisition, he rejoined us to head marketing for the GBU. Glenn Hobin, Wizard #62, had been the VP of Sales at Forethought during our critical final period just before the acquisition. He left then, but rejoined us more than four years later to sell PowerPoint to the Microsoft sales force. (Both of these stories come up in later sections in more detail.)

All the Wizards in Order of Appearance (Division I)

1	Bob Gaskins	7/5/84
2	Dennis Austin	10/22/84
3	Tom Rudkin	5/1/86
4	Keith Sturdivant	12/10/86
5	Robert Lotz	1/30/87
6	Kathi Baker	2/28/87

[First Customer Ship, PowerPoint 1.0 for Macintosh]

7	Harris Meyers	6/8/87
8	Aniko Somogyi	8/10/87
9	Dennis Abbe	10/26/87
10	Lewis Levin	11/16/87
11	Bob Lagier	12/16/87
12	Sharon Meyers	1/25/88
13	Tuan Nguyen	3/14/88
14	Bob Safir	3/14/88
15	Rick Hawes	3/28/88
16	Pam Miller	4/25/88

[First Customer Ship, PowerPoint 2.0 for Macintosh]

17	Judea Eden	7/18/88
18	Ron Ullmann	8/15/88
19	Don Miller	10/3/88
20	Barb Jernigan	10/24/88
21	Ralph Peterson	12/5/88
22	Nelia Craig	1/24/89
23	Lynette Moore	2/6/89
24	Andre Brogli	3/1/89
25	Joan Hoshino	3/6/89
26	Connie Clark	3/13/89
27	Dave Stearns	4/28/89
28	Cathy Harris	6/19/89

29	Dave Parker	6/19/89	
30	Pat Ford	7/3/89	
31	Charleen Mininfield	7/10/89	
32	Lucy Peterson	10/23/89	
33	Kathleen Richards	11/6/89	
34	Nola Donato	11/27/89	
35	Darrell Boyle	3/21/90	(also pre-1.0)
36	Kathy Friend	4/4/90	

[First Customer Ship, PowerPoint 2.0 for Windows]

37	Linda Fitzgerald	6/20/90
38	Soo Hahn	7/9/90
39	Jim Bartram	7/15/90
40	Laura Tillett	7/23/90
41	Paul Warrin	8/6/90
42	Yalin Chen	9/14/90
43	Bethann Martin	9/14/90
44	Bruce Lee	10/1/90
45	Amy Whitehurst	10/26/90
46	Cindy Goral	11/8/90
47	Bronwen Martin	11/8/90
48	Alice Wang	12/3/90
49	Eunice Yan	1/2/91
50	Pierre Aoun	1/7/91
51	Dan Hoffmann	2/4/91
52	Anders Kierulf	2/19/91
53	Kim Kinzie	2/19/91
54	Starlene Burgett	2/19/91
55	Dave Kesterson	4/19/91

[First Customer Ship, PowerPoint 3.0 for Windows]

56	Millani Lew	6/24/91
57	Brendan Busch	7/1/91
58	Christoph Ammann	9/2/91
59	Sue Ann Pratt	9/9/91
60	Annette Kronmiller	9/19/91

61	Karen Sipprell	10/8/91	
62	Glenn Hobin	10/21/91	(also pre-1.0)
63	Roz Ho	10/23/91	
64	Rich Sneiderman	10/31/91	
65	George Santino	10/31/91	
66	Brian Jackson	11/25/91	
67	Dorothy Adams	12/20/91	
68	Reidun Valo	1/6/92	
69	Hannes Ruescher	8/12/92	

[First Customer Ship, PowerPoint 3.0 for Macintosh]

There are also a handful of people who couldn't appear on the GBU roll of wizards, because they were never GBU employees, but were also critical to PowerPoint. These people come up in the story, and can be known as "Honorary Wizards." In no particular order:

Dick Kramlich (New Enterprise Associates)

Phil Lamoreaux (Lamoreaux Partners)

Rob Campbell (Forethought)

Tom Evslin (Solutions)

Tony Meadow (Bear River Associates)

Judith and Michael Maurier (Publishing Power)

Sandy Beetner (Genigraphics)

Rosemary Abowd (Genigraphics)

Mike Maples (Microsoft)

Jeff Raikes (Microsoft)

7 All the Wizards in Order of Appearance (Division II)

After my time, about 50 more people joined PowerPoint over the final two years that the group spent on Sand Hill Road before it was moved. There were still a lot of the early PowerPoint wizards around, so these later people could also make a substantial contribution.

A couple of names stand out in this second list. Vijay Vashee (Wizard #85) was a very early Microsoft person who was part of an internal group working to create a PowerPoint competitor prior to the acquisition of Forethought, and who played a role in the acquisition decisions.

After that he went on to do many other things at the company, during which time we kept in touch, and five years later, when I left, he was the one selected to move down from Redmond and take over management of the PowerPoint group. Ric Bretschneider (Wizard #77) joined just after I left, stayed with the group for 17 years (twice as long as I stayed), and in years to come headed the program management of PowerPoint for a long period. Doubtlessly many others among these people had distinguished careers at Microsoft, but they were after my time, and I didn't get to know most of them.

This list ends at the move from Sand Hill Road in late 1994, and of course there have been hundreds of people who contributed to Power-Point in the eighteen years since then, but this makes a convenient point at which to define the end of "the early days."

All the Wizards in Order of Appearance (Division II)

70	Neeraj Maithel	9/21/92
71	George Chinn	10/12/92
72	Mike Malloy	11/11/92
73	Rob Nixon	11/13/92
74	Bob Gregg	11/30/92
75	Donna Simonides	12/14/92
76	Mark Weigand	12/14/92
77	Ric Bretschneider	1/4/93
78	Jeremy Giddings	1/4/93
79	Susan Grabau	1/4/93
80	Marc Keller	1/4/93
81	Donna Reynolds	1/4/93
82	Cathy Albiez	1/11/93
83	Laura Hoffman	1/11/93
84	John Tafoya	2/15/93
85	Vijay Vashee	2/25/93
86	Chris Burroughs	3/1/93
87	Ly Hoang	3/1/93
88	Brian Rose	4/19/93
89	Merilee Shackleton	5/27/93
90	Jim Hansen	6/1/93

91	Mark Carlile	6/7/93
92	Teresa Fung	6/7/93
93	Robert Parker	6/14/93
94	Anil Mehra	6/21/93
95	Elliott Ng	6/28/93
96	Robert Scott	7/1/93
97	Peter Wu	8/16/93
98	Imran Qureshi	9/7/93
99	Howard Cooperstein	10/4/93
100	Melanie Pratt	11/9/93
101	Waltraut Monroe	11/15/93
102	Brian Henrikson	11/19/93
103	Shelly Albers	12/15/93
104	Dave Pond	12/15/93
105	Shubhangi Kanetkar	1/19/94
106	Peter Li	2/21/94
107	Farhang Zamani	5/2/94
108	Bakul Patel	6/6/94
109	Mike Kernaghan	6/13/94
110	Tony Lin	6/27/94
111	Eric Wilfrid	8/1/94
112	Liam Patel	8/8/94
113	Teresa Conway	8/15/94
114	Greg Nield	8/22/94
115	David Gorbet	9/6/94
116	May Quan	9/12/94
117	Chris Seitzinger	9/19/94
118	Kasia Kranz	9/26/94
119	John Bowler	10/20/94

8 Presentation Formats before PowerPoint

A student entering college today possibly never has seen an overhead transparency nor seen an overhead projector, and perhaps never has seen any presentational use of a 35mm slide or a 35mm projector.

PowerPoint, designed to produce those old formats, has actually re-placed them. Students entering college today almost certainly know how to use PowerPoint. They have grown up in a world (since 1995 or so) in which PowerPoint has always been the ordinary way to do things, not a novel replacement.

But for decades before PowerPoint, people made presentations and prepared visuals to be projected during those presentations. The tradi-tional pre-computer formats discussed here are no longer current, but they were the original inspiration for PowerPoint, and PowerPoint was designed to create them before it later replaced them. It will be helpful to know what these formats were, to understand how PowerPoint evolved, so I'll give a quick overview.

PowerPoint was originally designed to make it easier to prepare ac-tual overhead transparencies, actual 35mm slides, and video substi-tutes for the "multimedia" shows that used large banks of 35mm projectors, all sequenced and synchronized.

Overhead transparencies

Overhead transparencies were clear films, the size of a sheet of pa-per, and were projected from a lighted platform through a mirror and lens positioned "overhead" on a raised arm. They were usually produced by photocopying a page that had been typed by the department secre-tary (the only person with a typewriter, classically an IBM Selectric with Orator font typeball), with hand-drawn diagrams. (Before photocopi-ers, transparencies were written and drawn with opaque or transparent inks.) There was no color, because copiers produced only black-and-white images. A corrected overhead could be typed and brought to the meeting room "hot off the copier" in a few minutes, at a cost of pennies.

PowerPoint 1.0 (for Mac, April 1987) produced overhead transpar-encies on a black-and-white Macintosh for laser printing (normally on paper, to be photocopied to transparencies). Presenters could now directly control their own overheads and would no longer have to work through the person with the typewriter. PowerPoint handled the task of making the overheads all look alike; one change reformats them all. Typographic fonts were better than an Orator typeball, and charts and diagrams could be imported from MacDraw, MacPaint, and Excel, thanks to the new Mac clipboard.

Color 35mm slides

Color 35mm slides (image area measuring 24mm by 36mm) were placed in two-inch-square mounts in a circular tray for Kodak Carousel projectors. They were photographed from hand-lettered or typeset proofs or created on minicomputer workstations. Slides had to be prepared by a corporate art department or outside service bureau, for up to several hundred dollars per slide. A corrected 35mm slide could be reset, photographed, processed, and mounted in a few days, or overnight if corporate lives were at stake.

PowerPoint 2.0 (for Mac, May 1988, and for Windows, May 1990) added color 35mm slides, transmitting the resulting file over a modem to Genigraphics for imaging on Genigraphics' film recorders and photo processing in Genigraphics' labs overnight. Genigraphics was the leading professional service bureau, having developed its own computer systems for its artists (based on Digital Equipment Corporation PDP-11 minicomputers).

"Multimedia"

Multimedia was a name used for slide shows that added the illusion of motion, using a bank of from three up to two dozen slide projectors, all focused on the same screen, each with an external iris to control fades and dissolves, and all controlled by inaudible signals synchronized to an audiotape. Both the technology and the professional work needed to produce and perform such shows were expensive and time-consuming.

PowerPoint 3.0 (for Windows, May 1992, and for Mac, September 1992) added video out to feed the new video projectors, with effects that could replace a bank of synchronized slide projectors. This version added fades, dissolves, and other transitions, as well as animation of text and pictures, and could incorporate video clips with synchronized audio.

9 How Different Presentation Formats Were Used

In 1984, when work began on PowerPoint, a presenter could choose among overhead transparencies, color 35mm slides, and a "multimedia" show. These formats were prepared in different ways, with different equipment, and reflected orders-of-magnitude cost differences in terms of time, effort, and money, as just described.

Overhead presentations

Overhead presentations were used for "talking in meetings," designed for a fully lighted room (hence black letters on a clear background) where the speaker and others could see one another and inter-act. Transparencies were not a performance in and of themselves but a focus point. They were put on the projector manually one by one, and it was easy to leave the screen blank (lighted) to talk about something else or to answer a question. Overheads could be clear and elegant but couldn't have fancy decorations, because none was practical.

Color 35mm slide presentations

Color 35mm slide presentations were used for more finished "per-formances." The artists who produced them added drawings and graph-ic decorations. Slide projectors required a darkened room, hence light text on darker and subtly shaded backgrounds. Not only were the lis-teners in darkness, usually so were the presenters. It was nearly impos-sible to leave the screen blank (making the room pitch black), so discussion and questions were discouraged. The presenter's slides had to carry the entire show while the lights were down, so they needed higher finish and greater entertainment value.

"Multimedia" presentations

Multimedia shows were so costly that many people never saw one. With up to two dozen projectors synchronized to a sound track to create the illusion of motion from many hundreds of slides, a live pre-senter had to be rigidly scripted and had no way to tolerate interrup-tions. The purpose was to amaze the audience with technical and visual wizardry; content was largely secondary.

Among these options, overhead presentations, with the lowest level of finish, were appropriate for internal meetings (especially with execu-tives), for academic talks, and for classroom use, as well as for almost any everyday purpose. Color 35mm slide presentations, with a higher degree of finish, were appropriate for formal sales calls or for speeches to large audiences, where time and budget were available for their prep-aration. Multimedia presentations, with the most polished finish, were appropriate for only highly theatrical occasions with large audiences where entertainment was the main goal.

Against this background, we conceived PowerPoint to give control to the presenter by taking advantage of graphical personal computers, specifically Macintosh and Windows. We introduced three major ver-sions over its first five years, 1987 to 1992, corresponding to the three kinds of presentations: PowerPoint 1.0 made black-and-white overheads; PowerPoint 2.0 added color 35mm slides; and PowerPoint 3.0 added video effects to replace multimedia shows.

By 1992, PowerPoint could make presentations in all three styles, but there was no confusion, because physical media still imposed strict distinctions: overheads had to be black-and-white to be laser-printed and photocopied onto transparency film; color 35mm slides were sent over a modem to Genigraphics and returned in two-inch mounts; and multimedia-replacement shows (from PowerPoint) were delivered by connecting a computer directly to a video projector, which was still a very rare animal. Presenters used PowerPoint to make overheads and occasionally to make color 35mm slides; initially, most didn't have the chance to try video, because video projectors (and even large monitors) were of such unsatisfactory quality.

After 1992, over a period of about ten years, the combination of powerful laptops and small, bright, less expensive video projectors displaced all previous projection devices. Overhead projectors disappeared from conference rooms and classrooms, and in mid-2003 Kodak made the stunning announcement that it would stop manufacturing slide projectors the following year. In their place, you could use a laptop to project video.

This meant that every presentation could now mix the features of all three styles, so gradually the three styles became less distinct. With no constraints from physical media, presenters had no limitation and increasingly no firm intuition as to what was appropriate. Most presentations had previously been done using overheads, and most presenters had used nothing else. Presenters now began to experiment by adding features formerly used only with 35mm slides (such as vaguely related clip art, or subtly shaded backgrounds). They tried adding elements from multimedia shows (such as sound effects, attention-grabbing transitions between slides, moving text, and bullet points that "flew" to their places from somewhere off screen).

Much of this was novel and interesting the first few times, but virtually none of the extraneous decoration or entertainment had any purpose or benefit in the kinds of meetings where overheads had been used. Successive versions of PowerPoint made these elaborate features easier and more tempting to use, leading to more complaints about bad presentations. PowerPoint could still make very straightforward "overhead-style" presentations, but that style was not used as often as real overheads had been.

PART II: PREPARING FOR POWERPOINT

10 *"Why Did You Pick This Idea to Work On?"*

One of the questions on recent application forms of Y Combinator (for startup founders seeking initial funding) has been:

> Why did you pick this idea to work on?
> Do you have domain expertise in this area?
> How do you know people need what you're making?
> —Y Combinator application form, W2012 (Y Combinator 2012)

In my case, looking back, it seems as if I had spent many years gaining "domain expertise in the area"—so much so that it now seems inevitable that I would create PowerPoint, but it didn't seem at all that way at the time. I can identify six different strands in my background that converged to give me the idea for PowerPoint and the understanding of why people needed it and would eagerly pay for it:

> *1. I had grown up in the "audio-visual" industry, which included the traditional presentation business, and I had access to market research about that industry that was not widely available.*

This gave me information about what processes people had been using for decades to produce presentation visuals, how difficult it had been, and how much money they had actually been spending, so I could judge the size of the market and how much time and expense could be saved by using PowerPoint.

> *2. I had spent years at university studying "computers and the humanities," dealing with natural languages and their writing systems, typesetting, graphic art, and music on computers.*

21

This gave me knowledge of a lot of relevant software and hardware technology that was not generally known yet, because it was still impractical for use in products and was confined to research labs, but which was obviously going to become practical on future personal computers.

> *3. I had been employed at one of the companies whose culture at all levels was very heavily structured around standardized presentation formats, and I had given many hundreds of presentations in my job.*

This taught me how little control a traditional presenter had over the production of his presentation, and how valuable it would be to cut out the intermediaries and gain much better hands-on personal control—which was valuable for business success, and hence worth money from budgets.

> *4. I had put together a very cumbersome "Rube Goldberg" system of off-the-shelf computers and components to make rudimentary presentation visuals for internal use, and had been astonished to see what vast expenditures of time and energy other people would make just to use it.*

This demonstrated to me that many people wanted presentation visuals so much that they were willing to learn unrealistically difficult systems and to go through extremely complex procedures (or to task their subordinates to do so) in order to get them. From this experience, I concluded that people should be much more eager to use a system which would be simpler and more intuitive.

> *5. I had been on business trips through much of the world, buying technology from many vendors, and had seen first-hand how people at every vendor company used presentations in much the same fashion everywhere, worldwide.*

This taught me that a single presentation product could be used in all countries and languages, so localization would be straightforward, and sales would easily follow the penetration of personal computers in the emerging worldwide market.

> *6. I had engaged in a focused prediction exercise, trying to forecast what applications would become possible for the first time with the transition to WYSIWYG personal computers.*

This led me to formulate the idea that there was a very large class of documents which were sequences of single pages (that is, did not flow from page to page like a word processor), with complex layout of each page—such things as flyers, menus, brochures, sets of retail point-of-sale signs, and presentation visuals. Documents of this type were impractically hard to create using an Apple II or an MS-DOS PC, and would be much easier to create visually using "What You See Is What You Get" (WYSIWYG) systems such as Macintosh or Windows.

I'll expand briefly on each one of these six strands. Together they explain pretty well where I acquired "domain expertise," why I picked the PowerPoint idea to work on, and how I could be so certain that I could make the software and that, when I did, many people would buy it gratefully. As Paul Graham of Y Combinator further says,

> You can't build things users like without understanding them. I mentioned earlier that the most successful startups seem to have begun by trying to solve a problem their founders had. Perhaps there's a rule here: perhaps you create wealth [defined as "= how much people want something × the number who want it"] in proportion to how well you understand the problem you're solving, and the problems you understand best are your own.
>
> That's just a theory. What's not a theory is the converse: if you're trying to solve problems you don't understand, you're hosed. (Graham, Mistakes That Kill 2006)

11 The Audio-Visual Industry

From my earliest childhood, my father owned and ran a group of photographic businesses. These included retail sales of amateur cameras and projectors (still and movie), professional studio and press photographic equipment, industrial and scientific photographic equipment, and "audio-visual" equipment. Like most family businesses, ours dominated the life of the entire family. Our most memorable family vacations were every few years when we went to visit the Eastman Kodak Co. in Rochester, N.Y. (The idea that Kodak would file for bankruptcy in 2012 and exit the camera business is hard for me to believe; it was the most established institution of my childhood.) In later years my father was a principal in an unsuccessful startup to make the first all-automatic camera, which was a marketing success but with bad technology, and then was the head of the U.S. subsidiary of a major Japanese audio-visual manufacturer, Eiki Corporation, and in that role acquired a large American audio-visual manufacturer (Bell & Howell) to merge into the Japanese company.

The category of "audio-visual" is strangely named, but that was the term generally used for the whole industry; for instance, my father was prominent in the National Audio-Visual Association (NAVA) which held gigantic national conferences. His audio-visual business included motion-picture cameras and sound projectors, professional equipment for theaters and for scientific research, a local rental library of 16mm movies (a distant and cumbersome ancestor of Netflix), all kinds of audio recording equipment from broadcast use to tiny spy recorders, and even early photocopiers. There were also specialized presentation tools, from "flip charts" (large pads of paper, bound at the top and mounted on a tripod stand) to "flannel boards" (large flannel-covered panels to which prepared graphics could be stuck like an extremely gentle, and silent, hook-and-loop material).

The audio-visual business included all kinds of materials for making presentation visuals by hand—transparent films, colored adhesive films to cut into shapes, colored transparent inks and rub-down type for text, multiple strips of cardboard (one bullet point high) hinged together to be used for "progressive disclosure" of points, cardboard mounts for overheads (like picture frames, always with rounded corners), and stacks of transparent films all hinged to the edge of a single cardboard frame for "progressive additions" of elements to a diagram. There was a varied inventory of overhead projectors, from powerful auditorium models to ordinary classroom or boardroom models and folding semi-portable overhead projectors for sales calls. There were also ordinary and specialized 35m slide projectors, and tools for synchronizing, cross-fading, and sequencing them.

So, without even realizing my special information, I grew up with free access to all the technology and machines and supplies that were used for making presentation visuals in the time before computers.

There was later one other big advantage of my father's knowing people throughout the audio-visual industry. Among his friends was an old Army buddy from World War II named Tom Hope; Tom had been a long-time employee of Eastman Kodak in Rochester, and had left Kodak to write an insider newsletter, *Hope Reports*, with original market research about the audio-visual industry. When I got interested in PowerPoint, I was able to learn through my father's contacts with Tom Hope the basic market facts, such as how many overheads and how many 35mm slides were made each year, and how much money was spent on them. These numbers were not widely known and were not easily available to other people in computer software companies, but they convinced me (and helped me to convince investors) that a product like PowerPoint would find fully funded budgets, in innumerable companies, just waiting to be spent.

12 Computers and the Humanities

I was admitted to the Ph.D. program in the English Department at UC Berkeley in 1968. My intention was to specialize in Shakespeare and pursue an academic career teaching literature, but before I registered for my first classes, I read the catalogue and discovered classes in the Computer Science Department. At that time, Computer Science at Berkeley was a department in the College of Letters and Science, spun off from the Mathematics Department, with no connection at all to the Electrical Engineering Department in the Engineering School (to which it would much later be joined in a shotgun marriage); for this reason I was able to enroll in its courses.

My advisor, Josephine Miles, a noted poet, agreed that some exposure to computers would be broadening, so I enrolled in a beginning programming class. I was immediately enthralled, took all the classes I could (CDC 6400 assembly language from Butler Lampson was memorable), and soon I formally broadened my studies; I was approved to undertake an "individual interdisciplinary Ph.D. program" combining all of the degree requirements for a Ph.D. in each of the Departments of Computer Science, Linguistics, and English.

I soon met Laura Gould, daughter and granddaughter of celebrated Berkeley mathematical luminaries, who was teaching for the first time a course she had created about the use of computers for research in the humanities, and I learned a great deal from her. Laura and I wrote a textbook for her class about using the language Snobol4 for humanities research (Gaskins and Gould, Snobol4: A Computer Language for the Humanities 1972), because Berkeley had an excellent Snobol4 compiler for the CDC6400 computer. The Snobol4 compiler was being implemented by Charles Simonyi, a student then, who later would go on to work on the Bravo word processor at Xerox PARC, and then transplant Bravo ideas to Microsoft to be the basis for Word, where I met him again twenty years later. Laura's office mate was Jim Gray, at the time

25

also still a student himself, who put a copy of Donald Knuth's volume 1 in my hands and told me to read it until I understood why it was the greatest book ever written (sound advice).

When I was at Berkeley, beginning in the late 1960s, computers were still kept in large secure rooms with raised floors; users prepared programs and data by punching holes in cards, and received back output printed on big stacks of continuous-fold paper by printers that could only print fixed lines of characters (and most of the printers at Berkeley then could print only upper-case letters). This was an environment made for using computers to study physics or chemistry.

But I tried to use computers to study languages and literature and music and art. Among many other projects, I was the Chief Programmer for the Berkeley Machine Translation Project, trying to develop linguistic techniques to translate Chinese into English; we entered Chinese text using giant teleprinters with hundreds of keys to create Chinese telecodes on spools of paper tape for input, and for output we drew Chinese characters using very slow pen plotters (maybe an hour a page). I also worked on computer typesetting in multiple languages, including ancient Egyptian hieroglyphic for a Berkeley Dictionary of Late Egyptian, on writing computer poetry, and on a number of art and graphics and music projects. I learned a lot about representing human-language texts and documents in a computer, about representing tunes and musical structures, and about representing pictures and drawings. This often seemed mostly a waste of time, because it was so poorly matched to the batch-oriented large mainframe computers of the day and their limited input and output devices.

The advanced development projects at Berkeley, at that time, were time-sharing systems accessed through clunking teletype machines over slow telephone lines, which at that time were being widely touted as the great future systems that would allow many people to interactively share one of the large computers. Some of my friends were working at Berkeley Computer Corporation (BCC), creating another such system. But those systems were no more suitable for rich typeset text, graphics, or music. What were then called "compound documents" containing text, graphics, tables, foreign languages and much more could not be electronically produced in the age of teletype machines and character-mapped white-on-green screens with 24 lines of 80 characters each; they also could not be printed in the era of typewriter-like printers that could print only the characters on the typeball, and line printers that could print only the characters on a chain or drum.

So my interest was naturally drawn to a competing, but less-respectable, line of thought: that, somehow, every person should have an individual, dedicated, single-user computer—even though that was then almost unthinkably expensive. Most "smart" people in computer science thought large time-sharing systems with terminals would be far better and that the pathetically weak prototype personal computers wouldn't amount to much for a long time—John McCarthy, who was as smart as they come, is frequently cited as a proponent of this view. But there were hints of change. After all, Unix (early 1970s) was named in reaction to "Multics," an overly elaborate time-sharing system; Unix was to be "one of whatever Multics was many of." When BCC failed (also early 1970s), many of the people I knew there moved to Xerox PARC and began working on extravagant single-user computers, although they had to build their own emulation of a PDP-10 time-sharing system first, as a tool to run needed software. For the largely unappreciated story of how the idea of single-user computers evolved, see the excellent *Computing in the Middle Ages: A View from the Trenches 1955–1983*, by Severo M. Ornstein (Ornstein 2002).

Ten years after I arrived at Berkeley, I decided it was time to leave. I had completed a vast amount of work, everything but writing a dissertation after the topic had been defended, but I thought it was more important to move to Silicon Valley and work on software for personal computers. It was still fairly early—Bill Gates was still in Albuquerque writing software for the MITS Altair, and in the preceding year the Commodore PET, the Tandy TRS-80, and the Apple II had all been introduced. What had changed was that single-user computers seemed to some people like they might become practical. Even though the earliest personal computers were extremely limited, they almost immediately led many more people to think about creating word processors and other programs to manipulate human language, about creating spreadsheets to produce graphical charts and diagrams, about creating games with pictures and music, and about all kinds of things that I knew about. When I circulated my résumé, I found myself much in demand by real companies in Silicon Valley, with dozens of offers of jobs to continue working on the same kinds of problems that had recently been merely airy academic research.

So, without knowing it, I had a lot of preparation for working on the PowerPoint idea. PowerPoint would involve manipulating and combining text in different languages and scripts, typesetting in real time, creating diagrams, drawing pictures and charts, and even handling

video and sound, with output to many different kinds of graphics printers and displays. All the things I had studied when they were thought to
be impractical turned out to be practical on personal computers, at
least as seen through our optimism, and turned out to be just what I
needed to know to execute the PowerPoint idea and to avoid mistakes
and dead ends.

13 *Northern Telecom Company Culture*

It would be possible to write a book about how I came to join Bell-
Northern Research (BNR), about what kind of company it was, about
the many interesting experiences I had there, and about the remarkable
group of people I was able to gather to work in my new department
called Computer Science Research.

Here I want to focus on just one tiny aspect: the fact that everyone in
the company and in its parent companies used overheads all the time.

Bell-Northern Research was the counterpart of Bell Laboratories,
but for Canada. Its joint parents were also organized like the American
companies to which they had once been related, with Northern Telecom (formerly Northern Electric) being the counterpart of the manufacturer Western Electric, and Bell Canada being the counterpart of the
operating Bell telephone company. Bell-Northern Research had the
largest research and development operation in Canada, and had just
opened a new principal U.S. laboratory in Palo Alto.

BNR was an excellent place to experience a large company in which
almost everyone made and used presentation visuals. For some reason,
BNR and its parents, Bell Canada and Northern Telecom, had a corporate culture that was centered on overhead transparencies. The standard format for department and division reports was a set of pages, each
with a reduced-size overhead at the top, and the remainder of the page
filled with the written report corresponding to the topics on the overhead, carefully written in full sentences and paragraphs. For project
reviews, there was a standard "program" of slides in a prescribed order,
each slide on a prescribed topic, with money figures presented in
standardized tables and a lot of other standard features. The manager
seeking approval presented the slides in long meetings with a lot of
other comparable presentations, and also prepared the full-form "book"
of pages, each with a slide at the top and expansion below, including
fuller financials.

For big announcements, a set of overheads would be faxed down from Canada, the fax pages photocopied onto overhead transparencies, and then a local manager would place the overheads while a voice over a speakerphone from headquarters gave the presentation.

The fact that thousands of managers used overheads every day, in BNR and also in Northern Telecom and Bell Canada, gave rise to some of the same sociological network effects that Rich Gold of Xerox PARC wrote about insightfully twenty years later, after PowerPoint had become established. Presentations were definitely the way of building consensus around new project ideas; a proponent would go around from group to group, presenting and building solidarity, while dealing with objections. Standard corporate slides with very general content about goals would be included to indicate that the presenter was fully on board with corporate objectives. Individual slides would be exchanged between groups, with credits, to indicate ties of solidarity and trust between groups. (See Rich Gold (Gold 2002).) Even though overheads were still very hard to make—we're talking entirely about traditional manual techniques here—the community at BNR was so exceptionally intense in its devotion to overheads that one could get an idea of what might happen in a world with a program like PowerPoint that would make it much easier to produce overheads.

I had a related experience when I participated in the "Anpac" task force at Northern Telecom, an effort to formulate NT's corporate strategy for personal computers and networks. A group of fifteen or so people flew into Minneapolis every Monday morning for six months to work together until flying home on Friday. Our task was to prepare recommendations to the senior global management of Northern Telecom, and to deliver those recommendations as presentations. This was a very expensive task force; all its members were highly paid, we had expensive research and consultants, and we were provided with apartments and leased cars in Minneapolis for the whole period, with all expenses covered, including transportation home every weekend and back every Monday.

We would gather around a conference table and assemble our thoughts on whiteboards. Then we would watch as one of us sketched out an overhead transparency in pencil on a piece of paper. The paper drafts would be given to MaryAnn, our full-time dedicated assistant and the most important person, because MaryAnn had an IBM Selectric typewriter with an Orator typeball and a keycard to work the photocopier. The taskforce would sit around our conference room chatting, while we waited for MaryAnn to type the overhead drafts and photo-copy them. Then we would mark up her typing to correct typos, alter positioning, adjust prominence, and so forth, and give it back to her to retype and recopy while we chatted again. It seemed like such a bizarre way to waste time. But most of the taskforce members couldn't type, and those of us (programmers) who could type had utterly no way to get a typewriter. Eventually our senior executives would show up, and we would perform our carefully rehearsed and scripted overhead per-formance, and then go back to working on the next presentation.

I thought: what if we actually *had* this system of personal computers linked in networks that we are designing on these overheads and we are urging our managers to let us build? What would we do with it? We would make overheads.

14 How Much Pain Will They Endure?

One important reference point was the system that my group at BNR had built, between 1979 and 1982, to make overheads for our own presentations. This system was so cumbersome to use that it almost amounted to an unplanned laboratory experiment in how painful you could make a presentation system and still have the lab animals clamor to use it.

The text for overheads was typed into a plain text document using a terminal connected to the famously complex Emacs text editor on a PDP-11/70, with the desired content surrounded by a lot of formatting macro invocations written in Don Knuth's TEX language (we installed a copy of Stanford's distribution of the TEX system on our DEC-20 / PDP-10). No illustrations could be created in TEX, so they had to be drawn on a Three Rivers PERQ workstation running its own operating system, using a locally written bitmap editor with roughly the style of MacPaint (written by Karen Bedard). The text file from Emacs on the PDP-11 was then uploaded to the DEC-20 along with files of TEX macro definitions (written by Lynne A. Price, Whitfield Diffie, and me), and the picture files from the PERQ were uploaded to the DEC-20, using the lab's in-ternal network (all the DEC-20 stuff and TEX stuff was done by Patrick Milligan). Since TEX didn't know how to insert pictures, the pictures had to be post-processed on the DEC-20; the bitmap for each picture was torn into small tiles, each the size of a character, and one or more pseudo-fonts were created in TEX's font format, with each "character" in the pseudo-font being a tiny tile from the picture, and also pseudo-text was created to invoke those characters (text like "abcde" for five of the tiles) and was inserted into the TEX document where you wanted the picture to appear. TEX thought it was typesetting only characters from fonts, but some abutting blocks of characters looked like pictures. Then you ran the TEX program on the DEC-20, to create an output file.

At this point, you still had never seen *any* representation of the output! The user was entirely blind. Then, in a separate process, you ran the TEX output file through a program which reformatted it and spooled it to a Versatec plotter designed for Navy shipboard use, which printed the output on a continuous roll of grainy thermal paper, eleven inches wide—the output looked like that from an early Mac Image-Writer, but with inferior contrast from the thermal paper. The Versatec was supposed to slice its roll of paper into letter-size sheets, but the cutter usually didn't work, so we kept a pair of scissors tied to the printer on a string. Any mistake meant going back to Emacs on the PDP-11, editing the TEX formatting text in Emacs, uploading the corrected text file again to the DEC-20, and repeating the whole process. When the output looked OK, it could be photocopied onto overhead transparencies, enhancing the contrast in the photocopying. As an alternative output, we could generate a TEX output file on the DEC-20 for our Alphatype CRS phototypesetter (an exact duplicate of Knuth's setup at Stanford—Don Knuth would come over and use our typesetter occasionally when his own was down for maintenance). This machine had to be kept in our photographic darkroom, and generated individual pages of photographic paper, which were then developed in liquid chemicals that required constant maintenance. Needless to say, photo-typeset overheads were made very seldom. (My group at BNR later got a huge prototype laser marking engine from Canon, but we had to build our own hardware and software interface to drive it from the DEC-20, and that job wasn't completed when I left BNR in 1984, so not a sheet of paper ever went through it.)

Of course, we didn't intentionally put together such an obstacle course. It was just our best effort with our existing equipment to do our jobs, which involved making a lot of presentations. It was never intended for use by anyone else.

But the most amazing part of the experience in using the setup just described was that BNR people from outside my group, from the executive suite and from all the real development groups with deliverables and schedules, lined up to take classes on Emacs, on Unix for the PDP-

11/70, on the T$_E$X system and our local macros, on DEC's TOPS-20 operating system, on the Three Rivers PERQs and their operating system, on the locally written prototype bitmap editor, on the conversion of pictures to fonts, and on how the whole process worked. They actually learned how to do it all and soon filled the computers to overcapacity, which only made the whole process worse. People wanted better overheads badly enough to go through this entirely unrealistic amount of complex effort.

Note that the in-house system at BNR took *much* longer to use than just typing and drawing overheads; so working through all those complex processes did not save any time. It did improve quality somewhat. It required literally millions of dollars of computing equipment—the DEC-20s were hugely expensive mainframes, in a raised-floor computer center. Notably, for managers, who gave most of the presentations, it also did *not* bring them into personal control of their presentations; they still had to work through others, drawing up handwritten drafts for transparencies and handing off the work to be done either by an "assistant" (in those days much like a secretary) or by a Ph.D.-level "Member of Scientific Staff" in their department, often by both. The system at BNR did not let a content originator directly control the presentation, but forced working through other hands. It did not save any time or effort, and in fact cost more of both. But later, when I thought about making presentations on Mac and Windows, I realized that they could provide the higher quality, plus save time and effort, and let the person with the message control its presentation personally and directly as well.

Years later, the mistaken impression arose that the in-house BNR system had worked like PowerPoint, instead of being what it was—a painful example of the bad old days that PowerPoint would replace.

15 *The Global Presentation Grand Tour*

After the "Anpac" task force for which I had commuted to Minneapolis, NT had adopted as its strategy the "Office of the Future," a product line of personal computers connected by local networks and by the telephone network. To start executing this vision, it had purchased two established makers of computers for small and medium offices, one called "Sycor" and one called "Data100." Both companies had substantial customer bases in the U.S. and Europe, and the two had been combined into a company called Northern Telecom Systems Corporation (NTSC), then left without any new products, until the European division insisted on taking the lead in developing personal computers.

Beginning in 1983, I arranged to be seconded from BNR to NTSC for something called "Project Vienna," to quickly produce new products. From our headquarters in London, we traveled everywhere to buy the latest hardware components (motherboards, cases, disk controllers, disks, network cards, ...) and integrated the pieces into office networks of the first 286-based personal computers to be sold in Europe. We bought software from Microsoft, both MS-DOS and office applications such as Word and Multiplan—and that's how I met Bill Gates, while I was buying Microsoft software for this project. We produced documentation in nine languages, then sold and serviced these systems through the large NTSC network of sales offices and technicians.

The thing that impressed me, though, was the presentation visuals that we saw at every company we visited. We traveled around the world to buy components from many suppliers, going all over America (very deeply into Silicon Valley and New England), all over Europe including its far corners such as Finland, and Japan. Everywhere we went, the vendors had a pitch with presentation slides. I collected the printed copies of their overheads which they always passed out, and eventually I had a banker's box full of all the presentations. They were made in all kinds of ways—handwritten, on a typewriter, drawn on an old pen plotter, or made on many kinds of large computers. But I was struck by how they were very much the same all over the world. The basic style was essentially uniform everywhere, indicating that there was an international style for overheads. This meant that a single application to make presentation visuals would be saleable worldwide. It would require only the usual simple localization of language on menus and labels, not some more fundamental changes in style or format or features. And as GUI personal computers expanded worldwide, a presentation application would follow the hardware automatically.

Later, when we began work on PowerPoint, we went back to my "corpus" and went through it to tally features: how many presentations used bullet points? How many had a border around each slide? How many had a logo on each slide? How many used tables? How many charts? How many diagrams? How many "boxes and lines" diagrams? We used this data to prioritize features to be included in the early versions of PowerPoint.

16 *Focused Prediction of New Categories*

I prepared to leave BNR in 1983–84, as it became clear that Northern Telecom was having second thoughts, and wasn't going to approve the budgets needed to actually develop the "Office of the Future" systems that had been adopted as its strategy.

I spent the period working with Northern Telecom Systems Corporation on that new product line of conventional PCs for Europe, which kept me traveling abroad (and building my collection of presentations) about half the time. The other half I spent at the Palo Alto lab, writing reports on the PC business for them. I used my spare time, and my own NT 503 computer running CP/M with Word and Multiplan, to write business plans for several startup ideas; this was when I learned how to write business plans and construct spreadsheets of projections, activities which would become my regular duties at Forethought.

It seemed to me that the personal computer industry up until then had been shaped by hardware breakthroughs, such as the floppy disk and the daisy-wheel printer, that created new markets for software (database applications, word processing applications); these were the opportunities for new entrants. I thought that I knew for sure that the next big breakthrough would be graphical user interfaces, and any PC hardware that could run Mac or Windows could also run applications with graphical user interfaces. So what could be the *new* applications which would be enabled for the first time by GUI machines, along with the direct-drive pointing devices and high-quality graphic printers that would come with them? Those would be the opportunities for new software companies.

I had lots of ideas; at BNR I had even supported university research on TEX for Arabic, as an example of complex scripts which would become much easier to handle on GUI computers, with Japanese and Chinese as the most important instances. But one idea I wrote about was for software to make documents that were sequences of individual pages. By this I meant that such a document needed to have every page arranged visually one by one—in contrast, say, to Word which takes a long string of characters and pushes them automatically from page to page according to complex rules (*e.g.*, avoiding widows and orphans). My most immediate motivation was probably observing that whenever you wrote a one-page letter in Word it ended up pushing your complimentary close and signature line onto an otherwise-blank second sheet of paper, when what you really wanted was an opportunity to edit and shorten the letter so that the signature wasn't pushed to another page. There's a third class of software, "page layout," which combines both styles of working, where you have a set of individually arranged fixed containers on each page (like columns), plus rules for running text from one container to another, on the same or different pages. I was interested in all the documents for which neither word-processor software nor page-layout software was ideal.

There were dozens of examples of documents that were "sequences of single pages," such as brochures of all kinds, menus and wine lists, sets of retail point-of-sale signs, and (possibly the most promising) presentation visuals.

It was because presentation visuals belonged to this class of documents, I realized, that there had never been a successful presentation application on Apple II or MS-DOS despite many entrants, and that there never could be. But now I saw that the arrival of Mac and Windows would open up a land-rush into this major new application area, along with many others.

I realized that for all these new applications, it was important to completely write off the installed base of character-based PCs and make something as different from earlier competitors as it needed to be. This was an entirely new application area only open to GUI applications, and they would be the only competitors to matter.

At first, while I was doing this thinking at BNR, I thought that the application that I should develop was a very general editor for all kinds of "sequence of single page" documents, one that could be used equally well for wine lists and presentation visuals. But later, after I arrived at Forethought, I changed my mind and was inclined to think that presentation visuals specifically were the most valuable, the most desperately wanted, the most frequently used, and the most easily understood; so a new application should be marketed exclusively as an application to "create and manage presentations," and its features should be tailored to that specific use. Customers who bought it for that purpose would discover later that they could use it to produce wine lists and other examples of the larger document class.

17 This Wouldn't Make Sense with the Internet

I realize that a lot of what I describe in what follows might not seem to make sense, unless one remembers that the Internet was completely unknown outside a small research community in 1984. (We had an ARPAnet connection at the BNR lab in Palo Alto, but I had no real experience with it.) Lots of things about the way both startups and larger software companies worked prior to the Internet don't make any sense in the current age.

Today it's the fashion to make web services in a very "lightweight" way, to offer minimally viable web products free, and to iterate rapidly as experience is gained with initial web users. Without an Internet, none of that was possible. A software startup in the 1980s was a more difficult problem. You had to plan ahead a great distance and "call the shot" accurately, since a considerable investment was required before much in the way of feedback, let alone sales, could be available.

We couldn't reach potential customers directly (there was no web), so we had to groom editors of computer magazines and feed information to them, hoping they would print it in their magazines. We had to travel to the editors to demonstrate our software and leave copies for them. To get in touch with those editors, we had to maintain our own files of contact information, addresses and phone numbers, and employ a PR agency for whom that was their stock in trade. We traveled to meet industry consultants who were frequently quoted in the computer magazines, and we hired them at big prices to "advise" us, expecting them to say nice things to editors in the future.

Traveling imposed large information costs; people didn't have mobile phones, so had to call in periodically for updates, maybe getting a short document faxed to a hotel and delivered by a bellboy. Traveling abroad could mean being completely out of touch for several days.

We advertised in the computer magazines, hoping to interest potential customers. We paid for 800-number phone lines so that potential customers who wanted information or the names of dealers could call us; some people did call, a few called every day just to chat with our people at our expense. We spent a lot of money to try to collect registration cards, so we would even know the names and addresses of our actual customers who had already spent money with us, since they bought through retailers who bought through distributors.

Beyond the poor information flow, lack of the Internet imposed all kinds of costs and overheads and delays. The necessity to write and print physical books about the software led to long lead times, and complicated dependencies, such as that the number of pages in the manual had to be known before the dimensions of the box could be fixed for the box design, to be sure that the manual would exactly fit.

The same sorts of problems arose with all kinds of printed material that are no longer necessary because the information is now delivered over the net.

Since there was no way to deliver software over the Internet, we had to manufacture physical diskettes in physical boxes and place them in other companies' inventory stocks (and finance that inventory). Having to sell those boxes through distributors and then dealers imposed the high cost of a field sales force, which was hard to track and evaluate. Since every product in the hands of a customer had to pay for its manufacturing and overheads at each level of distribution, there was no possibility of free or minimal-cost versions early in a product's life, which implied some minimum level of function.

This system also imposed very high costs on making upgrades, with the result that the quality of the first-shipped product had to be high—the cost of an update forced by a single important bug was significant even for Microsoft, and could put a startup out of business. The software couldn't just run on our own servers with a known configuration and the possibility of easy updates, but had to run in the unpredictable environments of the users' own machines, a much harder problem for both development and testing. If a bug corrupted data on a user's machine, the update had to diagnose and correct such problems all by itself, working in an unknown disconnected environment.

I really envy people doing software with the Internet. One could do much better these days. But we didn't have it, and so we were forced to do many things that wouldn't be sensible today.

The situation reminds me of the oft-repeated story about a high school class studying *Romeo and Juliet*, who are mystified by all the tragic confusion at the end. "Why didn't Juliet just use her mobile phone to call Romeo when Friar Laurence gave her the sleeping potion, and get it straightened out with him?"

If you think about it, you realize that much of literature is built on plots that wouldn't make sense if mobile phones existed. I've listened to BBC Radio 4 interviews with detective-story writers who say that they purposely write stories set in the early twentieth century, so that they can take advantage of an age before mobile phones; but that ploy is only going to work for readers who can remember what that far away time was like.

The same is probably true for books about mid-1980s software startups; they can really only be understood by readers who were there.

PART III: FORETHOUGHT BEFORE POWERPOINT

18 Forethought's Earlier Idea

I wasn't around for the first year and more of Forethought's life. But when I joined the company, part of my job was to clean up the debris left from its beginnings, so I learned something about its past.

I wrote a short company history of Forethought in 1987, during the brief window of time after we shipped PowerPoint 1.0 and before we were acquired by Microsoft; it was for ourselves and for our long-time investors—that is, for the people who had lived through that history.

In that document, I started out by summing up what we all knew about the early period of Forethought:

> Forethought was started in January, 1983. The original business and product plan was certainly correct in its vision. The aim was to exploit the technology transition from character-mapped to graphics-oriented personal computers by focusing solely on graphics-oriented applications, and to build a major software company by growing rapidly with the newer market segment. The specific plan was to develop a proprietary graphics kernel and applications for IBM PCs.
>
> Many execution problems beset the company, primarily in development. A large number of unqualified people were added to the staff. Internal bickering and politics split the company, and resulted in wholesale defections. A failure by a supplier escalated into an expensive legal entanglement. The amount of development necessary was underestimated by orders of magnitude, and very little of that was ever accomplished.
>
> After 18 months and more than $2 million of invested capital spent (out of $3 million received) nothing of any real value had been accomplished. (Gaskins, Forethought History 1987)

This may sound harsh now, but at the time, when everyone recalled what had happened, that was a neutral description of the early history of Forethought, before the "restart" in July 1984 when I joined the company.

In January 1983, Forethought had been founded by Taylor Pohlman and Rob Campbell, both from Apple Computer. Taylor and Rob probably thought of their plan as being "deliver Xerox Alto software for IBM PC hardware." More than anything, the Forethought plan would have looked like the VisiOn project which shipped a year later, in December 1983, after more than two years of work by VisiCorp. This product resembled an early version of Microsoft Windows. It included VisiOn, a graphical window manager, plus VisiOn Calc spreadsheet, VisiOn Graph for charts, and VisiOn Word for word processing. (It's a small world: the VisiOn system developers included Tom Rudkin and Dennis Abbe, both of whom were early members of the PowerPoint group.)

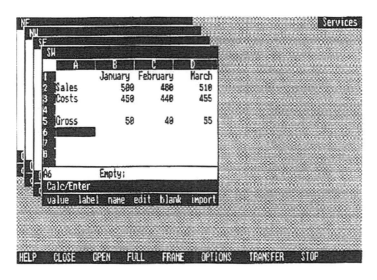

VisiOn with VisiOn Calc spreadsheet, circa 1983.

When I first met Taylor and Rob, in very early 1984, Forethought was in desperate straits. They had aspired to write (from scratch) a windowing system, a graphical file manager, graphics device drivers, a proprietary user interface standard with programming toolkit, a database system, and an integrated suite of office applications, all to run over MS-DOS on a standard IBM PC with the green monochrome display, plus required added hardware of a Hercules third-party graphics card for 720 x 348 resolution, a mouse, and a hard drive. (This hardware setup would have cost almost as much as the cost of a Lisa, thought then to be prohibitively expensive, and was more than VisiOn required.) All this would be a closed system, with no other sources for software, so Forethought had to provide everything. For example, Forethought was writing a piece-table based word processor modeled after Bravo, and was trying to create all its own fonts in-house.

By early 1984, the wheels had come off their idea. VisiCorp had already shipped a close approximation of what Forethought intended, but it had very poor sales; VisiOn was described as ugly and unacceptably slow, despite its requiring an expensive (and rare) hard drive. Opinions of VisiOn got worse after Apple introduced Mac, only a month or so later, with vastly better appearance and somewhat better performance (though also with extremely limited functionality) without a hard drive. Forethought was still nowhere close to a product.

It was clear that the product Forethought had planned would need an unrealistic amount of software development, and would require better hardware than customers could afford. Microsoft had announced Windows just a couple of months before, and Digital Research was working on the similar GEM system. Both of these efforts were much better planned and staffed, and even they didn't look obviously great (most people believed none of them would be successful).

Taking stock, there was nothing much to show for a year's work at Forethought. Piles of code were being created on a VAX, but no complete plan existed. The work so far was focused on the unglamorous lower levels of the system and was called "Foundation," frankly enough.

Although Forethought was far from having anything to sell, Taylor and Rob hadn't planned on being without a product for such a long time, and so had already hired a VP of Sales and a VP of Marketing, plus having the two business-development founders. This contributed to a high burn rate, with no products to produce revenue.

It happened that Forethought had no one who knew how to manage software projects, so they had hired a really random collection of about a dozen programmers, plus consultants.

After several months of work, the programming group had split into warring factions over some now-forgotten article of computing faith; one faction had withdrawn from the office and were working from their homes through access to the VAX over dial-up lines, holding parts of the source code hostage. The founders had nobody with the credibility to adjudicate the technical and personal disputes.

The funding history was very inconvenient. Some $700,000 had been raised initially in January and February of 1983; hopes were high enough that an extravagant burn rate was established, and another $2,500,000 had been raised later in 1983, not actually closing until December. Very soon after this round of funding, the situation was that over two million dollars had been spent, with another million still in the bank, and no concrete result had been produced.

Not unreasonably, the venture capital investors then called for a live demonstration of whatever had been accomplished. This was a command performance and could not be evaded, but there was really nothing to demonstrate. So it was imperative that by the date of the demo, which was sure to be extremely disappointing, management should have a plan to get back on track with new blood.

The important point about Forethought's difficulties is that it was mostly true, as I wrote, that "the original business and product plan was certainly correct in its vision." Doing something better than VisiOn in 1983 was a worthy idea, even if it was doomed to be crushed by Mac and Windows. But Forethought's founders had vastly underestimated the work and expertise needed for their plan, and shambolic execution of what they had begun left them on the verge of total failure.

All this, of course, was not uncommon in startups; Forethought was not the first.

19 The "Lab Day" Demonstration

I met with Forethought over several months, beginning on 16 February 1984. They were talking to several other people, including some extremely well-known programmers and software managers, so at first there wasn't much urgency with me. Gradually, I suppose, as time to the demo counted down and no one else could be hired to take over the disaster, I was the best choice they had. As the bar got emptier toward closing time, I began to look better and better.

I had come to the attention of Forethought through a recruiter who got my name from a friend of mine and, knowing nothing else about my background, sent my résumé to Forethought, mostly on the basis of "can't hurt to try." The recruiter played no role in the hiring process, and must have been astounded to eventually collect a fee for me without ever having set eyes on me. I'd never heard of Forethought before.

The big demonstration called for by the investors—given the name of "Lab Day" to emphasize its unfinished character—was set for 25 April 1984. Forethought became desperate to find someone before then.

They called me back a couple of months after our first talk, and two days before Lab Day, on 23 April 1984, I had a long formal meeting with the Forethought founders, who walked me through the entire organization and what they saw as the realities of the situation. As of then, at least based on what they represented to me, they still thought that there was some value in the work that had been done, if only they could straighten out the development process.

On 25 April 1984, I attended their Lab Day as an observer. An extraordinarily disappointing non-demo was sort of given—hours later than scheduled, with only the developers' fingers on the keyboard, and with nothing much at all visible on the display.

In my company history written in mid-1987, I summarized:

> On 25 April 1984, at a demonstration scheduled for the investors, the situation became clear: it was then approaching the planned shipment date, and no product was yet demonstrable. ... It was clear on that day that the original Forethought plan had failed. (Gaskins, Forethought History 1987)

During the long embarrassing delay on Lab Day, the investors had been left cooling their heels. We used the hours, while we all waited for the demonstration, as an opportunity for Taylor and Rob to introduce me to the investors and their associates and technical advisors, with the implication that I was the competent expert who was going to come in and straighten all this out. The occasion turned into a set of informal interviews, as all the attending technical advisors and investors got to probe me in depth.

The high point of my day was talking with independent board member Bob Metcalfe, inventor of Ethernet at Xerox PARC and by then chairman of 3Com; he gave me both his office and home telephone numbers in case I wanted to talk to him about any concerns I might have in joining Forethought. Bob, of course, was far and away the board member with the greatest technical vision to understand the Forethought idea to "deliver Xerox Alto software for IBM PC hardware," and I was very pleased to meet him. He lent Forethought a great deal of credibility in my mind, despite the failure of the demo.

20 Liquidate or Restart?

After Lab Day, the founders at Forethought understood that they were truly out of steam. Whatever the real value of the work that had been done (and they continued to think there was some value), they had lost credibility with their investors.

I was given the overhead presentation visuals from their next Board of Directors meeting in May 1984, held soon after Lab Day and before I was attending; they had met for the purpose of discussing going out of business. I still have the foils, and the first slide says:

THE PRIME QUESTION

LIQUIDATE	No special planning required
SELL	Requires rebuilding
REBUILD	Requires Major Plan Revision

You can't say that the Forethought founders were not being frank with themselves and with me, as evidenced by their giving me these foils. They realized that their development work had gone so wrong that they were facing either closing down immediately and returning the remaining money to their investors, or changing their plans to do something different that could build company value. So far, they had nothing worth selling.

It was also a good time to confess that the whole product strategy hadn't worked out, and it was not just the bungled execution. As the poor performance on original IBM PCs became evident, the Forethought target had quietly moved to possible new IBM machines that would be a lot more powerful, but nothing really adequate had been announced by IBM. Again from my company history written in 1987,

> ... no product was yet demonstrable. Even worse, the hypothesized market had never clearly materialized and IBM had still never shipped a suitable machine for the software to run on, if it *had* been developed. It was clear on that day that the original Forethought plan had failed. Work continued for another three months or so by momentum, while a plan was prepared for a restart. (Gaskins, Forethought History 1987)

And the longer it took for adequate machines to ship, the more likely it was that open environments such as Windows would be what they would run.

The good news was that the Forethought investors seemed to look at the situation in a very positive way. They shared the vision and realized that the company had gotten started badly. Dick Kramlich, of New Enterprise Associates, declared at an early board meeting that I attended that what we were doing was "a restart"—a familiar concept for a startup which has fizzled, and is started over again with revised ideas and new people added. The remaining $1 million was about the right amount to gamble on a restart. That is what I personally was prepared to join: a restart. (Recently the term "pivot" has been used for the related idea of a startup's dropping its original idea and turning to a different idea; I think "restart" was more accurate for Forethought's process.)

In addition to the good news that the investors were backing a restart, the other news was that apparently I had passed muster with all the investors, so we started moving toward my joining Forethought.

During May and June, the Forethought founders started preparing new plans—all involving me, although I wasn't there yet. By early June, I was consulting and meeting with them and with their developers at least a couple of times a week for long sessions, plus meeting with third parties they were considering using.

21 Why Would Forethought Want to Hire Me?

In retrospect, I now realize that I was far from being the most obvious candidate to rescue Forethought from its disaster, because I had never been responsible for any commercial product whatsoever, nor even for any important internal software. I knew a fair amount about programming, but not about programming for real "industrial" products.

Projects at university were the only programming projects I'd ever worked on directly. At BNR, my job was immediately that of being a manager, getting funding and approval for programming projects to be done by people whom I hired; and all the BNR projects were university-style research, not product development. I worked in the same building as people who were writing software to be embedded in products (telephone switches), so I saw a bit of how difficult it was, but I didn't attend their meetings or receive their progress reports. And when I was seconded to Northern Telecom in Europe, I constructed strategies for personal computer software products, but I never got close to actually executing the strategies—there were line organizations for that, and I was a staff guy working with other staff guys.

So I totally lacked any of the specific hands-on experience in real-world programming or in managing real-world software projects that you would expect from anyone hired by Forethought to fix the development of its software products. Moreover, I was over 40 years old, so you'd think that I would have had such experience by then, if I was ever going to have it. I presented myself more as someone recently out of school, which was true, rather than stressing that I'd left graduate school at age 35, but the facts were obvious on my résumé.

Startups, of course, are often founded by people who have no experience in products, just impassioned ideas. But it was very odd for Forethought to consider hiring me when the company was already established, had been in business for eighteen months, had a full management team (both the VP of Sales and VP of Marketing had been hired with track records), and had a board composed of seasoned venture capital investors with high-powered technical advisors. It was especially odd because the company had just demonstrated that it needed someone with lots of experience in developing software products. My résumé did not show any such experience.

Forethought was facing an old problem: how do you hire the first technical manager in a non-technical organization? It's hard. Paul Graham describes the problem well:

> ... when I think about what killed most of the startups in the e-commerce business back in the 90s, it was bad programmers. A lot of those companies were started by business guys who thought the way startups worked was that you had some clever idea and then hired programmers to implement it. That's actually much harder than it sounds—almost impossibly hard in fact—because business guys can't tell which are the good programmers. They don't even get a shot at the best ones, because no one really good wants a job implementing the vision of a business guy.
>
> In practice what happens is that the business guys choose people they think are good programmers (it says here on his resume that he's a Microsoft Certified Developer) but who aren't. Then they're mystified to find that their startup lumbers along like a World War II bomber while their competitors scream past like jet fighters. This kind of startup is in the same position as a big company, but without the advantages.

So how do you pick good programmers if you're not a programmer? I don't think there's an answer. I was about to say you'd have to find a good programmer to help you hire people. But if you can't recognize good programmers, how would you even do that? (Graham, Mistakes That Kill 2006)

I was, in fact, a good choice. I knew enough about programming, and I knew enough good programmers with industrial experience that I was, in fact, able to recognize and hire really great programmers. In the technical areas relevant to graphical user interface software, I wasn't just a "business guy," I knew what should be done, so that I wouldn't direct technical people into dead ends and waste their time, and I had enough advanced vision to inspire some desire on the part of technical people to join me and make that vision come true. I knew enough about research to distinguish it clearly from product development. Even though I would never have been able to architect and implement PowerPoint myself, I knew how to hire people who could. I knew enough about managing to be able to protect those people so they could get the job done, and I knew how to be sure I kept apprised of what they were doing.

But this set of abilities is almost impossible to promise credibly when you have no track record at all. It seems that someone in my situation needs blind luck to get into a position where there is a chance to demonstrate the claimed ability in practice.

So, why would Forethought have wanted to hire me? I can only conclude that their desperate situation, plus having no other candidates, led them to want to believe in me, and that I was just plausible enough to induce their willing suspension of disbelief. Blind luck, in other words.

22 Why Would I Want to Join Forethought?

Why, taking the question in the other direction, did I agree to join such a desperate organization as Forethought? To adapt a line from Groucho Marx, why would I join this club even though it would have me?

Forethought was one of the few companies I'd ever met that was interested in software for the impending generation of graphical personal computers. This was still pretty rare. At least three-quarters of the Valley didn't believe that systems like Mac or Windows would amount to anything, at least not until after a very long and slow evolution from the "huge installed base" of character-based PCs.

It was a pleasure to meet people who believed that graphical personal computers would be dominant, that this would happen as graphical user interfaces were introduced, that there would be widely sold platforms (comparable to Apple II or MS-DOS but even more widely used) on which new applications could be sold, and that the obvious growth path was to push functionality upwards as PCs improved. The agreement between me and Forethought on this basic vision was very attractive. The Forethought people were from Apple, but they were developing for IBM PCs, so that too was a basis for interest. (I had been convinced that Windows would come to dominate Macintosh ever since I attended the Microsoft Windows developer events in late 1983, based on my earlier dealings with Bill Gates.)

At Forethought, I'd met the board which included Dick Kramlich from New Enterprise Associates (NEA). Dick would ordinarily have been far too important to deal with a company like Forethought, but a more-junior colleague had made the investment in Forethought and then jumped ship, leaving Dick to take over the board seat. This was a huge advantage for Forethought. I've already mentioned Bob Metcalfe, inventor of Ethernet while at Xerox PARC and head of 3Com, another extremely smart guy. There were several other well-established investors involved.

I knew how hard it was to get to this point—to attract attention to the idea, get the first investment made, get the board recruited, choose and register a company name, find and rent offices, get set up to do business, get the corporate identity done, and on and on. Forethought had done all that, and still had about $1 million in the bank.

It would be a great savings of time to move into the shell of Forethought and take it over, like a hermit crab moving into the empty shell of a sea snail.

Adding it all up,

1. The company was funded for the fairly rare vision of doing software for graphical personal computer platforms.

2. The company had $1 million in the bank, and extremely smart investors and board members.

3. The company had all the tedious details of getting organized already completed.

4. The company was psychologically ready for a "restart," with a new business plan and new people.
5. The company was interested in me and my ideas for the new business plan.

I had grave doubts about almost all of the existing Forethought employees, but in a restart that need not matter, and it seemed to be no impediment to my accepting. In fact, we shed almost all the most-doubtful people immediately, and shed the rest of them soon after.

I was offered a very good salary, in fact higher than I'd been earning at BNR. I was also offered stock options on a meaningful chunk of the whole company (5%), more than a well-funded company with VC investors like Forethought would ordinarily have offered. My attorney insisted that I should also get a formal board resolution containing all the financial details needed to establish that my share of the company was a true fully diluted 5%.

This was a high-risk restart, so the 5% participation was appropriate. I was amazed that the VCs were willing to give me the board resolution I asked for; they must have thought it was a reasonable business precaution, given the disastrous state of the company. Carrying out the task of getting the promised documents for me was met with hostility from administrative employees—at the time, I thought they took my request to be distrust, but perhaps it was because they thought I was receiving too much of the company, compared to their friends among fellow employees who had arrived a year and a half earlier. But, after all, I *was* going to save the company or something like that.

23 Alternatives to Joining Forethought

Among those people who shared my vision of the impending revolution of graphical user interfaces, a majority were more interested in integrated systems of hardware and software, to get better performance.

Though it never made sense to me, a lot of smart people believed that the right evolution was to begin with high-performance custom-tailored special-purpose workstations, and then later move to personal computers when they grew up and became real. I always believed just the opposite: the correct path was to start with software on commodity personal computers as soon as they could do anything useful, and then grow up along with the market by adding features as PCs became more capable. I was sure that the initial victors in PC software would never be displaced by software evolved from workstations.

From the vantage point of twenty-five years later, this seems completely obvious, but it was a minority view in 1984. The hot business plan of that time was to build specialized computers from the new semiconductor parts or by adapting small minicomputers, tailor the hardware and software to a particular purpose, and sell high-value systems to companies at very high margins reflecting the tailored effectiveness.

Many firms designed and sold custom CAD workstations; they all went out of business, leaving CAD software on commodity PCs. Many firms designed and sold custom word processors and networks of them; they all went out of business, leaving word processors on commodity PCs. There must have been someone making accounting or planning workstations who lost out to spreadsheets on commodity PCs. The Xerox Star workstation was another example in the same genre.

Several companies including Genigraphics designed and sold custom presentation workstations (Genigraphics' was based on a PDP-11), but all went out of business, leaving PowerPoint on commodity PCs. Eventually, Genigraphics' professional service bureaus even replaced their own workstations with Macs and Windows machines running PowerPoint.

There were also higher-order manufacturers, such as Convergent Technologies, who made generalized computer workstations (incompatible with PCs) and basic software, and sold the result to other manufacturers, who would add more-specialized peripherals and tailored applications and then re-sell the resulting "vertical" workstations. This whole activity became an enormous business in total, but all of it failed in surprisingly short order, and just a few years later it was completely gone.

The market for moderately priced PC applications software on commodity multi-purpose generic PC hardware was so much larger, and the capabilities of PCs moved upscale so rapidly, that it was easy to evolve to become more capable. The workstation vendors, of all types, found it impossible to innovate as rapidly as PC manufacturers, and found it impossible to "cut back" their plans to a hardware base that they could not control—that's just not the kind of move that organizations do easily.

But before all those examples had worked themselves out, it was pretty rare to meet people who believed that personal computers would be dominant, that this would happen as graphical user interfaces were introduced, that there would be widely sold platforms on which new applications could be sold, and that the obvious growth path was to move functionality upwards as PCs improved. So agreement between me and Forethought on this basic vision was very attractive.

24 The Restart Strategy: Two Parallel Paths

My first day on the Forethought payroll was 5 July 1984. Two weeks later, on 19 July 1984, the first presentation to our Board of Directors (on overhead transparencies) preserves the top-level bullets of management's plan for the restart, which had two parts from the beginning:

PRODUCT ACQUISITION AND DEVELOPMENT

- **Products for Next-Generation PCs**
- **Independent development**
- **Internal development**
- **KEY: definition of internal products**

This slide sums up the next three years. The mission of Forethought was still software products for the coming generation of graphics-user-interface PCs. There were two sources of these products: (1) from "independent development" (we would license and publish products developed and owned by others), and also (2) from "internal development" (we would define and develop products so that we owned them). We would start by publishing products that independent developers had already written, making them easy to evaluate, which we would package and sell. At the same time, we would pursue longer-term internal development of higher-value products. Obviously, the "key" to success would be the quality of what we decided to develop internally, which was my task.

So we did not just wander into the "parallel tracks of publishing and developing" strategy by accident, we had carefully planned it.

The basic idea, as we explained it, was that we would use published products to build up the company as a delivery vehicle for software. In parallel, we would define and develop a high-value software product as our payload. By the time we had our internally developed software ready to ship, we would already have a company in place to deliver it rapidly and profitably. We would have made our mistakes by practicing on other people's software products. The revenue from the published products would allow us to pay for a sales force, to train phone support, and to establish a set of qualified manufacturers, long before we had any revenue from our own products.

Here's how I explained this strategy for the restart in my 1987 company history:

> In May and June of 1984, a restart plan was put in place. In its essentials, it was very simple: it aimed to preserve the vision of the original company, while changing everything else. Considerations went as follows.
>
> In early 1984, Apple's Macintosh had started to ship, in moderate volumes. Although far from the needed business machine that we had hoped IBM would ship, it was the first of the class of machines Forethought was interested in and IBM would have to eventually follow. Software for it was still scanty, barriers to entry and competitors were few.
>
> We believed that the sequence of successful software products (on Macintosh and later on IBM's similar machines) would begin with new graphics-oriented versions of programs in categories already known to dealers and end users (spreadsheet, database, word processing, ...). These could be developed quickly, especially by companies which had previously developed non-graphics equivalents. Eventually the large existing companies would probably enter these categories.
>
> But the major software opportunities would be in new categories—things that personal computers could do for the first time, because of the same hardware changes which made possible graphics user interfaces, and in which there were no large established competitors. Unfortunately, these were the categories which would also take the longest to develop, and for which markets were still uncertain.
>
> Hence the restart plan:
> - Locate other developers who had established products or expertise in established categories for older machines, and who were already interested in Macintosh versions.
> - Acquire marketing rights to their products (minimize upfront payments, even at the expense of larger royalties later) and publish these products quickly on Macintosh.

- Use these products to learn how to manufacture software, do advertising and PR, provide technical support, sell products, and collect receipts—in short, to build the company into a delivery vehicle for software.
- Meanwhile—in parallel—develop our own products internally, aiming at the new categories with the largest potential. We would consciously design products for high profitability, by focusing on software for specific high-value tasks which could command above-average prices with no higher than average development and marketing costs. Our products would be for the Macintosh, and for the similar environment of MS-Windows on IBM.

The royalty costs on published products, the lack of development control, and the fact that they were not our assets, would mean that they were not likely to be long-term opportunities. But, the revenue they would generate would let us finance the building of a fully functioning software company, pending the arrival of our own products.

If everything worked out, we would—at the completion of the restart plan—have both (1) a great product with the potential for high revenue and high profits, and also (2) the delivery mechanism necessary to turn that great product into actual sales and receipts. (Gaskins, Forethought History 1987)

This whole strategy has something of the flavor of the serious writer who dreams of churning out pot-boilers to finance the writing of the great American novel. But here the idea wasn't that our published products would be hack work. They were to be good products, the only thing necessarily "wrong" with them being that we didn't own them, implying that they would not be long-term profit opportunities for us.

25 Dual Paths Reflect Dual Managers

Of course, the two paths of the restart matched Rob Campbell's and my respective backgrounds. This is some variant of Conway's Law; if two different people had been doing the restart, it would have been structured differently.

Rob had never claimed to be able to manage difficult development, but (from what I knew) he had run a small company doing accounting software for small businesses, then worked at Apple on licensing outside software and creating Apple's software publishing group, and he knew a lot of people in other software publishing companies and in the industry. He was a master at—not surprisingly—PR, packaging, advertising, sales, and accounting, and so he envisioned extending his abilities at all these areas over software from multiple developers.

By contrast, I had never run a small business, and my strengths were in the definition and development of advanced products, what is really "product marketing," but I also knew enough computer science (particularly in the areas vital for the future new generation of PCs) to select, hire, and manage strong developers.

Each of us tended to focus on the part of a dual-path strategy which would utilize his specific personal strengths.

Rob's mind focused more on creating a publishing company, to publish software (handle documentation, manufacturing, packaging, advertising, PR, sales, and accounting) for many independent developers, among whom there would be one in-house developer ("the PowerPoint division"), as a device to assure that there were some technical people on staff.

In contrast, my mind focused more on creating a software company to develop PowerPoint, with the clever side-idea of having another group working on publishing outside software ("the publishing division"), so that we could practice how to handle writing and printing, manufacturing, packaging, advertising, PR, sales, and accounting in advance of completing our own development, thus preparing Forethought as a delivery channel all poised for action when PowerPoint was ready.

Through the sales of published products, so I thought, we would finance getting an organization in place to do those things and work out all the early mistakes so that nothing would impede PowerPoint's success, using essentially temporary products that would pay for themselves. We would also be able to talk with customers, as we sold and supported the published products, so we would learn about actual customers (wholesalers, dealers, and end users) while we worked on PowerPoint.

We set out our new organization chart on 9 July 1984, just four days after I arrived, in a management meeting.

We split company responsibilities in the way described above. Rob handled graphic identity, advertising, and PR, and dealt with the packaging design studio, the ad agency, and the PR agency. He also handled all sales and sales programs, and especially he headed the administration function that included working with investors, bookkeeping (still a great love of his), legal, invoicing, and collections. These were all activities required by the published products, and Rob also did all these things for PowerPoint.

Rob had six people reporting to him, but that included a VP of Sales and a VP of Marketing, so he had some firepower to get going.

I handled market research, product definition, development, testing and quality assurance, manufacturing (including print publishing), manuals and documentation, and everything that went on the disks. These were all activities required by the PowerPoint product, and I handled all of them also for all the published products.

I had twelve people reporting to me, but this was momentary, given that we had already agreed to immediately lay off most of them, and fairly soon all of them; I started layoffs on 23 July 1984, two weeks later. Taylor Pohlman, the other founder and the more technical one, was nominally in my organization but really was occupying a desk near the door as he considered other opportunities and worked on a plan to sell the failed Foundation development to some large company (a plan which obviously never got off the ground). So I was mostly on my own for the moment, but with the expectation of hiring.

Rob and I both handled pitching to raise money, since potential investors always wanted to see both of us. Of course, in every startup there are lots of menial tasks, and we both handled a lot of those, too.

Both Rob and I had the energy and optimism and nerve needed to survive in the often terrifying world of a startup. Rob and I both had the mindset of "doing the right thing," and we were able to trust each other—once either of us agreed to do something, he did it. So we didn't sabotage each other's projects. This is really a baseline requirement for a startup: at all times, each of us was dependent on the integrity of the other.

But there was no danger of faulty decision-making caused by groupthink or an emphasis on harmony. Rob's and my frequently differing points of view, about nearly everything, assured that any idea had to be well thought-out and well presented, and would be carefully considered before starting execution; we didn't casually make mistakes for lack of criticism. Most fundamentally, neither of us was in the mode of working for someone else and taking direction; each of us assumed he was in charge and insisted on that responsibility, which was not a bad situation.

It's important to be perfectly clear that the "dual companies" were not thought of as competing with each other; they were intended to be complementary parts of a single strategy, operating at different time depths into the future, each strengthening the other.

26 To Refocus: Applications for Standard Platforms

I started working first on the technical plan for the restart, which was due almost immediately, at the next Board of Directors meeting on 19 July 1984. Regaining technical credibility with the investors fell to me.

My contribution to the first presentation to our Board was to take exactly the same diagram of a stack of system layers that had been often presented to them by the founders as the Foundation development work under way, and to show that diagram again, but with a new box added at the bottom labeled "MS-Windows." There was by no means general agreement that Windows would do everything for us; people could hope that some parts of the proprietary system would live on as a level over Windows. But when I asserted that, at base, we would run on top of Windows and abandon our own low-level code for windowing and graphics and such, it was relatively easy for everyone to agree with me. It certainly put a lot of our failing internal projects out of their misery.

From my 1987 company history:

> By late July, 1984, wholesale layoffs took place, with a great deal of further attrition in the following months. A skeleton engineering staff was retained to see if anything could be done with the results of development, but it soon became apparent that (as Bob Metcalfe observed at the time) there was utterly no value in the work to date, and it was totally abandoned. (Gaskins, Forethought History 1987)

At the beginning of Forethought, the developers had needed the environment first, in order to write applications to run on it, so they began there. A year and a half later, when I came along, they were still deeply mired in the same lower levels of the system.

Windows was still merely a gleam in Bill Gates's eye, Digital Research's GEM was even less advanced, VisiOn was shipping but wasn't close to acceptable, so it was hard to give up and to agree to adopt something not as good as planned. But it was also becoming clear that whatever environment became successful would be some sort of industry standard.

When I arrived, I already knew that the idea of creating a proprietary windowing environment was futile. Between 1981 and 1984, I had carefully tracked (in weekly reports) how MS-DOS had overcome all the alternatives offered. So even if Forethought could have done something arguably better, I believed that it would be rejected by the market in favor of Windows. As to timing, there was no realistic chance of shipping anything before Microsoft could do better; Windows might be long delayed, but if so Forethought would be delayed even longer.

We didn't need to have months of technical discussion about the quality of the work done so far on the Foundation code. I just announced that we would adopt Microsoft Windows, and that changed everything positively. If I was wrong, then we would adopt some alternative to Windows, but we would not "roll our own" environment.

Interestingly, there was absolutely no internal debate about Windows versus Macintosh. Everyone agreed that we should publish products for Macintosh so as to ship immediately, and everyone agreed that we should develop our own products for Windows as the prime target.

I terminated the operating system people, and I started negotiating contract releases with the consultants. Within a few months, the process had taken its course; Taylor Pohlman, the more technical founder, was gone, and the old developers and all their projects were gone, save for one. I retained one developer who understood what had been done, because I needed that knowledge for my next project, as a tool to evaluate Windows. Forethought was now aimed purely at applications software: for Windows, in the future, for our own products; and for Mac, immediately, for published products licensed from other developers.

27 The MACWARE Brand

We started immediately on the published products from outside developers. In my 1987 company history, I wrote:

> We knew when we began the restart plan that we would soon need money. There was then somewhat less than $1,000,000 in cash, and it was being burned rapidly. The costs of shutting down the original effort in an orderly way and starting up the new effort would clearly consume all that cash by the end of the year—hence the importance to us of MACWARE products which could be shipped for revenue within 90 days. (Gaskins, Forethought History 1987)

We took precautions to protect ourselves against failures:

> ... In order to insulate these temporary published products from our longer-term plans, we adopted the trade name "MACWARE" to identify them, reserving Forethought for our future products. (Gaskins, Forethought History 1987)

This strategy to create a publishing division attracted exceptional effort and zeal within Forethought, in part because it gave the marketing and sales people in the company something to do—for the first time. While Forethought's Foundation product development was stalled, Rob Campbell, together with the VP of Marketing, Darrell Boyle, and the VP of Sales, Bob Wohl, had all been mostly standing around, nervously trying to discern what the programmers were doing behind the curtain. Now they were all released to create new brands and ship real products.

This division of the company got its own trademarked name, "MACWARE." We all got MACWARE business cards with the Forethought company name in much smaller letters, and our product boxes for published products emphasized the MACWARE name and logo, as did all our advertising and PR. We even got the phone number 1–800-MAC-WARE for our free customer service line (vanity 800 numbers were a *lot* easier to get in those days).

Before the end of July, 1984, we had identified three products, from three different developers who could work separately in parallel without interfering with one another; we thought we could introduce all of the products within six months. From my 1987 company history:

> Factfinder, a free-form filing product which had been very modestly successful on the Apple II, but which was far advanced in development for Macintosh. It appeared that Factfinder could be shipped in October, only 90 days later, and before Fall Comdex 1984.
>
> Typing Intrigue, a typing instruction program, which was new for the Macintosh, but was from a developer with experience in training development. This category had been very large on Apple II and on IBM PCs, and seemed to fit perfectly "the computer for the rest of us." Because it was very simple, it required very little work on testing and documentation. It, too, was expected to ship about the time of Comdex, in November.
>
> Nutshell (later FileMaker), a low-end single-file database which had been reasonably successful on the IBM PC. Our origi-

nal belief was that it could also be shipped in late 1984, although this definitely did not work out as planned. (Gaskins, Forethought History 1987)

We expected that these would be the first three products out of a much larger MACWARE portfolio, planning for at least half a dozen and perhaps even a dozen published products. That scope made it very sensible to spend a lot on the branding of the published product line.

We worked very hard to get Factfinder and Typing Intrigue finished. In about three months, we carefully vetted the software, got development fixes, and tested everything. We wrote simple documentation and printed it, designed and printed boxes, produced advertisements and PR materials, found contract manufacturing, printed diskette labels, duplicated diskettes, handled the press for the introductions, and sold the products to distributors. We printed dealer kits with backgrounders, data sheets, a contract, a credit application, an order form, and so forth. We set up free telephone support at our 800 number. It was a formidable effort, especially from people who were working together for the first time. From my 1987 company history:

> Factfinder was shipped in late October, and Typing Intrigue in November, essentially as planned and on schedule. Initial sales of both were promising, and in January, 1985, we made a big sale to First Software, but that was the last big sales month. (Gaskins, Forethought History 1987)

The problem was that customers were not buying Macs or Mac software, no matter how elegant our packaging or how memorable our 800 number. We got the products into distributors' inventories, but computer retailers didn't order them, because customers weren't buying as expected. Again from the 1987 company history:

> As predicted, we were entirely out of cash by late December, 1984. A January, 1985, sale to First Software with cash prepayment staved off disaster, but that was the last big sales month, because neither Factfinder nor Typing Intrigue sold through. Our products remained in distributors' warehouses, and both sales and collections dried up. (Gaskins, Forethought History 1987)

PART IV: POWERPOINT 1.0

28 The First Two-Page Description of PowerPoint

Even with all the focus on getting the MACWARE products published, so as to generate revenue for Forethought, I did not delay starting on the parallel path of internal development.

I wrote up a two-page description of PowerPoint for my product planning meeting held on 14 August 1984, just a month after I arrived at Forethought. This was the first description I had written for such a product (reproduced on the two following pages).

For some reason, I wrote it as a two-level (occasionally three-level) outline, which is not a format that I often used. I must have been aiming at compactness, perhaps also echoing the style of overheads themselves. Note also that it was printed on a coarse dot-matrix impact printer; we didn't have any high-quality graphical printers at the time when this was written (the LaserWriter wouldn't ship for another six months).

The "Presenter" [PowerPoint] idea was one example of the class of documents I was interested in: multi-page documents in which each page needed separate visual layout. This short document was written to show my new colleagues the kind of proposal I thought was necessary for candidates to become our internal products. (Gaskins, Presenter [PowerPoint] Original Proposal 1984)

This was a promising start, but there were lots of other things on my plate, such as terminating more developers, negotiating out of contracts with consultants, working on MACWARE products, and hiring new talent. I didn't do much more on the PowerPoint idea, other than thinking about it occasionally, for a couple of months, until after Dennis Austin joined Forethought on 22 October 1984.

14 August 1984
R. Gaskins

SAMPLE PRODUCT PROPOSAL:
PRESENTATION GRAPHICS FOR OVERHEAD PROJECTION

I. Target Market: People who make presentations to others: managers,
              professionals, knowledgeworkers, salespeople ...
                --people likely to justify PCs for multiple purposes
                --this purpose not served by word processors or spreadsheets
       A. In small companies, sales presentations to customers
       B. In large companies, project presentations to peers/superiors
                --both cases put a dollar value on effective communication
                --individuals' business success hinges on presentation

II. Market Size
       In 1982: Business presentations was $3.5 billion industry
                --520 million original 35mm slides
                --380 million overhead transparancies
       Computers could generate 60% [Hope Reports, courtesy DRI]
       (Percentage rises over time, as graphics devices get better,
        and percentage of overheads is likely close to 100%)

       Market may be concentrated in some Fortune 500 companies, e.g.:
                Intel for sales presentations
                Northern Telecom for internal presentations
       --can sell directly/refer dealers to local offices of such targets.

III. Product Concept: Personal Presentation Management
              --Create slide presentations
              --Create talking papers
              --Create handouts
                 all from one master data file

              --Outline aids for structuring/writing/reviewing *presentations*
              --Slides with border, logo, identification, sequence
              --Slides with high-quality typeset text, multi styles and sizes
              --Slides with diagrams, drawings, sketches, maps, org charts, ...
              --Slides with tables entered as spreadsheets
              --Slides with business chart graphics (from table entry)

              --display on PC screen, print on different-quality devices
              --produce printing-industry quality as one option

              --communicate high-quality slides via electronic mail, can
                   be used at far end with any output device (video to typeset)

              --[for high-volume users:]
              --Files of presentation/talking paper/handout for retrieval
              --Re-use parts of previous presentations
              --Create new sequences of old slides (new date, label, sequence)

Presenter Original Proposal, 14 August 1984, page 1.

62

```
                    --Standard templates for corporate graphic standards
                    --Standard templates for presentation structure standards
                    --Convert from/to IBM SNA document formats (DIA/DCA)
                    --Special facilities such as coordination of two projectors

        IV. User Benefits

                    --Improves effectiveness of presentation content
                    --Improves clarity of complex material
                    --Reduces time to prepare presentations (dramatically)
                    --Facilitates correct last-minute changes and revisions
                    --Allows compliance with company presentation standards
                    --Provides communication of high-quality presentations
                    --Reduces cost of presentations (dramatically)
                    --Allows the content-originator to control the presentation



        V. Technology Trends
                    --WYSIWYG required for sensible layout (better than PC graphics)
                    --Low cost printers (thermal transfer $500, laser $3000)=>originals
                    --Thermal transfer and ink-jet make slides (as do copiers)
                    --Color graphics plus color ink-jet for color

        VI. Match to Forethought Foundation Technology:

                    --Content-originator can improve result by controlling presentation
                        (no artists, no services, no clerical intervention, time is
                        of the essence)
                    --Requires typeset text, paragraphs, lists
                    --Requires graphics for diagrams and drawings
                    --Requires business charts from tables
                        (scaling to multiple sizes required)
                    --Requires simple spreadsheets (calculation in tables)
                    --Requires file cabinet of presentations and elements

                    --Would like link to mainframe databases for corporate data
                    --Would like simple link to 1-2-3
                    --(Ditto for project planners, word processors ... )

        VII. Joint Ventures with Large Manufacturers:

                    --3M very large player, in hardware (esp. compact models
                        for portable sales presentations) and in media
                    --Others include Bell & Howell, Charles Besseler, Elmo, Telex, ...
```

Presenter Original Proposal, 14 August 1984, page 2.

29 Enlisting Dennis Austin

The next event that was truly critical in PowerPoint history was enlisting Dennis Austin to join Forethought as my first hire. He arrived on 22 October 1984, only about four months after I had arrived myself.

I had known Dennis through our mutual friends when I was at Bell-Northern Research, and I had tried to recruit him there. Dennis had listened to my vision of networks of graphical personal computers, but refused to join us because he didn't believe that BNR and NT management was really supportive of what I wanted to do. In that judgment, he showed that he understood more about big companies than I did.

Dennis had a broad education and wide interests. He had a strong academic background, and had worked for Burroughs designing system software and languages for the elegant and innovative B1700 mainframe series, where he had taken advantage of the fact that Burroughs Fellow Edsger Dijkstra, my own long-time hero, visited the group at Santa Barbara periodically.

After that, in Silicon Valley, Dennis had been a senior architect at a startup called Gavilan Computers, which was trying to create the earliest really compact and battery-powered portable computers, recognizably the ancestors of modern laptops—with a (small, coarse) graphical screen and a touchpad above the keyboard. Dennis had worked on developing its broad software architecture, and particularly on its graphical user interface.

Dennis had limited previous exposure to Windows or Mac, but both of us knew that was irrelevant. He was familiar with the appropriate tactics and expectations for the microprocessors used in personal computers, and had little patience with the rough edges and poor performance of almost all personal computer software and applications.

Dennis was thoroughly on board with the view that the future belonged to graphical personal computers and their applications, as he recalls in a later reminiscence of his reasons for joining:

> ... I came with high hopes for great work at Forethought. There was no specific course mapped, but I was a true believer in Forethought's mission. (Austin, Beginnings 2009)

Even though our investors had decided on doing a restart rather than pulling the plug on Forethought, they were far from totally convinced that we could succeed. One bit of evidence is recalled by Dennis in the same document:

New Enterprise Associates financed both Forethought and my now defunct employer, Gavilan Computers. C. Woody Rea, a partner with NEA, nevertheless steered me away from Forethought. Not a promising company in his opinion. I had great respect for his judgment, but the Forethought mission was seductive. I joined Forethought in spite of its cloudy prospects. (Austin, Beginnings 2009)

This story (unknown to me at the time) underlines the fact that Forethought's mission of software for a new generation of graphical personal computers really was exciting to people, and really was exactly right for the time. It also confirms that Forethought had thoroughly destroyed its credibility with its investors, and the restart required swimming upstream.

Paul Graham has put his finger on one of the big advantages of a startup, which was exemplified in my hiring Dennis:

> ... the essence of a startup: having brilliant people do work that's beneath them. Big companies try to hire the right person for the job. Startups win because they don't—because they take people so smart that they would in a big company be doing "research," and set them to work instead on problems of the most immediate and mundane sort. Think Einstein designing refrigerators [as he actually did, with Leo Szilard]. (Graham, Smart People 2005)

In one sense, despite its excitement to me and to Dennis, designing an application like PowerPoint was something like designing a novel refrigerator, even to the positive impact of a great design on millions of people who use the result. All the people who use PowerPoint now, twenty-five years later, are still reaping the benefits of having Dennis work out the original design.

Dennis brought a lot of other talents. He was an excellent writer of English, sensitive to language and communication; being able to write clearly and effectively multiplied Dennis's effectiveness. He was particularly interested in the essays of E. B. White, paralleling my own interest in Harold Ross and the early circle of writers at the *New Yorker* magazine.

> Besides a mathematical inclination, an exceptionally good mastery of one's native tongue is the most vital asset of a competent programmer.
> —Edsger W. Dijkstra (Dijkstra, EWD498 1975)

We turned out to have many interests in common, and our daily contact was always a vast pleasure to me.

Dennis had a positive and resilient temperament, required for dealing with all the incoherence and disappointment in a startup. He was a true professional with independent spirit, always ready to assume responsibility, always maintaining frank and honest communication, and regularly producing miracles. He had an exceptional combination of aesthetic taste and technical judgment, which prevented many disasters. Dennis was never distracted by superficial issues, always returning to fundamental problems and giving them deep thought.

Dennis and I would work together on PowerPoint for about a year and a half before anyone else joined us. We worked together so long and so closely that it's impossible for me now to assign many of the ideas to an author. Our relationship with each other was purposely *not* like Paul Graham's recipe for startup failure, "business guys [who] had some clever idea and then hired programmers to implement it"! On the contrary, Dennis took part in considering all the business and market and customer strategies, understanding and approving it all, and I understood and approved every strategy about design and implementation.

The best description perhaps is Dennis's own: "Bob was building his dream house; Dennis was his architect" (Austin, PowerPoint Conception 2003). We both had to understand all of what we were doing, and all of why we were doing it. We also had separate responsibilities, of course; I knew little of the details of Dennis's negotiations with Apple over using CoreEdit for text, and a thousand other things, and Dennis knew little of the details of negotiations with venture capital investors and much else of the overhead of keeping the company on its rocky road. But our responsibilities overlapped heavily in creating PowerPoint.

We split the big conceptual ideas in PowerPoint, but Dennis came up with at least half of the major design ideas. He also came up with a great preponderance of the medium and smaller details of architecture and operation which were so delightful to discover and learn and which contributed so much to PowerPoint. And, of course, he was completely responsible for the fluid performance and the polished finish of the implementation, which marks products that have both smart architecture and smart detailed execution. It's a good bet that if Dennis had not been the person designing PowerPoint, no one would ever have heard of it.

(Tom Rudkin later also made large contributions (described in their place) both to the final year of work on the first version and after that time in heading work on the Windows version. There were other people who were later important to further design work. I myself never contributed a line of code to PowerPoint, although I would read the code periodically.)

My fingers were the ones on the keyboard for the product definition documents and business plans, balancing all the ideas, no matter where they came from. Dennis's fingers were on the keyboard for the detailed product specs that weighed and integrated all the ideas from all sources into a design.

Dennis began as the sole architect and designer for PowerPoint, and left Microsoft more than ten years later, a couple of years after I'd left, as the head of an organization of some 35 developers, all working on PowerPoint. Such prolonged consistency of technical vision is what makes for exceptionally successful products.

30 Evaluating Microsoft Windows Before It Shipped

I had thrown out the lower levels of the old Foundation work when I announced that we were adopting Windows. A good way to learn about Windows would be to try porting the document formatting code from Forethought's Foundation project to Windows and see how that worked. This would incidentally verify that we were not throwing away anything valuable, but the bigger purpose would be to learn a lot more about Windows and about Microsoft's commitment to it.

At this point, we had two developers: Peter Bishop, ex-PARC and the only early Forethought developer left, who had been there while the Foundation project was designed and who knew a lot about its theory and its implementation, and Dennis Austin, newly hired, who had wide experience with successful real software design, and who had no investment in the earlier Foundation work.

Peter and Dennis spent some time together experimenting with how hard it would be to separate and discard the lower levels of the Foundation code, which would be replaced by Microsoft Windows, and whether it was possible to port some of the remaining upper-level code dealing with document formatting to run on Windows.

After a few months, juggling many other responsibilities and distractions caused by work on the MACWARE products, Dennis came to two conclusions: (1) the document code from Foundation was poorly designed, so it would be best to throw it away and start over regardless of our goal; and (2) Microsoft Windows was extremely far from being a viable platform for graphical applications development.

The first conclusion wasn't very surprising, and I had foreseen it long before, from talking with its developers. But you can't discard the project that everyone has been developing and defending and funding for a year and a half without being seen to give the decision proper attention.

The porting project was worth doing mainly because it gave us a way to evaluate Windows. Having a real project with substantial amounts of code to actually try to run on Windows gave us some visibility and attention at Microsoft, because there weren't many companies with even one developer committed to apps for Windows, so that assured us we were getting whatever information Microsoft knew. Dennis's conclusion that Windows wasn't nearly ready for serious use was a valuable one, although unwelcome; it was going to be a *lot* of years until Windows would be capable of supporting a graphics application. The underpinnings of Windows just didn't provide facilities to support the level of graphics and typography that we would need. In theory, there was code in the Foundation project which might have been helpful to fill in for some of the deficiencies of Windows, but the analysis of Foundation's design was that it would not actually help at all.

Making a sensible decision at this time about Microsoft Windows as a strategy for PowerPoint was very complex, full of misleading and mistaken information.

On 19 June 1984, even before I was on the payroll at Forethought, I had met with Steve Greene, from Microsoft's sales office in Mountain View; he had given me the inside word on when Microsoft expected to ship its own applications on Windows over the next six months (quoted from my contemporaneous notes):

> Microsoft Schedule for MS-Windows Applications:
> End of 1984: Basic, Paint, Plan
> First Q 1985: Word, File, Chart

Actually, Windows itself would slip by a full year and didn't ship until almost a year and a half after our conversation. Excel (a different development, but roughly "Plan" [visual Multiplan] plus "Chart") shipped on Windows in 1987 (two to three years later), and Word in 1989 (more than five years later). PowerPoint shipped on Windows in

1990, almost six years later. If Word for Windows actually had shipped in "First Q 1985," then we might have more reasonably expected to ship PowerPoint for Windows in 1986. But there turned out to be a "reality adjustment" of several years to all these schedules. Microsoft was not trying to mislead us, but even they had limited visibility into their own code and schedules.

It was Dennis's first-hand investigation that convinced us that Microsoft was itself mistaken in when it could expect to ship its own applications on Windows, and even mistaken in when it could expect to ship Windows.

Windows 1.0 was shipped in November of 1985, more than a year later than had been expected, with Forethought prominently listed as one of the original Independent Software Vendors supporting it (Ozzie, Windows 1.0 Press Kit 1985); but, long before then, we had learned enough to decide that Windows 1.0 would be inadequate for our purposes, and had switched strategies to target Macintosh first. Having mounted a small project on Windows was the best way to find that out.

While working on the port of the document code to Windows, we began to concentrate on how we would use it to create documents like presentations—bulleted lists, for instance. This gave us the opportunity to talk about lots of presentation ideas, even though it became clear that the Foundation code wasn't very well matched to these requirements. Toward May 1985, Dennis and I spent our meetings about the Foundation port talking more about features of a presentation application. Basic concepts such as the "model slide" (later master slide) emerge as early as this in my notes.

From my company history written in 1987:

> We believed we should get the MACWARE products launched first, so we did nothing until after the first of the year—and by then, with our sales below forecast, we were utterly without cash and struggling to get FileMaker out for revenue until May 1985. The result was that we did essentially nothing but talk about the PowerPoint proposal until late May 1985, when the first round of convertible debentures closed. (Gaskins, Forethought History 1987)

In May 1985, with some more money received, we stopped work on the Foundation port completely. Peter Bishop left a couple of months later. Dennis Austin moved to officially designing PowerPoint, half time.

31 Shipping FileMaker in the Mac Doldrums of 1985

While the evaluation of Windows as the platform for PowerPoint went on, it already began to be clear that the MACWARE plan was not going to work out as hoped; MACWARE was not going to turn into a large stable of a dozen products, all selling in large volumes for a rapidly growing Mac market. The fact was that Mac was not selling well, and our own two initial products were not so insanely great that they could overcome that. Our third product, FileMaker, had slipped badly.

From my 1987 company history:

> Meanwhile, Nashoba's FileMaker had slipped for legal and contractual reasons, plus delays at both Nashoba and Forethought. It moved from January to March, and ultimately would be shipped in May, 1985—almost a full year after the restart plan was begun. We continued to cut back during this period, dragging it out further.
>
> Despite anticipation, FileMaker never really did sell well—we had entered the dread year of 1985, the worst time for Macintosh software companies. Its initial sell-in [stocking all the distributors] was fewer than 900 units, and it settled down to a couple of hundred units a month. Our other products did no better. (Gaskins, Forethought History 1987)

As John Sculley described it much later, the Mac "was failing in early 1985":

> [Sculley:] ... the Macintosh, which he [Steve Jobs] developed, was failing in early 1985. His vision was ahead of its time, the power of the microprocessor wasn't enough to do what he wanted to do and Mac sales were falling off. (Guyon 2011)

I wrote in my 1987 company history:

> ... after the first of the year [1985] ... with our sales below forecast, we were utterly without cash and struggling to get FileMaker out for revenue until May 1985 ... .
>
> Through early 1985 we lived with the monthly prospect of liquidation. In May, 1985, we received $1,000,000 from the first round of convertible debentures. But by then we were substantially negative, and when FileMaker failed to sell well, we rapidly ran out of cash again. (Gaskins, Forethought History 1987)

By early May 1985, we had a new million dollars, and we finally shipped FileMaker, but, with the extremely disappointing initial sales of FileMaker, it was clear that dramatic cutbacks were needed.

We reduced all possible headcount, and stopped looking for new products. Rob took over marketing and sales directly and dispensed with our two Vice Presidents for those areas; I took over all facets of product marketing as well as my previous responsibilities, and we focused on existing products.

Sales did not improve, and by our Board of Directors meeting on 25 July 1985, the discussion was about an idea for "an effort to help the best Mac software companies to survive" by promoting a series of mergers and acquisitions to build a single strong Mac software company that would be well financed.

Looking ahead, this set off a grueling marathon of seemingly endless negotiations with every Mac software company in the world about how we would all merge to form "Mac Software United." When that failed, it ignited a further flurry of fruitless activity on various side deals. The venture investors in all the companies were desperate for follow-on investments from outsiders to keep their companies alive, so each looked to all the others to fill the gap, leading to universal disappointment.

From my 1987 company history:

> Then followed a long period of another year—from May 1985 to April 1986—during which we tried every stratagem we could think of to improve our business, but basically without result. We continued to lose money steadily during the entire period. We also considered structural changes in the company, such as acquiring VisiCorp/Paladin, being acquired, merging with UMF Systems, forming a marketing consortium for other struggling Macintosh developers, and so on. Ultimately these came to nothing, and so we continued with our original plan.
>
> Gradually, our competitors went out of business. Purely because we were able to continue to raise capital, we stayed in business. (Gaskins, Forethought History 1987)

All the frantic activity did encourage our investors and did bring us another $250,000 in November 1985, but was otherwise a total waste of time.

32 Starting on PowerPoint Planning

By May 1985, the choice between Windows and Macintosh as the first target for PowerPoint had gotten very cloudy.

Mac sales and Mac software sales were very poor (as we knew from our own sales reports), so—reasonably enough—it was quite a challenge for anyone in the whole industry to get funding to develop Mac applications. As Mac stalled out, many developers concluded that Mac could fail totally, leaving Windows to be the first major graphical platform.

Our experimentation with early Windows 1.0, and our interactions with Microsoft, had tended to convince us of the opposite: that Windows was much further behind than was generally believed or was admitted by Microsoft. Even so, we always believed that Windows would eventually be the major platform. And on the other hand, we certainly had to admit that Mac was selling very poorly, including our own Mac products.

We began to think that a robust Mac market was some distance away, perhaps not until new Mac models were shipped, and prices came down, but a robust Windows market might be even further away. Our faith in the graphical platforms as a whole never wavered, but it was disappointing to see both of them succeed so slowly. We continued to work on the PowerPoint idea with Windows as its target, but with growing suspicions that we might change our minds.

In May 1985, just about six months after Dennis had arrived, he started working seriously on PowerPoint as a product. At the same time he was spending up to half of his time answering calls from end users about technical problems they were having with our published products, not at all a bad way to get a sense of the Mac's early users.

> In May 1985, after the debentures round closed for $1,000,000, we finally were able to assign one person half time to beginning development of PowerPoint (the other half was spent answering technical support calls!). About $25,000 was invested over six months. (Gaskins, Forethought History 1987)

Dennis and I both started spending serious time on PowerPoint, and my notebooks recording these meetings show a constant flow of the important ideas underlying PowerPoint. Dennis later wrote:

> The product design details required a lot of invention. Bob was able to spend many hours with me hashing over ideas. It was a

productive process and the quality of my designs reflected Bob's support and feedback. I have compared our collaboration to a building design project: Bob wanted to build a dream house and I was his architect. My spec went through several revisions and was ready for its first distribution in August of 1985. I listed both our names as authors. (Austin, Beginnings 2009)

At the time when Dennis and I had started thinking about Power-Point, the only other person in the company who had been seriously interested in the idea was Darrell Boyle, our VP of Marketing. Unfortunately, almost at the same moment when serious work began, Darrell left as part of the necessary cost-cutting and downsizing—of which he was the leading advocate. We had not made much progress up until then, but Darrell liked so much what he had heard about the Power-Point product concept that he didn't let the fact of his leaving get in the way of working on it. Darrell formed his own consulting practice to advise Apple and others on "desktop presentations," and thus did a lot of good for us, as well as for any competitors, as he independently became an industry guru on the subject. We kept in touch and cooperated, although Forethought wasn't a very good client for Darrell because we had no money. Years later, after the acquisition by Microsoft, Darrell came back to head marketing for PowerPoint at the Microsoft Graphics Business Unit.

33 But Isn't PowerPoint Too Simple?

There was one specific continuing problem. The grandiose visions of the early Forethought Foundation project, which had attracted the initial VC investment, made anything more attainable appear puny and unimpressive. After that, the months of jawboning about imaginary mergers that would unite dozens of products in a single huge company made my modest page and a half about making black-and-white over-heads seem like a laughably small idea, not large and complex enough for an important VC-funded startup in Silicon Valley.

Paul Graham has summed up the reaction to his own startup, and I recognize what he's talking about:

I like to find (a) simple solutions (b) to overlooked problems (c) that actually need to be solved, and (d) deliver them as informally as possible, (e) starting with a very crude version 1, then (f) iterating rapidly.

When I first laid out these principles explicitly, I noticed something striking: this is practically a recipe for generating a contemptuous initial reaction. Though simple solutions are better, they don't seem as impressive as complex ones. *Overlooked problems are by definition problems that most people think don't matter.* Delivering solutions in an informal way means that instead of judging something by the way it's presented, people have to actually understand it, which is more work. And starting with a crude version 1 means your initial effort is always small and incomplete. (Graham, New Things 2008, emphasis supplied)

So the initial reaction within Forethought, outside of Dennis and Darrell Boyle and me, was tepid. Most people thought it was one idea which we might do, yes, okay, but surely we would be doing dozens or hundreds of other things too! The longer I worked on ideas for applications, though, the more I became convinced that this was the one—this was the problem that many people actually needed to solve, and that could become a major reason for adopting future systems like Mac and Windows as they matured. I was soon writing business plans in which I claimed that presentation graphics would become a category comparable to spreadsheets, which seemed deeply implausible to most people at the time. (Now, of course, the once-great spreadsheet category has been easily exceeded by PowerPoint.)

For many, many months, no one else at Forethought would really commit whole-heartedly to PowerPoint; partly this was because of the urgency to focus on the publishing business to get immediate revenue, but partly it was because the idea seemed slightly disappointing to them. I tried to combat this by composing more persuasive pitches for the idea. The continuing reservations within Forethought about PowerPoint kept alive all the competing ideas to expand by buying other products, which consumed so much time, energy, and money. Dennis and I met together regularly for creative sessions, which were a refuge, and we spun out the PowerPoint idea in ways that were progressively more and more delightful, at least to us.

34 Why I Thought Many People Wanted PowerPoint

I also lavished time on the endless stratagems to keep Forethought alive, but at the same time I tried writing up plans and expositions about PowerPoint. I started with the basic explanation of why many people would want to buy PowerPoint, and why the precise moment made such a product possible:

> Preparation of business presentations—overhead transparencies, 35mm color slides, and their equivalents for video projection—is a new application area for personal computers. Personal computers and the programs which have been available in the past to make presentations have produced results of such low quality and have required so much effort that really only dedicated computer enthusiasts would put up with using them.
>
> We expect that this will change over the next two years, so that presentations will become one of the broadest and largest horizontal applications for personal computer software. As it happens, personal computer equipment for preparing presentations and audio-visual equipment for displaying presentations are both changing radically so as to be easier to use together. The new personal computers can for the first time support the graphics needed to make presentations. The new audio-visual devices can for the first time economically image and project presentations originated from personal computers. The mutual reinforcement of these changes in the two industries makes presentation graphics on personal computers, at just this moment, a unique opportunity. (Gaskins, PowerPoint Marketing 1986)

35 Leveraging Personal Motivations

I needed to make clear that "presentations" were actually used in businesses all the time, not just on a few ceremonial occasions:

> Everyday presentations are much more common than the very formal occasions for which thousands of dollars are spent to prepare stylized color slides. In fact, a very large number of businesspeople make "presentations" to others all the time as part of their work. These are semi-formal meetings in which an individual attempts to persuade others to make a decision, to approve a course of action, or to accept a result. Almost any manager, professional, or consultant considers presentations of this sort a major part of the job. Sales people perform these presentations with almost every customer. As knowledge workers come to play an increasing role in companies, those people too—the analysts, engineers, and the like—spend a large amount of time on presentations to share information and to gain consensus.

There is a difference between the use of presentations in smaller companies and in larger companies. In smaller companies, it appears, most of the presentations are given to customers or to other outsiders. Such events as proposals to clients, progress reports, and major sales approaches are regularly handled by giving a presentation, even though the managers may seldom sit down themselves and show one another transparencies.

By contrast, in larger companies the great bulk of presentations are held for management and other insiders. Because of the increased difficulty of communicating with larger numbers of people, presentations are regularly used for project reports, internal proposals, status reports, and staff briefings. Very large multi-location companies often institutionalize the presentation and its associated "foils" as a standard form of memorandum. Compared to the vast number of internal presentations, the occasional preparation of slides for the annual meeting or for a standard sales presentation may be much less important.

Whether in small or large companies, however, the individuals making the presentations are united by common motivations which make them a single market for personal computer presentation software:

— an individual's business success can often hinge upon the success of the presentation, yielding a strong personal motivation to do the best job (and to have the best tools) possible; and

— an economic value can be put on effective communication.

(Gaskins, PowerPoint Marketing 1986)

The contrast I described between small and large company usage was purely based on my personal observations. The important thing, though, was the common motivation for all business users: to enhance their personal individual business success, which led them to put an economic value on more effective communication, and thus to be willing to buy the product.

Note that I did *not* target other existing large groups of users of presentations, such as school teachers or military officers. I did not think that bureaucratic organizations would be early to adopt graphical personal computers, because they are driven more by political than economic factors.

I also did *not* plan to target people who were not existing users of presentations. Some of these groups have become very large PowerPoint users, such as clergy and school children, but we left those markets to develop. Our focus was purely on business users, in small and large companies, from one person to the largest multinationals.

36 Potential Customers Are Spending Heavily Now

Every startup always tries to claim some astronomically large "served market," often with numbers pulled from the air and then multiplied several times.

I didn't need to exaggerate. I actually had very persuasive numbers, thanks to the personal connection which gave me access to otherwise-obscure data from the audio-visual industry. Our potential customers, just in the U.S., were already making well over a billion presentation slides every year, even though the work was slow, cumbersome, and expensive. That's certainly a big enough market for a startup to address:

The Presentation Graphics Market is Huge

The total volume of business done annually in the U.S. for "Business Presentations" is generally estimated to be over $6 Billion in 1985, rising to $10 Billion by 1990. (This includes hardware, software, services, and program material for 35mm slides and for overhead transparencies only. It does not include video, films, filmstrips, or other audio-visual market segments.)

The best market research in this area comes from Hope Reports, Inc., headed by Tom Hope, a former employee of Eastman Kodak, now a consultant in Rochester, N.Y. According to his work (all numbers are aggregated and rounded off for simplicity), people in the U.S. produced:

- over 600 million original 35mm slides in 1985;
- over 500 million original overhead transparencies in 1985;
- together, over 1.1 billion presentation slides last year!

It is possible to gain an appreciation for the size of these numbers by hypothesizing that the average "presenter," a serious maker of presentations, makes about 100 slides per year, equivalent to 12 monthly presentations of 8 slides each, or 4 quarterly presentations of 25 slides each. (One study found that the average sales and marketing professional makes between 7 and 9 presentations a year, using between 7 and 10 slides each time—which adds up to 50 to 90 slides per year. That is the average, and our customers are at the upper end of that, so 100 slides per year is reasonable.) If we divide our 1.1 billion slides by 100 slides per presenter, we get the very rough estimate that there are—today—over 10 million people in the U.S. who:

— need presentation software and hardware enough to buy it; and

— would consider presentation capability a major factor when purchasing a personal computer or peripherals.

(Gaskins, PowerPoint Marketing 1986)

Of course, when you're two guys in a tiny startup, a billion presentation slides carry a fair amount of unreality. I left unsaid the usual startup pitch: "if we could get just 0.001% of that market … ." As it turned out, by 2003, it was estimated that PowerPoint was selling more than $1 billion of product per year, and in 2010, Microsoft announced that PowerPoint was installed on over a billion computers (including trialware and pirated copies). Back in 1985, I was just glad to be able to use the word "billion" in my business plan at all.

37 There Are No Successful Competitors

Ordinarily, you'd expect that such a large and coherent market of business buyers would already have been served by developers of personal computer software. Fortunately, I had credible numbers to say the opposite and personal observation corroborated the numbers: essentially *none* of the huge market of presentation customers were using personal computers; they were still using manual methods, even if they owned first-generation, character-mapped personal computers. There was something that had prevented earlier competitors from having any success in this market.

Despite the large number of people making presentations, and the large dollar value of the market, so far presentation graphics has been a rather small category in personal computer software. Again, Hope Reports has some eye-opening numbers:

For 35mm color slides:

— Of the 600 million original slides made in 1985, only 12% were produced using any kind of computer at all (mainframe, service bureau, minicomputer, or personal computer). This number is surprising small, but is rising rapidly, up from 3% in 1983 and 1/10 of 1% in 1978.

— Most of the initial growth has been in centralized systems for corporate communications departments, either dedicated minicomputers or personal computers tied to a larger computer at the vendor's site, not in systems for use by individual presenters.

For overhead transparencies:

— Of the 500 million original transparencies, only 1/2 of 1% were produced using any kind of computer in 1985! This is a very small percentage, given the rise recorded in number of overhead transparencies (500 million in 1985, up from 450 million in 1984 and 400 million in 1983).

— Production of overhead transparencies is typically much more widely distributed than that of 35mm slides (lots and lots of people typing with Orator type balls and IBM Selectrics on pre-printed slide frames), and central services often don't produce them at all.

Hence, if the initial computer systems have been for central service organizations, that explains why they are not being used for overheads.

So Tom Hope's numbers leave us with the realization that 88% of 35mm slides—and 99% of overhead transparencies—are still being produced manually, by people typing, or drawing, or using rub-down lettering or Kroy machines, or using photographic processes.

Why don't those ten million people use personal computers to help them?" (Gaskins, PowerPoint Marketing 1986)

38 Presentations Require Graphical PCs

My answer as to why all earlier competitors had been unsuccessful was obvious to me: this was a category that would be unlocked for the first time only when Windows and Mac replaced first-generation PCs. Categories that would take advantage of that transition were, after all, the original Forethought mission.

Presentations demanded graphical layout of each slide, and earlier PC software had been unable to provide that because of the underpowered and unsuitable hardware:

The reason is simple: Previous generations of personal computers were not powerful enough to do the job. They couldn't address enough code, or execute it fast enough, or both, to support a really simple user interface for graphics tasks.

— Displays with limited resolution, whether text-only or coarse graphics, could not show a presentation on the screen adequately, so a user had to work 'blind.'

— Printers and film recorders were inadequate to produce finished output, so eventually some manual work had to be done to get professional quality.

Limited by all these hardware shortcomings, software for presentation graphics had a hopeless task, and as a result no existing program for use on Apple II or IBM PC machines really does a good job.

This is all changing very rapidly. The current generation of graphics personal computers can support great applications for presentations:

- Both adequate processing power and adequate memory are available in 80286-based machines from IBM (the 'AT' series) and from others (Compaq, ATT, H-P, NEC, Tandy, Zenith, and many more), and in 68000-based Macintoshes from Apple.

- Graphics environments (MS-Windows for IBM and compatibles, Macintosh for Mac) provide a software base of hundreds of person/years each, plus data interchange among programs.

- Current widely sold displays are for the first time adequate to display a presentation slide (640 x 350 color for IBM's EGA, 512 x 342 mono for Macintosh).

- New printers make professional-quality overhead transparencies very easily, particularly color printers and laser printers with PostScript interfaces, or the comparable Xerox Interpress interface.

- New film recording cameras utilizing similar techniques (in fact, some new film recorders will actually use PostScript or Interpress) can produce professional-quality color 35mm slides.

- New video projectors based on Liquid Crystal Displays are just beginning to make possible high-quality and inexpensive direct projection of computer images.

This new generation of personal computers and display peripherals could easily produce at least 80% of all 35mm presentation slides. (According to Hope, about 20% of all slides use photographic images, which would require additional equipment; but availability of alternative computer graphics such as scanned photographs might well cover much of that requirement.)

For overhead transparencies, this new hardware can produce effectively 100% of what anybody wants.

But the new hardware does not make the old software any better. Existing programs have been designed for the limitations of the last generation, and for use by technical specialists, by AV [audio-visual] experts, and by computer enthusiasts. It is still almost always easier for a presenter to sketch out a presentation using pencil and paper, then hand it off to a specialist who manipulates the computer. The further step of new software is required to deliver the advantages promised by the new generation of hardware. (Gaskins, PowerPoint Marketing 1986)

An interesting detail there is that "personal computers ... could easily produce at least 80% of all 35mm presentation slides," and not more, because "about 20% of all slides use photographic images," which was then a barrier to producing them on personal computers.

In fact, digital photographs were hardly known in 1985. There were no common digital cameras or common scanners—no sources for digital images. Even professional slide producers would incorporate photography by creating digital 35mm slides with solid masks for the photo areas, and then double-exposing the final slide with an inverse mask and an analog photo source. Today, this situation is very hard to imagine.

39 Presentations Will Be One of the Largest Markets

If you believe that Windows and Mac will eventually rule the computing roost, then you must conclude that the same new hardware that will be capable of running those graphical environments will also produce new graphical application software markets that will be very broad, with huge numbers of customers—comparable to the great successes of the day, such as Lotus 1–2–3.

I found two other researchers, from the PC industry, who added verisimilitude to the claim that this would be a huge opportunity. For those within Forethought, the message again was: how can it be that a market of this size would not be big enough to be appropriate for a startup? I wrote:

As a new generation of software becomes available for the new hardware, presentation graphics will become a major horizontal category. There have been similar cases before.

• Introduction of floppy diskettes, and then later of inexpensive hard disks, gave rise to two successive generations of successes in widely used horizontal database software.

• The introduction of adequate keyboards and printers gave rise to successes in horizontal word processing software.

• The introduction of 16-bit machines with vastly larger address spaces gave rise to the success of 1–2–3 and other horizontal integrated software.

In the same way, the introduction of the new generation of machines capable of handling high-quality graphics will give rise to new categories of widely sold software for the graphics tasks that large numbers of people want to do, such as making presentations.

This is backed up by some 1985 predictions from International Data Corporation, concerning the percentage of personal computers which will be used for presentation graphics.

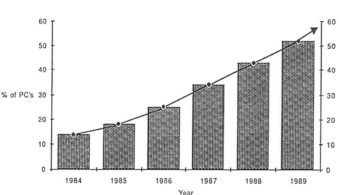

PC's Used for Presentation Graphics

—International Data Corporation, 1985

According to IDC's analysis, in 1984 only 14% of personal computers were used for presentation graphics (a number which is equal to 406,000 machines, when applied to their estimate of the number of personal computers in use).

By 1989, this will increase to 52% of all personal computers— which coincidentally they calculate as equal to 10,600,000 machines, so by 1989 all of our 10 million presenters will finally be able to use appropriate tools.

As a point of comparison, note that IDC thinks (on comparable methodology) that 43% of all personal computers were used for spreadsheets in 1985; they are predicting that presentation graphics will be a more important horizontal than spread sheets.

It is interesting that Future Computing believes the same thing. In their 1985 predictions of unit sales for personal computer software packages, they predict that unit sales for presentation graphics will surpass those of spreadsheets in 1988.

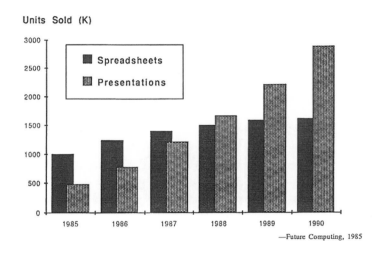

—Future Computing, 1985

Both of these groups of analysts seem to confirm the opinion that making presentations is a widely desired task, and that sales of software to make presentations will increase dramatically as soon as better packages are available to exploit the new hardware just being introduced. (Gaskins, PowerPoint Marketing 1986)

40 This Is More Than a Replacement Market

One of the perpetual fears of startups and their investors is that there is only a short-term market for replacing the old methods of existing users with a new and better method, and then, once the replacement market has been satisfied, the business will stall out and sales will plateau.

My approach to arguing against that fear was to claim that business people got real personal advantages from using presentation visuals, but that existing manual methods were too expensive and cumbersome to allow people to get all they wanted. As new software made it easier, quicker, and cheaper to use presentation visuals, the already huge market actually had the potential to become much larger.

When I made this pitch to Forethought people and investors, and to outsiders, this claim was probably the one most often challenged. It's interesting, from the perspective of twenty-five years later, that it's probably the claim most strikingly demonstrated. Certainly a much higher proportion of business meetings now use PowerPoint than the "1 out of 40" estimated in 1981, and that's not to mention all the non-business uses of PowerPoint that have emerged. I wrote:

Presentation Graphics has Real Benefits

One reason for thinking that these predictions will in fact come true with greatly increased use of personal computers for presentation graphics is that graphic visual aids used in presentations deliver real benefits to users.

A well-known experiment conducted by the Wharton School of the University of Pennsylvania in 1981, studied "Effects of the Use of Overhead Transparencies on Business Meetings." (The study was issued by the Wharton Applied Research Center and was funded in part by the 3M Corporation.) The results were astounding:

- Presenters using overhead transparencies were "perceived as significantly better prepared, more professional, more persuasive, more highly credible, and more interesting" than speakers without visuals.
- Speakers supported by overheads won approval for their projects twice as often as speakers without visuals.
- Speakers with overheads generated on-the-spot decisions 33% more often.
- Use of overheads reduced average meeting length by 28% (equivalent to 42 days per year for the average manager).
- Use of overheads raised retention to as high as 50% from about 10%.

But, despite all these measurable advantages, only one business meeting out of 40 makes use of visuals of any kind!

This suggests that, in the future, even more people could make use of presentation graphics than our 10 million current presenters, if the new personal computers can make it easy enough. The total market size on personal computers may be even larger than substitution for the present manual preparation market alone. (Gaskins, PowerPoint Marketing 1986)

41 The Best Feature Was Hard to Understand

Here is what I personally thought was the most important reason why people would really want to buy PowerPoint, and it really was enough all by itself to understand the pitch:

> All these advantages are important, and the time and cost advantages are critical for cost justification. But from a sales standpoint, the most important advantage of using a program like the one envisioned here is control. When successfully completed, this program will allow the content originators to directly and personally control their own presentations. For anyone who makes presentations regularly, the advantage (in time and in quality) of gaining enough leverage to directly and personally create all needed presentation materials far outweighs all other advantages. (Gaskins, PowerPoint Marketing 1986)

But, to appreciate this advantage, you pretty much had to personally be a presenter.

I noticed early that other people who themselves made lots of presentations "got" this aspect of personal control and immediately understood the leverage it would give them.

But people who hadn't experienced the frustrations of working on this task through other people didn't really understand. Unfortunately, venture capital investors did not make many presentations, they were professional *consumers* of presentations and demonstrations; and so they hadn't experienced those daily frustrations. For them, the presentations just appeared, apparently effortlessly.

I always mentioned the feature of "personal control," but I didn't rely on it to convince anyone who didn't viscerally feel the flexibility and the quality improvement that would be possible by cutting out all those people in the middle.

> The Wharton School study demonstrated advantages of presentation visuals, no matter how they are produced. There are addi-

tional benefits to using a personal computer to prepare presentation graphics.

First, the ability to see and refine presentations on a flexible medium such as a graphic display screen allows the presenter to improve the effectiveness of presentation content, particularly in clarifying complex material. This advantage is analogous to the higher quality of writing which is widely observed to be possible using word processing software on a personal computer, as opposed to dictating and correcting typed drafts.

By using a representation on personal computers, parts of a single presentation can be prepared by several individuals, then put together in a common format. With convenient tools for exchanging information via communications, several individuals can collaborate on a presentation—even if they are not in the same location.

Digital communication of presentations from one location to another is also useful for preparing a presentation in one location, then sending the files via communications to a distant location where they are imaged (on a laser printer or a film recorder) at full original quality. Most managers in multi-location companies are all too practiced at trying to make out blurry presentation foils sent by facsimile transmission from a distant site for a conference-telephone announcement or meeting. If the presentations were prepared on personal computers, then the files could be sent instead and the foils produced locally at the highest quality. Similarly, data for color slides can be prepared in California, sent electronically, and imaged on a film recorder in Boston, to produce 35mm slides in Boston in an hour—much faster than if physical slides had to be transported.

Substitution of personal computers for human assistants can reduce the time required to produce presentations (often dramatically), and reduce the cost to prepare presentations (equally dramatically). More important in practice is the gain in flexibility; a presenter can work through lunch hours, into the night, or on weekends, without requiring typists and artists. In this way, also, last minute corrections, changes, and revisions can be made ... correctly. How many times has every presenter had to explain mistakes and missing slides caused by last-minute revisions gone awry?

All these advantages are important, and the time and cost advantages are critical for cost justification. But from a sales standpoint, the most important advantage of using a program like the one envisioned here is control. When successfully completed, this program will allow the content originators to directly and personally control their own presentations. For anyone who makes presentations regularly, the advantage (in time and in quality) of gaining enough leverage to directly and personally create all needed presentation materials far outweighs all other advantages. (Gaskins, PowerPoint Marketing 1986)

42 There Is No Market Leader to Displace

Another great fear of startups and of their investors is that the startup will create a good product but then be unable to displace a competitor who is much larger, much better financed, and has much more control of sales channels and of customer purchasing organizations. In such a case, the large and dominant competitor may manage to buy time until it can copy the innovation and succeed in crushing the small startup, or even a larger innovator. You don't want to pick a fight of this kind.

For example, Excel, even though it was the first successful spreadsheet on Mac, still had a great battle to displace Lotus 1–2–3 on PCs. Word, even being a successful early word processor on Mac, still had a mighty struggle to displace WordPerfect on PCs. And this despite the fact that Excel and Word had all the advantages: they were from Microsoft, the maker of Windows; Microsoft had oceans of money and had excellent connections in sales channels and with customers; and both Lotus and WordPerfect were extremely dilatory in producing Windows versions.

My counter to this fear was to say that because presentations had never been even adequately good on character-mapped PCs, there *were* no successful competitors. There were lots of aspiring competitors, as I listed elsewhere, but none of them had any devoted or even satisfied users. This always makes it easier to enter a market.

The first success is yet to come

Writing in *InfoWorld* in early 1985 on the topic "What's ahead for Software," William J. Coggshall summed up this situation when he wrote:

Graphics will come into its own. Currently, there is no market leader.

If you try to name the top five spreadsheet companies, you can tick them right off. Try to name the top five graphics companies, and they don't come readily to mind—for presentation graphics in particular.

> There is an opportunity there to maintain substantial growth by providing professionals with a way to express their words and figures graphically ... .

We believe that the first successful competitor will leverage off of MS-Windows and Macintosh on the new generation of graphics personal computers to provide, for the first time, an adequate approach to using personal computers to create the kind of presentation lots of people need to create. The result will be a very successful software product, and our plan is to make Forethought that first successful competitor. (Gaskins, PowerPoint Marketing 1986)

43 Analyzing My Corpus of Slides from the Grand Tour

We started early on the task of trying to find out with what frequency different kinds of slides were actually made by users, and thus how we should prioritize features in PowerPoint. A second use for this data would be to decide on what the default styles in PowerPoint should be.

We started with a collection of real-world overhead slides, a part of those that I had collected in my banker's box during my Grand Tour of technology vendors for Northern Telecom.

I find the first such tally, made with Dennis Austin, in my notes for June 1985 (from which this recap is taken).

We found lots of diagrams, by far the largest number being simple "boxes and lines" with labels—that is, multiple boxes of various shapes containing labels, connected by lines or arrows that were often also labeled. We found large numbers of bulleted lists, both alone and combined with the diagrams in various patterns; the great majority of text was in lists of bulleted phrases, not in full sentences. Of the bulleted lists, by far the most were only a single level; very few used a two-level "outline" style, and we had only one example of a three-level outline. There were very few paragraphs of text (full sentences written continuously), often a quotation being presented for its exact content. About 55% of the overheads contained bulleted lists, about 70% of the overheads contained diagrams, and about 35% of the overheads combined both. Virtually every overhead had a title at the top. The "Other" category of slides included slides containing tables, about 2% of the total collection; of these, a majority were text-only tables.

This overall simplicity came about partly because the overheads had been produced manually or with poor tools, and so it was difficult to fine-tune the slide layouts. Most of them had been sketched in pencil first and then typed by someone else, so it hadn't been easy to vary the layout to match the actual sizes of text items or diagram parts. Also, since most of the slides were typed, there was no opportunity to use variation in typography to direct attention within text; this tended to incline presenters to use visuals for graphical diagrams more than "word slides" to support live presentations.

In the first batch of about 400 overheads, we found:

Title above a diagram	30%
Title above a diagram above a single-level bullet list	28%
Title above a single-level bullet list	12%
Title only, or diagram only	6%
Title above diagram and a single-level bullet list, side by side	4%
Title above diagram and a single-level bullet list, overlapping	3%
Title above a two-level bullet list (multiple items at top level)	4%
Title above a two-level bullet list (one item at top level)	2%
Title above a three-level bullet list [only one example found]	0%
Title above two single-level bullet lists, side by side	2%
Title above a paragraph of text	2%
Other (including tables)	7%

It wasn't difficult to conclude that (1) a way of constructing "boxes and lines" diagrams with labels, plus (2) a way of constructing single-level and multi-level bulleted lists, and (3) a way of combining those freely below a title, together would make it easy to duplicate almost all the overheads in the corpus.

A similar tally could be repeated now, using modern PowerPoint slides found on Internet slide-sharing sites. My guess is that current PowerPoint slides would exhibit somewhat greater novelty, because novelty is so much easier, even despite the fact that most organizations use the PowerPoint defaults ultimately derived from these patterns of more than twenty-five years ago.

44 The Design Spec Was Vital Before the Internet

These days, we don't really remember how difficult it was to get information prior to the age of the Internet. This made product development completely different, as a passage from Eric Ries about current techniques suggests:

> Some people misunderstand the Lean Startup model as simply applying pull to customer wants. This assumes that customers could tell us what products to build and that this would act as the pull signal to product development to make them ... .
>
> [But] customers often don't know what they want. Our goal in building products is to be able to run experiments ... . Thus, the right way to think about the product development process in a Lean Startup is that it is responding to pull requests in the form of experiments that need to be run.
>
> As soon as we formulate a hypothesis that we want to test, the product development team should be engineered to design and run this experiment as quickly as possible, using the smallest batch size that will get the job done. (Ries 2011)

This is all very well when a prototype can be crafted, put on a server, and exposed to potential customers in a few hours or a day.

But back in the mid-1980s, none of that was possible. You could put together faked "screen shots" and talk someone through the idea (which is what we did), but it was impossible to write an application quickly and distribute it to anyone with an expectation that it would work. The result was that a far larger investment was needed before feedback was possible, and so the people doing the innovation had to imagine the product and its use in far more detail than is necessary today, and apply careful judgment to their precise imaginings. The result was a full design specification. For PowerPoint, every pixel in the design drawings was considered and accurately placed, like making precise architectural drawings.

Having worked in print shops back in the days of moveable metal type, I compare this to the change in typesetting. Today, you type your headline in any font you want and just experiment with sizes, styles, and alternate fonts until it looks right. Back in the days of moveable type, you had to imagine very carefully and precisely what all the letter forms would look like and exactly what size you wanted, and write down the font, size, and style of every bit of type on the page—and then edit that marked-up spec, long before you saw a proof from the typesetter. When a proof came back, only small changes could be made without incurring punitive costs. I find that today I can no longer imagine type in advance as well as I could then. It's so much easier to just give it a try.

In the mid-1980s, we had to be very careful to work out a fully detailed hypothesis of what customers wanted, judge all the parts of it ourselves, get what feedback we could, and invest with the expectation that we would get one experiment—and if that single experiment failed, so would the product and the company.

45 PowerPoint Design Beginnings

While I was writing all these reasons why PowerPoint was big enough and would be successful enough to be the Forethought internal product, Dennis Austin and I kept working on its design and Dennis began writing a design spec.

We had both been impatient about all the other calls on our time that delayed work on PowerPoint, but one result of the slow process of hashing out the spec was that it was becoming very clearly imagined, even in the earliest versions.

Dennis has described how this started:

> Starting from Bob's proposal from a year prior, I sat down to write a specification for a product. The product design details required a lot of invention. Bob was able to spend many hours with me hashing over ideas. It was a productive process and the quality of my designs reflected Bob's support and feedback. I have compared our collaboration to a building design project: Bob wanted to build a dream house and I was his architect. My spec went through several revisions and was ready for its first distribution in August of 1985. I listed both our names as authors. [See (Austin and Gaskins, Presenter [PowerPoint] Design 1985) and (Austin and Gaskins, Output Samples 1985).]
>
> Bob Gaskins had a clear vision for the kind of product he wanted to create and there were several key insights that would

guide the design. Presenter was to create presentations—not simply slides. It was to provide a means for structuring, writing, and reviewing a presentation as a whole. That would also make it easy to re-sequence old slides and to re-use parts of old presentations to make new ones. It would construct a consistent layout for all slides in a presentation. The layout included items like a graphics border, corporate logo, running heads, and slide numbers. The Presenter package would also use templates with such features to support corporate graphic standards.

It should allow the production of various presentation materials from a single master file. This would include both presentations slides (overhead transparencies, but also on-screen presentations, and perhaps eventually 35mm slides) and printed handouts. The potential high quality of output should be matched by high-resolution graphics and typeset-quality text. Bob was good at communicating his vision to the management of Forethought, to potential sources of financing, and to me. When I sat down to design the details of Presenter, the goals were crystal clear." (Austin, Beginnings 2009)

This first spec for PowerPoint took an unusual form, almost entirely in pictures. It consisted of mocked-up screen shots with limited "discussion" captions, then mock-ups of all the menus, dialog boxes, and sample output pages. All the screen shots, menus, and dialogs were set up to look like Microsoft Windows, not like Macintosh. This graphical format required a great number of particular points to be fully decided and precisely documented in the mock-ups, and was easy to grasp.

46 *Initial Design: Principles*

From Dennis Austin:

In the presentation graphics category, the conventional model was to describe an intended slide and then have the program produce it. You described the slide by filling in forms. You selected a type of slide and then detailed its precise characteristics. Then you could preview the results. This was obviously not the way Presenter would work.

Our model was the what-you-see-is-what-you-get paradigm, popularized at Xerox using a phrase borrowed from the popular 60's TV show, *Laugh-In*. Presenter displayed the "preview" at all times, and the user interacted with the finished appearance. All this seems pretty obvious to modern thinking. To Bob and me and to pretty much anybody else at Forethought, it seemed obvious even in 1985. But the general industry thought much differently. Anyway, even with our fervent devotion to the graphics user interface model, I needed some design rules for this particular effort.

I took ideas from the wisdom of the day:

The principle of least surprise: You might not be able to make things obvious, but at least you could design them so that they made sense once discovered. Once you realize that software is designed with this principle in mind, you can sometimes guess how something works.

Make easy things easy and hard things possible: this idea, later sloganized by Eric Wall, emphasized the commonplace activities. Make sure that the everyday stuff is straightforward. Other stuff needs to be there, but don't worry about how easy it is.

More narrowly, though, I was aiming at a particular audience—an audience identified by Bob Gaskins. Our users were familiar with computers, but probably not graphics software. They were highly motivated to look their best in front of others, but they weren't savvy in graphics design. It was my job to make Presenter easy to learn and use for this audience specifically. (Austin, Beginnings 2009)

47 Initial Design: Slides

Dennis Austin recalls designing the basic foundations of what was a slide:

Apple was selling a vector drawing program for the Macintosh. Named MacDraw, it was patterned after their earlier effort, LisaDraw. I had used LisaDraw during my time at Gavilan. I made my own presentations with MacDraw and printed them on the LaserWriter, and this influenced my design thinking. Very early I decided that drawing vector "objects" would be the basic metaphor for Presenter. I respected the precedents being set in MacDraw, but still thought the details of drawing would need to be a lot different in Presenter.

I could simplify the usage considerably by targeting precisely the features needed for creating typical presentation slides—not elaborate drawings. The Presenter drawing surface, a single slide, had known bounds. These could be adjusted, of course, but the output of the drawing had a set real-world size. For MacDraw and similar programs, the drawing was abstract and expanded as needed. Scaling and fitting to an output medium was a separate problem and output might even spread across multiple pages.

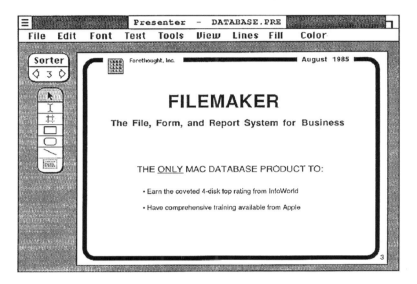

Mock-up of design for a slide in the first PowerPoint spec.

The default slide size I chose was 7.5 by 10 inches. This seemed ideal, because it had a 3:4 aspect ratio that was the same as computer monitors of the day, and it also fit US letter paper with exactly 0.5 inch margins. In contrast to every other application I'd seen, my default page (slide) had a horizontal or landscape orientation. This was appropriate for on-screen presentations, obviously, but I thought it was also best for overhead projectors where the bottom part of vertical slides was often hard for the audience to see. The Macintosh system software accommodated landscape printing, but it didn't support that orientation as a default. Unsupported software tricks were necessary to accomplish my ends, along with a lobbying campaign at Apple to make the feature a standard capability. (Austin, Beginnings 2009)

48 Initial Design: Drawing

Drawings were the most common elements we had found on overheads. Dennis Austin recalls how the design of PowerPoint drawing evolved:

> Presenter users would build slides using the drawing metaphor, but the "drawings" would be only simple diagrams and text. As already mentioned, that simplified the interface considerably and also permitted specialization in the areas we thought important. I omitted many features offered by MacDraw, including dimensioning, arbitrary polygons, and freehand curves. More interestingly, we largely obscured the significance of stacking order. Most objects would have no fill (we had no color, remember) and we were trying only to build diagrams.
>
> MacDraw had other complexities to be reckoned with. You could click on an object to select it, but you could also simply drag the object to reposition it. Since a click sometimes entailed a slight, accidental mouse movement, the difference was one of timing. It was confusing to new users and sloppy clickers because an attempted selection often resulted in unintentional movement of an object. I addressed the problem by inventing a different kind of selection highlighting and requiring that you could only move or resize a selected object. You couldn't select and move in one mouse motion.
>
> For graphic balance it was typically appropriate to arrange objects symmetrically, or at least carefully, with respect to the slide area. For that reason, I adopted a measurement system having the origin at the center of the slide rather than the usual upper left corner. That way it was easier to place content in a pleasing design.
>
> I added movable guidelines, at first called T-squares, to aid in the positioning of objects. (The name T-square was borrowed from FileMaker, Forethought's hot product at the time.) When a T-square was being dragged, its measured position appeared next to the cursor. By holding down the Macintosh Option key, the measured position was shown in relative numbers so it was easy to measure relative distances without resorting to rulers and doing arithmetic. The T-squares appeared, by default, crossing at the center of the slide and thus again allowed easy positioning of objects at the center, horizontally or vertically, of the slide. T-squares were "magnetic" in that objects being dragged with the mouse would snap to positions relative to the guideline. The edg-

es would snap, but so would the object centers—another aid to centering and symmetry.

I noticed that objects often needed to be resized without changing their position. That gave rise to the Option key resize modifier that resized the object but anchored it at the center. Of course it could be used in combination with the already-traditional Shift modifier that maintained aspect ratio while resizing. (MacPaint inspired the Option key idea, but MacPaint didn't have the concept of resizing.)

One additional problem of object placement was accuracy. The Macintosh screen was small, but, luckily, slides typically contain items large enough to be seen from the back of the room. Consequently, you could usually work with the entire slide on view—50% scale. We provided other scales, of course, for detail work. I selected a limited set of scales with simple multiples. It allowed use of integer arithmetic (*i.e.* fast arithmetic) in calculation, and, at the same time, preserved perfect registration of pixels. Two points placed coincidentally at one scale would be coincident at all scales. (Austin, Beginnings 2009)

49 Initial Design: Text

Text was the next most common element we had found on overheads. Dennis Austin explains how much work went into designing Power-Point text:

Text Boxes

Unlike MacDraw, beautiful text was a centerpiece of Presenter. Instead of simple labels with a single text style, Presenter had to provide full typeset-quality text as a word processor might. Unlike word processors, though, text appeared in graphics elements that I called text boxes. A text box was like other graphic objects in that it could have a line border or a fill, but its contents were a miniature document. It was a "word processor in a box," including not only typefaces, sizes and styles, but word wrap, line and paragraph spacing, margins, tabs, etc.

Presenter's text was even more specialized. Presentations often included bulleted lists, and sometimes sub-lists with their own bullets. I chose this as the default format of Presenter's text box. A bulleted list consisted of paragraphs with a hanging indent, *i.e.* a paragraph where the margin of the first line is left of the subsequent lines, and with paragraph spacing that separates the items in the list. The indention of the paragraph was fully adjustable, but this was the default style.

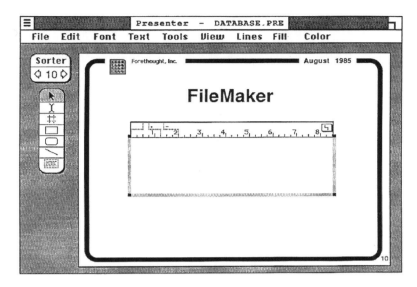

Mock-up of design for text box in the first PowerPoint spec.

To cater to sub-lists, enabling an outline of sorts, paragraphs had a "level." Each level had its own margins of indention, so you could easily type in a simple bulleted outline without fussing with formatting. Full formatting was, of course, available if the defaults weren't suitable.

Label Text

Text boxes weren't the only kind of text needed. For diagrams, it was important to be able to create simple text labels. In MacDraw labels were pieces of text in a single font and style. Presenter had these simple labels (although the text could be fully styled), but it also allowed graphic objects to contain text.

Text contained in an object (rectangle, oval, etc.) was centered in the object both horizontally and vertically. This made it very convenient to construct typical diagrams and simple tables out of labeled boxes. If needed, it was possible to anchor the text as needed instead of centering it. Labels were created with the label tool and had, by default, left alignment. If you edited the text, the upper left corner of the object on the slide did not change. Here too the anchor point could be changed if needed.

The distinction between simple label objects and graphic-objects-containing-text was made by an attribute called size-to-text. The size of label was determined by the text it contained. Even if you later added a frame or a fill, these objects automatically resized when their text was changed. Graphic objects that contained text, however, had a set size and were resized by adjusting handles in the usual way. The text display was centered in the object. If the object wasn't big enough to contain the text, it simply stuck out of the frame. By the way, text boxes (the full word-processor kind of text) also were size-to-text. Because their text word-wrapped, the width of a text box was fixed. The bottom of the frame, though, was automatically set by the size of the content. (Austin, Beginnings 2009)

50 Initial Design: Pictures

Dennis Austin explains how the Mac "picture" format was central to PowerPoint:

> With simple drawing tools plus the elaborate text tools, Presenter was ready to create most of the content of presentations.
>
> It was our intention to leverage the rich world of other Macintosh applications to provide more specialized content. Doing so made our job easier, of course, but it also made it easier for the user. Content could be created using the tools most appropriate for the job by experts in those particular tools, and then pulled into the presentation where needed. It seemed far better to create graphs in Excel for example, than to introduce our own set of tools for the same purpose. And those who missed polygons or other features from MacDraw could create their complex drawings there and then paste them into a presentation.
>
> Presenter achieved this with deep support for the Macintosh concept of a picture. Picture was a standard format of the platform and could contain vector drawing, bitmap art, and text in any combination and arrangement. Arbitrary visual content could be captured in a picture, placed on the clipboard, and pasted onto a slide. Pictures scaled well, so a picture could be resized on the slide and placed as needed. (Austin, Beginnings 2009)

51 Initial Design: Master Slide

The problems caused by working at too low a level are very real, and so once we decided that PowerPoint would need to be "direct drive," we had to find new solutions to make that possible.

For instance, the simple "direct-drive" approach to putting a border on every slide would be to just draw a line around the edges of every slide. But then, when you wanted to change the border, you'd have to go back and redraw it on every slide—earlier products for PCs in fact worked just this way, or at least required resetting a parameter on every slide individually and resaving each slide as an independent file.

So PowerPoint introduced the "slide master," an extra sort of ghost slide in every presentation, whose content appeared as a background on all the other slides; you draw a border once on the slide master, and an uneditable border appears on all the slides in that presentation (it can only be edited on the master); this preserves the direct-drive interface, but raises the level at which you are working. (Eventually, in future versions, this line of thought would be elaborated into "templates.")

The idea is similar to that of "headers" and "footers" in word processing documents, and we extended it in similar ways. For example, a code typed on the slide master would turn into the page number on each different slide, just as a code typed in a header will turn into the page number on each page of a document. Similarly, the master slide evolved to include the idea of a different master for the first slide versus all others (like a special header for the first page in a document), and eventually to multiple masters associated with different parts of a presentation (like multiple headers for different chapters of a report).

Dennis Austin on the origins of the "master slide" in PowerPoint:

> Building presentations out of slides demanded some sort of structural similarity among slides. There was to be a graphics theme uniting slides, but in terms of content, the main structuring elements were a title and a body. Titles were to be text, of course. A body could be text or a graphics element, but text was the unifying theme Presenter could provide. Slides had two distinguished objects: a title and a body. The titles could be extracted for help in organizing the slides. Body items, text or otherwise, weren't used for organization in the initial version of PowerPoint.
>
> My main idea for unifying the look of slides was to provide a "model slide" whose attributes were copied for other slides. The model slide had two functions. It provided background art—a

border, logo identification or any other consistent information—and provided the location and format of the title and body objects. Background art was the same for all slides (it could be omitted for exceptions), but title and body formatting was only the default. Any slide could change after it was created.

The background art capability was also the vehicle for providing slide numbers, dates, and similar text substitutions in a standard location. About the same time, Aldus Corporation invented a very similar device for their new product, PageMaker. They used the name "master page," though, so by the time Presenter got to market we decided to change the name of our model slide to master slide. (Austin, Beginnings 2009)

52 Initial Design: Title Sorter and Slide Sorter

Every slide in the corpus we had examined had a title. Dennis Austin recalls how the first devices for organizing slides were designed:

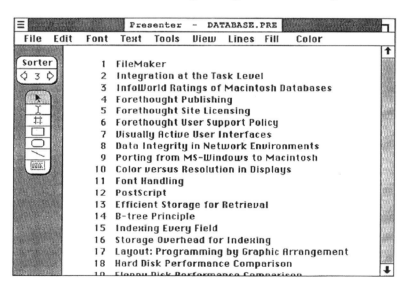

Mock-up of design for title sorter in first PowerPoint spec.

Title Sorter

Every slide had a title. It could be empty, or invisible, but it existed. The title provided a name for every slide and Presenter gathered those names to display a list of slides by title. The view was called Title Sorter in the original version of the product. It eventually became the Outline view when the text in the body object (if any) was included.

Slide Sorter

Thanks to a surprisingly capable graphics system in the Macintosh tool kit, it was possible to display images of slides at greatly reduced scale. That allowed a special view of the presentation showing slides as thumbnail images. The effect was much like sorting slides on a light table, an extremely novel feature at the time. The slide images could be copied, deleted, or dragged on-screen to reorder the presentation.

Making this feature practical required that the program construct thumbnail bitmaps of the slides to optimize rather slow slide drawing times. The approach was practical, though, and never failed to impress new customers. (Austin, Beginnings 2009)

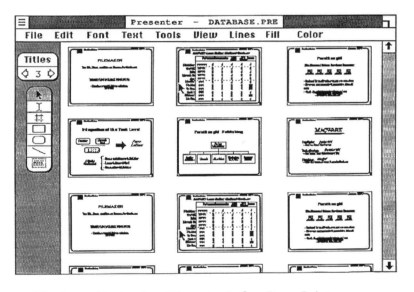

Mock-up of design for slide sorter in first PowerPoint spec.

53 Initial Design: Slide Show

Dennis Austin describes how "slide show" was designed, even though for the first versions of PowerPoint it could only be used for looking at shows on the screen of the computer itself; early Macs did not offer video-out connectors, so there was no way to put the show on external monitors or projectors:

> It was sometimes useful to give a presentation with the slides displayed directly on the screen with no other clutter. It could be used for a one-on-one presentation and, with bigger displays in the future, for larger groups.
>
> Scaling slides to fill the screen and hiding the menu bar were not too difficult, but Apple didn't officially support it. In fact, it was a violation of the Macintosh user interface rules. Presenter was the first Macintosh application with a convincing reason to hide the menu bar and break out of the windowing environment. I showed this to the user interface experts at Apple and lobbied them for support.
>
> Once the menu bar and all controls were removed from the screen, the user was in a mode from which there was no obvious exit. The mouse button was used to advance the slide, so that didn't help. We settled on using the ESC key as the emergency exit. It didn't have much precedent in the Macintosh UI, but it was the standard shortcut to cancel modal dialog boxes. That seemed like a precedent. (Austin, Beginnings 2009)

54 *Initial Design: Notes and Handouts*

In the last of his notes on the initial design, Dennis Austin describes the "notes pages" and "handout pages" which could be produced by PowerPoint in addition to slides:

> It was easy to take advantage of Macintosh graphics scaling to produce handout pages from the slides. Using a model handout page, analogous to the model slide, you could set up the background graphics, page numbering, etc. and then Presenter could produce handout pages with two, three, or six slides printed at reduced scale on each page.
>
> Reusing the same idea, we created notes pages. Each notes page showed a single slide at half scale leaving the other half of the page for notes. You could flip through notes pages the same as you could slides, adding notes as appropriate. The notes pages were actually a type of "slide" in themselves, so anything you could draw on a slide you could draw on a notes page.

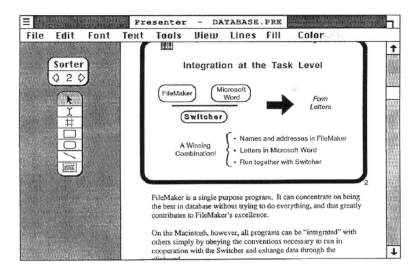

Mock-up of design for a notes page in first PowerPoint spec.

Both handouts and notes pages were printed at the opposite orientation from the slides. The default, then, was to print them vertically. This gave an efficient use of space on the page, and vertically oriented pages were more convenient as handouts in any case. (Austin, Beginnings 2009)

The notes page format was directly patterned after a standard format that I had been required to use at Bell-Northern Research and Northern Telecom, created by the corporate art department; the books handed out at presentations had on each page a small reproduction of a slide at the top and amplifying text or tables (which could be what was to be spoken at the presentation) below. The handout pages, two, three, or six slides per page, with or without space to take notes, didn't have a precursor at BNR and NT.

55 Design for a Particular Task (Don't Generalize)

By this time in the design process, I had become firmly convinced that the right thing to do was to design for the very particular task of making presentation visuals. I still understood this as an instance of the larger class of documents which were sequences of single pages that needed visual layout, but we agreed not to give consideration to anything other than presentations. This was a help in making progress on the spec:

In order to maximize the power of the Presenter program and at the same time keep its use as simple and intuitive as possible, it is essential that every element and feature be sharply focused on the particular task of making presentations.

Many programs are used for making presentations today, and all of them have some helpful features, but each of them also has a host of lacking features and irrelevant complexities which make them much harder to use than necessary. Part of the Presenter design is to extract and utilize the successful features from other applications, adding only the special features especially required for presentations.

The same technical features which are present in Presenter could be used to make any number of other one-page documents—flyers, posters, point-of-sale information, bill stuffers, sales bulletins, and so on. We expect some customers to discover this, and to use the product for purposes other than presentations. But design will concentrate on tuning all the features to be in the form which is best for the narrow task of presentations. (Gaskins, PowerPoint Marketing 1986)

56 *PowerPoint Development Begins for Macintosh*

Six months later, in November 1985, when we managed to extend the debentures by another $250,000, we felt we could assign the one person full time. We invested about $40,000 over the next six months. (Gaskins, Forethought History 1987)

The decision on whether to start development of PowerPoint for Windows or Mac remained a difficult one. During the initial planning, the spec had assumed Windows as the default, but our own experience with Windows made us very cautious.

Information that could be misleading was very common. I talked with Paul Brainerd at Aldus, who told me (according to my notes of 27 August 1985) that Aldus was completely committed to Windows, and at that time already had their flagship PageMaker running on Windows. He pronounced Windows as better designed and more robust than Mac. Even though that's what he said, it was the final details that mattered, and PageMaker did not actually ship on Windows until February 1987, about a year and a half later, and even then had to ship with a Windows 1.0 runtime, so that users could use it without buying Windows. Here again, our first-hand experiments with Windows had given us some insight to match up against the reports of others.

I learned very early during the PowerPoint planning period that Microsoft was going to introduce its own applications first on Macintosh. They did so (Mac Word earlier in 1985, and then Mac Excel in September 1985), both before Windows 1.0 shipped.

From this confirmation, I deduced that Windows was going to be delayed, and that it would change to become more like Mac in order to ultimately become the winner on PC hardware. That made it sensible for Microsoft to ship first on Mac, where there was better development support, all the while planning to ship the same applications on Windows. All that reasoning turned out to be true—although we had then no idea how long it would take for Windows to come up to speed. Excel shipped on Windows in 1987; Word didn't ship on Windows until very late 1989—just six months before PowerPoint for Windows.

Twenty-five years later, Tandy Trower (then the manager of Windows at Microsoft) recalled:

> Even at Microsoft, getting developers to write Windows software was a challenge. Microsoft's own applications group was currently mostly focused on the applications they were developing for the Apple Macintosh, to some extent because Microsoft's chief competition, Lotus and WordPerfect were largely ignoring the Mac as a platform. (Trower 2010)

Lotus and WordPerfect were equally ignoring Windows. Tandy could have said that the focus on Mac at Microsoft was also because the Applications Division needed to ship products. Excel could ship two years earlier on Mac than on Windows, and Word could ship four and a half years earlier on Mac than on Windows.

We all had much the same information. Forethought was one of the smallest Windows ISVs (Independent Software Vendors), and yet Tandy Trower made personal calls on us to tell us about the Windows strategy. We just didn't think we could successfully ship a product for Windows, yet, though we planned to later. Excel and Word obviously thought the same.

Many of the larger ISVs got a lot of attention from IBM and came to a different conclusion, which was that neither Mac nor Windows was all that important, and that they could coast on MS-DOS and a character-mapped windowing system for DOS from IBM called "TopView" until OS/2 and Presentation Manager became its replacement. This strategy mistake brought low a number of previously successful companies.

Dennis Austin remembers this period of decision making:

> An odd thing had happened during the design phase. We started by assuming that we were targeting Microsoft Windows. That seemed like the path to long-term success because Microsoft ran on the mainstream, open system and was likely to form an eventual standard. I had acquired a good bit of experience with Windows during the previous effort with Foundation, though, and I didn't really think Windows could meet our needs. Its graphics and typographic support were weak and it was immature in all respects.
>
> We decided that the better strategy was to build for Macintosh first and to move to Windows when it was ready. It may seem ludicrous to view the Macintosh, at 16 months old, as being mature. But, perhaps owing to earlier experience with Lisa, Apple had this simple machine quite well buttoned-down. It had a simpler programming model and a more complete and well-documented toolkit. It had an effective graphics system that was easy to control precisely. More important, it had a well-designed text subsystem. All this is not to mention that the system was already proven to be efficient for the kind of work we wanted to do.
>
> The Macintosh had a key feature that Windows didn't even appreciate—the Apple LaserWriter. Unlike laser printers available for the IBM PC, LaserWriters were based on Adobe PostScript. PostScript could produce the graphics we needed and, more particularly, the text. Beautiful fonts in any size, and printable in "landscape" orientation. Some companies were already buying a Macintosh and a LaserWriter for the sole purpose of preparing presentation slides—in MacWrite or MacDraw!
>
> What's more, Apple's admittedly small market was genuinely excited about using the machine. Microsoft's customers were extremely skeptical about Windows and you couldn't even install it without upgrading your configuration and buying a mouse. It was our opinion that the Macintosh was the machine that would break the ice and eventually prepare a market for Windows.
>
> To understand our new target environment more deeply, I switched to using a Macintosh at the office. Although limited in scope, it was a delightful machine to use with interesting surprises around every corner. I wrote specifications in MacWrite and I drew up sample screen images in MacPaint. (Austin, Beginnings 2009)

It was pretty clear that Mac was way ahead of Windows, and everything we had learned by experimenting with both platforms confirmed this. Nevertheless, it was important to keep our commitment to a near-term Windows version strong, if only to head off any temptation to take shortcuts in the Mac implementation that would make it harder to port to Windows. In fact, we knew that Windows was missing large facilities that Mac provided; we were betting that Windows would be augmented so that it would become easier to write applications for it comparable to those on Mac, basing this hope on the fact that Microsoft's own apps were being shipped first for Mac.

That was a correct bet, but we overestimated how soon that could happen for a graphics-intensive application. We ended up investing *three times* the development work on PowerPoint 2.0 for Windows as we had previously invested in PowerPoint 1.0 and 2.0 together for Mac, and we didn't ship our first Windows version until mid-1990, three years later than on Mac (rather than the six months glibly predicted).

Despite our decision to do our own PowerPoint first for Mac, we kept pushing the developers of our published Mac products to come up with Windows versions of their products. We did this because the published MACWARE products were less graphics-demanding than PowerPoint, and we hoped that shipping a Windows product would teach us something. None of the developers could produce a Windows version—they didn't want to learn, they couldn't afford development machines, they thought it was too disappointing. All that tended to confirm our decision to start PowerPoint on Mac.

57 *Explaining the Decision to Develop for Mac First*

The decision to prioritize Mac PowerPoint first was controversial because of all the conflicting information and opinions. Once that decision was made, I spent some months polishing what I hoped was a persuasive rationale for the decision.

We were going to commit our major product development to the same Mac platform which had so far produced only disappointing sales for us. We could hardly afford to lose technical credibility with our investors again, so the explanation had to be convincing to someone who didn't really understand the technical gaps in Windows. Here's my version of the explanation as it appeared in June 1986 (very similar drafts were much earlier):

Relative Timing of Macintosh and MS-Windows Versions

During the last several months, we have been discussing the product with Apple and with Macintosh users, we have also been discussing it with MS-DOS users and with presentation hardware companies. It has been interesting to observe that the Macintosh users grasp immediately the nature of the breakthrough, because Presenter is the natural way of making presentations in the Macintosh (or MS-Windows) environment. But MS-DOS users have had much more difficulty grasping the clear differentiation of Presenter from its older competitors.

In thinking about the reasons for this, we have realized that to fully grasp the Presenter product concept you must hypothesize an environment in which

— most personal computers have a high-quality graphics display, a mouse pointing device, and software to exploit them;

— most personal computers have a graphics printer, capable of printing multiple fonts and arbitrary graphics at moderate to very high quality;

— many other graphics programs exist, all observing the same standards of data interchange, so that text and graphics data can be received from them;

— many programs utilize the same user interface standards, so that moving rapidly from one program to another is smooth and not disorienting;

— some method exists for instantly switching from the context of using one program to using another, rather than quitting one application and opening another;

— device-independent graphics standards permit proofing documents on one device, then printing them on another substantially more expensive device, with some assurance that they will print correctly (*e.g.*, a laser printer or a $30,000 phototypesetter).

We believe that precisely these conditions will evolve under the influence of MS-Windows, eventually—but all of them are already true on Macintosh today. Thus it is no wonder that Macintosh users can understand immediately how Presenter would work and why they want it.

Just when all these conditions will be true on the IBM base is hard to predict. If IBM were to introduce a 286 machine with

EGA (or better) graphics built-in, at a PC price level, include a mouse as standard, and bundle MS-Windows, then it could happen very fast. Without that help, it could be much slower.

The most problematic condition is when the other software will exist, because Presenter requires that programs such as Excel, MacPaint, MacDraw, and the like exist in the same environment to be of maximum value. Microsoft has announced that it will ship Excel for Windows, but has not announced a time (rumor says February 1987). In February 1986, they were announcing further changes in the Windows user interface (in the direction of Macintosh) to facilitate a version of Excel. There are still some missing pieces of MS-Windows (support for rich text editing, a standard for rich text interchange, fonts, device drivers, a standard for PostScript- or Interpress-level device drivers, etc. These gaps may delay much software longer than we would have hoped.

None of these considerations is decisive. But it is at least reasonable that for the next year the market on MS-Windows machines may be no larger than the Macintosh market, and perhaps considerably smaller. This being the case, it appears that the lowest-risk strategy is to introduce Presenter on Macintosh, get maximum leverage from aiding Apple's strategy, and sell first in the Macintosh market, where the product will be warmly received. Then, aided by that introduction, extend the product to MS-Windows a few months later.

This is our current intention. Forethought schedules the Macintosh version of Presenter for first customer shipment in February 1987, and the MS-Windows version of Presenter for first customer shipment in August 1987, presuming that schedules for funding and development can be achieved. A "Beta" pre-release of the Macintosh version for marketing purposes can be available in late November 1986. (Gaskins, PowerPoint Marketing 1986)

Clearly, from the aggressive promised schedule for PowerPoint on Windows (six months after the Mac version—it actually took three years), we were continuing our swaggering braggadocio just like everyone else who wasn't actually shipping Windows applications. We didn't want anyone to think that we lacked commitment to Windows! But to ourselves, as the text above says, we admitted that the gaps in Windows "may delay much software longer than we would have hoped."

58 Cross Development of Mac PowerPoint on Lisa

Dennis Austin recalls how he started on the implementation of Power-Point:

> Apple made available a native development environment for the Macintosh, but there were no compilers. There was only a crude text editor and an assembler.
>
> A superior, though expensive, option used the development environment on the Lisa. It had a reasonable command-line interpreter with a reasonable set of commands—certainly not Unix, but far better than MS-DOS.
>
> I think there was a C compiler, but the featured language was a very good version of Pascal. All the interfaces were documented in Pascal, so this was a clear favorite. I knew the language well and, in fact, had developed two different Pascal compilers in the past. Bob remarked once that he liked the idea of developing in Pascal because it felt like relying on a 1968 Mercedes-Benz.
>
> Luckily, cash-poor Forethought already owned a Lisa. I dragged the Lisa down to my office, joining the PC and the Macintosh already on my desk, and started learning the ropes. The Lisa took up a lot of space, especially since its hard disk was external. I was lucky enough to have two Apple ProFile external disks, each with five megabytes, connected to the machine's parallel port.
>
> ... The Lisa development system wasn't exactly a powerhouse either.
>
> 5 MHz processor
> 1000 K (1 Mbyte) main memory
> 5 MB hard disk connected to the parallel port
> 12-inch black and white monitor, 720 x 360 pixels.
>
> (Austin, Beginnings 2009)

59 The Target Environment for Macintosh PowerPoint

Dennis Austin also recalls what the early Macintosh application environment was like, and how it was different in expecting user interfaces from independent software vendors to be consistent with Apple's own user interface standards:

The Macintosh was not only a new kind of personal computer; it was a new kind of approach to personal computers. It was open to (and desperate for) third-party software, but for the system to succeed applications needed consistency in user interface. That required evangelizing the independent software developers and selling them on the benefits of standardization.

It helped that Apple had developed a fairly large toolkit of services that developers could rely on and avoid building a lot of their own software. Using the toolkit saved time and it also provided a lot of the standardization automatically. The downside was that developers were accustomed to doing things exactly as they pleased. They didn't like following rules or standards.

We, on the other hand, were not from the personal computer world and we embraced this new way of doing software. We hoped to not only save time, but to leverage the Apple marketing machine to our ends so they could use us in promotions of how to write a great Macintosh application. Eventually this hope was more than realized in the form of an investment by Apple—their first in another company.

As I remember it, the first Macintoshes weren't really bad performers. Well, there was that 128K version that didn't really work, but the "fat Mac," the 512K version, was decent. That memory belies just how modest the hardware was by modern standards:

8 MHz processor
512 K main memory
No hard disk at all
9 inch black and white screen (no gray), 512 x 384 pixels

The core operating system was scarcely more advanced than DOS, but it had a very nice user interface toolkit and enough programming at the graphics level that there was no command line system at all.

I took all these limitations seriously. The 1.0 product had to succeed or there would be no second chance. Performance had to be there. (Austin, Beginnings 2009)

60 Arguments for Leaving Out Features

As the spec for PowerPoint matured and the explanation of its features expanded, the task of producing PowerPoint got bigger and bigger. We were on the lookout for good reasons why any feature could be left out.

One of the best lines of thought was that Apple was promoting consistency of user interface among all the applications for Mac, those from independent developers (like us) as well as from Apple. This argued for an approach of many cooperating apps, rather than a monolithic single app full of compromises.

Here's how I explained why we would be so different from what might have been expected:

> The requirements, and the opportunities, of new environments such as MS-Windows and Macintosh, lead to a product concept very different from any existing package sold to make presentations.
>
> Most strikingly, virtually all existing presentation packages stress the creation of business charts (pie charts, bar charts, line charts) as their most important function; some very popular packages will do nothing else at all. They have a lot of function connected with data entry and editing, and chart attributes. In sharp contrast, *Presenter will have no tools at all within itself for making business charts!*
>
> This decision comes about because of the difference in assumed environments. The existing packages were designed for a standard MS-DOS environment, where the numbers to be charted might come from many incompatible sources, where there was no standard form for graphics, and where just making a single chart which could be used as a slide was a difficult task.
>
> More recently, it has been discovered that users really benefit from a single program which can do both spreadsheets and charts (such as Microsoft's Excel) because much of the information from the spreadsheet can be used directly to annotate the charts, and users need to go back and forth between numbers and graphics while tuning plans and assumptions. The spreadsheet itself serves as the data entry and editing interface for charting, with a consequent unification and simplification of the whole process.
>
> At the same time, in the new environments, Presenter can depend on standard data interchange formats for use with other programs, and methods for instantaneous context switching from one program to another (via multi-tasking and Windows-level macros in MS-Windows, or even hot-links between two running programs, and via Switcher in Macintosh). Once this is true, it would clearly be a poor choice to duplicate the charting function in Presenter; users would have to learn a new way of doing things, in addition to what they use in their spreadsheet/charting pro-

gram, move numbers and then do redundant formatting, and so on. It is clearly better to let users do charts in their spreadsheet/charting programs that they use for analysis, then optimize the use of the same charts in the presentation program.

Some existing presentation programs are specialized to other kinds of drawings than business charts, such as signs, organization charts, project charts, CAD-type drawings, and so forth. For each of these, the same argument holds as for pie charts: users already create specialized art using programs which manage that kind of data for them, and should be able to use the same art easily in presentations. Someone who manages projects using a scheduling program will be creating and using Gantt charts and PERT charts every day through a familiar interface; it should be possible to use that same program and the same schedule charts in presentations, not to have to duplicate effort and learn something new.

Similarly, existing presentation packages come in multiple versions designed for specific output devices—different packages for 35mm, for overheads, and so forth. In the new environments, this is unnecessary complexity. Both MS-Windows and Macintosh offer device-independent graphics standards and system device drivers. A presentation should be capable of being generated for any device.

A diagram will show our model of how Presenter integrates into the new richer graphics environments:

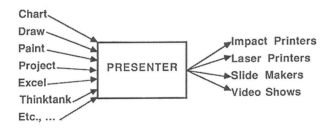

On the left are samples of the many specialized sources of graphics and data elements: various tools that a presenter might (or might not) use to manage data. Whatever combination of these a presenter uses, the output of all can be used directly in presentations.

On the right are the various output devices supported. Presenter will create paper output, or overheads on transparencies, or 35mm slides, or video for a live presentation, all in monochrome or color. Presenter works with whatever devices are supported in the environment.

Between these two standards for data exchange, there is a coherent task for a presentation program regardless of the specific data to be presented.

Presenter provides facilities for:

- organizing and composing a presentation, editing and merging presentations;
- laying out slides, creating and editing their content;
- creating text, both editing and formatting and graphics layout;
- creating multi-column tables, whether numeric or words;
- doing general drawing of the type used for simple diagrams;
- clipping and resizing art from any source;
- setting standard repeating elements, formats, and tools for the presentation;
- previewing the completed presentation on the screen;
- page layout for slides, talking papers, handouts, etc.

This is a substantially new concept for a presentation product, made possible only by the new environments of MS-Windows and Macintosh.

Just as Presenter would not be appropriate for the old environments of the previous generation, so too existing programs designed for those limitations will be strikingly poor in the new environments. For presentation graphics, this change makes possible a breakthrough in product design. (Gaskins, PowerPoint Marketing 1986)

We were not only trying to cut down on the feature set of our first product. We really believed that PowerPoint would be the stronger for not including business charting, at all, rather than something minimal; better to concentrate on making it easy to draw the "boxes and lines" diagrams that were much more common. But that was a tough sell, both inside and outside of Forethought, when the feature set of every existing presentation application was approximately 90% simple business charting, even though such charts were comparatively rare in actual presentations.

61 Sharpening the Focus for PowerPoint 1.0

While the earliest description of PowerPoint had described a product that could replace overhead transparencies, 35mm slides, and multimedia shows, the decision to make the first product only for Macintosh helped focus on only one bit of that market: overheads.

A basic reason was the Mac's lack of color; there was just no possibility of competing for the 35mm slide market in black and white, whereas virtually all overheads were black and white anyway.

But also there was a difference in the prospective customers. I wanted a product for "content originators" to use directly, not a product to sell to professional service bureaus. The number of business presenters was very much larger than the number of professional graphics producers; that made a much bigger market for both Macs and for Mac application software, even despite the fact that business people weren't buying very many Macs in 1985.

This narrowing (or sharpening) of focus was another decision that provoked doubts both inside and outside of Forethought, since it seemed to make the PowerPoint idea "smaller" again. Big 35mm slide shows were impressive! Overheads were just hacked out for the internal meeting and could be done perfectly well in MacDraw or even on a typewriter, or so the critics said. (As I quoted Paul Graham earlier, "Overlooked problems are by definition problems that most people think don't matter.")

Here was my attempt to describe the decision to make only overheads in version 1.0:

> Preparing presentations in the style associated with "35mm slides" is a vertical market, where the customers are graphics arts producers and central graphics service departments who prepare slides on behalf of clients. A much larger horizontal market is that for preparing presentations in the style associated with 'overheads,' where the customers are all the people who prepare presentations for themselves.
>
> Personal computer users who are content originators rather than artists are better suited to preparing overheads than 35mm slides. Presenter, and other personal computer software, will best fulfill the cluster of expectations surrounding overheads— informal, for lighted rooms, for smaller groups, for working meetings where content is more important than form or fancy

graphics, for situations where speed and personal control are important.

The conclusion is that we should focus on the overhead market, while pointing out that we support color and that anything designed for an overhead can also be imaged on 35mm film. We should not position ourselves as an alternative to Genigraphics, nor think that our customers will be in the central services department which concentrates on professionally artistic slides.

Our targets for Presenter should be people who want (in order):

1. conventional overheads printed on a laser printer or impact printer in monochrome, for monochrome copying;

2. color overheads, generated on color inkjet or thermal printers;

3. "electronic overheads" generated for direct video projection; and

4. what we might call "35mm overheads," slides which must be in 35mm format for some reason but have the content more often associated with overhead transparencies.

All of these can be produced by the customer who is the content originator or an immediate staff member in the same department. (Gaskins, PowerPoint Marketing 1986)

It's necessary, when trying to ship a product, to clearly separate issues that are different time depths into the future. Here I said "we should not position ourselves as an alternative to Genigraphics" for PowerPoint version 1.0, even though for version 2.0, shipped only a year later, we would do exactly that, and with Genigraphics as our partner.

62 Overheads as a Growing Business Market

I tried to legitimize the idea of a product sharply focused on overheads by providing evidence that overhead transparencies were really a modern and rapidly growing presentation segment; moreover, almost all makers of overheads were business customers, who had the budgets to buy personal computers and software. Again, the goal was to make the idea seem "big enough."

This was in contrast to the rather dowdy past of overheads, which was better known. Here again, I drew on my personal experience of how overheads had been made manually thirty years before, and drew on audio-visual industry research showing that buyers of overhead projectors had changed from schools to business.

Note that, despite my finding that over 90% of individual U.S. classrooms still contained an overhead projector in 1985, I did not for a moment suggest targeting educational customers. PowerPoint was a business product:

> Overheads are a slightly later invention [than 35mm slides], having been devised first as a format for Army training and briefings in World War II. Overhead projectors were large and bulky, but because they projected a transparency almost as big as a sheet of paper, transparencies could be made quickly by hand—even drawn on clear transparencies in real time during discussions. (This use is still seen today in the arrangements for rolls of transparency material which provide a speaker with a scratch pad visible to the audience.)
>
> After the war, the principal use of overhead projectors was at first in bowling alleys, to project score sheets as they were updated. They became popular with schools, because teachers could prepare customized instructional material cheaply. A whole industry of transparency materials (for grease pencil, for typewriters, for ballpoint pen) and colored films, tapes, and inks grew up.
>
> Eventually, the popularity of overheads saturated the schools—even today, there is an overhead projector for more than 9 out of 10 U.S. classrooms—and sales of new hardware fell dramatically. (Sales of supplies for making overheads continued strong.)
>
> Two things changed about ten years ago: (1) 3M invented lower-cost portable machines with reflective stages, which folded up to become practical to carry as sales aids; and (2) Xerox and other copier companies made overheads much easier to produce, since any paper document could be easily copied onto transparency film.
>
> Since then, sales of new overhead projectors have rebounded to surpass their historical highs. In 1965, there were about 100,000 overhead projector units sold; in 1975, about 50,000 units; in 1985, over 120,000 units. Today, sales of overhead projectors are virtually all made to businesses. (Gaskins, PowerPoint Marketing 1986)

Everybody knew about the invention of transparency film that could endure the fusing heat of a laser copier without melting; that had made overheads vastly more practical to use, since anything on a sheet of paper could be photocopied onto an overhead.

I knew about the recent invention of portable folding overhead projectors the size of a thin attaché case, because my father's company Eiki in Japan had also invented one and was selling it to businesses in large quantities. The new design was made possible by replacing the traditional large and hot light box in the base with a thin reflective mirror surface and a Fresnel lens, illuminated from above by a tiny high-output bulb.

My father gave me one of these projectors, and I often took it along and used it in pitches for further rounds of investment, to surprise and impress my auditors with how modern overheads had become. I still have that overhead projector, now rendered entirely useless by Power-Point.

63 When I Learned about Overhead vs. 35mm Style

As we prepared a product focused on overheads, I thought a lot about how presentations made with overheads differed from presentations made with 35mm slides. I had a particular reason for dwelling on this topic, since it had once caused me extreme embarrassment.

One holiday season while I was at Bell-Northern Research, I got a call on Christmas Eve from the boss of my boss's boss, the head of the U.S. subsidiary for all the U.S. labs. He told me that he was committed to give a talk as part of a keynote panel at a large telecommunications conference to be held immediately after New Year in a city far away, but unfortunately he was ill and wouldn't be able to go. Would I go and make the address for him? Thanks very much. Oh, and he had not yet prepared his talk, so I would have to take care of that, too. Thanks again.

I had no choice but to do the talk, so over the holiday week, I put together something to say (about communication in future wide-area networks of personal computers, I'm sure). I had no way to prepare any visuals except overheads—BNR didn't use a service bureau like Genigraphics, we used our corporate art department in Ottawa to make 35mm slides, and there was no chance to do that over the holidays. I thought overheads would be okay. (I didn't know it then, but what I should have done was to call Genigraphics, who had made an excellent business of working all night, even over holidays, to save the skins of

CEOs who hadn't prepared in time, and of charging very robust rush premiums for such service. I'm sure that, when I sent the extremely large bill to the same big boss who palmed his keynote panel off onto me, he would have approved my expenses without question.)

I took a red-eye and arrived at the big conference on the day after New Year. I found the producers who were holding a rehearsal for the panel at which I was to fill in. It turned out that the auditorium would hold several thousand people. There were several other speakers who had proper 35mm slides, and the auditorium had high-end projection of 35mm slides from an acoustically sealed projection booth high in the back wall. They had apoplexy when I showed them my overhead transparencies and said that I intended to use them.

But the session was the next day, and we were all wedged. The producers rented an extremely bright industrial overhead projector, and jury-rigged it in the middle of their stage set where it stuck out like a sore thumb. Since I had to change the overheads by hand, I also had to talk from the middle of the set, instead of from the podium at one side where the proper microphones were. My overheads were severely distorted into a "keystone" shape because of the angle necessary to reach the giant screen large enough for thousands of people to see. (This problem has gone away with digital projectors that can distort images to counteract keystoning; the 35mm slides were fine, of course, since the screen over the stage was level with the projection booth located at the back of the hall.)

The rehearsal didn't go smoothly. Afterward, I worked hard on practicing my talk overnight.

> Depend upon it, Sir, when any man knows he is to be hanged in a fortnight, it concentrates his mind wonderfully.
> —Samuel Johnson, 19 September 1777

The next day, at our performance, another speaker gave the first talk, speaking from a podium at one side, with a spotlight on him and a hidden microphone, using excellent professional 35mm slides. Then my turn: I walked from the panel's seating area to the middle of the lighted stage, got my temporary microphone, put my first overhead on the projector, looked back at the distorted trapezoid, and tried to convince several thousand people that my view of the future of telecommunications was worth listening to.

Even allowing that it may not have been the best talk I ever gave, it should have been passable; it was on a topic I understood, felt passionate about, and had presented on many important occasions. But I certainly did not get a warm reception for my ideas from the huge audience. The session chairman and the other panelists ridiculed what I had to say and treated me like a fool.

I realized, while I stood there and shuffled the overheads on the projector, that the whole style of my presentation was fatally wrong for the occasion, in every way. After that, I thought deeply about different styles of presentations.

This distinction was important all through PowerPoint's history. It was important first to get PowerPoint 1.0 focused on overhead style, and it was important later to clearly add the separate 35mm style in PowerPoint 2.0. So long as the physical media and their projectors were differentiated, we could help presenters not to contaminate either style with the other. But by the mid-1990s, as video projectors replaced everything else, there was no longer a mechanical separation of the two styles, so a presenter was required to use experience and taste.

Twenty years after PowerPoint shipped, I wrote an article for *Communications of the ACM* (Gaskins, Back to Basics 2007), explaining how PowerPoint 3.0 and video projectors introduced the original sin of confusing the two styles I had distinguished, which brought death by PowerPoint into the world, and all our woe.

64 How Overhead Style Differs from 35mm Style

My observations about how overhead style differed from 35mm style were based on my personal experiences, and always seemed to me both insightful and original. I don't think very many people ever appreciated them as much as I did, but I made use of them in designing Power-Point.

If we were going to focus sharply on a product to make overheads, then we needed to be sure that we selected all the proper marks of style for that market in our design. Dennis and I discussed this endlessly until no further subtleties could be distinguished. Here is what I observed at the time:

> Overhead transparencies and 35mm slides can be looked at as simply two different sizes of film, and in principle anything which can be imaged at one size can be imaged at the other size.

But in fact there are very strong differences in the habits and expectations associated with the two formats and in the way they are used.

Historically, these differences may stem from the fact that professional graphic artists made the material which they photographed onto 35mm slides for clients, whereas overhead transparencies were mostly produced by the same people who used them—Army officers preparing briefings, teachers preparing classroom materials, and eventually businesspeople photocopying overheads for meetings.

Whatever the historical source, today the markets and uses for overheads and 35mm slides are completely different. Video for presentations, as it begins to be used, seems to be splitting the same way into "video replacements for overheads" and "video replacements for 35mm." A computer program to make overheads should be different from a computer program to make 35mm slides in ways that go far beyond the output device drivers.

• Light Room *vs.* Darkened Room

Overheads are typically designed for presentation in a lighted room, whereas 35mm slides are typically designed for showing in a darkened room.

This observation is more important than it may at first appear. In a lighted room using overheads, the human presenter is visible. There is opportunity for two-way discussion and interaction, since faces and expressions can be seen and reacted to. Documents (drawings, financial statements, site maps, contracts, ...) can be handed out for consultation and discussion. Overheads permit most of the activities of a regular business meeting to go on, with the transparencies as a device to focus attention.

But in a darkened room using 35mm slides, the human presenter is very likely invisible (very few setups have light on the presenter at a podium). It is not possible to see audience reactions or requests to be recognized, so the session tends to be one-way with the audience passively listening. It is not easy to take notes or to consult documents. All eyes are on the screen, because there is nothing much else visible.

• Low *vs.* High Entertainment Value

This difference means that overheads should have a very subdued "entertainment value," and should not attract so much attention that they overshadow all else. Overheads use dark letters on a light background, visible in lighted rooms. They do not have fancy transitions (being changed by hand). The screen can be left light (without a transparency) for discussion of an extraneous point easily. The presenter will point with a hand or a pencil, casually, to points of interest. Overheads, a surprising part of the time, consist simply of word charts. Overheads have very abstract diagrams, usually schematic with simple labeled boxes and lines. Charts and graphs are as plain as will do the job. There is never a synchronized sound track, since the overheads do not constitute a performance by themselves; they accompany a meeting.

35mm slides, in contrast, need a much higher "entertainment value" so they can carry interest all by themselves—as they must, since nothing else is visible and they must be a performance on their own. They have light letters on dark backgrounds, so as not to be dazzling in a darkened room. They may have fancy transitions or fades. It is very difficult to leave the screen dark (without a slide) since then the audience is in total darkness, so extraneous points are discussed with a useless slide visible (another reason to discourage them). The presenter needs a lighted arrow pointer to point, and so usually no pointing is done. Word charts are avoided if at all possible. Diagrams are fancier, and realistic photography will help to maintain interest. Charts and graphs are as fancy as possible—shading, three dimensions, etc.; these refinements do not add more information to the charts, but make them graphically more interesting to look at. Synchronized sound effects or narration are sometimes used.

• Meeting Size and Formality

There are other differences connected with these. Overheads are used in small group meetings, where discussion is possible. Indeed, overheads are frequently used in a one-on-one meeting, where they are not projected at all but just turned over in sequence for discussion. Thus, the overhead merges with the flip chart for single-person sales presentations.

As a group gets too large to support discussion, then using 35mm slides in a darkened room serves to control audience interference—slide show first, questions or discussion later. Overheads are not sufficiently formal for a really large group, whereas 35mm slides are pretentious shown to a single person (unless photography is required for information value).

In sum, overheads are usually used in situations where the audience is asked to concentrate on the information, and not to be awed by artistry. 35mm slides are usually used in situations where the audience should appreciate the artistic sophistication of the presentation as well as its content.

(There are, of course, exceptions to the generalizations made above, but upon close inspection these often support the distinction. "Overhead" material will sometimes be reshot onto 35mm slides for better visibility in a moderately large company meeting, without changing its essential character. "35mm" material will sometimes be reproduced onto overhead foils for presentation in a small conference room without 35mm projection equipment, or where a lighted room is required. The distinction between the two styles of use is not exactly coextensive with the distinction between the transparency sizes, but it is surprisingly close.)

• Preparation

Overheads are almost always prepared by the person who will give the presentation or by an immediate staff member in the same department. It is extremely uncommon for overheads to be prepared by a centralized corporate graphics service department. And, even if a centralized service were willing, they would almost always be too slow; most overheads are made hurriedly, within a day of their being used, and copied to transparency film on office copiers. Color would be useful, but is seldom used since copiers do not copy in color. Thus, the layout and artistic quality of overheads is almost always in the hands of amateurs who have little knowledge of effective presentation styles, no graphics training, and very poor tools.

35mm slides are more often prepared by a corporate- or division-level graphics service department. It will take some time to make them and process them anyway, so there is more advance planning. As befits a larger event at which they will be the center of attention, the slides are very frequently designed by professional artists and illustrators working from rough ideas submitted by the presenter. Color is mandatory. These people have very good (often expensive) equipment, and their work takes time. So 35mm slides must be planned well in advance, and cannot be easily changed at the last minute. (Gaskins, PowerPoint Marketing 1986)

The fact, almost accidental, that overheads were produced on printers and copiers which only supported black and white, whereas 35mm slides were always produced on color film, presented a very easy way to separate templates and styles in the early products. But the central point was:

... overheads are usually used in situations where the audience is asked to concentrate on the information, and not to be awed by artistry. 35mm slides are usually used in situations where the audience should appreciate the artistic sophistication of the presentation as well as its content. (Gaskins, PowerPoint Marketing 1986)

65 *PowerPoint 1.0 Feature Prioritization*

I began to think about other product components that would have to go on the disks, beyond the program code. Such items as clip art, frames and borders, ribbons and scrolls, and maps would need to be sourced and licensed:

> Based on the foregoing considerations, the features of the initial release of Presenter (for both Macintosh and MS-Windows) will be focused on overheads, and primarily on those imaged statically on film for projection by conventional overhead projectors. Features include capabilities to:
> - create, structure, and lay out presentations;
> - lay out slides, do direct word processing of word charts;
> - do general drawing, clip and resize art from any source;
> - utilize master formats, custom tools, libraries of art and of formats;
> - lay out pages to print slides, talking papers, and handouts;
> - preview a slide show using the whole computer display.
>
> It is also important to ship as part of the initial product a "template" library of clip art, such things as:
> - borders, arrows, headline scrolls, sized to fit slides;
> - thematic and decorative art for vertical specialties;
> - maps of states, countries, SMSA's.
>
> International versions could be of major importance, since there is relatively little cultural content in Presenter and the product could be used easily in many language areas. Development will be carried out so as to permit easy localization. (Gaskins, PowerPoint Marketing 1986)

The line about "little cultural content" went back to my personal observations on my "grand tour." It made sense to plan for localization from the very first.

66 Windows 1.0 Ships, with Forethought as an ISV

Microsoft finally shipped Windows 1.0 in November of 1985, a year or so later than it had expected.

Although we had decided to develop first for Mac, we were keeping the door wide open to Windows. And all our work with Windows had qualified us to be an official Windows Independent Software Vendor.

**WINDOWS
ISV SUPPORT**

Company	Contact Name	Address/Phone Number
Advanced Analysis	Chris Doner	344 Westline Drive Suite C12 Alameda, CA 94501 415/865-7531
Aldus	Paul Brainerd	616 First Avenue Suite 400 Seattle, WA 98104 206/467-8165
Arity	Peter Gabel/ Meredith Bartlett	358 Baker Avenue Concord, MA 01742 617/371-1234
Arrays Continental	Jim Sadlier/ Jim Buddle	11223 S. Hendrix Avenue Los Angeles, CA 90045 213/410-9466
Atron	Perry Lynne	20665 Fourth Street Saratoga, CA 95070 408/741-5900
Forethought	Robert Gaskins	1973 Landings Drive Mountain View, CA 94043 415/961-4720
Future Tech	Leon Stucki	724 West Hi-Crest Blvd. Auburn, WA 98001 206/939-7552
Hayden Software	Lars Stenson	60050 Suffolk Street Lowell, MA 01854 617/937-0200
Hewlett Packard	Rosemary Wicowski	10520 Ridgeview Court Cupertino, CA 95014 408/865-6475
Hypergraphics	Darrell Ward/ Phillip Crews	308 N. Carroll Denton, TX 76201 817/565-0004

(This document prepared on Microsoft Windows using Windows Write.)

THE WAGGENER GROUP • 6915 • W. SW. ADAM AVENUE • SUITE 550 • PORTLAND, OREGON 97219• 503-245-0905

The Windows 1.0 press kit (20 November 1985) included a list of all the committed Independent Software Vendors who planned to develop Windows products—including Robert Gaskins at Forethought. This was a year and a half before we shipped on Mac. (Ray Ozzie posted a scan of the whole press kit on the web. (Ozzie, Windows 1.0 Press Kit 1985) This is page 29 of 32 pages.)

If you look at the whole list of ISVs, out of 26 ISVs listed, only two companies remain in business: Microsoft's own Apps Division, and Hewlett-Packard. Everyone else (even Aldus, Micrografx, and T/Maker) either went out of business or was acquired, usually in negative circumstances because of poor sales. Being on this list was not a guarantee of success in software.

Still, PowerPoint really was committed to Windows early. Our strong belief in Windows, beginning very early and never being seriously diluted by Mac, is what ultimately made PowerPoint a big success. We expected that Windows would be at least 90% of the market, whenever it arrived; that turned out to be true, and remained true for twenty-five years. Developing PowerPoint for Mac first never took our eyes off this eventual prize.

67 FileMaker and Other Distractions

Amidst all this progress on the spec for PowerPoint, we had the background of continuing problems in our operations centered around the published FileMaker product. Here is the summary of the period from my company history written in 1987:

> Gradually, our competitors [for FileMaker] went out of business. Purely because we were able to continue to raise capital, we stayed in business. By early 1986, FileMaker was one of the few products left in its category. We thought there was a possibility to stem the losses from MACWARE products by introducing an upgrade version of FileMaker (FileMaker Plus) and discontinuing our other [published] products. We consciously delayed PowerPoint for about six months, so as to get FileMaker Plus out first and cut our losses. In doing so, we stretched ourselves out to the uttermost limit of the PowerPoint market window.
>
> We planned that a new version of FileMaker Plus would bring us to break-even, since we could increase the price (from $195 to $295) and could expect a sales increase. We knew that it would not produce sustained profitability—only PowerPoint could do that. But it should cut our MACWARE losses.
>
> Again we were delayed by legal problems at Nashoba, and by development delays of theirs and of ours. It was particularly difficult to negotiate a contract, and the contract eventually agreed upon reflected the weakness of our bargaining position. A planned introduction in March moved out twice. FileMaker Plus was introduced in August of 1986.
>
> FileMaker Plus sold well at introduction, particularly in the non-recurring upgrade of previous FileMaker owners, producing a blip of profitability, and then settled down to somewhat below

break-even. We ended the year [1986] slightly ahead of our revenue and profit plan, though still having lost money. (Gaskins, Forethought History 1987)

In another document also written in 1987, I refer to the FileMaker Plus contract as a mistake that we made, in "accepting a contract which was ludicrously unfavorable to ourselves" (Gaskins, Restart Lessons 1987). The details of this contract will be described in a later section.

We also discovered in this period that the publisher of an MS-DOS product similar to FileMaker and developed by the same developers was claiming all rights to any future Windows version of FileMaker. We didn't even have a contractual right to any possible Windows version; but this competing claim would guarantee that it would be impossible for us to profit on the larger Windows platform from the reputation FileMaker would have built on Mac.

But we went through all the rigmarole of a complete product release—software validation and testing, new book, new boxes, new inserts, all the printing, disk manufacturing, disk labels, dealer information, advertising, PR, sales, update offers and fulfillment, lots of customer support. We ended up with little to show for it, but with considerable distraction from the concentration on PowerPoint.

During this same period, we also were raising another round of money,

> ... in May 1986, ... we managed to close the first part of the Preferred C round ($408,000) (Gaskins, Forethought History 1987)

Inevitably, this was tied to the FileMaker Plus product we were just about to ship, so events in mid- to late-1986 produced some disappointment in the investors when the large amount of effort spent on FileMaker Plus did not actually bring Forethought to break-even:

> We had expected the MACWARE products to be self-funding, and perhaps even to finance our product development at least in part. If the MACWARE products turned out not to be self-funding—as in fact happened—then we had to come up with a great deal of capital to fund our operations during the entire period of development, in addition to the funds needed for development. Worse, since we needed to stay in business, the continued money-losing operations had first call on our limited resources, and further delayed our development efforts. By further delaying our development efforts, we further delayed profitability. (Gaskins, Forethought History 1987)

68 *Designing to the Limit of Macintosh Capabilities*

What was strikingly new about the design of PowerPoint for Mac was that, based on the attractive and simple examples of MacWrite and MacPaint, users wanted to somehow create a presentation slide "directly" by typing and drawing on a screen image representing the slide. We thought that was the right model, too, but most previous work in computer graphics had been in very different directions.

Most computer graphics research had involved creating some sort of description of the result, by writing macros, setting parameters, and typing un-styled text into forms, and then waiting while the result was computed and a representation sent to some output device—often to a graphical screen, usually different from the screen where the description was typed. In part, this was because the low power of computers, not only personal computers, allowed no possibility of computing the complex appearance incrementally as changes were made; any computer which could do such work was a mainframe shared among scores of people. There had been the minority-interest work at Xerox PARC and elsewhere, but there were no near prototypes for PowerPoint.

All the earlier presentation software had worked "indirectly," by first creating a description for each slide and then "rendering" it. This was true of the limited-function programs for DOS on IBM PCs, such as Software Publishing Corporation's new Harvard Graphics product and many others; it was equally true for the very high-function programs for workstations with lots of special hardware, such as Genigraphics' PDP-11 based workstations. As is often the case, people working on such systems came to consider the limitations of this way of working as actually an advantage.

The "direct drive" interface for PowerPoint was just on the edge of what was possible to do on a Mac while delivering really great performance, thanks to the very same "trick" that made Macintosh itself possible in 1984: that is, to restrict the possible function enough so that it can be delivered with astonishing speed and smoothness by the computer power that is realistically available. Deciding precisely what function to provide, without letting the limitations show, is, as Dennis Austin says, "almost an art, and I think the Mac's successful practice of it was mostly responsible for the appeal it held."

The first Mac was dismissed as a toy by serious computer graphics people: a tiny screen (512 x 342) by their standards, only black and white, very limited memory, no video out, grainy low-res printers. What could be done with MacWrite and MacPaint was, in truth, extremely limited—but it could be done in "What You See Is What You Get" (WYSIWYG) style, with excellent performance and polish. Function was not improved until the introduction of the LaserWriter (1985), a much more powerful computer than the Mac itself, which allowed high-res typeset output, but even after that many limitations remained.

For PowerPoint, it would have been unrealistic to compute the appearance of really complex color video presentations directly with each keystroke, back in those days. But the problem was changed when we sharply restricted it to what could be done on a Mac, which was overhead transparencies. Though it was not obvious, there was a narrow overlap between what black and white overheads required, and what a Mac could accomplish well.

The Mac's limited screen resolution was very low for showing a whole slide at a time, but it was the right shape ("landscape") and the low resolution meant that not so many dots had to be computed for each screen update; luckily, the large letters and simple diagrams used on overheads could be shown fairly legibly. The Mac's limitation to black and white, with no color on screen and no video out (hence no expectation of projected color or of 35mm slides), was a great simplification; it was also fine for overheads, because laser printers were also black and white only, and their output had to be copied onto foils for projection using a photocopier that was then also black and white only, so on-screen color would have been no use for overheads. Elaborate high-resolution typesetting took a lot of horsepower, but that could be offloaded from a Mac to the computer in a LaserWriter. So it was just barely possible to use a Mac to produce overheads directly, in the same way as other Mac apps demonstrated every day. But this restriction of the problem to what was feasible on the existing hardware wasn't obvious to people working in the field, and required inventing a number of new techniques.

Looking ahead, as computer processing and memory increased, Apple added color to Macs, and so PowerPoint 2.0 could accomplish the job of making color slides with gradated backgrounds; as with offloading typesetting to the LaserWriter for making typeset overheads, this was partly achieved by offloading the actual generation of the bits for 35mm slides to larger imaging computers located at Genigraphics' processing laboratories, followed by FedEx overnight shipping.

With still further improvements in computer power, PowerPoint 3.0 could accomplish the job of producing live color video slideshows to feed to video projectors, which themselves were still grossly impractical even when PowerPoint 3.0 was shipped. In each of these generations—black and white overheads, color slides, color video and sound—the user experience improved dramatically in the first few years after each was shipped, because affordable PC hardware and peripherals caught up to the software, but the software was complete and offered really very good performance from its first release.

69 Forget Earlier Software, Match What Presenters Do

We thought that it was not important to be consistent with the user interfaces of earlier presentation software products, because nobody much used them. But, at the same time, we did not underestimate the importance of matching the expectations of the many users who were still using manual processes to produce presentation visuals:

> Presentations are today handled by a variety of graphics arts and photographic techniques, and form a major part of the "audio-visual" (AV) industry. As personal computer programs are introduced to take over some of this work, they will exist at the intersection of the audio-visual and personal computer markets. It is essential to understand and fit into the expectations of both of these worlds if we are to be successful.
>
> Compare the situation in word processing a few years back, as word processing software on personal computers took over the market from dedicated word processing equipment. Programs such as Microsoft Word, which took maximum advantage of the new designs made possible by the personal computer, did not become the biggest sellers. Instead, programs which preserved some of the limitations of earlier dedicated word processors, such as MultiMate (modeled after Wang's word processor) and Display-Write (modeled after IBM's DisplayWriter) achieved the widest acceptance. Despite their—technically unnecessary—limitations, they did a better job of meeting the expectations of people who were actually using and buying word processing equipment. (Gaskins, PowerPoint Marketing 1986)

Part of this strategy was to match the style of overheads in use. For example, if lots of manually prepared overheads contained a pre-printed border in the shape of a rounded rectangle with breaks to fill in a date and an occasion (and many did), then it was important to be sure that the same format could be produced easily in the direct-drive PowerPoint interface.

70 Unsuccessful Competitors Prior to PowerPoint

We expected that the market for presentation software on Mac and Windows would be distinct from that for software on Apple II and MS-DOS, because the new products would be so much more usable. Even so, we paid careful attention to the very large number of competitors who had tried to make presentation software for the first-generation PCs. All of them had recognized the application category, and they were in touch with real customers, however dissatisfied.

What we suspected was that these first-generation competitors would be inclined to design follow-on products for Mac and Windows by keeping too much compatibility with their older products. Our course, as just explained, was to break decisively with how earlier software had approached presentations, but not with the expectations of users of manual techniques.

From the viewpoint of twenty-five years later, it's interesting to see what high prices were being charged for character-oriented PC software in 1986, despite its comparatively low functionality; a number of the competitors were charging $400 to $700 per copy.

What interested me the most in 1986 was that, in the specific sub-category of "Overhead Presentations," there were five entries, and three of those were distributed by IBM Corporation, though all of them had been written by other developers. I thought that IBM probably knew better than anyone what they were being asked to provide on the IBM PC, and that tended to confirm my decision to focus exclusively on overheads for the first version of PowerPoint:

> Since no existing program for Apple II or for the IBM PC does a good job, there is as yet no really successful competitor in the category of presentation graphics. No product is really widely accepted, no product generates a lot of revenue to permit expensive marketing, and no large installed base of users exists.
>
> No program known to us combines even the features we have identified as critical for Presenter—rich text for wordcharts, drawing, import of charts, and graphical construction/editing of a presentation—let alone the other features.

Most of the programs listed here are not really competitors for Presenter at all, but rather sources of art that Presenter can incorporate and work with. Nevertheless, they are graphics programs which people might expect (incorrectly in many cases) to use for generally the same class of problem.

Business and Professional Software Inc. has products such as Business Graphics ($350) for charting, 35mm Express ($695), and Overhead Express ($195). Company revenues for 1985 were about $2 million. IBM has licensed Overhead Express for non-exclusive distribution.

Graphic Communications, Inc. has products such as Graphwriter ($595), a charting package, and Freelance, ($395) a free-hand drawing package used to touch-up single charts imported from Graphwriter or from Lotus 1–2–3. Revenues had been about $5 million per year. The company was very recently purchased by Lotus.

Decision Resources Inc. publishes Chart Master ($375) for organization and schedule charts, Sign Master ($245) for simple signs, and Diagram Master ($345) for simple diagrams. Company revenues have been about $8 million per year. Decision Resources claims to have 25% of the business graphics market, and published reports say it is about to go public. Ashton-Tate has very recently signed a letter of intent to acquire the company.

Digital Research Inc. has published DR Graph and GEM Draw and GEM Wordchart for its own operating environment. DRI considers itself a graphics application company, but the decisive rejection of GEM by developers and manufacturers assures that these products will never find much of a market in their current forms.

Apart from Lotus's very recent acquisition of GCI, major software companies have not done much yet. Microsoft has had Chart, for charting, but rather obsoleted it when Excel was introduced with built-in charting. Ashton-Tate does not have a product in the area (but will have if the acquisition of Decision Resources goes through). H-P has a charting program and a drawing program, but H-P is not a major software company.

The best entry is probably Software Publishing's Harvard Presentation Graphics ($395), introduced in March of 1986, as a stand-alone application. Less well-known companies include Enertronics Research (EnerCharts, $395), Micrografx (Draw!, $195), Visual Communications Network (VCN Execuvision, $520), and Zenographics (Autumn, $395, and Mirage, $695).

Product Categories:

Business and/or Scientific Charts

BPS	*Business Graphics*	$350
GCI (Lotus)	*Graphwriter*	$595
Microsoft	*Chart*	$350
Microsoft	*Excel*	$495
Hewlett-Packard	*Charting Gallery*	$295
Computer Support	*Picture Perfect*	$295
Cricket Software	*Cricket Graph*	$195–$495

35mm Presentations

BPS	*35mm Express*	$695
Software Publishing	*Harvard Presentation Graphics*	$395
Enertronics Research	*EnerCharts*	$395
Zenographics	*Mirage*	$695
Zenographics	*Autumn* ['Auto-Mirage' add-on]	$395

Overhead Presentations

Living VideoText	*MORE* [Outliner]	$295
Digital Research	*GEM Wordchart*	$195
BPS (dist. IBM)	*Overhead Express*	$195
IBM Corp.	*SlideWrite*	$225
IBM Corp.	*PC Storyboard*	$250

Paint and/or Draw Programs

Digital Research	*GEM Draw*	$195
Digital Research	*GEM Paint*	$195
CGI (Lotus)	*Freelance*	$395

Micrografx	In*a*Vision	$495
Micrografx	Draw!	$195
Hewlett-Packard	Drawing Gallery	$395
Microsoft	Windows Paint	free
Computer Support	Diagraph	$395

Signs and Diagrams

Decision Resources	Chart Master	$375
Decision Resources	Sign Master	$245
Decision Resources	Diagram Master	$345
Decision Resources	Map Master	$395

Animation

| Zsoft Corp. | PC Presentation | $ 95 |
| VCN | VCN Execuvision Concorde | $695 |

Of all these, the real competitors are the ones listed under Overhead Presentations. It is fascinating to note that no less than 3 of those 5 programs are distributed by IBM—all created by outside companies. (Gaskins, PowerPoint Marketing 1986)

71 PowerPoint Fails an Assessment

On one occasion, our senior investor, Dick Kramlich of New Enterprise Associates, tried to validate for himself and for other investors my technical vision—or at least I thought at the time that's all he was doing.

Dick asked me to make a technical pitch in his presence to a technical advisor for his VC partnership. This advisor, Herbert Baskin, was a professor of EECS at UC Berkeley (not in the department I'd studied in, in liberal arts, but the other one, in engineering), and was the director of the graphics research laboratory at the university. He had a colossal reputation; he had started a computer graphics group at IBM Research as early as 1968, designed successful commercial computer color graphics systems for the large computer manufacturer Datapoint, and at this time, in addition to his appointment at Berkeley, he was also

CEO of a successful startup company called General Parametrics, which he had founded in Berkeley.

His company, General Parametrics, had developed a dedicated computer called VideoShow, price about $5,000, which did nothing but generate a video signal from a floppy diskette written in a special compact graphics format. The video signal from the VideoShow could be fed either to an external video monitor or to an external video projector, though projectors hardly existed. This device was only for playing back the diskettes containing video; it could not also be used as a personal computer.

They also had developed software for ordinary IBM PCs running MS-DOS (called PictureIt), to prepare the slide show presentations on diskettes that could be transferred to the VideoShow unit to feed video to a monitor. This whole system seems ridiculously expensive and impossibly cumbersome now, but it had sold very well. A review in *InfoWorld* for 11 March 1985 had raved that "A combination of software and a special, compact hardware unit, the images produced via your computer are stunning, and the whole system is incredibly simple to use. ... If you can afford it, we highly recommend it." (p. 37).

So, if anyone could have seemed perfectly qualified to evaluate my idea, it was Herb Baskin.

Dick Kramlich and I visited Professor Baskin at his General Parametrics office on 11 March 1986, and I gave Baskin a short presentation and talked him through my mocked-up "screen shots" and my mocked-up "sample output" of what would someday become PowerPoint. No demo, because there was nothing running to demo.

Baskin listened carefully, and then told me (and my listening investor) that my idea was all very well, but naively impossible. He explained patiently, in avuncular style, that it was not really feasible to type on a computer screen and have the text appear immediately in final position and in the correct font, size, and style; instead, you should type unstyled "typewriter" text into a "form" of some kind, and have a "render" command which would interpret the data for the finished slide and draw a picture of it on the screen. If what you saw wasn't right, then you cancelled the preview and went back and edited the input form. Very simple. Everybody did it this way (and that was true). And, he went on, this abstractness was in fact a big advantage, because you could separate the content from its particular format.

I was nonplussed. On this day when he seemed to be denying that you could type on a computer and see WYSIWYG text in correct font, size, and style, the Macintosh had been shipping for some two years, and Mac did exactly that! But the "computer graphics" establishment had not embraced the Mac or the earlier work at PARC, and Baskin had perhaps not paid attention to how a Mac worked—in any case, he had not appreciated how the Mac and Windows style of working could impact the products of his own company.

Professor Baskin pronounced my unimplemented idea for Power-Point to be impossible, unfeasible, certainly a bad idea. Yet, for some reason Dick Kramlich afterward chose to believe in my vision, and to doubt Herb Baskin's authoritative assertions that it was impossible.

At the time, I believed that this whole interaction had been just an examination of my PowerPoint idea, so I wondered why Dick would have believed me rather than the undoubted expert. But I now realize there must have been more to the story.

Dick is a very smart guy, and it's very likely that he had already realized that there could not be bright futures both for his investment in the General Parametrics proprietary hardware approach with non-WYSIWYG software, and also for his investment in my graphical WYSIWYG personal computer software approach to the same market. I didn't even think of this at the time, but that would have been a basic observation for anyone considering the consistency of his portfolio of investments, as Dick surely would have done.

Dick must have been figuring out the resolution of the conflict by using Baskin and me to criticize each other's approaches, much as the 18th-century bookseller Bernard Lintott, when he commissioned translations from languages that he couldn't himself read, checked their accuracy by getting multiple translators to correct one another.

I now think that Dick was *both* testing me by seeing how someone in the graphics establishment reacted to my (yet unimplemented) plan, and also at the same time was using me to test whether Baskin appreciated the coming paradigm shift that, if it were to happen as I predicted, would eventually threaten the General Parametrics business and Dick's investment in it.

Baskin was doubtless right that the kind of complex color graphics he was thinking of couldn't be edited in real time on a Mac, and it didn't occur to him that the functionality could be restricted to be practical, while still being extremely useful.

Baskin's General Parametrics startup had excellent initial success and actually went public in an IPO later in 1986, but it faltered eventually for exactly the expected reason: its product was displaced by PowerPoint, as soon as video from mainstream PCs and Macs improved in the early 1990s. In 1995, the General Parametrics corporate shell was sold to Metal Management, Inc., a full-service metal recycling conglomerate in Chicago, as a way for Metal Management to get a public stock listing, so the company's name was changed to Metal Management. Less than five years later, the company filed for chapter 11 bankruptcy protection.

In any case, the planning and early development of PowerPoint continued along, as if nothing had happened.

> *Alexander Pope, writing to the Earl of Burlington, November 1716, about Bernard Lintott the bookseller: " 'Pray, Mr. Lintott,' said I, 'now you talk of translators, what is your method of managing them?'—'Sir,' replied he, 'those are the saddest pack of rogues in the world. In a hungry fit, they'll swear they understand all the languages in the universe. I have known one of them take down a Greek book upon my counter and cry, "Ay, this is Hebrew, I must read it from the latter end." By God, I can never be sure in these fellows, for I neither understand Greek, Latin, French, nor Italian myself. But this is my way: I agree with them for ten shillings per sheet, with a proviso, that I will have their doings corrected by whom I please; so by one or other they are led at last to the true sense of an author; my judgement giving the negative to all my translators.' "*

72 The PowerPoint Idea Is Leaked, but Misapplied

The PowerPoint plan to focus on overheads was, apparently, suggested to another company in early 1986. We knew nothing about this at the time; the story only came out years later when a contemporaneous history written in 1988 was published on the web. Fortunately, the recipients of the information chose not to use it properly, since they didn't understand what was significant about it.

The background is that there had been a well-known "outline processor" for Apple II called ThinkTank, developed by Dave Winer at his company called Living VideoText. It was the latest in a series of outliners he had developed, and it had also been released for character-mapped IBM PCs. This program had an option to print an outline as overheads for a presentation; to do that, it printed each top-level item of the outline as a "title" at the top of a new page, and then printed all the lower-level items underneath that top-level item in multi-level indented outline format. (If the lower-level items exceeded a page, the top-level item was repeated on another page with something like "[Continued]" appended.) Winer might have been surprised by my tally of the corpus slides, which had taught me that lists with more than a single sub-level were extremely rare on overheads.

For the Mac platform, Winer was refining ThinkTank in early 1986 into a program called "MORE." MORE was still an outline processor; you typed into a text outline as on an Apple II, and printed in much the same way, but MORE took incidental advantage of the fonts and graphics on the Mac. Winer, writing a history in 1988, recorded how it came about that MORE was able to dramatically improve its presentation features:

> An interesting thing happened when we demoed an early version of MORE to Guy Kawasaki and Alain Rossman at Apple. The Bullet Chart idea was Guy's. We showed him the enhanced slide show. He asked if it could print. We printed for him. He went to the LaserWriter down the hall and brought back our printout, marked up with a box around the text, and bullets on each of the subheads on the printout. He said if we could do that, everyone at Apple would use this product. We got the idea! For the next couple of weeks, Peter and I iterated over the design of what would become the Bullet Chart feature of MORE 1.0. Bullet Charts were a real score for us and our users. We already knew from reading reg[istration] cards that a very major use of ThinkTank was preparing for presentations. It only made sense that we should go the next step, and print the outline in presentation form. (Winer, Outliners 1988)

Apple's Guy Kawasaki and Alain Rossman were friends of ours who knew Forethought very well, knew all about PowerPoint, and were generally informed about its development as Apple insiders. If they had not had their awareness of the importance of overhead presentations dramatically raised by us, then we hadn't been doing our jobs. So at their suggestion ("the Bullet Chart idea was Guy's"), Winer added to MORE 1.0 the option to print an outline as a "bullet chart," with a frame around the pages and bullets prefixed to sub-items, to be copied to make overheads. MORE 1.0 was shipped in June 1986, ten months ahead of PowerPoint 1.0.

Winer later said that adding the bullet chart idea made a big difference for his company:

"By early '86 ... we were in desperate shape. ... Guy Kawasaki showed us where the market opportunity was [for MORE]. In June of '86, we came out with MORE for the Macintosh, and we never had cash problems again." (Swaine 1991)

What was missing, of course, was the direct-drive user interface of typing directly on a representation of the finished slide, so as to see visually how the bullet points would fit on a page along with other elements—for that matter, the other elements were missing too. But, just as in my encounter with Herb Baskin, this "indirect" way of working was actually considered by Winer to be a positive benefit. He continues in his Outliners history document:

> I've always felt that graphics products like page layout programs, draw programs, paint programs, were too low-level to be useful to word and concept people. With MORE, the process of producing graphics was automated. The user didn't get control over every pixel in the presentation, that's the usual tradeoff, but you could produce a sequence of bullet charts in MORE simply by typing in an outline and flipping a switch. It was this instant graphics, its very high leverage, that made MORE a powerful product. ... I look back on MORE as the perfect product. (Winer, Outliners 1988)

There were always "outlining people" who thought this way—that a hierarchical outline was the natural structure for representing anything, and that the advantages of being able to achieve precise graphical control were less important than the disadvantage of having to bother with that precise graphical control. The challenge in designing PowerPoint was to reverse that balance in favor of direct visual control by the user. In years to come, I occasionally met "outlining people" who wanted to work in the MORE way, but deep multi-level outlines on overheads have never been popular. The structure of a presentation is not the tree of a multi-level outline, but is a single ordered sequence of slides, with each slide having a separate internal structure.

This minority design preference of Winer's ultimately had some consequences: a year later, Microsoft would decide between acquiring either Winer's Living VideoText or PowerPoint in a direct comparison, and chose PowerPoint. But Winer had other acquisition offers at the time, much the same ones as Forethought had, and promptly sold his company to Symantec, after which he continued his career as a serial entrepreneur.

Winer didn't do anything wrong in gaining information about PowerPoint; he couldn't have known the sources of the Apple folks who "evangelized" him. And, in fact, the Apple people may have considered an "outlining-based" product to be completely different from the visual-based PowerPoint they knew about, and merely wanted more presentation options for Mac.

Fortunately for us, Winer's own design preferences led him to use the information in a way that was non-competitive, even though he personally considered his work to be "the perfect product."

73 Resistance Was the Problem, not Espionage

The story about Apple evangelists carrying what could have been PowerPoint ideas to a competitor who welcomed them is pretty much an isolated instance. The far bigger problem during development was that people didn't "get" why PowerPoint would be so great, not that they tried to steal the idea.

In the early months of working on PowerPoint, I felt very protective about the idea; it seemed so obviously great that anyone who heard of it would copy it immediately. Over the three years of pitching the idea hundreds of times, I more or less came to the opposite conclusion: that no one would want to copy it, and I would talk about it to almost anyone for a business reason.

In those days, I first heard a line attributed to Howard Aiken (designer of IBM's Harvard Mark I computer during World War II):

> Don't worry about people stealing your ideas. If your ideas are any good, you'll have to ram them down people's throats.
> —Howard Aiken

> (I don't know where I originally found the quote back in those days, but it is also now quoted by Paul Graham (Graham, More Googles 2008).)

I realized immediately that he had been exactly right. The ideas that everyone recognizes immediately as worth stealing are going to be just barely in front of the current commercial frontier and can't be successfully stolen quickly enough, while an idea just a little further away in time will seem to have objections that make it appear a bad idea to most people.

During the three years of development, I talked about PowerPoint to many people in many companies. Despite that, I think only a few other people saw the idea clearly. Our competitors who were already in the DOS or Apple II presentations business by and large didn't see it, either. One time, another company with whom we were working on a different project started to pitch me on the idea for something like PowerPoint—I cut them off nearly at the first sentence, saying that we had some other commitments, so we couldn't discuss that, and it apparently was never pursued.

The idea of PowerPoint, which seemed so blindingly great to me, didn't immediately grab many other people. Even within Forethought, there was the continuing unease that the presentation category might not be big enough or important enough, and that presenters might be content to use a word processor or a drawing program rather than to buy a special-purpose program.

Some categories of people in particular were relatively insensitive to the appeal I saw in PowerPoint. Even later, after years of talking to me and interviewing users, journalists almost always failed to really understand PowerPoint. I always thought the reason was simple: journalists are the targets of a lot of presentations, but they don't make them.

Similarly, as mentioned earlier, some investors just didn't get the idea (our own did, of course). Same reason, I think: VCs receive pitches all the time, but they seldom make them, so they don't really feel as keenly the benefits of PowerPoint.

On the other side, industry consultants and gurus who made their livings giving presentations about their work could always be counted on to understand some of PowerPoint's great features. Thus, for every version, we would go around and show the product to PC industry consultants and collect glowing endorsements, which could be quoted by the journalists. But even consultants didn't understand the category as well as customers in companies where presentations were a way of life and served a wide spectrum of communication needs; see the discussion in (Gold 2002).

74 System Requirements for PowerPoint 1.0

When we started real implementation of PowerPoint, we had to set firm minimum system requirements for the machines on which it would ever run. Since we had decided to start with Macintosh, we specified a PC with about the same level of function. The plan clearly depended on Windows continuing to evolve to be more like Mac.

> The Presenter program will be tailored for two personal computer environments:
> — MS-Windows, running on a machine with at least an 80286 processor, 512K of memory, and EGA-level (640 x 350) or better color graphics (from IBM, Compaq, Tandy, Zenith, H-P, NEC, ATT, ...);
> — Macintosh, with a 68000 processor, 512K of memory, and monochrome graphics.
> These two environments are very much alike, and are becoming even more alike as MS-Windows continues to gain features more like Macintosh. Still, we think both will constitute significant markets. Fortunately, it is possible to develop related programs for the two environments; but scrupulous adherence to even the smallest conventions of each environment separately will be required.
> Almost all questions of hardware compatibility are answered by saying that we will support these two environments fully, but only these two environments. (Gaskins, PowerPoint Marketing 1986)

There are points of interest here. Note that we never planned to support the 128K original Mac; a screen image of a PowerPoint slide was about 200K. Bill Gates is widely quoted as saying that "Anybody who could write a good application [to run] on a 128K Mac deserves a medal." (quoted in (Linzmayer 2008, 116)).

Unlike many other early Windows developers, and unlike VisiOn, we never planned to support IBM's CGA display (640 x 200) and never planned to support PCs with 8088 or 8086 CPUs, even if Windows did.

In 1984, most VCs didn't understand that Mac and Windows would replace DOS, and they were worried that we didn't have a strategy for compatibility with the "installed base" of DOS machines. When raising money, I used to tell the VCs, dramatically, that we were totally writing off 100% of the installed base of PCs and 99% of what would be shipped that year. We were so totally convinced that there was a new opportunity on Mac and Windows that, like Cortez, we were burning our ships so we could not return to the old world. Our entire design and our code would only work on Mac and Windows; we were that sure that the new graphics PCs would obsolete the entire old DOS base, and our future was in the new world. If we were wrong, we would die, because we had no fallback position; but we were not wrong.

That was dramatic enough to assure that if they invested in us, they knew what they were doing.

75 The State of Macintosh at Predicted Shipment

This was our prediction of what Macintosh hardware capabilities would be available to PowerPoint at its first ship, all tending to back up the idea that it would be wise to start by concentrating on overheads:

> Macintosh is being sold today intensively for "desktop publishing" applications, and it actually delivers the printers, the fonts, and the software necessary to do the job. Apple is clearly positioning Mac as the kind of machine on which one would make presentations, so many users already look to Mac for this application.
>
> Mac lacks a large screen, color display, and color peripherals. Apple says it will inform developers (under non-disclosure requirements) about its color strategy in July of 1986. If this is so, it is quite likely that color on Macintoshes will not be available when Presenter is first shipped.

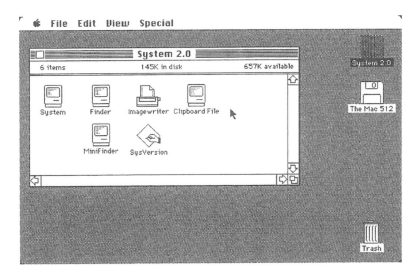

Even if Macintoshes get color displays, there will certainly not be a color LaserWriter soon. ImageWriter II is not a suitable color device, since the colored ribbon segments pick up contamination from other colors (and Apple support on Mac is sub-minimal). For color overheads, Apple would have to add a high-resolution color inkjet or color thermal transfer printer. For color 35mm slides, Apple would have to add a film recorder (very likely with a PostScript interface).

Neither the Mac nor the Mac Plus contains a video-out jack, so the installed base sold through 1986 at least will not be able to directly show video presentations of any kind, monochrome or color.

But the same hardware configuration being sold today for page layout use could also be used to make outstanding (monochrome) overhead transparencies by adding only our software. Hence, the initial positioning on Macintosh would be for producing overheads using LaserWriters (or ImageWriters). This could be introduced to dealers and salespeople as an extension of "Desktop Publishing." (Gaskins, PowerPoint Marketing 1986)

76 Macintosh Implementation Considerations

Dennis Austin has written about some of the many considerations that were presented to implementers by the constraints and limitations of the early Mac hardware and system environment:

Integer Arithmetic

I was determined to avoid the use of floating point arithmetic in the graphics calculations. I was sure that the processor was too slow to permit the constant calculation needed for real arithmetic. QuickDraw itself, the Macintosh graphics engine, worked in integer arithmetic and that certainly seemed good enough for the resolution of a ten-inch slide.

This decision led to some slightly odd features of the design, such as fixed scaling factors for the view. It did give the intended result, though: Lightning speeds for hit testing and drawing.

Compact file size

The Macintosh had no hard disk. The single floppy disk had to contain the operating system, the application program, and the data files. Compact files were de rigueur. Luckily, presentations don't generally require large data volumes. Descriptions of the graphics are generally small. The text is perhaps the bulkiest part of the data, and that isn't much compared to a word processor.

The main consumers of space were pictures pasted into the presentation. The Mac format for vector graphics was very compact, but bitmap graphics take more space. Pictures' bulk was unavoidable, but we did our best to keep the storage of the rest extremely compact.

To avoid wasting space with pictures used more than once, pictures were kept in a reference-counted pool. That saved memory during operation as well as file space, but introduced the possibility of reference-count errors, especially given the tricky aspects of copies on the clipboard, in the undo buffer, etc. We did have a few such errors, of course.

While open, a presentation was kept completely in memory. Main memory was fairly commodious compared to disk, so this seemed obviously right. It also made for snappy response. The problem was in managing the available memory.

This was not a virtual memory system. The OS could manage data segments, but the application controlled which segments were movable or discardable. Data had to be locked during access lest the OS move it while the app is holding a pointer to it. But data needed to be unlocked most of the time or the heap would get too fragmented.

The user could set heap space. There was a lot of data that Presenter could not allow to be discarded, but could be moved around as needed. We wanted to take advantage of more heap space, though, if it were available. One good use was the thumbnail images displayed in the slide sorter. These took a while to draw, but we could retain a bitmap of each thumbnail whenever memory was available. We devoted a lot of resources to optimizing use of memory for the thumbnail images.

Code segments were completely managed by the operating system, but it was up to us to decide the segmentation. We carefully planned the segments so that uncommon code could demand space when more common code could be unloaded. Printing is an archetype for this kind of analysis. Presenter's printing code needed to be loaded, and a print driver as well, but lots of UI code could be discarded while printing.

Text

Text for slides was a special problem. It was critically important that text on the screen be a faithful preview of text on the slide. This was manifested particularly with respect to line

145

lengths and word wrap. Users would line up their graphics with their text, and that alignment had to remain the same at different scales and at different resolutions.

Amazingly, even in its primitive form, QuickDraw measured text in fractional pixels so that measurement and spacing could, in theory, be retained at different resolutions. Presenter was the first application where the theory had to work in actual practice, and it was a continuing source of difficulties.

CoreEdit

The Macintosh toolkit handled styled text, but only in the simplest form of a single run of characters in a particular font and size. There had been ambition to provide more complete toolkit support with word wrap, mixed styles, and so forth, but it never made it to production.

The basic tools for complete text processing had been written into a package called CoreEdit, but it was used only by MacWrite and was not part of the toolkit. Apple made the source (assembler) available for licensing, but there was no support for it.

Presenter needed to have extremely high-performance text and it obviously needed to be written in machine language. CoreEdit seemed like it was the shortcut to our goal. It was indeed fast, but I found that it played fast and loose with the Macintosh rules to gain that speed. It took heavy modification to adapt it to the Presenter graphics environment and change it to follow the Macintosh standards more closely. It might have been easier to write a new text module from scratch, but I learned a lot from reading the code. In the end, PowerPoint 1.0 ran on much later Macintosh systems than MacWrite did!

Slide show

It was obviously important for slide shows to snap quickly between slides. The only way to do that was have the next slide ready in an off-screen bitmap. There was only enough memory to keep one or two off-screen bitmaps as large as the entire screen, but we could rely on each slide remaining on display long enough for us to draw the next one in the background. Backing up to the previous slide could be a problem, but there was sometimes enough memory to keep that bitmap available for a while.

Slide Sorter

To implement the Slide Sorter, we drew thumbnail images of slides off-screen and saved them in bitmaps. Presenter tried to prepare thumbnails in the background so that the slide sorter would pop quickly into view when needed. There was no multitasking in the operating system, of course, so this was do-it-yourself multiprocessing. When a slide was being drawn into an off-screen bitmap, it constantly checked for user input and abandoned the drawing whenever demanded.

The thumbnails also consumed valuable memory. They were simply discarded when memory was needed for another purpose, and drawn anew when memory became available again. (Austin, Beginnings 2009)

77 The State of Windows at Predicted Shipment

Windows was not as well known to us, but that was not much of a problem, since we were aiming at Macintosh first.

The principal issue was that the great bulk (95% or more) of the installed base of PCs were 8088-based, and had poor displays, and we intended to write off all those machines as below our minimum system requirements. A lot of people, from investors to sales people, wanted a product which could be sold into that "enormous" installed base; the only problem was that performance of Windows on such machines was impossibly bad.

So my argument was that the installed base would turn over rapidly enough to make an interesting market. Not accidentally, writing off most of the PC installed base was another argument for starting on Mac; the number of 286-based PCs wasn't all that much larger, and Windows wasn't installed on enough of them to make the initial Windows market size very different from the Mac market size, small though Mac was.

> MS-Windows clearly will be the equivalent environment on IBM and compatible machines. According to a January 1986 survey of developers by Future Computing, 40% of developers intend to develop software for MS-Windows (as against 12% for TopView, and 6% for GEM). The dominance of Windows is probably even greater today. Not only does Windows provide the same high level of system support as Mac, but Microsoft has promised developers that software which runs on Windows and uses its multitasking and memory management will continue to run on the new (incompatible) protected-mode "DOS 5.0" for 286 machines

only, due early in 1987; this is an offer developers can hardly afford to refuse.

There is already an installed base of over one million IBM PC-AT compatible machines, and over half of these have been sold with high resolution graphics display cards (either the Hercules monochrome or the IBM EGA color). Hence, the number of existing machines already in use which could adequately run Windows and provide a Macintosh-like level of performance is already about as large as the Macintosh installed base.

Note that our programs will *not* be optimized for use on the largest part of the installed base of personal computers, namely 8088-based IBM Personal Computers with either IBM Monochrome (character-mapped) Displays or IBM Color/Graphics Adapters (640 x 200). We do not believe that an adequate program can be written for such hardware, and notice that MS-Windows itself does not deliver an adequate graphics interface on such older machines.

All evidence is that that older generation is at the end of its life.

Compaq expects 60% to 80% of its sales in 1986 to be 286-based models; Tandy, Zenith, and NEC have made similar announcements, and it is widely believed that IBM will introduce a lower-priced 286-based machine soon, to replace the aging PC and XT as mainstream business machines. (The way in which this is done may be by introducing a new power machine and re-pricing the AT, or by actually introducing new PC and XT models. The 8088-based machines presumably have a future at still lower prices, for use at home and in very small businesses.) For the installed base, plug-in 286 accelerator cards ($800 with a megabyte of memory), EGA cards ($400), and expanded memory and hard disk cards offer a realistic upgrade path. For these reasons we think it is reasonable not to design new products for the old lower level of performance.

Lotus was widely criticized in January of 1983 for introducing a new spreadsheet program (1–2–3) which required the address space of an 8088, and which could not be engineered to work on the dominant 8-bit installed base. Subsequent events have demonstrated that they were right to fully exploit the power of what was then the emerging generation of machines, at the expense of forgetting the old installed base, because the new generation rapidly grew to dominate the old. We think the situation is precisely analogous with respect to the new generation of graphics-oriented personal computers today. (Gaskins, PowerPoint Marketing 1986)

```
≡              MS-DOS Executive              ⌐
 File  View  Special
 A ⌐—⌐  C ⌐——⌐  D ⌐—⌐  E ⌐—⌐  F ⌐—⌐  C: \WINDOWS1
 CALC      .EXE    24992  11/15/85    5:42am                      ↑
 CALE┌─────────────────────────────────────────┐
 CARDF│           Microsoft Windows             │
 CLIPB│           MS-DOS Executive              │
 CLOCK│  ┌──┐                                   │
 COMM │  │  │       Version 1.01                │
 CONTR│  └──┘                                   │
 GDI  │      Copyright @ 1985, Microsoft Corp.  │
 KERNE│            ┌────────────┐               │
 MSDOS│            │     Ok     │               │
 MSDOS│            └────────────┘               │
 NOTEP│      Disk Space Free:   519168K         │
 PAINT│      Memory Free:          381K         │
 REVERSI  .EXE    14816  11/15/85    5:42am
 SETUP    .EXE    33974  11/15/85    5:42am
 SPOOLER  .EXE    13216  11/15/85    5:42am
 TERMINAL .EXE    43968  11/15/85    5:42am
 USER     .EXE   122408  11/15/85    5:42am
 WIN      .COM     4867  11/15/85    5:42am                       ↓
```

78 Enlisting Tom Rudkin

The second big milestone in PowerPoint history, after enlisting Dennis Austin in October of 1984, was enlisting Tom Rudkin, who joined us on the first of May, 1986, eighteen months later. This gave PowerPoint two full-time developers plus my services.

> Six months later, in May 1986, when we managed to close the first part of the Preferred C round ($408,000), we felt we were able to hire a second person full time (with whom we had been talking since the previous January). We invested about $70,000 over the next six months. (Gaskins, Forethought History 1987)

Tom was extremely bright, had just the experience for PowerPoint, and, like Dennis and me, he was a real believer in graphical user interfaces and in the fact that they were just about to revolutionize personal computing.

Tom had a strong academic background, and then had worked at Intel where he was the lead software developer for the ICE-85 and ICE-86 products and designed the common command language for the family of In-Circuit Emulators.

After Intel, he had joined my group at Bell-Northern Research, where he implemented several Smalltalk systems on our DEC-20. This led to a memorable day when we entertained a group of visitors from Xerox PARC, including Adele Goldberg, and we demonstrated to them

Tom's implementation of Smalltalk-76 (vast approval) and then Tom's implementation of Smalltalk-80. We didn't know that Adele believed Smalltalk-80 to be a deep secret except to their non-disclosure partners—true, we had implemented it from a document picked up by someone in a cafeteria at MIT and passed along to us, but we didn't realize the level of corporate security to which Xerox aspired. Adele was livid with fury, and the encounter did not lead to the future pleasant collegial relations with her group at PARC that we had hoped for.

After leaving BNR in October 1982, Tom had joined VisiCorp, where he was a senior designer and architect on the VisiOn project, the very system that delivered what pre-PowerPoint Forethought had been failing to deliver. This system had been actually shipped at the end of 1983, just about the same time that Mac shipped and Windows was announced. Sales were slow, though; the VisiOn assets were sold to Control Data Corporation in mid-1984 and, by the end of 1985, VisiCorp was merged into Paladin Software.

I had been very impressed by Tom's abilities when we worked at BNR, so when I heard he was available I was very keen to interest him in the PowerPoint project. Tom had outstanding technical judgment, honed by his experience in shipping a graphical environment on PCs to customers like ours. Tom also had the personal qualities of strength and integrity needed in a startup, and was another independent voice to be sure we were doing the right things. I had always enjoyed very much working with Tom, and he made an excellent third colleague for our tiny PowerPoint group.

Tom also fit in well, because he shared Dennis's and my interest in language and writing. He had spent a year abroad in France while in college, and was a good addition to "the most literate programmers in the valley."

Tom first worked with Dennis Austin in the whole final year of development of PowerPoint 1.0 for Mac. But Tom had joined us specifically to head PowerPoint for Windows, and as soon as the first product shipped he did just that, heading the incredible three-year effort that followed, to ship our vitally important first Windows product.

Tom's VisiOn experience was very useful in judging the progress of Windows, and eventually in contributing ideas to the Windows group to help improve Windows. VisiOn had run on low-end IBM PCs and on low-end 640 x 200 CGA monochrome displays, so Tom knew all the problems that Windows would have to solve, and then some.

Tom worked at the Microsoft GBU until February 1995, having run a large department of many developers on PowerPoint, then run other related development projects. Thus, as with Dennis Austin, Tom provided PowerPoint with continuity of development management with the same leaders for more than ten years.

An experienced developer who had worked for Microsoft in Redmond, and who joined us later at the GBU, remarked once that PowerPoint was the best-structured large program he had ever seen. That's one advantage of this kind of continuity. It is only possible by hiring absolutely the best people first.

79 Startup Ingenuity for Source Code Control

Dennis Austin has also written about Tom Rudkin's arrival and the imaginative way in which they instituted a source code control system consistent both with Forethought's limited budgets and, more importantly, with the lack of programmer time to invest in infrastructure (we didn't have junior programmers or system administrators):

> I began development of Presenter by myself. I implemented a basic application structure and simple drawing. After that, I tackled text because it seemed like the area most difficult to get right. To my surprise and pleasure, the implementation work went fairly well and the performance of drawing and text seemed excellent.
>
> There was obviously too little time to complete the entire application on my own, however, so, with the company finances temporarily stable, we hired another programmer. Tom Rudkin had worked for Bob back at Bell-Northern, and had since been employed at VisiCorp. He and I worked very well together and our two-person team was at least twice as fast as I was working by myself.
>
> We acquired a second-hand Lisa for Tom to use, but we had to solve the source control problem. There was no software solution at hand, but we soon invented a practical alternative.
>
> We bought one of those card racks that hangs on the wall intended to hold employee time cards for punching in and punching out. In each of the slots we put a 4x6 card corresponding to a single source file. When you wanted to modify a file, you pulled the card out of the rack and took it to your office. To check in, you made a dated notation on the card about what had been done and

then returned the card to the rack. The actual file was, at this point, copied to our network repository.

This crude system worked remarkably well for us. We also had neighboring offices, so it was well supplemented with other communication. This was the only time in my career where I was called upon to work in such intense cooperation with a single other individual, and it will always be a highlight. Tom was a consummate professional as well as a warm, spirited and dedicated compatriot." (Austin, Beginnings 2009)

Tom Rudkin suggested that he and Dennis should write an article for the April issue of *Software Practice and Experience*, describing how the new source code control system was "immune to race conditions on multiple users checking in or out at the same time" (Rudkin 2012). This system continued to work up to First Customer Ship.

80 The PowerPoint Paper Blizzard of 1986

With Tom Rudkin on board, the first step was to bring him up to speed on everything done previously, and the best way to do that was by writing an updated spec for the product, incorporating everything learned and decided in the previous nine months. This was also the first comprehensive spec to be illustrated with mocked-up Mac formats rather than Windows. (Austin, Rudkin and Gaskins, PowerPoint Spec 1986)

For the first time, also, this spec was tied to a detailed schedule, based on Dennis's and Tom's estimates for every work item. We had been talking to Tom for some time before his formal first day, but, even so, a mere three weeks to bring him up to speed, have him take part in estimates for everything, and write a 45-page spec was pretty quick work. (Again, it was written with Dennis Austin's fingers on the keyboard, and his was the largest contribution.)

But the spec was only the tip of an iceberg of paper for PowerPoint that I was preparing at the same time.

On the same day, 22 May 1986, the 45-page spec was accompanied by my 16-page listing of all the tasks that everyone in the company would have to undertake to get PowerPoint shipped, and my 4-page critical-path chart of boxes and lines. It showed First Customer Ship on Mac to be 16 February 1987 (about two months earlier than actually happened).

Three weeks later, 10 June 1986, I had a 15-page spreadsheet showing PowerPoint Financials: Sales Forecasts, Budgets, and Cash Flow. Along with it was a 15-page spreadsheet showing the Forethought Pro Forma Income Statement with Cash Flow, FY1987-FY1991. As usual, I authored these, but the latter one was specifically agreed with Rob Campbell and co-signed by him. These were presented to the Board of Directors for approval.

Two weeks or so after that, 27 June 1986, I published a rewritten version of the PowerPoint Product Marketing Analysis (53 pages), frequently quoted here (Gaskins, PowerPoint Marketing 1986).

Three weeks later, 15 July 1986, I published a formal Forethought Business Plan (54 pages), again with Rob Campbell's buy-in. The same day, I also published two presentations, one about the business plan (10 slides) and one about the long Marketing Analysis (28 slides), called a "New Product Summary and Review" (Gaskins, NPSR 1986).

Part of the motivation for this huge blizzard of paper was that I was still having problems getting Forethought to begin to turn attention away from published products and to focus on PowerPoint. If we couldn't accomplish that, we couldn't become profitable.

A month after the blizzard, on 14 August 1986, I issued a Power-Point Project Status Update (9 slides), summing up what was in all the other documents. The date was chosen to be exactly two years since my first two-page description written 14 August 1984. This document put everyone on notice that the time to focus on PowerPoint had come, or else it would not get shipped. The parting injunction was:

> We believe it is almost certainly not too late for us right now, but any further delay would jeopardize success. (Gaskins, PowerPoint Status 1986)

At the time that all this material got written and issued, we were carrying out all the final tasks for shipping FileMaker Plus, a dizzy whirl of activity, providing constant interruptions that could not be deferred.

81 Invasion of the Xeroids

At the same time as that blizzard of activity, our investors, having just done a Preferred C round of $408,000, surprised us by telling us that there was "no chance of bringing in a new VC," which would be necessary to raise any further money, because "software deals [were] not being funded." That was bad news, because we were, perversely, spending all the money we had just received to ship the FileMaker Plus upgrade. Money in the bank would not possibly stretch to finish PowerPoint. Also, a longstanding plan to merge with a public company shell called UMF was dead, because we were not delivering our numbers (*i.e.*, not selling enough FileMaker to meet our forecasts). Our only future funding source, the investors suggested, would be to find some customer to finance further work.

Coincidentally, we had been approached by Xerox, who were very interested in PowerPoint. This was an immense irony, given that the whole paradigm of graphics user interfaces had been pioneered at Xerox's own Palo Alto Research Center, and people from PARC had been giving presentations prepared on their Altos for more than ten years.

Xerox wanted to talk about acquiring rights to PowerPoint, believing they could use it to sell Xerox printers. They proposed, with endless complications, to prepay us about $750,000 over ten months, partly to induce us to make a co-labeled private version for Xerox to sell, partly as pre-payment for product. We met Xerox people in what seemed like almost every major city in the United States for extended talks.

The longer they kept us talking, the bigger the deal got. They wanted to create a new line of software supporting color to make a market for a new line of Xerox color printers; PowerPoint would be perfect for that. They had an unannounced clone of the IBM PC AT, to support color and color printers.

They also wanted to re-design our software; "little" things, like adding color, and like adding the ability to read and write Harvard-compatible and Freelance-compatible formats (not realizing how different those DOS products were). And, they needed business charting to be in the product, not imported from Excel. And, they weren't much interested in Mac; they wanted the Windows version first. But really, their boss "preferred" the GEM environment from Digital Research instead of Windows, so we should aim the product at GEM rather than Windows; they were going to ship GEM on their AT-clone. (Preferring GEM was such a lapse of taste and judgment that I could hardly believe my ears.)

All this was totally unrealistic, but, with more meetings, the Xerox people became even more grandiose. They might want all MS-DOS rights, no sales to anyone but them. They might want to buy a Windows version of FileMaker. They could introduce us to venture capitalists who would be happy to invest on the basis of a Xerox contract; and they did have us actually talk to a Xerox internal VC group (no result). They wanted a comprehensive business plan proposal for all of this.

Later, just at the end of Forethought's life, Xerox proposed that they wanted exclusive marketing rights to PowerPoint, for which they would pay something above $18 million. They would pay us $100,000 in "earnest money," a breakup fee of $1 million if no deal was completed within 60 days (they realized that their credibility was exceptionally weak after their months of talking), $125,000 a month in development fees, and then $18 million minimum guarantee against product payments over three years. This was mostly about the Windows version, and had lots of distasteful details, such as a request for us to write Windows drivers for old non-graphical printers, highlighting a lack of shared vision. Xerox specifically did not want to acquire the company, just exclusive marketing rights, leaving the biggest part of the risk with us.

We spent days with them, soaring with their fantasies, but in the end they were never able to make a commitment of any kind. We were never able to write them off and ignore them, since they might be our only funding possibility to finish PowerPoint.

82 Problems with Publishing

A nagging problem throughout late-1986 was that there wasn't really clear action at Forethought to assure that the "booster rocket" of the publishing business would be thrown away when PowerPoint was ready to take over.

On paper, it was perfectly clear. In June of 1986, we had adopted a formal five-year plan for Forethought, ratified by our Board of Directors, which consisted of me and Rob Campbell and our two largest investors. That plan showed PowerPoint as 25% of total sales for FY87 (the then-current fiscal year), 75% of sales and 85% of profits for FY88 (the next fiscal year), and 100% of sales and profits for FY89-FY91 (the following three fiscal years). Forethought's fiscal years ended on March 31, so "FY88" began in April 1987 and ended in March 1988. (This caused endless confusion.)

To achieve this plan, clearly PowerPoint had to be completed soon, and publishing would have to be phased out in favor of higher-profit internal products. That was what was on paper.

But as time went by, the publishing business became more prominent. Most people at Forethought were working on it; it provided a lot of drama and a lot of fun for those people; and no concrete plan emerged to ever wind it down. Rob still operated as though he thought he was building up a publishing company, a fairly small and peripheral part of which was my PowerPoint activity. I thought I was building up a PowerPoint company, a small and temporary part of which was his publishing activity. This ambiguity was able to continue for a surprisingly long time without requiring resolution.

For the first period after the restart, the conflict of these two views of Forethought wasn't too important. We raised several rounds of money, we went through endless perils and barely survived, but the ambiguity continued.

Gradually, PowerPoint began to get better and better, so its outlook improved. We were committing to real forecasts for its revenue, and needed to get it finished and shipped in order to meet those commitments.

The MACWARE publishing business had begun rather well, but the initial two products (Factfinder and Typing Intrigue) were little more than toys for the original Mac, and rather quickly ran out of steam after we had practiced upon them. The third product, FileMaker, had very good developers (Nashoba) and became more than just a throw-away product to practice upon; but it grew so much that it required a lot of investment, just at the time when Mac sales in 1985–1986 were very poor. The result was that Forethought's contract with Nashoba had to be renegotiated several times, each time giving more of the revenue split to Nashoba, until the product became relatively unprofitable for Forethought. Worse yet, we were building no asset value in the product, since we had no rights to it. The publishing business had been supposed to finance PowerPoint, but had ended up unable to even reach break-even, so it sapped PowerPoint resources.

I later summed up what the situation was in mid-1986, in a memo on Forethought business strategy, which I wrote in May of 1987:

> In order to get a Nashoba renewal in March 1986, and in order to conserve cash, we had to agree to extreme terms in our agreement covering FileMaker. We have no ownership of the name FileMaker. We have no rights to any future versions of the product for Macintosh. We have no rights to any future versions for other machines, including IBM. We have exceedingly onerous reporting requirements, which involve disclosing almost all of our financial

information to the developer. We have very limited control over the evolution of the product. We have virtually no ability to transfer our limited right to sell FileMaker to others. And—sufficient all by itself—we pay royalties under a complicated formula which works out to about four times the going rate! In our FY1987 just completed, including all the introduction costs of FileMaker Plus, we paid 26% of revenue as royalties to Nashoba. On a multi-year basis, we estimate that 30% or more of FileMaker revenue will be paid to Nashoba.

By agreeing to these terms, we in effect guaranteed that the effort invested in FileMaker Plus would not increase the asset value of Forethought.

... the FileMaker business is just busy work. And think of the huge amount of wasted effort! The salespeople frantically trying to make a monthly FileMaker target of 1500 units, 12 times in a year; the constant attention to manufacturing, entering orders, fulfillment, answering inquiries about why FileMaker has not arrived; the expense and creative effort of trying to revamp all the advertising and collateral material; the late-night sessions trying to get the highly detailed Nashoba statement out of accounting every month for 12 months; the customer support reps trying to answer detailed technical questions from customers all day every day; all the work of specifying a new version of the product, trying to influence development without much success, and all the expense and attention required during documentation and testing; and so on, and so on. All wasted. At the end of the year we will have virtually no profit left to show for all our work. Since we own nothing in the product, we have only increased the value of an asset of Nashoba's. (Gaskins, Forethought Strategy 1987)

All this was grim for the people working on the publishing business. Rob Campbell really liked the FileMaker product, and he contributed a great deal to it; we all liked it and put a lot into it, but Rob was its real champion. But FileMaker now had this deep unprofitability built into it, and we had no way to fix that. Without FileMaker, we had no publishing division—it was the only published product left.

As PowerPoint progressed toward its distant goal, there were always shorter-term proposals to enlarge the publishing business, which had to be squashed to avoid delaying PowerPoint. The lingering dissatisfaction with the PowerPoint idea made these proposals attractive to the publishing arm, so each one was compared carefully to the alternative of finishing PowerPoint, and I had to make the case over and over.

157

At one point, just for a single example, one of the original developers of AutoCAD came to us with a proposal that we should complete and publish an unfinished CAD program for Mac and Windows that he had mostly written. This would be an expansion of the publishing division, but the developer wasn't self-contained like Nashoba, so we would have had to manage development at the expense of PowerPoint. I knew that the product wouldn't be a good idea because it required so much technical and market knowledge that we didn't have. What we didn't know then was that AutoDesk itself wouldn't be able to release AutoCAD for Windows until 1993, seven or eight years later, well after the *third* version of PowerPoint had shipped on both Windows and Mac! Thank goodness that, after a lot of travel and analysis, we concluded that we would not go ahead.

We also got constant proposals to merge with other small software companies, the aim being to get big enough to launch an IPO, often with product baggage; these proposals had appeal to our investors, so they demanded consideration. The appeal was always made that we could quickly increase the number of products available for sale, so as to reach break-even on the publishing business.

All these proposals to expand the publishing business were rejected, either by management or by our investors, but only after distracting work on every one. To keep PowerPoint going required a lot of energy to assure that it got resources. If I had not personally believed in Power-Point and worked constantly to keep it moving forward, it would never have been shipped before Forethought got bogged down in publishing and went out of business. The "paper blizzard" described earlier had some effect, as it became somewhat less responsible to ignore Power-Point, now that it was our whole official plan for future profitability.

As PowerPoint neared completion, the indecision about what kind of company Forethought would be was always exacting an overhead of struggle, and projects were competing for attention and resources in a way that is more typical of life in a large company. That is no help in a startup, which should ideally be united on a single strategy.

83 Apple Gets Interested in Investing

The background of Apple's making its first ever venture capital investment in PowerPoint goes back a long way.

When we were running out of money in early 1986, the prospect surfaced at a Forethought board meeting on 15 April 1986; Dick Kramlich mentioned, among a long string of prospective investors, that we might look for $750,000 from Apple Venture Capital. The idea was to structure it as an R&D partnership: it would be specifically for PowerPoint only, and if Forethought went out of business, ownership of the PowerPoint product would go to Apple.

We got in touch with Dan Eilers at Apple, who was interested. Contacts dragged on into May; eventually, the funding round was completed without Apple, and their interest was on hold.

Then, after we got the news that the investors planned on no further funding, and after we had Xerox consume a lot of time and come to nothing, Apple suddenly resurrected itself in early September of 1986. We got a call out of the blue: Dan Eilers of Apple, head of the new Strategic Investment Group, and Horace Inea, his technical advisor, would like to come over for two hours. Their agenda was to get a current Forethought business update, and get the latest FileMaker update, but especially to find out about PowerPoint.

We met, and things appeared to move rapidly. They wanted to make a "long-term equity investment," and they called back the next day to get the name of our audit partner at Arthur Young (our accountants), so they could follow up on their due diligence.

One big issue, though, was that this new Strategic Investment Group had not yet made its first investment, though they had been organized for six months. Our existing VCs thought that Eilers and Inea were extremely cautious because they wanted their first deals to be big successes. Woody Rea from NEA thought that the biggest problem was that Dan Eilers was afraid that Forethought would go out of business, so PowerPoint would never get to market and its value would be lost— an analysis later confirmed by Dan Eilers himself.

That certainly was a big risk, because we really were running out of money once more. We again entered into all kinds of negotiations. One, rather serious, was to be acquired by Ashton-Tate. Another was to get an investment from Broderbund, although they thought we were making a big mistake in our "overlooking" the "vanilla MS-DOS market," a view that guaranteed there would be no meeting of minds. We explored an exchange of software with a company called Presentation Technologies; an investment from Adobe, after we talked with John Warnock and with some of his investors in Adobe; a separate sale of the international rights to PowerPoint. We had further fruitless talks with

Xerox, again with complex plans and promises of letters of intent that didn't materialize. All this took up huge amounts of time in October and November.

But, Apple stayed around in the background. By November, we were meeting with operational people at Apple and with Darrell Boyle, our own former VP of marketing, who was now a consultant to Apple on Desktop Presentations, about Apple's adopting PowerPoint for internal company use and giving us lots of marketing support—not an investment, but a hopeful sign.

Apple support would be great, so long as we could stay in business, but we were down to nothing in the bank because, after a sales blip from the August upgrade, FileMaker was still hemorrhaging money. By our Board of Directors meeting on 19 November, Dick Kramlich was asking "Can't we renegotiate the Nashoba deal [for FileMaker], get out of it some way?" My company history written in 1987 records:

> ... by November, 1986, we were once again actively considering liquidation. We managed now to close the second part of the Preferred C round for $325,000. (Gaskins, Forethought History 1987)

This round was accomplished because, gradually, Forethought's investors were becoming optimistic that Apple could be talked into making an investment, but thought that the money wouldn't be in the bank before January 1987, for some Apple internal reasons. So, once more, our investors came through for us; yet again, we abandoned all the other negotiations, and continued working on PowerPoint.

84 Why We Thought Apple Should Invest

In addition to the interaction that our investors had with Apple's Strategic Investment Group, which tended toward confidence that they would invest, I had previously written a summary of the strategic reasons why Apple should be interested:

> Apple is surely not the most important partner for Presenter since it is surely not the dominant vendor of personal computers to people who make presentations. Nevertheless, Apple's partnership is particularly important in view of our decision to proceed with the Macintosh version of Presenter first. Until we have an IBM version, other partners are reluctant to get seriously involved

(very few of them believe that Macintosh has any importance for them). With Apple's active help and investment, we can use this situation to launch the product inexpensively.

Over the last three months, Forethought has held a number of discussions with the marketing management at Apple Computer responsible for Macintosh sales in the markets addressed by Presenter. We have shown them prototypes of the product and discussed its proposed features and positioning at length. Their response to us has been:

- The Presenter product is of critical strategic importance in Apple's intended positioning of Macintosh. Even today, they are running three-page ads in the *Wall Street Journal* including an overhead projector, but they have no presentation product to recommend for that function.
- Presenter's planned ability to work with larger screen sizes, to support color presentations, and to drive color slide making peripherals, could all be of the greatest importance in connection with models of Macintosh and new peripherals which could be available in the foreseeable future. [This careful language means we actually had received some nondisclosure information about these from Apple, of course.]
- Presenter is so important that, if it can be developed and delivered, Apple "would provide support on the same scale as that given to Aldus." For Aldus (developers of PageMaker) Apple has run steady multi-page advertising in national magazines and the *Wall Street Journal,* promoted dealer tours through the major markets at Apple's expense, hired and trained a 62-person force to focus on sales of Aldus's software with Apple hardware to dealers and corporate accounts, provided support for internationalization, and provided a range of other services.
- Apple knows of no other developer working on a comparable or competitive product, so they would particularly like to see Presenter finished promptly. They would look forward to working with Forethought on its introduction, based on our experiences working together in the past.
- Apple is not offended by our intention to also do a version of the product for Microsoft Windows on IBM, but would be pleased if there were an initial period of up to six months during which the product was available only on Macintosh. After that, they would welcome a compatible product for

> MS-Windows which could exchange data with the Macintosh version, as part of their strategy of compatibility through data communication.
> (Gaskins, PowerPoint Marketing 1986)

All this was on the basis of the interaction we had had back in April and May of 1986, during the first consideration of an Apple investment. If it were true that Apple's greatest fear was that we wouldn't stay in business long enough to ship PowerPoint, then the solution was clear: give us the tools—the investment and the marketing support—and we would finish the job.

85 Adding Final Resources for PowerPoint Ship

By November 1986, then, we had some more money and were no longer about to liquidate the company and, in fact, we could hire. But Dennis, Tom, and I had all read Fred Brooks, and we all knew and believed his "Brooks's Law" that "Adding manpower to a late software project makes it later." We decided not to add developers to PowerPoint.

From my 1987 company history:

> Six months later, in November 1986, when we had closed the second part of the Preferred C round for $325,000, we felt we could hire contractors to help us finish the PowerPoint program and manual—by that time it was too late to add employees.
> (Gaskins, Forethought History 1987)

We found two sources for code that we needed for our First Customer Ship. First was Bear River Associates. Tony Meadow and his partner had done some development of Mac printing for other applications, and they were able to provide us with a lot of the custom printing code that we needed, working independently and not slowing down the main development. They did very well, were intelligent to work with, and delivered what they said they would, on schedule. We used Bear River Associates again, repeatedly, on important parts of PowerPoint 2.0 and 3.0, after we became part of Microsoft, and they are remembered fondly for their critical contribution to our making the first ship.

The other help was from Tom Evslin, then heading Solutions, Inc., of Vermont. Tom was developing some utilities for Mac that did graphical operations with multiple scrapbooks, which would facilitate a lot of uses of PowerPoint, and could license us to ship that with our product.

He also could supply code for reading ThinkTank and MORE files, so that we could convert their outlines to presentations. Tom delivered on time, and after that we found ourselves consulting Tom repeatedly to do difficult tasks well into PowerPoint 2.0 and 3.0, and he also provided critical consulting aid to Genigraphics. Ultimately, Tom joined Microsoft, where he headed another business unit that developed Microsoft Exchange. Then he joined ATT, where he started the flat-rate ISP called WorldNet, and, after that, he founded ITXC, which became the world's leading provider of wholesale voice-over-IP networks, where he was chairman and CEO. Somewhere along here he stopped having time to consult with us, but he remained a friend to PowerPoint.

The decision not to add developers and only to contract cleanly separable functions worked out perfectly.

86 How PowerPoint Got Its Name

We called our product "Presenter" for the three years of its development, and never imagined that the name wouldn't be available for the final product.

In those days, it was no concern that the corresponding domain name might not be available; there were only 115 domains registered (.com, .org, .edu, and .net) on the date that PowerPoint 1.0 shipped, and the web wouldn't come along for a while—Tim Berners-Lee made the web publicly available for the first time on August 6, 1991, and the Mosaic browser wasn't released until 1993, after I had left Microsoft! If we had wanted a domain name, just about any domain name, it would have been no problem.

Toward the end of the development, we needed to register our product name as a trademark. Not all companies bothered about this; Microsoft, for instance, couldn't trademark either "Word" or "Excel"— or even, for a long time, "Windows." But we thought it was prudent to have the name trademarked, and venture capital investors always liked to see "defensible" intellectual property being created, because that can add value at a liquidity event.

Much to our surprise, when the name went to our intellectual property lawyers for a pro-forma review, they responded that "Presenter" had been previously used for presentation software shipped along with presentation hardware by some company in New Jersey. So, very suddenly and very unexpectedly, we lacked a name for our product at the last minute. There was great pressure to come up with the name, because it was fundamental for preparing lots of printed materials with long lead times, which had to be ready to go in the box on ship day—the manual, the reference cards, the box itself—not to mention advertising and PR materials, and work on all that already had begun.

We spent at least a week with everyone trying to think up a new name. We had already used a name based on Aldus's PageMaker for our published database product FileMaker, so naturally there was some lobbying for another "family member"—SlideMaker? OverheadMaker? For those with mostly short-term interest, these seemed ideal: such a name would clearly express what the product does, would show the family resemblance of Forethought product names, and would use a model that customers already understood. From my longer-term outlook, though, it was entirely wrong to focus on the physical embodiment created by the first release of the product; that turned out to be an excellent call, after slides and overheads disappeared! And anyway, the product didn't make "slides," it made entire "presentations," composed of many slides plus other elements such as notes and handouts.

So, I resisted the family-style names and continued to think. Then one morning, when I was taking a shower (where most of history's great discoveries seem to have occurred), I thought of the name PowerPoint, for no obvious reason. I went in to work and proposed it to other people. No one else much liked it, but I became attached to it. Later that same day, Glenn Hobin, our VP of Sales, returned from a sales trip, and he had an idea for a name: when his plane home was taking off, he had seen out the window along the runway a sign reading "POWER POINT." I took his independent discovery as a favorable omen, and we were truly out of time; so I forced the issue, and we sent the name PowerPoint off to our lawyers. Use of the extra internal upper-case letter was mandatory in those days for Mac software, based on Apple's style in product naming.

The lawyers reported that "powerpoint" had been registered in a number of classes of products, including fishing hooks and ballpoint pens (a PaperMate product in the 1970s), but hadn't been registered for software—we could use it. So we committed and started revising the drafts of our printed materials. This really was at the very last minute: in my notebooks, I was using "Presenter" as late as 13 January 1987, in a presentation to Apple's VC group; but an entry from 21 January 1987, about a presentation to our Board of Directors, for the first time includes "PowerPoint (new name)." So the change was made just barely one month before our formal announcement, and three months before the first shipments of completed product boxes went to customers.

Int. Cl.: 9

Prior U.S. Cl.: 38

Reg. No. 1,475,795

United States Patent and Trademark Office   Registered Feb. 9, 1988

TRADEMARK
PRINCIPAL REGISTER

POWERPOINT

FORETHOUGHT, INC. (CALIFORNIA CORPO-   FIRST   USE   4-20-1987;   IN   COMMERCE
  RATION)   4-20-1987.
250 SOBRANTE WAY
SUNNYVALE, CA 94086
                                              SER. NO. 669,735, FILED 6-29-1987.

    FOR: PRERECORDED   COMPUTER   PRO-
GRAMS RECORDED ON MAGNETIC DISKS,   JODY HALLER DRAKE, EXAMINING ATTOR-
IN CLASS 9 (U.S. CL. 38).   NEY

"PowerPoint" was properly registered as a trademark from the first ship of PowerPoint 1.0 on 20 April 1987, for "Prerecorded computer programs recorded on magnetic disks, in Class 9 (U.S. Cl. 38)."

In retrospect, it was great that we found a name so distinctive that it could come to mean "any presentation" or "any materials for delivering a presentation," as well as naming our specific product, and so abstract that it could survive the obsolescence of overheads and 35mm slides.

Plus, it suggested our goal of putting power into the hands of the individual content originator. The "Power" in "PowerPoint" was thought of, not as in "Powerful," but as in "Empowerment."

"PowerPoint" is a much better name, but if "Presenter" had been available, we would never have considered anything else.

87 *Columbus Becomes the PowerPoint Mascot*

As we prepared the user manual for PowerPoint 1.0, we needed some sample content to work with for illustrating the procedures described in the text. This sample content needed to be clearly arbitrary, so it would be self-evidently just an illustration of how the program worked.

At the time, it was customary, including at Microsoft, for the writers of manuals and collateral to make up some business such as "Mike's Dog Grooming" or whatever, and to make very cursory attempts at realism. The examples were trivial and boring.

I came up with what I thought was a much better idea: the device of a notional proposal being made to Queen Isabella by Christopher Columbus seeking financing to sail to America. This topic was obviously merely illustrative, so we wouldn't need to even mention that fact. It gave opportunities to include bullet lists (of objectives), pie charts (of colonial market shares), org charts (of the commanders of the three ships), schedule charts (of the expedition schedule), financial tables (of projected plunder), maps (of the proposed routes), and so on. "Mike's Dog Grooming" offered much less scope for creativity.

I bought a number of books about Columbus, including illustrated volumes, so we could get the details of the Spanish monarchy's coats of arms, and the right names (in full) for all the senior commanders in the org chart. Much of what was in the sample presentations was historically accurate.

After using the Columbus theme in writing the manual and help files, we extended the same theme to all our marketing materials, packaging, and even advertising; you have to include sample slides in advertising, and it's extremely useful to make clear instantly that the ad is about presentations and not about, say, dog grooming by Mike. We created demonstration presentations for the Columbus theme.

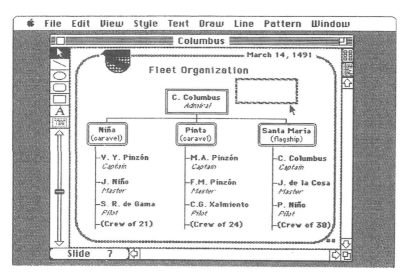

Columbus theme as shipped with PowerPoint 1.0.

Columbus served us very well for many years. It continued as our only theme used in our manuals, our product packaging, our advertising and collateral materials, and even our demos for five more years, through PowerPoint 3.0 shipped in 1992, and it became a consistently recognizable PowerPoint feature across multiple versions and platforms.

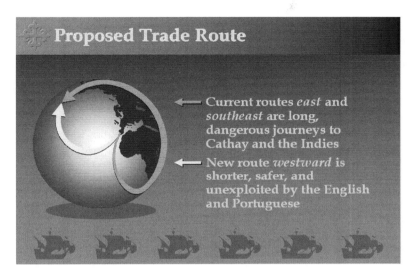

Columbus theme as shipped (in color) with PowerPoint 3.0.

Soon after PowerPoint 1.0, the internal Microsoft corporate communications people professed to be "tired" of the Columbus theme, although the customers didn't get tired of it. The corporate communications people claimed that they could absolutely do no more, they needed the creative stimulus of "Mike's Dog Grooming," and they spent my money to offer me terrible alternatives to Columbus. Fortunately, the professionals at Genigraphics had no trouble in thinking up endless fascinating variants on the Columbus theme, so I just outsourced the work to them, with great results.

In consequence of this long-running theme, the GBU half-celebrated Columbus Day, the second Monday in October, as an informal business-unit holiday. The last use of the theme, for the 1992–1993 launch of PowerPoint 3.0, coincided precisely with the 500th anniversary of Columbus's 1492 voyage to America, so the ship awards for employees and friends incorporated real antique U.S. Columbian half-dollar coins bearing Columbus's portrait, minted for the Columbian Exposition exactly a century earlier in 1892 (Windows ship) and 1893 (Macintosh ship).

Ship awards for PowerPoint 3.0, for Windows and for Mac, incorporating Columbian half-dollar coins minted 1892–93.

My original inspiration to create a presentation for Columbus's project came from the best book I know about how to make presentations, *Moving Mountains: or The Art of Letting Others See Things Your Way,* by Henry M. Boettinger (Boettinger 1969), frequently reprinted but now out of print. Because Boettinger wrote twenty years before Power-Point was invented, he focuses on the communication techniques of presentations, without being distracted by the irrelevant mechanics of any software application, and he really knows what he's talking about. In later years, I bought cases of the paperback edition of his book and distributed it to all hands at the Graphics Business Unit. Boettinger did not use Columbus's voyage to discuss visuals, but instead used it as an example of how to organize communication about the progress of a large project, writing out a plan for Columbus's voyage in Army "Field Order" format. He got the same advantages of having his readers focus on the structure rather than the content of what he was illustrating.

88 The Countdown to First Customer Ship

There was some planning in December of 1986, but the real progress toward an introduction started in January 1987. By now, everyone at Forethought was getting on board the train. Apple was gearing up to help with the rollout, with much of the planning in the hands of Darrell Boyle, acting as a consultant. Glenn Hobin was pre-selling the product, and by the time of shipment he had managed to sell more than we manufactured, so we were going to sell out immediately. Every day things were decided and committed. Rob Campbell was fully engaged, and every day reported that he had managed to schmooze one more important contact.

We would introduce 22 February 1987 at PC Forum, then show the product at Apple World and at the Seybold desktop publishing event. First Customer Ship would be in the window of April 15 to 20.

Fortunately, the software was also falling into place. The careful approach to development was paying off, and there were no last-minute surprises.

Beginning in January, there were disks available that we could use for real demos. The demos didn't look very surprising to Dennis, Tom, or me, because we had visualized precisely the same behavior from the specs. But we found that many people weren't able to do that and didn't really believe until they could see the software work in front of their eyes.

We began to get rave early reviews from PC experts:

> I see about one product a year I get this excited about ... people will buy a Macintosh just to get access to this product.
> —Amy Wohl (industry consultant/guru), *Wall Street Journal,* 6 March 1987

Gradually, all the moving parts were synchronized, and we set 20 April 1987 as the official ship date for PowerPoint.

89 *Apple's Very First Ever Investment, in PowerPoint*

As PowerPoint became visibly real, Apple reappeared, ready to invest.

On 13 January 1987, we met with Dan Eilers and Horace Inea again. I gave them a near-final demo of PowerPoint, putting a disk in a Macintosh and showing them that the whole product worked.

On the spot, they told me that now they were "in." PowerPoint was strategic to the future of the Macintosh. They hoped to have a firm decision to move within just a few days.

The principal reason that they had held off before, they volunteered, was that they were afraid that we wouldn't be able to complete PowerPoint, the "risk of development"; but, they said, they had always loved PowerPoint and were delighted that it was turning out so well. They could invest $432,000 and would expect their money to be spent on "very aggressive launch programs."

They did caution that they did not want to invest in FileMaker and that it "should pay its own way without subsidization." A second reason they had hesitated to invest, in fact, was our "bad royalty deal with Nashoba," which made FileMaker unprofitable. (All quotes here from my contemporaneous notes.)

The next day, I had a further due-diligence meeting with Horace Inea, and we went over the history of PowerPoint development and the remaining schedule in full detail—they knew everything about the amount of development risk remaining (which was very little).

But then we didn't hear back from Apple. At our Board of Directors meeting a week later, Dick Kramlich told us he had talked to Dan Eilers. Eilers would like to invest $432,000, and if he did so, NEA would invest another $250,000 of its own plus a further $50,000 from another investor. But Dick had heard that Apple's Board of Directors might be just about to kill Eilers' whole department, the Strategic Investment Group which had yet to make any deals, and then the investment wouldn't happen. We passed all the needed board resolutions, anyway.

The Apple investment did happen, although it didn't actually close until March—two months later, and almost a year after their first expression of interest! By that time, when we had already introduced the product and were already getting very strong reviews and had already sold out, there wasn't any appreciable risk left at all. Thus did PowerPoint become the very first venture capital investment ever made by Apple's Strategic Investment Group.

At the time, I thought of the similarity to Samuel Johnson's reaction to a late offer of help when he was trying to get his great dictionary completed:

> Is not a Patron, my Lord, one who looks with unconcern on a man struggling for life in the water, and, when he has reached ground, encumbers him with help? The notice which you have been pleased to take of my labors, had it been early, had been kind; but it has been delayed till I am indifferent, and cannot enjoy it; till I am solitary, and cannot impart it; till I am known, and do not want it. I hope it is no very cynical asperity not to confess obligations where no benefit has been received, or to be unwilling that the Public should consider me as owing that to a Patron, which Providence has enabled me to do for myself.
>
> — Samuel Johnson, letter to Lord Chesterfield, 7 February 1755

The situation was not really the same. Apple's apparent interest in making an eventual investment had been critical to saving us from death a few months earlier, and we appreciated it. But really, if our product was strategic to the success of the Macintosh, and their great fear was that it wouldn't get finished, they could have been more helpful by investing in it much earlier, while we were still drowning and struggling for life in the water.

By the time they invested, we were already talking with Microsoft.

90 Apple's Private Side Letter

Apple's Strategic Investment Group invested by extending our Preferred C round on its standard terms, but to do so, they required a private "side letter" from Forethought.

They required two agreements in the side letter from us (plus some technical points):

(1) We would spend 100% of Apple's investment on PowerPoint, none on any other product and specifically none on FileMaker.

Apple really wanted and needed PowerPoint, to sell Macs. Apple people had been attending some of our board meetings as observers, and they had set the world record for due diligence, so they knew all about the unprofitable terms of our FileMaker deal; they also knew that FileMaker wasn't selling Macs in the quantities that PageMaker was, and that they hoped PowerPoint would. So they wanted all their money spent on making PowerPoint as successful as possible.

(2) We would [repeat, *would*] agree to use best efforts to produce an equivalent and compatible product for MS-Windows, after a brief delay.

Apple's concern was that corporations would standardize on Windows PCs and their software, thus excluding Macs because of software incompatibilities; but if the same software were to exist on both platforms, with easy file compatibility between them, then that would remove choice of software as a reason to ban Macs. I thought this was enlightened reasoning, and that was our plan anyway.

I was temperamentally opposed to delaying software, but committing to the very brief delay they wanted was no problem; I knew that it would take a while to make a Windows version, so I was comfortable that we would not have it done too early, and that nothing would really be delayed by the agreement—the delays would come for other reasons.

91 Microsoft Invites Itself to See PowerPoint

Even before Apple confirmed its investment in PowerPoint, Microsoft had already come calling to see the product.

We had been dealing with Microsoft people to get information about Windows as a platform for PowerPoint since I arrived in mid-1984. In addition to the local evangelists, Tandy Trower himself had come down from Redmond to visit us, small as we were. I always considered that to be proof of the exhaustiveness of Microsoft's campaign for Windows adoption. My own contacts within Microsoft went back to when I was buying MS-DOS and Microsoft applications (Word, Multiplan, Chart, and so forth) for that project to build 286-based workstations for Northern Telecom Systems Corporation in Europe in 1983. That project had involved repeated trips to Redmond, where I'd talked with Bill Gates, Scott Oki, the newly-arrived Jon Shirley, and all the other top people. I'd also attended the developer introduction of Windows in Redmond.

The idea of getting Microsoft interested in PowerPoint was by no means new. I had considered whether we should take the initiative in my marketing analysis of June 1986:

> Microsoft, as the manufacturer of Windows, obviously has much to gain from a very successful version of Presenter on Windows. They have already encouraged Micrografx in marketing In*a*Vision, a rather poor sort of drawing program, as a "presentation graphics" offering, so perhaps they understand that really good overheads would be a help to Windows.
>
> Up till now, we have avoided telling Microsoft much about our product plans. Now with Bill Gates personally heading up applications, it might be wiser to tell him everything and see what results. (Attempts to test the waters by making a presentation to Dave Marquardt of Technology Ventures, who sits on their board, have so far been unavailing. That would still be the best first step, if it can be done.)
>
> Microsoft also has much to gain from Presenter in that we aim to work really well with Excel charts—not only via cut and paste as on Macintosh, but also via Dynamic Data Exchange (DDE) on Windows. In this respect they are the most prominent of a set of potential software partners: companies with products whose output we turn into great presentations (*i.e.*, those below us in the food chain of data exchange). We will work really well with these

people via our Copy from... command, cut and paste, and (on Windows) DDE. (Gaskins, PowerPoint Marketing 1986)

Now, in January 1987, six months later, we were finally out talking to people about PowerPoint, getting ready to introduce it on 22 February. Word got around, and soon Microsoft called up and offered to come down to Sunnyvale for a whole-day meeting. They would like a demo of PowerPoint and a discussion of our product and marketing strategy for it; then lunch, and in the afternoon they would give us a presentation on Windows futures that would be helpful to us in planning a Windows version.

We had that all-day meeting on 6 February 1987, at which I gave a full demonstration of PowerPoint; the disk was just about final at this date. Microsoft was from the beginning completely honest about the fact that they wanted to work on a similar product, and had a preliminary group in place to do so. Even though we had thought about this meeting for so long, afterwards we were hardly able to focus on its importance because we were so buried in the mountain of details for our launch.

92 Staffing Up for the PowerPoint Launch

The original plan for the restart had been that we would build up a functioning company of experienced people by practicing on published products, and those people would be ready to use their well-honed skills on PowerPoint when it was ready.

As it turned out, because of the long periods of unprofitability from published products and the recurring money-famines which reduced headcount, we ended up preparing for the launch of PowerPoint by hiring new people—but, as noted, not more developers. We could do this, because, increasingly, everyone believed that the Apple investment would arrive and be money in the bank.

My 1987 company history pointed this out sharply:

> In part because it took so long, our original operations in fact had to be shut down or replaced before PowerPoint came to market. ... There really is very little continuity: the Forethought group in our PowerPoint era is almost entirely new people:
>
> Software Development—two software developers, hired to do PowerPoint—one [Dennis Austin] very early, in October 1984, but the other [Tom Rudkin] just in May 1986.

Software Test—entirely new person [Robert Lotz], hired for PowerPoint in January 1987.

Product Manager—new person [Keith Sturdivant], hired from outside specifically for PowerPoint, in December 1986. Manuals and sample presentations done by contract writers.

Sales—entirely new people. One sales person was hired in early 1986, but the real difference came when Glenn Hobin joined us in July 1986. The remainder of the sales group has been hired very recently.

Marketing—no people left at all. We eventually lost our good people such as Darrell Boyle during the low spots of the struggle. Advertising, brochures, etc. done by outside agencies and contractors anyway.

Customer Support—new manager and entirely new representatives, all hired in the last 90 days in connection with the PowerPoint introduction.

Finance/Admin—entirely new people, with the big difference coming with the hiring of Susie Allen in November, 1986.

We absolutely benefitted from staying in business for the three years, in the sense that we had a continuous presence in the product channels and in the industry press; having just shipped $1 million of PowerPoint in its first 30 days demonstrates the value. On the other hand, this was an expensive strategy, and thus high-risk because the expense so often put us on the edge of going out of business altogether. We may possibly have been wrong to think that it was so hard to build a new company around a new product; to a major extent, we have just done so. (Gaskins, Forethought History 1987)

93 New Manufacturing for PowerPoint Launch

Another part of the original plan for the restart had been that, by practicing on published products, we would build up a stable of trusted suppliers for all the tasks of manufacturing software, and these suppliers would be ready to execute for PowerPoint. But this was another of the theoretical advantages of publishing that hadn't worked out.

For MACWARE, we had indeed built up an infrastructure of extremely competent suppliers—to print boxes, to print books, to duplicate disks, to print disk labels, and then to assemble finished product from the parts list. For PowerPoint, however, we didn't use them.

Just as the PowerPoint launch neared, the software products business was looking attractive to big commercial printers, and the giant firm R. R. Donnelley & Sons opened a division to handle complete software product production. Donnelley would accept copy and art for the manuals and inserts and registration cards and all the other printed parts and a master set of diskettes, and they would print boxes and books and duplicate disks with labels in disk-holders and assemble completed products, taking all the management of inventory and logistics out of our hands. Moreover, they had the capital to print and hold partially completed components (*e.g.*, printing great stocks of the manual pages at once, leaving them unbound, and then binding them into books closer to need), which we did not, lowering our costs.

At the time, almost all manuals for software followed a design made standard by IBM for the PC. Manuals were shipped as small ring binders with a shrink-wrapped set of loose punched pages, the assumption being that there would inevitably be so many mistakes that updates would be published, and the user could replace the updated individual pages. This is how IBM had long produced documentation for programmers and IT personnel, but it didn't work so well for the consumers who bought personal computers. There were indeed lots of mistakes in every manual, and millions of updated pages were sent out, but no one ever actually replaced the pages; update sets were just added loose inside the covers of the binder, and often the original set of pages had never even been opened and put on the rings. The whole industry format for manuals was dysfunctional.

For PowerPoint, thanks to Donnelley, we did something very different. We produced a slim hardback book, what the trade calls "case binding," in boards covered with blind-stamped cloth. It was actually a set of pages finished like a paperback, with a glued spine rather than sewn, but glued in a special way to lie flat when open; and then, instead of having a soft cover added, the book block was inserted with its end papers glued to the inside of the standard hard cover. This hardback appeared much more expensive than a paperback, but cost only a few cents more. It was much less expensive than the standard ring binders or the alternative "cased wire-O" formats, so it reduced our cost of goods substantially.

The hardback book format served clear notice that we had written our manuals carefully; if an update was needed, we would have to send out whole new hardback books. One reviewer (Bill Coggshall) said later, after we had been acquired by Microsoft, that the format gave the impression that "Microsoft is really sure about what it's doing, like somebody who works the *New York Times* crossword puzzle in ink." We were that sure from the very beginning.

We dealt with a single project manager at Donnelley, rather than a whole network of suppliers. We didn't need to invest in component inventories. Donnelley charged us a single contracted price only for finished shrink-wrapped products on pallets when they were handed over to transport companies, not for progress payments along the way. They also handled all the shipping.

I was the manufacturing guy, so I adopted Donnelley's service for PowerPoint, and it worked well. We would send a person to do press checks and approve printing, and we would send a Q. A. engineer to check the disks duplicated from our golden masters. Pallets emerged from Donnelley and went to distributors.

Donnelley later took a part of the front of the box and used it to make a plaque for my office wall:

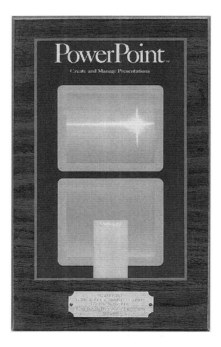

Wall plaque made for R. R. Donnelley & Sons from the box for PowerPoint 1.0 to commemorate its first production.

So ultimately, the trusted suppliers we'd built up earlier weren't of direct use for PowerPoint after all. This was a poor outcome, since many of them had given us favorable treatment over the years in anticipation of profits when our big product arrived, in the fashion so common in Silicon Valley, and doubtless they thought we had strung them along.

But the integrated service from Donnelley saved us vast amounts of administrative trivia when we had no people to engage in it, and saved us capital when we were, if only out of habit, conserving every dollar.

94 Microsoft's First Offer to Acquire PowerPoint

We did the introduction of PowerPoint on 22 February. Five days later, we had an internal meeting to consider an unexpected Microsoft offer for PowerPoint. Bill Gates had said that Microsoft would definitely be in the presentation market one way or another, and wanted PowerPoint as the best product. He wanted to do an acquisition of the product for cash, immediately. Development would stay in Sunnyvale, at least initially; all other functions would be handled in Redmond.

Three weeks later, 13 March 1987, we had dinner in Silicon Valley with Jon Shirley (the President of Microsoft) and Jeff Raikes (head of Applications marketing). They repeated a similar offer, with more details. They offered $5.3 million to the investors, plus incentives to the developers. They were interested only in PowerPoint; they said that they expected that FileMaker Plus would not be popular on Windows.

This offer seemed a positive vote of confidence in PowerPoint, but the rest of the terms weren't so attractive; especially, the amount of money offered would not have provided much return for our investors. Also, we had received two other serious offers of acquisition in the preceding week, one from Ron Posner and Ben Rosen of Ansa, and one from Gordon Eubanks of Symantec; both were variations of the many "combine our products and go public within a year" proposals.

We decided to sit tight and ship PowerPoint before taking any other step. This decision was ratified at our board meeting on 17 March 1987. Further possibilities were swirling around. The first potential underwriter of an IPO, Baer & Co., had scheduled a meeting with us.

The final details of the PowerPoint software continued to come together on schedule, thanks to calmly heroic efforts by Dennis and Tom.

95 *The Golden Masters for PowerPoint 1.0*

By 10 April 1987, the bug count was down to less than the fingers of one hand, and the only moderately serious problem occurred on a small number of early Macintosh machines that had been manufactured with older buggy ROMs. Dennis, Tom, and I declared that we were ready to make the Golden Masters for PowerPoint 1.0.

Back in the days of diskettes for distribution, the steps of getting the proper software into manufacturing were complicated. Procedures were needed to assemble and verify the "bill of materials" for the distribution disks—the proper versions of the software plus everything else ("read-me" files, clip art, templates, help files, and so forth). It was easy to make mistakes and get the wrong version of some file unless meticulous care was taken in maintaining libraries. The proper files then all had to be written on a floppy that had to be perfect—every bit on the recording medium had to be exactly right.

When the creation of precisely one perfect disk was verified, this became the "Golden Master." Quality Assurance would hand-deliver this master to manufacturing. At the manufacturing plant, the single master received would be used only on specialized duplicating machines to make further masters, called "silvers"; the Golden Master was then locked up in a secure cabinet. The silver masters were used on duplicating machines to manufacture product disks, which were verified against silvers. If more silvers were needed, they were made from the unique Golden Master. Golden Masters were never de-accessioned, but remained permanently in secure storage, so later questions about what was on them could always be answered with assurance. The whole Golden Master process helped to prevent errors, and also made it easy to assign responsibility for any mistakes discovered in products.

All this care was taken to assure that what went on the product disks exactly matched what was on the Golden Master. That was fine so long as the Golden Master was correct. A single momentary lapse of attention in making the Golden Master would automatically result in manufacturing the wrong thing. Even if a mistake were somehow caught before shipment, the cost of reduplicating, and then tearing open shrink-wrapped boxes and rebuilding them, was very high.

Much more commonly, the boxes went to customers before a mistake was discovered, and then the cost was astronomically high. With no Internet, we would have to try to contact every customer who had returned a registration card, and mail them replacement disks. We would have to staff customer service for a wave of calls about the problem, sending replacement disks to complainants. We would have to recall product in inventory at distributors and replace it, and replace the inventory in stock at dealers. Every step took a lot of people and a lot of time, cost a lot of money, and, even in the best case, such an episode tarnished the reputation of the product. A tiny oversight on a Golden Master was a good way for a small company to go out of business.

Dennis Austin has recalled our procedure for getting Golden Masters right, which was something like a flight check list:

> I learned a lot from Bob Gaskins, but few lessons come to mind more pointedly than the Golden Master procedure. "Golden Master" was a term widely used for the disk delivered to the duplication house that made disks for shipping. (The general culture used the word disk to refer to floppy disks that IBM insisted should be called diskettes. This minor dispute ended when distribution moved to CD's, which, because of their earlier use in audio, have always been called discs.) Bob's experience in shipping software was recent, but he had learned the danger of trivial errors. The software may be debugged, but one little error in setting up the disk could mean the re-manufacturing of hundreds or thousands of copies. When you make a golden master, you better be absolutely certain it is perfect.

> The key to perfection was twofold. First, plan and document every detail of the disk to be created and the precise procedure for creating it. Second, use redundant care in following procedure to the letter. Once the steps were documented, we made a huge ceremony out of the actual procedure. We first recognized that two people were required to do the work. One would follow the steps on paper and the other carry out the instructions. The two would monitor one another's actions to be sure no one slipped up. (The two people were generally Bob and I.) We donned special robes to signify that we were engaged in a solemn rite. (Our robes were actually some old purple T-shirts from Bell-Northern Research, but it's the idea that's important.) Step by step we soberly followed the instructions to guarantee the perfection of our master. We practiced this routine several times building FileMaker releases, so we wasted no time on the night of PowerPoint's Golden Master. (Austin, Beginnings 2009)

It is entirely characteristic that both Dennis and I worried a lot about the usage of "disk" versus "diskette" versus "disc." Hardly anyone else cared, which we also noted.

The precautions we took were extreme, but so were the risks. In fact, we never made a mistake in preparing a Golden Master. In later years, the same ceremonial rituals (including wearing special costumes) were taught to everyone in the GBU who made masters, eventually usually a pair consisting of a Program Manager and a Quality Assurance Engineer, and our perfect record continued.

The final step in development was adding the "About box" to the software. Dennis took care of that, and remembers what he did:

> The Macintosh style introduced a standard "About" command (in the Apple-character menu, back then). It displayed a box that was supposed to give details of the application, but invariably added some stylistic flair and gave credit to the programmers that created it. We didn't have any artists on staff, so I concocted an image myself. I drew a fixed bitmap (using MacPaint) that we could display when needed. Only the exact version number was inserted dynamically.

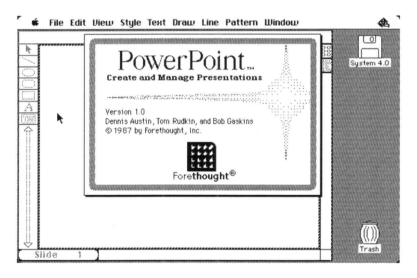

The "About box" for PowerPoint 1.0 with the credits.

I tried to capture the spirit of the box art in black and white. My artistic efforts didn't draw any raves, but time was short. I was only too proud to put my name and Tom's name in the credits.

On reflection, though, Tom and I realized that Bob Gaskins' name deserved to be added too. Tom and I may have created the program, but Bob created the idea and shepherded it through the violent storms of management and financing that made it happen. We built his vision.

Late in the evening on Sunday, April 12, 1987, we finalized the golden master disk for PowerPoint 1.0. The date on the files was set to the planned ship date of April 20. The time stamp was set at 4:30 p.m., and that rather arbitrary time became a tradition that was maintained through many subsequent releases. (Austin, Beginnings 2009)

The next morning, Monday, I was asked at the weekly executive staff meeting whether or not we were still on schedule to ship PowerPoint by 20 April. Since I remembered the time stamps we had put on the golden masters, I was able to assure everyone that not only would we ship on 20 April as promised, in fact we would ship at 4:30 p.m. precisely.

96 PowerPoint 1.0 Ships

The PowerPoint 1.0 ship went essentially as planned. We were able to report to our Board of Directors on 22 April 1987 that we were sold out of product, and had shipped 8,000 units and realized that revenue in two days. Dan Eilers, attending from Apple, exuberantly announced new Apple research that "16% of Macs sold in the previous 12 months are used *primarily* for presentations." He added that the "primary product used is MORE, second (by far) is MacDraw—hence most of the charts must be word charts (all that MORE does)." The enthusiasm among the investors for PowerPoint's future was now unbounded.

By 24 April 1987, we had shipped all of the product boxes we had (10,000 units), and Donnelley was busily manufacturing more. There were a few delays in the shipping, but nothing that interfered with stocking the distribution channels. The mistakes could have been Donnelley's, but perhaps also the Forethought person administering that area hadn't been watching all our eggs in Donnelley's basket carefully enough; she won an instant air trip to Crawfordsville, Indiana, to sort it out at the Donnelley factory.

We got no reports of bugs on our 800 customer service number, but lots of enthusiastic callers who had begun using the product. Real customers loved it. At one of the first demonstrations of PowerPoint

1.0 at a Mac event, I was speaking from the platform in our booth, when I was interrupted by a loud man in a suit. "Can you make presentations? God, I do that all day long. I'll buy a Macintosh if you can do that!" (PC users in corporations often went to early Mac events to see what they expected to be coming along on Windows.) I couldn't have planted a better shill to convince the folks at Apple that PowerPoint would sell Macs.

But we were not lingering over our past successes. I had two more meetings on 20 April 1987, the official First Customer Ship day, and both were about the future that was about to overwhelm us.

One was a product planning meeting to plan the next version of PowerPoint, which we expected to be in color and to run on Windows as well as Mac. This was the longer meeting. The strategy was emerging to *not* make a Windows version of PowerPoint 1.0 after all, but rather to make a new color product for Mac, and make that the first version for Windows.

The other meeting that afternoon was to discuss two new financial offers. One was from Baer & Co., an offer to underwrite an IPO planned for 1 September 1987, which would offer 20% of Forethought for $5 million; that would give the company a post-money value of $25 million, implying that we were worth around $20 million now.

The other offer was an updated offer from Microsoft, offering $10 million to $12 million, maybe $15 million, with the main goal to be a Windows version of PowerPoint in a year's time.

97 The Restart is Complete

My company history, written a month later in May 1987, finished here. I felt that we had kept the promises made at the time I joined the company for the restart. The relief I was feeling is obvious in the last words of the history:

> In this way, we finally completed executing the Restart Plan we had set out upon three years before. We had in fact built both a great product in PowerPoint and a delivery vehicle for it. We completed PowerPoint so as to ship it on schedule on April 20. By early May, we had shipped about $1,000,000 worth of PowerPoint and exhausted the first printing of 10,000 copies. (For comparison, InfoCorp believes that Lotus shipped only 16,000 copies of Freelance [on MS-DOS for IBM PCs] in all of 1986.) In the first

month of shipment we showed a net profit of just over $400,000—almost exactly the amount spent on developing PowerPoint.

It is reasonable to forecast that, during the next twelve months, our revenue from PowerPoint will total about $7.5 million (about 80% of our revenue), and net profits before taxes from PowerPoint will be over $2.5 million (over 95% of our profits). The value of the company has been increased by our sales success with PowerPoint from $3 million (post-money at the last funding) to the range of $15 million (offer from Microsoft) to $20 million (pre-money value from Baer & Co. letter of intent to underwrite an IPO). This all seems a reasonable return on the $3 million invested since the restart.

Although we had suffered myriad problems along the way, we had finally delivered exactly what we said we would deliver under the Restart Plan of 1984. (Gaskins, Forethought History 1987)

PART V: MICROSOFT ACQUISITION OF POWERPOINT

98 Are We Planning for an IPO or an Acquisition?

We had held everything together to get PowerPoint shipped to wide acclaim. But rather than basking in the warm glow of success, we all realized that we had stretched as far as we could, and we needed to make some fundamental changes.

In the Board of Directors meeting on 22 April 1987, just two days after the formal shipment of PowerPoint, we started discussing profound changes, on all fronts.

The first topic was how to get an IPO done as soon as possible. Dick Kramlich thought that the offer from Baer & Co. was excellent news, and that "Baer & Co. is just exactly right for Forethought." It was a quality firm. We should also try to provoke a competitive offer from Whale Securities; Dick would contact them himself. We should do this immediately, "now." (Dick knew to strike while the iron is hot—remember Harold Macmillan's answer when asked what was most likely to derail future plans: "Events, dear boy, events.") Both Dick and Phil Lamoreaux agreed that it would be easier for us to do an IPO than to do a private placement at the same valuation.

But to actually do an IPO, we would need more senior management. We had been doing just fine with Rob handling all the bookkeeping, but now we needed to hire a CFO immediately. Dick knew a candidate who had just left Software Publishing Corporation, and suggested that we offer her 2%-2.5% in stock, on the theory that she would add 10%-15% to the value of Forethought at the IPO.

The investors wanted to delay looking for a new VP of Marketing ("as late as possible"), but wanted to hire a new President and CEO to replace Rob immediately. Companies commonly react to initial success by bringing in an experienced CEO to manage the needed growth, especially when an IPO is in prospect; it is not necessarily any reflection on the people being replaced.

Their best CEO candidate was Bill Campbell, who was a senior sales and marketing executive at John Sculley's Apple. Bill had come to Apple from Eastman Kodak, before that had worked for J. Walter Thompson advertising agency, and before that had been head football coach at Columbia University. (People in the industry who wanted to ingratiate themselves addressed him as "Coach.") He was pretty much the inverse of Bill Gates in every imaginable dimension, but he was very "bankable" with venture capital investors. The investors' feeling was to offer him 5% of the company, and to go up to 8% if necessary. Rob could then be the marketing guy under Bill Campbell.

Dick undertook to personally talk to Bill Campbell about the CEO position, and also to personally call the CFO candidate, and to personally get in touch with Whale Securities, and to do all three immediately.

The second topic was acquisition offers. A surprising development was that Apple was now planning to set up a new software subsidiary, acquire enough products for it to do $90 million in business immediately, and spin off the subsidiary as a public company in early 1988. This new subsidiary intended to compete with PowerPoint, or else was a potential bidder for an acquisition. Thus Dan Eilers, who just a month before had made his investment and joined our board, would be considering resignation over the conflict of interest. The good news was that this was potentially another large bidder for Forethought.

Microsoft was back with another offer, and wanted to come down for a major meeting within a week. Dick Kramlich's advice again was to immediately get a letter of intent from Baer, and if possible from Whale, and use their valuations to provoke richer offers from Microsoft and from Apple. In the meantime, encourage Microsoft, and tell them that there is a floor of $15 million in MSFT stock to buy us, because "we're talking with an underwriter at $20 million pre-money valuation."

If we were going for an acquisition, we didn't need a new CEO who would get 8% of the company, and in fact we didn't need a CFO either, for another 2.5%. If we were going for an IPO, we needed both immediately. To get the acquisition done at a good price, we needed IPO offers from underwriters; to get those offers, we needed for them to see that we could hire a CEO and a CFO. To pursue both goals at the same time would be tricky.

Just two days after shipping PowerPoint, our reward was not an opportunity to recline on our couches and be fed peeled grapes by gracious attendants. We were now running faster than when we were trying to get the product out.

99 Progressively Better Offers from Microsoft

We continued to get a trickle of offers from Microsoft, usually each one better than the last, but with a changing profile of complications from one offer to the next. There was clearly some improvisation going on.

On Tuesday 28 April 1987, just about a week after our ship, we spent a whole day entertaining a Microsoft delegation at Forethought. Our visitors were Jeff Raikes, Director of Applications Marketing; Jeff Harbers, Director of Applications Development; Vijay Vashee, heading the internal group specifying a new graphical presentation product; and Pete Higgins, in Raikes's department. Raikes and Harbers were the top marketing and development people in the Applications Division, reporting to Bill Gates as Acting VP of Applications, so this was an ample show of force to convince us that Microsoft was taking the idea of an acquisition seriously.

The meeting had two parts: (1) in the morning, a general discussion of how we could make a success of PowerPoint on Mac, with additional meetings between me and Jeff Harbers on development issues, and between Rob Campbell, Vijay Vashee, and Pete Higgins on marketing plans, and (2) in the afternoon, a general discussion of PowerPoint for Windows, both our plans to get there, and Microsoft's plans to improve Windows to make our job easier.

After that, there was a discussion about the acquisition structure. The Microsoft group had thought about it a lot more than we had and suggested three models: (1) a "development center," just developers working remotely and visiting Redmond often to liaise; (2) a "product center," with program management doing product specification, plus development, documentation, and testing; or (3) a "business center," an independent business unit. Their choice was (2), a product center, with marketing and everything else consolidated in Redmond. In any of the three choices, the developers would remain in Silicon Valley.

The Microsoft people told us that there had been about 450,000 Macs sold in the U.S., about 600,000 worldwide. They estimated the PC base for Windows at about eight times the size of Mac. So they thought it reasonable to sell about 100,000 units of Mac PowerPoint annually, and 500,000 or more units of Windows PowerPoint.

On 13 May 1987, two weeks or so later (after time for legal review), Microsoft faxed us a formal letter of intent.

The amount of this offer was 100,000 shares of MSFT stock, worth about $12 million at the time; the stock had sextupled since the IPO a year earlier. That was more than twice the amount offered on the 13th of March, two months earlier and before our ship, so we'd made progress in raising the price.

Some of the details in the letter of intent were surprising. Unlike the discussion we had just held at Forethought, the entire business now was to be completely relocated to Redmond, including development, with nothing left in California. Key personnel, to be named (but certainly including all the senior developers and me), would be required to agree to relocate to Redmond as a condition of the deal.

Also, there was a command performance: "An essential part of the technical and due diligence investigation will be Bill Gates' meeting with Bob Gaskins of Forethought during the week of May 18 or as soon thereafter as possible ... ." (Microsoft Corporation 1987) I was the only person named in the letter of intent as requiring such vetting.

A couple of weeks after that, on 27 May 1987, there was a telephone call with another revised offer.

The new revised offer was extremely complex. It was a base of 90,000 shares of MSFT stock, plus multiple "bonuses" that could take the total up to 130,000 shares (then worth about $14.3 million). The bonus levels were based separately on sales volume goals for Mac PowerPoint, for Windows PowerPoint, and for the total, plus bonuses for shipping the Windows version by June of 1988, and for shipping an OS/2 version within 30 days of IBM's release of OS/2 Presentation Manager.

Also, rather than moving everything to Redmond immediately, now the proposal was the opposite: to run PowerPoint as a "business center" in Sunnyvale, but only for one year, after which everybody would be relocated to Redmond—how this would work was hard to understand.

Neither the complicated pricing nor the "move in one year" terms were attractive.

We considered this latest Microsoft offer at a Board of Directors meeting the same day. There was a lot going on other than Microsoft. We had current open merger opportunities with Aldus, with Ansa, and Symantec, all just re-verified as active.

We also had received an actual letter of intent from the people at Baer & Co., who were ready to go out and sell our IPO now—they declared it to have "lots of sizzle." Whale Securities reported by phone that they were eager to send us their competing letter of intent.

These developments on the IPO front encouraged our investors, who again stressed the need to get the IPO done immediately, without hesitating. We were too small for a really top-tier underwriter, but once we were public, the aftermarket would find its own level for us, better not to wait for any reason. Baer & Co. was thought to be the "perfect underwriter for Forethought," high quality, capable of delivering even in bad markets, a very acceptable way to go public.

The discussion then formally considered the relative risks of the Microsoft offer versus the risks of an IPO.

For a Microsoft acquisition, our investors perceived the risks as being that there was little upside in MSFT stock, hence we needed the maximum cash value now, and that Microsoft's seriousness hadn't really been demonstrated.

For an IPO, our investors perceived the risks as being that the hot market for IPOs might be over within as little as three months, thus eluding us no matter how fast we moved, and/or that our sales of PowerPoint might be flat after the initial sell-in, which would be during the period of an immediate IPO and would kill it.

Dick Kramlich's final pronouncement was that the "danger is to be too conservative."

100 How Microsoft Decided to Pursue PowerPoint

When Microsoft first approached us to acquire PowerPoint, we didn't know anything about the background of how they decided to get into presentations, or how they chose PowerPoint. But over the years since then, I've reconstructed part of the story.

In my reconstruction, by 1986, there were apparently two different plans for a presentation application at Microsoft in Redmond, perhaps complementary to each other. One plan was to design and develop a new application for presentations, like PowerPoint. The other was to add a feature to Word that could print Word outlines as overheads.

The "new application" plan was being worked on by a small number of people in the Applications Division, including Vijay Vashee and Trish May. They were chartered to come up with the specification for a new application, envisioned to be based on a graphical "direct-drive" design. The most senior person involved, who was managing and driving the activity, was apparently Jeff Raikes.

At the same time, according to Jeff, Bill Gates was thinking that a quick way to offer customers some way to make presentations might well be to add a feature to Microsoft Word, so that an outline created in Word could be reformatted for printing as overhead transparencies. This would have had a lot of advantages, not least that Word on character-mapped IBM PCs (by far the largest number of machines supported by Microsoft) would have gained the same feature, and so overheads could have been made easily on the huge installed base. Better quality would have come with future evolution.

This idea of Bill's was not merely theoretical, of course; there had been a well-known "outline processor" for Apple IIs and IBM PCs called ThinkTank, developed by Dave Winer at Living VideoText. This program had an option to print an outline as overheads for a presentation, by printing each top-level item of the outline as a "title" at the top of a new page, and then printing the lower-level items underneath that top-level item in multi-level outline format. Winer had added racing stripes to the basic paint job for the Mac version, called MORE, by simply drawing a rounded frame around each page and inserting a bullet before each item—as I described in more detail earlier. Before Power-Point, based on information I gained about the same time from Apple's private surveys, it appears that Winer's MORE was the program most often used to make presentations on Macs.

Winer says that Bill approached him in February 1987 at Esther Dyson's conference (which took place on 22–25 February), with a proposal to buy Living VideoText, and soon after sent a letter of intent. (Winer, Rejection 2010)

Within just a few days of that approach by Bill Gates to Winer, we at Forethought were approached (on 27 February 1987) by Jeff Raikes with the same inquiry, about buying PowerPoint and Forethought. Jeff was Director of Marketing for Microsoft's Applications Division, and Bill Gates at the time was the Acting VP for the Applications Division, so they were working closely together. That first approach to us was followed by a dinner with Jon Shirley and Jeff Raikes on 13 March 1987, which included a concrete offer, and then another offer at a higher price on 6 April 1987.

PowerPoint 1.0 shipped on schedule on Monday, 20 April 1987, and was sold out immediately (10,000 copies, worth $1 million) with heavy press coverage and great reviews. ("I see about one product a year I get this excited about ... people will buy a Macintosh just to get access to this product." —Amy Wohl, industry consultant and guru, in the *Wall Street Journal*, 6 March 1987.)

About a week after we shipped, on Tuesday 28 April 1987, we received the plenary delegation from Microsoft (Jeff Raikes, Jeff Harbers, Vijay Vashee, and Pete Higgins), who spent the entire day at Forethought, talking about PowerPoint's initial sales and reception on Mac, and about our plans for future PowerPoint on Windows, gauging our knowledge and interest in the Windows product.

The very next day after their visit, on Wednesday 29 April 1987, Frank Gaudette, Microsoft's CFO, sent Dave Winer a letter to say that Microsoft would not proceed under the letter of intent to buy Winer's company, Living VideoText.

Winer replied with a letter in response, but was answered by a firm and final rejection dated 4 May 1987 from Microsoft's President, Jon Shirley: "Bill Gates, Frank Gaudette, and I ... are not persuaded by your letter to change our position ... which is that we will not proceed under the letter of intent." Winer published a scan of this final rejection letter from Microsoft (Winer, Rejection 2010).

Years later, at the celebration for the twentieth anniversary of PowerPoint 1.0, Jeff Raikes briefly told the whole group the story of how he had championed the view that presentations should be graphically created by a separate application such as PowerPoint, in contrast to Bill's view that Microsoft should begin with overheads auto-generated from outlines as a feature in Word. (Jeff has since told a briefer version of the same story in a video released on Microsoft's Channel 9 website, so it's now in the public record (Raikes 2010).)

From all this, it seems that, in the early months of 1987, Jeff Raikes had managed to convince Bill Gates that a fully graphical "direct-drive" model for a presentation app was superior, probably using information gathered by his internal group. But probably both of them agreed that the internal group was too far away from shipping—that group had not yet begun active development, so they had at least a year or two left to go (longer, actually, since they were aiming at Windows, but they didn't know that at the time).

So (1) they continued the internal spec work in Redmond; (2) they left in place the letter of intent to acquire Living VideoText, and they may have had another active candidate—we later heard that there had been three companies considered; and (3) they waited to see whether PowerPoint would make its announced ship date of 20 April 1987.

When PowerPoint did ship, to first-day sales of ten thousand units, $1 million, and rave reviews, they sent down a group of senior people to perform a day of last-minute due diligence, and that confirmed the wisdom of following up the PowerPoint acquisition plan. By the end of the day, Microsoft had enough information to cancel the potential purchase of the MORE outliner, and then further Microsoft people returned to negotiate the purchase of PowerPoint with us. As soon as the acquisition was firm, the internal group was disbanded.

Dave Winer thought it was likely that MORE was not purchased by Microsoft specifically because he wanted to insist on retaining some independence for Living VideoText and to stay in Silicon Valley:

> We lost the deal in a meeting with Shirley over exactly this issue. Shirley said that they'd offer everyone at LVT [Living VideoText] jobs, but that we'd become a product team and nothing more. "Oh the waste!" I thought. (Winer, Could Have Been 1999)

Yet, within a few weeks, Jon Shirley was standing up at Forethought and explaining how important it was to have an independent Business Unit for PowerPoint permanently located in Silicon Valley. The difference is most likely that the initial idea of acquiring Living VideoText was really to gain developers to add a particular feature to Word, which would marginally increase Word's revenue, so of course they would join the Word group in Redmond. In contrast, the idea of acquiring Power-Point was thought of as acquiring an independent product that would generate a much larger new revenue stream, enough to justify its own organization.

Winer later described in an interview how it turned out for his company:

> I had a meeting with Bill Gates in, I guess it was February of '87, and he just blurted out, "Why don't we just buy you?" We worked out a letter of intent. It was all happening incredibly fast. And then the deal fell apart, but I had got committed to my board. Meanwhile, Gordon Eubanks and John Doerr [of Symantec, who wanted to merge with Forethought at the same time] were saying, "We really want to buy you guys." So when the Microsoft deal fell through, I called up Gordon and said, "OK, tell me how much you want to pay. It's yours." (Swaine 1991)

Footnote: As clearly noted on the box for PowerPoint 1.0, the first shipped version of PowerPoint—shipped before we had any real discussions with Microsoft—would directly open and convert existing files created in ThinkTank or MORE, providing a free instant upgrade path. We did this because we knew Living VideoText had been selling to customers who wanted to make presentations, and we wanted to give those customers a much better experience while preserving their previous work. Not all MORE outlines made great presentations, however.

101 Forethought Managers Decide for Acquisition

Two days after that Board of Directors meeting where the investors had been so enthusiastic for an IPO with Baer & Co., on 29 May 1987, we had a meeting of the Forethought senior managers of all parts of the company—just four of us, at the time (a fifth had recently resigned for unrelated reasons).

We met to consider the same question as we had discussed at the Board of Directors meeting: should we do an IPO or an acquisition?

There were four options put up on the whiteboard:

1. Sell to Microsoft for a price of $15 million;
2. Do some kind of deal with Xerox [who were still pestering us];
3. Do an IPO at a value of $20 million pre-money, stay independent;
4. Do nothing, grow organically and slowly.

Rob Campbell voted tentatively for (3) do an IPO, but all the other managers, including me, voted for (1) sell to Microsoft. We all felt that the IPO could never happen. A week later, at Rob's staff meeting on 8 June 1987, Rob announced that he had changed his mind: he no longer thought that we could pull off the IPO, either. He now supported first (1) sell to Microsoft, or second (4) do nothing, grow organically and slowly. So management ended up unanimous in supporting an acquisition.

There were many reasons, obvious to all of us, why an IPO was too risky. I had written down my opinion in a document dated 25 May 1987, four days earlier:

> There has been a poor job of putting systems in place by which to manage the business. All of our administration, finance, and operations areas have always been on the edge of collapse, and they are so today. ... [I]nsiders know that Forethought does not now

have the strength to deliver on that potential. Because of the mistakes listed above, we have not built a strong company structure. (Gaskins, Restart Lessons 1987)

And there was no time for rebuilding. Our investors were stressing that an IPO must happen immediately, this minute, before the window can close. That would have been difficult even if we had been equipped to carry it out, but we had already decided that we had to recruit both a new CEO and CFO, and such senior-level hires don't work out in a substantial proportion of cases, especially when there is pressure to get someone into the job quickly.

We all saw that the prospect of an IPO was too risky, and that it wouldn't happen, so we all voted against it and in favor of selling to Microsoft.

The specific concern was that the period of easy market access and high valuations for IPOs that we were then experiencing was brief and would close, and that we would not be able to successfully launch an IPO in the available time.

In late May and early June of 1987, that fear might have seemed exaggerated; but then five months later (shortly after the acquisition) came 19 October 1987, "Black Monday," when the DJIA plunged 22.6%. The crash was well before any conceivable Forethought IPO could have been mounted, and the IPO window closed.

Paul Richter reported in the *Los Angeles Times* for 6 December 1987: "1987, which began as the best of years for initial public stock offerings, became the worst in memory overnight as the stock market collapsed. 'It's a scene of devastation,' said Paul Simmonds, research director for the Institute for Econometric Research, the Largo, Fla., publisher of the IPO Letter. 'Offerings have been withdrawn, prospectuses aren't being printed, institutions aren't buying. The market's dead in the water.' "

It wasn't until nearly four years later, June 1991, that the IPO market recovered (the broader market bounced back before then). Forethought's record had not made it an exceptional IPO candidate anyway, even during the bubble, and after Black Monday, the decision we had taken to sell out earlier appeared to have been brilliantly prescient. PowerPoint would never have survived if it had depended on the proceeds of an IPO in late 1987 or early 1988 for funding—the IPO would never have happened.

102 Reasons Why I Favored Joining Microsoft

All of those reasons why an IPO was too risky were true, and were sufficient to reject the possibility. As a Director, I had a responsibility to adopt the most favorable strategy for all of Forethought's shareholders. I absolutely believed, then and now, that a sale to Microsoft would be best for all our shareholders, including our large investors, and best for all our employees (who were also all shareholders).

I had additional reasons to be in favor of the acquisition by Microsoft. One reason was very simple: the acquisition by Microsoft could cleanly isolate PowerPoint in a new stand-alone business, and definitively put an end to the doomed publishing business and the whole dual-company strategy.

In the alternative, an IPO would very likely result in an attempt to indefinitely prolong the life of the MACWARE software publishing business, so as to make Forethought appear to be a "full line software company." To do that, we would have to make a plausible case in the IPO documents that the publishing business was successful and would continue to be. I would have to write that business plan, and I couldn't do it because I didn't believe it. I thought the publishing business had served its purpose, and then some, and would never be part of a successful long-term strategy.

Beyond that basic reason not to consider an IPO, I was strongly attracted by Microsoft. I thought that it would be the ideal home for PowerPoint. This turned out to be especially true when Windows itself took longer than expected to become popular, which slowed down Windows development at every applications company. Only at Microsoft were we able to command resources so as to be ready with an excellent product at the earliest possible moment, on Windows 3.0, and then again on Windows 3.1.

I invested a lot of time during these weeks in making the case to my fellow directors and my fellow managers for the superiority of the Microsoft acquisition option, and my arguments persuaded both.

I'd known Microsoft's senior managers and many lower-level people in the company for the last four years, and had been impressed by everyone. Both Bill Gates and Jon Shirley were the right people. Microsoft appeared to have even less in the way of company politics than Forethought did (and that turned out to be true, at that time). I believed that Microsoft would be exceptionally successful, so the chance for all of the PowerPoint people to participate in that success meaningfully was a great opportunity. I knew that Microsoft understood the revolution of graphical personal computers, so it would be the right home for PowerPoint. I thought that Windows would be the big success in that market, so being closer to the developers of Windows could only be helpful.

I advised my fellow directors to put no post-acquisition conditions, at all, on our accepting a Microsoft offer.

> We should not delay looking for other potential acquirers who are only vapor. We also should not worry at all about trying to negotiate any terms on which this location is to be run after the acquisition—once the purchase is made, Microsoft should do whatever they think is best. The only negotiation should be to make the deal as rich as possible and as risk-free as possible for our shareholders. (Gaskins, Response 2 (15 June) 1987)

But I hoped that we could end up staying in Silicon Valley rather than moving to Redmond. To be part of Microsoft would be bliss, but to be part of Microsoft and yet be able to stay in San Francisco would be very heaven. If we could avoid forced relocation, things would be perfect.

I used to joke, afterward, that the whole dramatic enterprise of Forethought had been merely an elaborate scheme that I used in order to get a job with Microsoft without having to move to Seattle.

103 Bill Gates Has to Approve Bob Gaskins

The Microsoft letter of intent dated 13 May 1987 had said: "An essential part of the technical and due diligence investigation will be Bill Gates' meeting with Bob Gaskins of Forethought during the week of May 18 or as soon thereafter as possible ... ." I was the only person named in the letter of intent as being required to perform.

At first, I had delayed setting the appointment, since the details of the offer were not what we would have wished for, and there was serious concern within Forethought about the risk and reward of acquisition by Microsoft versus an IPO with Baer & Co.

But as the consensus of Forethought managers emerged for acquisition, we also got renewed encouragement from Microsoft. Rob Campbell had met Jeff Raikes at a convention in Atlanta on 3 June 1987, and Jeff had said again that they were "very motivated to do the deal." Jeff also was encouraging about improving the proposal for how we would be organized, now suggesting a "business center" be created, which would retain all functions at Sunnyvale (mysteriously, for the moment, even including a supplementary sales force of our own); this sounded like the plan to move everyone to Redmond was not cast in stone.

Rob pointed out the issues that were bothering our investors: the complex "bonus" terms of the pricing, he suggested, might "inhibit integration" (though they actually might have made sense, if the group were to be operated as a stand-alone "business center" for one year to earn the bonuses, and only then folded into Microsoft, which was the preceding offer), and he also suggested that it would be necessary to "collar" the stock price, so that the value of the agreement was not totally dependent on the price of MSFT stock, because the investors thought that MSFT had a lot of risk on the downside. Jeff repeated that they were "very interested."

This all sounded like progress, so I made an appointment to meet Bill Gates in Redmond, on Saturday 6 June 1987 at 3:00 p.m.

I went up to Redmond alone, and met with Bill in his office, one-on-one. We had had a number of personal meetings before, going back to the 1983 period when I was buying software for Northern Telecom, so we knew each other slightly.

Even so, it certainly concentrates the mind to be personally interviewed by Bill, with the whole $14 million acquisition and the best chance of liquidity for our investors and financial reward for our employees all riding on his evaluation.

Bill had a normal conversation with me, probing me about technical details of the software and the Mac platform, about marketing positioning and plans, about business numbers and ratios, and about individual employees. It went very well, since I had all those areas at my fingertips. I had just written my history of the company's restart in the prior two weeks, I prepared all the business plans, I lived and breathed the technical details, and I had had six weeks to recover from the First Customer Ship.

I didn't expect anything different, but just for the record, Bill did *not* ask me why manhole covers are round, or how many gas stations there are in the U.S., or whether I could code FizzBuzz in a language of my choice on the whiteboard. We just had a perfectly normal and pleasant conversation, all of it at the enhanced level of intellectual intensity characteristic of Bill.

I came away feeling that things had gone very well. By Monday, two days later, word came in a telephone call that Bill had approved me and was in agreement with the deal, but was leaving the details of that deal to others.

104 Forethought Investors Decide for Acquisition

We held our Annual Meeting of the Forethought Board of Directors on Wednesday, two days later, 10 June 1987. By now, Dan Eilers had re-signed because of his Apple conflict of interest, so we were back to four directors (Dick Kramlich, Phil Lamoreaux, Bob Gaskins, and Rob Campbell).

We discussed all the acquisition offers. First was Microsoft. Rob and I put on record the current state of negotiations. I had previously pre-pared my written recommendation to the Board that we should pursue the acquisition by Microsoft (Gaskins, Response (1 June) 1987). After the meeting, I supplemented this with an extended version of the same document (Gaskins, Response 2 (15 June) 1987), based on what I said at the meeting.

Next was Apple. Bill Campbell had turned down the offer to be our CEO, and was now involved instead with the effort to set up an Apple software subsidiary that might want to buy us. But he had phoned to say that it was too early for them to consider an immediate acquisition, so Apple would pass on making an offer for Forethought.

There were a number of what were the usual cats and dogs. Ansa wanted to merge for an IPO in the fall, to be done by Alex. Brown at a $75 million value. We had a "firm" offer from Borland to acquire Fore-thought for $18 million in cash, with action absolutely guaranteed within the week (never happened). We had an immensely complex offer from Xerox (after hours of negotiations) for exclusive sales rights to PowerPoint, for which they would pay something above $18 million.

There were other offers for acquisitions, but Dick Kramlich summed up the state of play and the Board's unanimous conclusion: "It's Mi-crosoft or nothing."

Moving on to consideration of the IPO, the discussion was different than in the past. Dick Kramlich began by reporting that Baer & Co. "really wants to do this deal now," and we had their letter of intent; there was no word from Whale Securities, but there was maybe a little new interest from Alex. Brown.

But, Dick continued, the "whole key is the CEO choice." With Bill Campbell having ruled himself out, Dick half-heartedly mentioned a couple of other possible candidates, but suggested that we retain the recruiting consultants Heidrick & Struggles to perform a search for us. Rob Campbell echoed the importance of the CEO search, agreeing that we had to locate a new CEO to do an IPO.

Phil Lamoreaux injected that he was "more cautious" and would take $15 million from Microsoft. Dick summed up: "no IPO today, we need a new CEO."

The meeting ended with a summary of the agreed directions to management (that is, to Rob and me):

1. Tell Baer & Co. we want to postpone any IPO until we can staff up;
2. Open a search with Heidrick & Struggles in Palo Alto for a CEO;
3. Make the sales goal for the month, don't lose momentum;
4. "Our real agenda is to get a clean, high offer from Microsoft."

And on Microsoft, the specific direction was: contact Microsoft immediately and see if it were possible to get a deal which was higher in value and with fewer complications. If so, accept it. If not, then get in touch with Dave Marquardt (the VC who served on Microsoft's board) and connect him to Phil and Dick to continue negotiations.

This was the decision point: "Our real agenda is to get a clean, high offer from Microsoft." The directors were unanimous in prioritizing this goal, and the management was unanimously behind it.

105 Final Negotiations on the Microsoft Deal

The call to Microsoft resulted in a further offer which was different, but not one which was cleaner. Now the offer was to make us a "product/marketing center," which would include development and limited marketing in Silicon Valley, for a total of 15–20 people. All else, including again all sales, would be in Redmond. The price was upped to a maximum of $15 million, but computed as a $9 million base plus a "royalty" of $75 per unit of Mac product shipped for eight months, and further bonuses for releasing Windows and OS/2 versions by agreed dates. The new offer, however, was for cash rather than MSFT stock, overcoming one hesitation of our investors.

The prospect of remaining in Silicon Valley was good, but the new idea of "royalties" seemed unnecessarily complex, so we moved on to the plan of trying to make progress through negotiations between the VCs for the two companies.

Phil Lamoreaux managed to meet Dave Marquardt for two and a half hours at 6:00 p.m. on Sunday, 21 June 1987. His pitch was that the VCs who had invested in Forethought were interested to conclude the Microsoft offer and were able to make it happen, but (1) the offer was a little light and (2) the structure could be improved. The aim was closure, fairly quickly.

Phil reported that the meeting had gone well. Phil asked for $20 million value (based on the IPO letter of intent from Baer & Co.), but would take $17 million in cash.

Dave Marquardt had allowed that the structure should be simpler. He also agreed that the whole concept of an "earn-out" (the bonuses and royalties for shipment volumes and development milestones) would cause problems rather than solve them. This was because, after the acquisition, the achievement of those volumes and milestones was up to Microsoft management, not to Forethought's previous investors, and their interests might not be aligned.

Marquardt further volunteered that it was a "make *vs.* buy" decision for Microsoft, and they had concluded that they had to buy. They had looked at three companies, and we were the only ones left on their list, so they were also motivated to close. (I still know of only one of the other two possibilities, which was Dave Winer's MORE.) Marquardt would ask Jon Shirley the following day, 22 June 1987, to get involved and try to get closure within a week. Phil expected a prompt and positive response.

And three days later, Thursday, 25 June 1987, about 11:30 a.m., we got the word: Microsoft had agreed to a very clean deal, at a price of $14 million in cash. This was not a definitive agreement or anything to announce, but it appeared to be a meeting of the minds.

Rob Campbell went up to Redmond to meet Jon Shirley two days later, Saturday, 27 June 1987, to get details of what had been agreed. We had a special meeting back in Sunnyvale on Sunday, 28 June 1987, for Rob to report back what happened.

The participants from Microsoft had been Jon Shirley, Jeff Raikes, Bill Neukom from legal, and Vijay Vashee from the internal project that was just being replaced by PowerPoint.

Jon Shirley had said that he considered the acquisition a firm deal, subject to due diligence in the areas of accounting, legal, and technical. Contrary to previous offers, we were to be a permanent installation in

California, and we would be a "Business Unit," the first such group in the Apps Division, comparable to a few similar, self-contained organizations that already existed in the Systems Division.

As part of the Applications Division, we would report to Bill Gates as Acting VP of Applications, but for better accessibility during the transition, Jeff Raikes would be our primary point of contact. The transaction would be for $14 million in cash, plus possibly some incentives to be defined for our employees joining Microsoft. Everyone at Forethought who would not be part of the PowerPoint Business Unit would be offered a suitable job with Microsoft in Redmond or in local field offices, or outplaced with severance, and Microsoft wanted to "go the extra mile" to be sure everyone was treated well.

Final due diligence would be at Forethought the following Tuesday and Wednesday, 30 June 1987 and 1 July 1987. Steve Grey would meet with our Arthur Young partner and with internal bookkeeping. Bill Neukom would meet with our local attorneys. Jeff Harbers and Dave Moore would arrange to interview all our developers and look over all our source code. This last step of due diligence impressed me with the wisdom of our decision; none of the score or more of our former suitors had ever realized that it might be a good idea to at least look at the code to get an idea how competent we were.

We would aim to have a definitive agreement and a public announcement by the week of 20 July 1987.

106 *The Internal Announcement of the Acquisition*

We had the internal announcement at Forethought on Thursday, 9 July 1987, at 3:00 p.m. Jon Shirley and Jeff Raikes came down to be there in person. It impressed me that Jon was willing to go to so much trouble to make a brief appearance before all our people.

In the morning, we handled several peripheral notifications. Nashoba, developers of FileMaker, were told about the deal, for the first time, and given a slot to travel to Redmond to talk to Microsoft independently (Forethought couldn't negotiate for them). It had been definitely decided that the new Graphics Business Unit (GBU) in California would deal with graphics only, and initially PowerPoint only. Whatever the future was for FileMaker, it would be elsewhere.

Letters of notification to all shareholders would go out the following Monday. A party was planned for 24 July 1987 (actually held on the 25th, at the Ching Gallery in San Francisco).

In the midst of all this, with Jon Shirley on site, I did not lose track of the priorities: the same day, I finalized an offer to Dennis Abbe to join the development group. Dennis Abbe, with Scott Warren, had formed a small Texas company called Rosetta where they created the celebrated Rosetta Smalltalk that ran on Z-80 machines, and after that Rosetta had created much of the early VisiOn operating system under contract to VisiCorp, a project where Dennis had met and worked with Tom Rudkin. Dennis Abbe was grandfathered into the PowerPoint group to be eligible for Microsoft's previously-offered incentives (although these turned out to be unnecessary in the final terms of the deal). We were very keen to have Dennis join us, and he played an extremely important role in PowerPoint development in years to come, so it was definitely worth taking time on this day of all days to be sure that he got a timely offer.

At 3:00 p.m., the whole company assembled in the only room we had large enough for everyone, an unfinished expansion space that was under construction adjacent to our offices. I was so struck by the importance of the occasion that I began a fresh new lab notebook in which to take notes for the new epoch (the only time I failed to fill one lab notebook before beginning a new one).

Rob made a brief announcement to all hands: a letter of intent had just been signed. We would be the "Graphics Business Unit," a permanent Microsoft installation focused on the presentation graphics market. Full vesting of all options in Forethought would occur at the transition for all employees. Then he turned the occasion over to Jon.

I had dealt with Jon Shirley fairly often in the past, going back to 1983, and had always been particularly impressed by his intelligence and plain speaking. His talk on this occasion was simple and convincing, nothing canned or pompous, and very thoughtfully aimed at precisely the concerns of the Forethought people who were hearing about this, as a fact rather than a rumor, for the first time.

Jon began by saying that this was the "first major acquisition by Microsoft." What they were looking for were great products, great people, and complementary visions, and Forethought met all three criteria.

He went on to say that PowerPoint was "not only great, but [was] a pioneering product—a major new category, a leadership product." (I did think how much easier the preceding three years would have been if I had had that quote available to use at the beginning of the project.)

Jon said a lot of things that reassured even me. Microsoft wanted to build up a real team, here, to do graphics products. The location in Silicon Valley was important to them; not all the best people in the world could be hired in Redmond. It would be important for Microsoft to have other development centers in other locations, and this was the first. A year from now, there would be more people in the GBU than were in all of Forethought at the acquisition; within a year, we would need to move to a larger building in our area. (This specific detail confirmed to me that the "permanent unit" plan was true.)

The major assets of Microsoft were people, and the aim was to place all of Forethought's people within Microsoft; they had "never laid off a person at Microsoft."

The charter for the new GBU would be specifying, developing, documenting, testing, and marketing PowerPoint. Phone support would be in Redmond, sales would be in the existing national and international sales organizations. (This faced honestly the fact that most of the Forethought people listening wouldn't be in the GBU—most of them were in phone support, sales, and marketing administration.)

Jon ended by saying that the acquisition would be "super-synergistic": "we'll put a lot of resources into here, to put out great products."

Jeff Raikes then spoke. He confirmed the "Business Unit" organization, saying that it was familiar to Microsoft in a few existing groups in Systems Division (programming languages, Xenix), and that it "fosters a small-company approach." A business unit turned out to be a self-contained P&L unit under a General Manager. Organized that way, we were a bad fit in the sprawling Applications Division at first, but a year later, Apps was reorganized into other Business Units, parallel to us, each similarly self-contained and with its own P&L statement; that made things much easier.

Jeff stressed that we would be first-class citizens of Microsoft, even though residing in a distant part of the empire, with all the same advantages as people in Redmond: private enclosed offices for everyone, worldwide email access (a rare perq in 1987), all the lavish company benefits, and we would all attend the next company meeting in Seattle in October (this was true, and most impressive).

Rob closed by cautioning everyone that the deal was not yet definitive, that it was not public knowledge, but that we expected it to be final by 1 August at the latest.

Rob and I had a short private meeting with Jon and Jeff after the all-hands event. Jon told us that Microsoft had held a telephone board meeting the day before to approve the deal. In that conference call, several of the detailed terms had been simplified in Forethought's favor, even during that final formality. Earlier thoughts of requiring non-compete clauses from everyone had been abandoned, and only Rob and I would be required to sign such agreements, for one year—perfectly reasonable.

107 Agreeing on the Organization (and No P-Code)

Over the next couple of days after the internal announcement, we settled the organization of the new Graphics Business Unit. Two people from the Microsoft Human Relations group came down and talked individually with every single Forethought employee, providing each person with a trustworthy, non-management source of information about personal concerns.

We had a few bumps over the future organization, so I talked with Forethought's lawyer who was negotiating the text of the final agreement with Microsoft's lawyers. He consulted his counterparts, who consulted Jon Shirley and Jeff Raikes, and our lawyer reported back to me that Microsoft "would like to please [me]" in any future arrangements, because they thought that I was the one who "has the business and product vision." I called Jeff Raikes to confirm this. With that assurance, we settled our arrangements very quickly.

I was the General Manager of the new business unit, at a "Director" level in the Microsoft organization, reporting to the VP of Applications (at the time, Bill Gates, "acting"). Rob Campbell would be reporting to Bill separately, as a consultant under Jeff Raikes's direction for three months, with the aim of a smooth transition.

Rob would be in charge of keeping Forethought together until the Definitive Agreement. After that, he and I would jointly work on the closing down of Forethought's corporate existence. I would be in charge of starting up the new Microsoft business unit.

On Saturday, 19 July 1987, I hosted Bill Gates in Sunnyvale, along with Jeff Raikes and Jeff Harbers, for a full-day transition planning session, focusing on the "starting up" part of my job.

We confirmed the new GBU organization and considered whether one or two people from Redmond might be useful transplants. We immediately agreed to make Dennis Austin and Tom Rudkin the heads of two development groups, and to hire aggressively for them; Bill was adamant that I should never fail to hire a good developer, regardless of any headcount plans. We settled on headcount goals for immediate hiring as soon as possible: about 7 people for development, about 5 people for program management, 2 or 3 people for QA, thus a total of about 15 developer-type folks. We also penciled in a couple of product marketing people, perhaps one person for user education materials, one receptionist/telephonist, one person to handle the administrative tasks of the business unit, for a total of about 20 people, plus Rob Campbell keeping an office with us for a short time.

On development, there were lots of suggestions from Jeff Harbers about how we might take advantage of work already done on Excel and Word for Windows. This began to worry me, since I was not impressed by what I had heard, and I was very wary of getting entangled in the way that some other development group worked. Bill cut through all this by the decree, very surprising to Harbers, that the GBU would *not* use Redmond's internal development environment.

The background is that, beginning in the 1960s and 1970s, it had been common to implement applications (and other programs) using languages based on compilers that produced a compact intermediate language (called "p-code" from its use in Wirth's Pascal) that could be interpreted by a simple interpreter on target machines. Such an approach can work well, and there are many good reasons why it is still widely used in the proper situations.

In Redmond, the Applications Division had adopted a whole private ecosystem of special tools to produce and interpret its own p-code, back in the days of 8-bit machines with tiny memory and at a time when it seemed a competitive advantage to port easily to many incompatible PCs. By 1987, both situations had changed, making that way of working much less attractive, but the internal development environment lived on.

Besides its advantages, the Applications Division system also caused some problems, mostly because it was an internal tool set that was not finished, documented, or tested to product standards; its use was only tolerable because its maintainers and its users were all part of the same group. The Applications Division back then had a unified development group under Harbers, who produced all the tools and also used them to develop all the applications (Multiplan, Word, Chart, File, and so forth) for the product groups. As a Business Unit, for the first time, we would have a separate dedicated development group reporting to me, rather than sharing Harbers's group.

By decreeing that we would not use the internal tools at the GBU, Bill was saying that we should use the very same commercial development tools and compilers that Microsoft made and sold to every other developer in the world, tools which were better maintained and supported for remote use. This shrewd decision saved us enormous trouble, by making us independent of the Apps development group in Redmond, and thus made all our development much easier; but with the long history and huge investment in the internal development tools for Apps, only Bill could have made the decision to abandon them.

108 Final Steps to a Definitive Agreement and a Price

We held our final regular meeting of the Forethought Board of Directors on 21 July 1987.

The sales report was that FileMaker was below plan for the quarter, but PowerPoint was actually ahead of plan for its introductory quarter. These sales results assured that the acquisition would stay on track.

There was still concern expressed among some less-involved investors that Microsoft would not complete the acquisition, but those of us who had been involved in the negotiations didn't share those fears. We passed all the formal resolutions needed for the acquisition to occur. The Forethought books would be closed 31 July 1987.

After that meeting, I got a telephone call from Jeff Raikes, to say that Microsoft offer letters would be couriered overnight for the six people whom we had agreed to retain at the new GBU, so I could hand them out in the morning.

There was a formal shareholders' meeting on 24 July 1987, and a great party thrown by our investors for all Forethought people on Saturday night, 25 July 1987, at the Ching Gallery in San Francisco.

On Thursday, 30 July 1987, Microsoft and Forethought issued public announcements that the sale of Forethought had been concluded, effective 31 July 1987, at a price of $14 million cash.

(Comparing values at different dates is imprecise, and there are several approaches, but one common calculation is that such a price from 1987 should be multiplied by 1.875 to give the equivalent price in 2010. In those terms, $14,000,000 in 1987 would be the equivalent of $26,250,000 in 2010.)

The *New York Times* printed the story the following day and got all the facts correct (they didn't yet print PowerPoint in the typographic form we used—they do now!):

COMPANY NEWS
Microsoft Buys Software Unit
Special to the *New York Times*
July 31, 1987

The Microsoft Corporation announced its first significant software acquisition today, paying $14 million for Forethought Inc. of Sunnyvale, Calif.

Forethought makes a program called Powerpoint that allows users of Apple Macintosh computers to make overhead transparencies or flip charts. Some industry officials think such "desktop presentations" have the potential to be as big a market as "desktop publishing," which involves using computers to lay out newsletters and other publications. Microsoft is already the leading software supplier for the Macintosh.

The personal software industry has been buzzing with acquisitions lately. Microsoft has purchased a 10-employee Berkeley company called Dynamical Systems and has invested in another company, Natural Language Inc. But the acquisition of Forethought is the first significant one for Microsoft, which is based in Redmond, Wash. Forethought would remain in Sunnyvale, giving Microsoft a Silicon Valley presence. The unit will be headed by Robert Gaskins, Forethought's vice president of product development.

(New York Times 1987)

109 *The Payout at the Acquisition*

Before we sold to Microsoft, the Forethought stock options of all the employees had been substantially eroded in value—they wouldn't have been worth very much. Many very difficult funding rounds at barely increasing valuations, even if not literally "down" rounds, can only be closed with generous preferences for investors. The VCs have antidilution provisions, but founders and early employees can be very heavily diluted.

But then in the final days just before the acquisition, the VC investors who owned a dominating majority of the company unexpectedly initiated and voted very generous final make-good option grants to current employees, in some cases fully reversing the dilution of the preceding three years for the recipient. I don't think I ever knew which employees received the make-good option grants—it wasn't a management action, it was an investors' action, and there was no requirement for them to do it. All along, Forethought's investors had been invariably supportive and positive, with none of the struggle between management and VCs that you sometimes hear about, and this was merely the last in a long series of contributions to the success of Forethought and of the people who worked there. The effect of these generous grants was to further dilute the original founders and long-gone employees; it did so by concentrating ownership more in the final employee team, the people who had produced PowerPoint and gotten it sold to Microsoft, alongside the VC investors.

Forethought had used about $3 million of VC investment while carrying out the PowerPoint plan from restart in July 1984 to acquisition by Microsoft in July 1987 (we had most of a million dollars in the bank when I joined, and roughly the same amount at the acquisition). Of the $14 million sales price, about $12 million went to the investors, thus giving them about a 3-times to 4-times return. This was respectable, but not any big success given the effort invested.

This distribution demonstrates that, in terms of the most basic measure of success in a startup, Forethought had not been successful in achieving much value for its founders and employees. Before the company had built any appreciable value, about 85% of the company was in the hands of outside investors, a share that would have been even larger if not for their generous last-minute grants. This was not unfair, and reflected both the initial flame-out and all the problems after the restart; but it did mean that any big payday for the employees would have to come from the next step (in our case, as part of Microsoft, where in fact all the PowerPoint people did very well).

The VCs, too, would have preferred a company in which they owned less than 85% of the stock but which grew wildly, and was ultimately acquired or went public at a huge valuation, giving 100-times or more returns. But that doesn't happen very often. Our VCs, after their generosity, got back a return which was at the low end of their aspirations, but much more than they had been expecting for a long time (four and a half years since the founding of the company, during most of which time we were about to liquidate), so they were relatively happy at what could be presented as a success.

Dick Kramlich, at an NEA partners meeting in Baltimore, was knighted "Sir Never-Give-Up" and awarded four weeks of mandatory incremental vacation by his often-skeptical partners, for his long-term dedication to working out Forethought. In 2012, having invested in myriads of successful companies since, Dick still mentions PowerPoint among a dozen selectively chosen investments in his biography on the NEA website, which pleases me very much.

For my part, I had been convinced that the Microsoft acquisition would return more to our investors than any other feasible option could return, more than any IPO. I was sure of that at the time, and I was sure of it four months later when Black Monday struck and killed the IPO market.

My tension didn't end until the money went out. I have never been so relieved as when the purchase price was released and wired to our investors. I had a deep sense of responsibility to the investors who had backed us for so long, and I was much gratified by having engineered a decent return for them after long periods when it seemed likely they would end up with nothing.

110 The Outcome for People Who Didn't Get Acquired

At the end of July 1987, it became strikingly clear what Forethought had become when we released the initial Microsoft GBU org chart. All the people who had worked in the "publishing division," including Rob, were gone, having either accepted or turned down jobs in other parts of Microsoft, and all the people who had worked in the "PowerPoint division" remained as part of the new Graphics Business Unit.

This was the perfect focusing step that we needed. Going forward from the acquisition, the goal was to have the GBU concentrate on developing the second (color) version of Mac PowerPoint and the corresponding Windows version of PowerPoint, and to have the rest of Microsoft concentrate on selling the existing Mac product. We had time to build up our marketing side, and we began that by importing a marketing manager from Redmond, a rare exception to the policy of "no transfers." The Graphics Business Unit worked very much as I had always seen Forethought, with Microsoft support groups in Redmond taking over roughly the functions that Rob's "publishing division" had given to the PowerPoint group in the past (accounting, sales, and the like).

No one ever planned to lose Rob Campbell at the acquisition, unless that was Rob's own private plan. I know that the Microsoft people handling the acquisition thought very highly of Rob, and very much wanted to keep him on within Microsoft, but that was hard to work out. It wasn't really possible for Rob to be parachuted in as a senior manager in some other Microsoft group; in those days, Microsoft seriously followed the rule that everyone, including in marketing and sales, should report to someone more technical than himself, all the way up to Bill at the top (and this was the same reason given for not hiring Forethought's senior sales people). Rob didn't want a staff job; in fact, Rob may well have preferred another startup to any job Microsoft could offer. So Rob went on to continue his successful career as a serial entrepreneur, possessing the possibly unique distinction of having reported directly to both Steve Jobs at Apple and (however briefly) to Bill Gates at Microsoft.

It's true that the PowerPoint group lost all our sales and marketing people at the acquisition in a very clean break, but the loss wasn't irrevocable. Both the Forethought VP of Marketing and Forethought VP of Sales ultimately rejoined us as part of the Microsoft GBU.

Darrell Boyle had been the VP of Marketing in the early days of Forethought (he joined before I did, and he was responsible for some exceptional actions such as the impossible sale to First Software in early 1985), but he had laid himself off to cut our burn rate in one of the early cash crunches, even before we got started on PowerPoint. But Darrell believed in the PowerPoint product concept so strongly that he formed his own consultancy to advise Apple and others on "desktop presentations," and became an industry guru championing our category. About three years after the acquisition, as we grew rapidly and our imported marketing guy returned to Redmond, Darrell came back to head marketing for PowerPoint at the GBU.

Glenn Hobin had been the VP of Sales at Forethought up through its final days, and had saved Forethought many times by his insight (Glenn was an academic psychologist as well as a master salesman). At the acquisition, we retained no sales function, and the sales group up in Redmond wasn't overly welcoming (again, the claim of "not technical enough" to be a senior manager at Microsoft, but I thought the problem was in the Microsoft sales group). Instead, Glenn joined up with the Nashoba developers who still owned FileMaker (since it had not been sold to Microsoft), reorganized Nashoba, got the product back into the market very quickly, and soon thereafter sold FileMaker to Apple for its new Claris software division (headed by "Coach" Bill Campbell who had been sought to head Forethought). Glenn thus had the distinction of selling Forethought's PowerPoint to Microsoft (for $14 million) and Nashoba's FileMaker to Apple (at an unreported price, rumored at the time to be about $5 million), both products whose value he had established by selling them to users. After accomplishing that coup, and selling his new company out from under himself, he later rejoined the growing GBU to head our one-man sales department, to be an "ambassador" to the Microsoft sales force in Redmond, and to help them sell PowerPoint to major accounts.

111 What If There Had Been No Acquisition?

Just as a thought experiment, we might forget the actual situation of Forethought, and make the heroic assumption that the company could have hired a new CEO and CFO and pulled off an IPO within three months, and could have done reasonably well thereafter as a company focusing on desktop presentations. How would history have played out for an independent company?

The most important strategic circumstance that happened after we sold Forethought to Microsoft was that the market for Microsoft Windows didn't develop as quickly as we (or Microsoft) had expected. In the final business plan that I wrote for Forethought, dated 27 June 1986, there was a passage where I said " ... it is at least reasonable that for the next year the market on MS-Windows machines may be no larger than the Macintosh market, and perhaps considerably smaller." Thus, I went on to conclude, it is reasonable to start with PowerPoint on Macintosh first.

As things turned out, my prediction of a tiny market for Windows PowerPoint, smaller even than that for Mac PowerPoint, was a good call for 1987—and also a good call for 1988, for 1989, and for 1990 (calls that I failed to make). Sales of PowerPoint on Windows were not larger than Macintosh until 1991, because it wasn't possible to ship an application until then (all dates here are in Forethought fiscal years, ending in March, not calendar years). Yet, the most important development to be doing during all those years was Windows, because, after1990, it was the Windows market that expanded rapidly, with the earliest arrival (PowerPoint) the biggest winner.

With the insight of afterthought, we can see how wise it was to sell Forethought to Microsoft. If PowerPoint had not been acquired by Microsoft, we would have been faced with zero Windows sales for another three or four years, but with a need for heavy development investment in a Windows product (which was not easy to raise after Black Monday in late 1987). That long delay was ample time for Microsoft to have developed its own new presentation application for Windows, leaving PowerPoint in a poor position. Obviously, we could not have developed PowerPoint for Windows much earlier than an internal Microsoft team could have done; we might possibly have done a better job, but lacking close cooperation with the Windows developers, even that might have been less likely.

And, however well we would have done in that first round, almost immediately—by 1992—we would have been hit by the move to "Office suite" products, and if we had lasted that long, we would have soon been out of business, along with our other competitors. Recommending the acquisition turned out to have been an astute move.

112 *Resolution of the Dual Companies Strategy*

The acquisition by Microsoft wrote the final chapter of the "dual companies" strategy—the plan both to develop PowerPoint as our flagship application and at the same time to publish applications developed by others under our MACWARE brand, as a self-financing way to prepare for PowerPoint's delivery. As I've described, this publishing activity had tended to take on a life of its own, and we were never able to formulate the plans to end it. The new priority after the acquisition was to jettison MACWARE immediately.

There were several points of view among Forethought employees about being acquired by Microsoft. Microsoft was not in need of a software publishing division, and it was obvious that the publishing business would end. Those in Forethought who were interested in the publishing business mostly (but not universally) opposed the sale to Microsoft. On the other side, Microsoft was in need of a presentation product, so much so that they were developing one, and it was obvious that the PowerPoint business would have a great opportunity as part of

212

Microsoft. Those in Forethought who were interested in the PowerPoint business mostly supported the sale to Microsoft, though with serious regret for our lost independence. I shared that regret, and it made me feel that I would need to do everything possible to assure that I could salvage as much independence as possible.

After the Definitive Agreement, the publishing division disappeared overnight. At Redmond's instruction, we immediately destroyed all traces of the published products and everything bearing their trademarks, and we made video recordings of the destruction (since Microsoft had no agreements with the developers, and didn't want lawsuits). We boxed up all records of dealing with the developers of the published products and sent them to Redmond, in case they were ever needed. We stopped selling everything, and cancelled distributor and dealer agreements of those not on Microsoft's approved lists. We set up intercepts on our phone support lines to refer people who called about published products to their respective developers. MACWARE just vaporized and disappeared from our lives.

So in the end, the whole publishing activity was indeed shed just like booster rockets, leaving PowerPoint to continue its journey unencumbered.

Why did the dual-companies ambiguity go on for so long without clear resolution? Probably both Rob and I were hedging our bets.

From my point of view, building up the service departments through the publishing activities was good, but only because it was a rehearsal for the delivery of PowerPoint, which should increase the chances of PowerPoint's success; and if it should happen that PowerPoint wasn't immediately a big hit, publishing perhaps could provide a revenue stream to finance whatever steps it took to fix any problems.

From Rob's point of view, having the people and organization to create software internally made for a much better publisher, because we possessed technical knowledge; and if it should happen that publishing wasn't very successful, maybe PowerPoint would be a big hit.

All the time, of course, we had our Board of Directors, who were all savvy venture capital investors and independent entrepreneurs, and they could have directed us to close down either activity at any time. But we were able for several years to write and present business plans that made the dual-track plan seem at least plausible, and our investors may have been hedging their bets in the same way.

113 Did the Dual Strategy Help PowerPoint?

At the restart, when just beginning the development of PowerPoint, at first I very much agreed with the dual-track plan to publish software developed by others as practice to build the delivery vehicle for Power-Point, and thought it very clever.

During the development, I came to feel that our actual experience showed that to be mostly wrong; the published products did not pay for themselves, but ran huge deficits that repeatedly brought us close to liquidation and very nearly killed PowerPoint. Partly this was because of the poor market for Mac software in 1985 and 1986, and I thought we were stubborn not to recognize that fact and cut our losses on what was after all a sideshow.

In retrospect, neither of those two positions is clearly the correct one.

All the messy complexity of the sideshow had one advantage, in that it provided a continuing drama of operational problems and successes for investors and board members to discuss. Since we began as a "re-start" with a million dollars in the bank, and with a board full of important people and legendary top-tier investors and their funds already in place, we probably didn't have the opportunity to adopt a very slow and low-burn strategy. Those leading VCs were used to going to board meetings where management reported lots of real-world action, and not just product planning details for the first two years. Even the repeated episodes of running out of money and facing shutdown were occasions when the VCs could play an exciting role. The publishing company dual-track model, with its bustling energy, looked at the time like the "swinging for the fences" strategy, although actually focusing on PowerPoint might well have produced a much larger return for Fore-thought's investors.

The distraction afforded by the sideshow allowed PowerPoint to be defined and developed slowly and carefully, building for the long term. It also kept us from finishing and shipping a less-polished version of PowerPoint a year earlier, when the poor market for Macs and the state of the product might have made it unsuccessful; the delay may actually have been an advantage, in that it brought PowerPoint to the market when Apple was shipping new machines, interest in Mac and Windows was higher, and PowerPoint was fully ready.

Publishing did give us early experience with the steps of finishing a software product while we were still in the early stages of working on

PowerPoint, so, as PowerPoint progressed, we understood better exactly the steps we were going to need to take to complete it, and we avoided last-minute realizations that we had overlooked critical preparations. Finally, it also did teach us about shipping and publicizing software for Mac, which had value (though perhaps not as much as we paid— experience keeps a dear school).

When we got down to the Microsoft acquisition, all the capacity we'd developed for customer support and for sales and accounting turned out to be useless; those were the parts that Microsoft could do better. On the other hand, we needed to be able to book sales and collect money and support customers in order to successfully ship PowerPoint, and thus attract a large valuation from Microsoft. If the successful ship event tripled the value of the company (or nearly so— Microsoft raised its offer from $5.3 million before ship to $14 million after ship), and if (a bigger if) the publishing strategy was what made that possible, then it was worth it. It's not clear whether that was true.

Having real products shipping for almost three years had given us something to talk about so as to become known, had allowed us to enter into Apple promotions and to talk with analysts, and had also made us an established multi-product company in the eyes of distributors and dealers. All these were real advantages.

Even before the acquisition, though, some of the theoretical advantages of publishing hadn't worked out. For MACWARE, we had built up an infrastructure of extremely competent suppliers—to print boxes, to print books, to duplicate disks, to print disk labels, and then to assemble finished product from the bill of materials. For PowerPoint, however, we didn't use those suppliers. Just as the PowerPoint launch neared, the software products business was looking attractive to big printers, and the giant firm R. R. Donnelley & Sons opened a division to handle complete software product production. As I've described at more length, I adopted Donnelley's service for PowerPoint, and it worked well; we were able to set up wholly new manufacturing at the last minute, with no glitches.

We also had expected the publishing business to build up an experienced staff ready to deliver PowerPoint. That also didn't work out, perhaps because of the cumulative delay, and we ended up hiring almost all new people for the PowerPoint introduction.

The dual-companies strategy did help PowerPoint in a way which should not be underestimated. In those days, before the Internet, it was usually necessary to work for a long time before being able to release anything to customers. During this long period, there was much investment of both funding and development time, but very little feedback from real purchasers (insiders and consultants are rather different from customers). Then, at the end of two or three years, it was time to roll the dice, to invest in manufacturing a large inventory of product and to ship it to distributors and dealers, with advertising and PR to try to get end users to buy it.

It was very common for the product to go wrong in a lot of large and small ways during this long incubation period, so that when it finally shipped, it could easily fail, even if the concept was sound, because it had so many non-optimal parts. Our involvement in the publishing business was a way to help avoid that problem. In particular, through our continuing involvement in the development of FileMaker, and our exclusive contact with all its customers (we did all marketing and sales, all PR and advertising, and handled all the free 800-number customer and technical support), we gained a good evolving insight into product features and user interface conventions as seen by actual Mac customers. This provided some amount of help to keep development on track during the three years of PowerPoint development.

We actually required contact with customers by every employee. Tom Rudkin recalls that "Forethought policy was for everyone in the company to take turns answering the support phone line during lunch breaks. This turned out to be a wonderful experience for me, because it allowed me to talk with real customers using Macintosh programs and learn what kinds of problems they were having" (Rudkin 2012).

What was perhaps a final benefit of the dual-companies strategy was completely non-obvious and unplanned: the strategy may have contributed to the comparative autonomy of the group in the first five years following the acquisition by Microsoft. Because we had been a fully functioning stand-alone company for a long time, and had more than one shipping product, it seemed plausible (and to us seemed an achievable negotiating position) to make us the first "Business Unit" within Microsoft's Applications Division, and to allow us to continue independently. If we had been mostly just a handful of developers, it might have been a non-negotiable and obvious move to just insert us into some existing organization in Redmond.

It was our gaining five years more of real independence, with all the clout and resources of Microsoft at our backs, that enabled us to equip PowerPoint for long-term success even beyond its original uses and that, not incidentally, brought the large rewards to the people who had worked on it. If the dual-company strategy contributed to that, then it was ultimately a big win.

114 How Much Did the Dual Strategy Cost?

From my company history written in 1987, just before the acquisition:

> During the whole period, we invested about $400,000 on developing PowerPoint, or roughly 10% of our total $4 million venture capital investment (that is the almost $1 million left unspent at the restart, plus the $3 million raised since then). Probably another $400,000 or so went into costs of shutting down the original operations, for another 10%. About 17% ($700,000) was left in the bank at the PowerPoint ship—but that was the same $700,000 we had received at the last minute, when it was too late to help our plans. This leaves about 63% of our investment ($2,500,000) which went to losses on our operations, almost all in connection with the published MACWARE products, building the delivery mechanism. (Gaskins, Forethought History 1987)

An additional real cost of having a run-rate that required spending so much was that we had to spend the time to raise all that money. Rob Campbell and I had to spend a great deal of time pitching potential investors, both venture capital and corporate.

In my appointment books from the period between the restart and the acquisition, I find that 133 of my formal meetings were with potential investors, and that doesn't include all the internal meetings and board meetings devoted to the topic.

In addition to the two investment rounds prior to the restart (February 1983 and December 1983), we did *five* more investment rounds afterward, during two and a half years: May 1985, November 1985, May 1986, November 1986, and March 1987.

From my company history written in 1987:

> Thus ... we were faced with the real prospect of liquidation at least every six months. We had to raise $3,000,000 in additional venture capital investment to keep going, during tough times for software investments, which meant that fund raising took up as much time as running the business. We were always short of the proper resources, always forced into short-term decisions, then always playing catch-up. (Gaskins, Forethought History 1987)

217

The overhead of that constant money raising shouldn't be underestimated. The fact that we were so often faced with the prospect of being out of business assured that money raising would take top priority. Paul Graham, who has seen startups do a lot of raising money, says

> I'd noticed startups got way less done when they started raising money, but it was not till we ourselves raised money that I understood why. The problem is not the actual time it takes to meet with investors. The problem is that once you start raising money, raising money becomes the top idea in your mind. That becomes what you think about when you take a shower in the morning. And that means other questions aren't. (Graham, Top Idea 2010)

Pitching new prospective investors always involves going back to the beginning and trying to explain the idea you're working on to people who haven't heard it before. This can become frustrating (though far from useless). An astute commenter wrote on the *Hacker News* website:

> It's been my experience that raising money can feel like a cross between prostitution and social work.
> —Chuck McManis (McManis 2011)

115 *Could the Publishing Business Have Succeeded?*

Perhaps the MACWARE publishing-company strategy was a useful throw-away to help PowerPoint, but could it have been more than that? Did Forethought make just one big mistake, that being to get wedged into bad FileMaker contracts with Nashoba, so that the product was profitable for its developers but not for us? If we had been stronger negotiators or in luckier circumstances for Mac sales, could MACWARE publishing have become another successful business, alongside PowerPoint?

That possibility could be plausible only if the publishing model in general had turned out to be successful for software. The consensus now is that software publishing never worked. Here is Paul Graham writing in late 2009:

> But this model [publishing] doesn't work for software. It doesn't work for an intermediary to own the user. The software business learned that in the early 1980s, when companies like VisiCorp showed that although the words 'software' and 'publisher' fit together, the underlying concepts don't. Software isn't like music or

books. It's too complicated for a third party to act as an interme-
diary between developer and user.

If software publishing didn't work in 1980, it works even less
now that software development has evolved from a small number
of big releases to a constant stream of small ones. (Graham,
Apple's Mistake 2009)

Paul is right, but he can't help speaking from the position of knowing what happened later. For a period in the early 1980s, successful
software companies on MS-DOS and Apple II were often publishers of
licensed software, companies such as Software Publishing Corporation
or VisiCorp—both once very strong, though both ended badly. Such
publishers were able to sell lines of related products that worked together, at least a little. At that time, it could seem plausible that there
should be an opening for such a publisher concentrating exclusively on
the Mac, as with our MACWARE.

But it's not so clear why Mac exclusivity should be much of a lasting
advantage over a good company like Software Publishing, which could
apply what it already knew about customers and the publishing business to the new platform of Mac. There was a brief moment when
developers were quicker to embrace the tiny Mac platform than publishers were—after all, the publishers had to put up most of the money;
for that moment, there was an opening for a Mac specialist publisher.
But even then, it was clear to me that developing a new high-value
category on a new generation of graphical PCs, on Mac and Windows,
should be a much better business. I argued at the time, in some detail,
that the existing publishing companies were already failing (Gaskins,
Forethought Strategy 1987).

Also, Forethought's weakness relative to the developer of FileMaker
wasn't an accident. The developer, it seems to me, can fairly easily replace the publisher, either with a different publisher or with an in-house
activity, whereas the publisher can't really replace the developer of an
established and successful product. The publisher typically never even
has possession of the source code, and could hardly reverse engineer it
credibly against the competition of the original.

The afterlife of FileMaker illustrates this. Nashoba, after its publishing contract was cancelled by Microsoft, had little problem in replacing
Forethought and getting back into the market, with negligible loss of
momentum. Forethought even owned the copyrights to the FileMaker
boxes and manuals and all other printed materials, since we wrote them

and published them, but Nashoba found it easy to get everything re-written.

It seems in retrospect that the temporary success of software pub-lishing companies in establishing families of products was an accident of the very early days, and that model couldn't compete after more knowledge and more capital became available to developers. I thought I knew by 1984 that software publishing was not a successful model, and that already it was on its last legs. But you could never be sure at the time.

116 Did the Slow Development of PowerPoint Hurt?

During the early development of PowerPoint, I was extremely impatient with the delays. It seemed to me that we were constantly falling behind. I worried that someone else would beat us to market. I resented the time wasted on the publishing operation, once the revised contracts made it clear that publishing could never be profitable for us.

But in retrospect, I wonder: did the slow pace of development on PowerPoint really hurt the product, or help it?

What else we did at the same time has been documented above. We had lots of distractions, we applied only so many man-months of effort to PowerPoint, beginning very slowly, and we lacked resources. But many of those distractions were educational for people working on new software, even if not appreciated. Our distractions, the published products, kept us in close touch with Mac software and with Mac users, which was a useful context.

What if we had not had the distractions or resource constraints, and had had a dozen programmers on staff and assigned to the job? We probably could have worked a little faster, but not in proportion to the larger headcount. There is a certain elapsed time needed to think up great software products. The long incubation period, and the fact that only two or three minds were working on the detail, made for a product with both superior design and robust implementation. It also allowed development to go smoothly at the end, without the discovery of over-looked mistakes. If PowerPoint had been done much more quickly, I doubt it would have been as good.

And, despite my impatience, it turned out that there really wasn't a good reason to ship earlier.

For one thing, everyone now agrees that through 1985 and 1986, Apple's sales of Macintosh hardware were very poor, and that necessarily implied poor sales of all Macintosh software.

> "I think we'll break the cumulative two million total in 1985. Sure."—Steve Jobs, predicting Mac sales prior to its introduction.
> Apple sold only 500,000 Macs by the end of 1985, and didn't break the two million mark until 1988. (Linzmayer 2008, 123)

John Sculley, who became the CEO of Apple a year before the start of PowerPoint's development, and remained CEO through all of its first three versions, later wrote:

> ... the Macintosh ... was failing in early 1985. His [Steve Jobs's] vision was ahead of its time, the power of the microprocessor wasn't enough to do what he wanted to do and Mac sales were falling off. (Guyon 2011)

Indeed, all of 1984, 1985 and 1986—while we worked on Power-Point—were tough times for Macintosh and Mac software developers. Any PowerPoint that we could have shipped twelve or eighteen months earlier wouldn't have had as many potential buyers, and would likely not have had the requisite sales, even apart from the fact that it wouldn't have been as good.

Early Macs were great at what they did but were exceptionally low function, and it took Apple a very long time to make upgraded Macs that approached adequacy. Early on, I coined the phrase for presentations that "there is no other application which is so valuable to people who can sign $10,000 purchase orders," but the early Macs really weren't nearly powerful enough to attract those people.

Mac didn't begin to be adequate until the introduction of the Mac Plus in January, 1986. The Plus came with new features of 1MB memory, a SCSI port for peripherals such as hard disks, an 800KB floppy drive, and the first 128KB ROM with the new Hierarchical File System. This was just beginning to move out of the toy category, and a lot of earlier Mac software (such as ThinkTank 512) wouldn't run on the Plus.

That was all there was until the next models, the Mac II (expansible) and the Mac SE (with internal hard disk), were introduced in March 1987—only days before PowerPoint 1.0 shipped. These models began to work decently. Equally important was the LaserWriter, shipped in March 1986 but at a price of $6,995; it was indeed the most powerful computer Apple had shipped, but it took some time for customers to get used to the price point. LaserWriter II wasn't introduced until 1988.

Apple's slowness to introduce better Mac models was very hard to understand.

> "We were too tired, too arrogant, too stupid, I don't know what."
> —Apple evangelist Guy Kawasaki explaining why Apple took so long to fix some of the early Mac's speed and memory [limitations].
>
> "We thought: It's there, it's beautiful, it can't be improved, we did it. Everyone was burnt out and we wanted to get the hell out of there." —Apple Fellow Steve P. Capps. (Linzmayer 2008, 121)

So there was almost no motivation to ship any major Mac application at all until early 1986, and that increased greatly with the next generation of Macs, at the end of the first quarter of 1987. PowerPoint shipped just one month after that next generation, and was in a good position to take advantage of the interest in the features of the new and more powerful Macs and the LaserWriter. Shipping PowerPoint even a few months earlier might have been initially disappointing.

At the time, of course, I felt incredible pressure to get PowerPoint shipped by the date we achieved, since we knew about the new Mac models well before their announcement. I made presentations at board meetings about the lack of wisdom of our continuing to spend too much time on the unprofitable FileMaker at the expense of the Power-Point ship date. (Gaskins, PowerPoint Status 1986)

As it turned out, we were still at least a year to two years (or more) ahead of Microsoft's own effort to develop a competitor to PowerPoint. And the customer reaction to the new Mac models of 1987 (which Microsoft had also known about all along, of course), at the same time as it made the moment right for PowerPoint's introduction, also served to focus the attention of people at Microsoft on the fact that they were too far behind, leading to the decision to buy PowerPoint. Those same Mac models introduced in March of 1987 were still the only models announced when we shipped PowerPoint 2.0 for Mac in May of 1988, so we got to take advantage of a long stable plateau in Mac evolution.

Later, the same thing was true on Windows. Excel for Windows shipped as early as 1987, but it obviously wasn't very graphical. There were so few machines with Windows 1.0 installed in 1987 that Excel shipped with a Windows runtime, which started up when Excel was summoned from MS-DOS. Customer reactions to Excel on PCs were not as positive as on Mac, particularly against Lotus 1–2–3.

Word for Windows shipped in late 1989, six months earlier than PowerPoint for Windows, on Windows 2.0, but it didn't demand much in the way of graphics either. Word for Windows also shipped with a runtime to start up from MS-DOS, because still so few machines had Windows. There were many doubts and complaints about Windows.

The first adequate version of Windows was 3.0, shipped in May 1990—and PowerPoint 2.0 for Windows shipped at the same time, with Bill Gates using PowerPoint to demo the new version of Windows. Windows 3.0 was still a partial platform, but with three years of work, we had filled in many of the gaps. The big leap forward (much bigger than was reflected in the version numbering) was Windows 3.1 in 1992, which introduced TrueType fonts, and once again we shipped the new PowerPoint 3.0 for Windows at precisely the same time.

As will be discussed later, Lotus Freelance and Aldus Persuasion both were about one year later than PowerPoint on Windows, and Harvard Graphics was about two years later than PowerPoint on Windows—we were well ahead of our most-determined competitors.

So, in retrospect, it appears that we were developing PowerPoint pretty much at the optimum rate. We used the early time to get the spec right, and then were able to build that with no missteps. We built solidly, using the minimum number of people who had deep insight into the purpose of the category, the structure of the application, and the limitations of the platforms. We had no big slips, no persistent bugs, and no limitations caused by inadequate architecture. Dennis Austin's assessment is that our work "was slow, but highly efficient. Maybe efficiency makes it easier to achieve quality, even in general."

Looking back, I'm entirely content with the ship dates for both Mac and Windows PowerPoint. It was essential for us to hustle to be sure that we had versions ready to ship at the earliest date that they were needed, but we always did; and shipping before the platform can support a great product doesn't win lasting friends.

117 Was PowerPoint Just Luck? How Risky Was It?

Any startup founder (or re-founder) will be the first to say that luck plays a big role in every startup; there are so many ways to screw up, so many ways to get into a disaster.

Or, more likely, many disasters. Many of them you bring on yourself, but others are lobbed in by outside forces. If you have the luck to avoid them all, one way or another, you succeed.

But was PowerPoint only luck? I don't think so.

Even at the inception, in mid-1984, I had data to show that presentations were something many people were paying big money to do, already. It was clear that tools for doing presentations better were worth money. It was clear that the people who wanted to give better presentations also had the signing authority to spend that money for that purpose. Mac was barely shipping, and Windows was a year and a half away, both initially very weak, but many people knew, from "expensive prototypes" (at Xerox PARC, or even in my own lab at BNR where we had Wirth's Lilith and Three Rivers PERQ workstations running for experimental programming), how Mac and Windows were going to evolve—even if the future evolved more slowly than seemed possible.

Rather than being lucky that the idea succeeded, it still seems to me (as it did then) that PowerPoint was inevitable. If we had not succeeded at it, someone else would have, and fairly soon after we did.

But what were the chances that Forethought would be the group to deliver that inevitable result? Lots of luck, there. We were simultaneously doing so many things right, and doing so many things wrong, that the outcome was always finely balanced.

There are a number of types of risk in a startup, which applied to PowerPoint very differently. Here's the standard list:

Business model risk—how are you going to get paid, and will that be profitable? No risk for PowerPoint: how to package and sell productivity applications was well understood (databases, word processors, spreadsheets, even graphics) in the DOS and Apple II worlds. PowerPoint would use the same existing delivery channels and pricing.

Technology risk—can you do it? Very little risk for PowerPoint: designing and programming PowerPoint was definitely very difficult, it required working near the edge of hardware capabilities, and it could be done very well or done not so well. But there was not really any doubt that the project was feasible.

The specific engineer who was going to design and implement it, Dennis Austin, believed he knew how to do it, and then later Tom Rudkin agreed and believed that he also knew how to do it. Both of them had the specific backgrounds to be able to make that judgment. (I get points for being able to tell whether someone else really knows what he can do.) This was not a research project, even though neither the

Mac nor Windows versions could have been done at all by any random group of industrial programmers.

Market risk—will anyone buy the application? I felt that my data from Hope Reports demonstrated that the existing market was there, and even DOS products had done okay, even though their platform was obviously inadequate. Very little risk.

Execution risk—do you know how to manage it, and can this team do it? Many other personal computer application projects had been done, but that's no guarantee that I or people I hired could do it. PowerPoint definitely had this risk. There were people in other companies who had successfully managed other similar projects, but I wasn't one of them. I had never managed any product development, so I was a minus factor. (But I'd had a lot of success doing things for the first time.) Dennis and Tom had developed software products, so their experience was a plus factor. Assuming they were right about the technology risk, they could probably execute.

Financial risk—can the project attract enough financing to get all the way to returns? PowerPoint *really* had this risk. No matter how vivid the future was to me, it seemed much more pale and shimmering to potential investors. Forethought's financing was a long series of improvisations, but the bright spot here was that we had Dick Kramlich from NEA, who stage-managed those improvisations and reached into his own pocket to tide us over when all else failed at critical moments.

I conclude that we were lucky that we managed our financial risk and our execution risk (of management incompetence); either of those could have brought us down. But the technology risk, the market risk, and the business model risk were all very safe bets. It was the logic of those strengths that pulled us through.

I was completely confident that PowerPoint would succeed, but my "contempt of risk and ... presumptuous hope of success" (Adam Smith, in *The Wealth of Nations*) were thoroughly illogical. I really believed that personal single-user computers would revolutionize the world, and that graphics PCs would replace all existing PCs, and I was sure I knew that millions of people wanted to make presentation visuals, so it was easy to conclude that the hardware trend would push this application to success. What isn't clear is why it never occurred to me, even fleetingly, that even if all that were true, it was extremely presumptuous to think that it would be my own product which became the inevitable success.

PART VI: POWERPOINT JOINS MICROSOFT

118 Reverse-Acquiring a Senior Management Team

By becoming a Business Unit of Microsoft, and retaining our identity while gaining access to a full portfolio of resources, we were going to be able to go through the scale-up that every successful startup faces.

We had spent three years perfecting the PowerPoint product, and had now discovered that it was a perfect fit to a very large market. We had confirmed that our business model was essentially the same as other productivity apps (such as Word and Excel). We had people (ourselves) in place who could manage the initial version of the Power-Point product, as was proven when we did so.

Then suddenly, the first-day sales of PowerPoint brought us above cash-flow break-even and to substantial profitability; but we had no scalable company structure or systems. We sold out of inventory, and had customers eager to buy the product. We needed to rapidly scale up the production of our product, and especially to expand to sales outside the U.S. We needed to immediately scale up the development of our follow-on versions. We needed to scale up all our departments to handle large numbers of interactions with the outside world.

We had already been (formally) searching for a new CEO and a new CFO, who would have the experience to handle those challenges. But instead of hiring a senior management team for Forethought, we "reverse-acquired" such a team by joining Microsoft.

The acquisition gave the PowerPoint group a ready-made team of senior management people: Jon Shirley as President and COO, Frank Gaudette as CFO, Scott Oki heading Sales, Bill Neukom heading Legal, Pam Edstrom heading PR, and Bill Gates as the CEO and, above all, the chief technical resource. These were all some of the most able people in the world—we could never have hired senior managers even vaguely in the same league for PowerPoint (compare these people to the suggestions made for senior hires at Forethought!). They were heading a company of 1,200 people—exactly what we needed. Their own IPO had occurred less than a year earlier, so they remembered how a small company operated.

These people were precisely the people I needed to talk to, as General Manager of the Graphics Business Unit, and they were the people who could run superlative administrative departments, which I had no desire (and no experience) to manage.

A year later, we gained Mike Maples as the architect of innovative management for still further growth. Starting out as VP of Applications (and hence my boss), he was the best source of advice I could have had.

The whole experience, in fact, was somewhat reminiscent of the restart story, when PowerPoint moved into the empty shell of Forethought's original plan and made use of its resources; now, having outgrown that shell, PowerPoint needed to find a larger shell and transfer into it, so as to continue growing with more resources.

This is not a common strategy for making the startup transition. Most acquirers would not have been so unprepared as Microsoft was to interfere (or else so wise as to not interfere); most acquirers would have come in and stomped us to death almost immediately. By contrast, PowerPoint got five more years, during which Microsoft unloaded from our shoulders all the difficult work of supporting growth, and left us pretty much alone to work out the elaboration of the PowerPoint vision.

119 Action Items to Enter Heaven

The effective date of the Microsoft acquisition was 31 July 1987, a Friday. On the following Monday, 3 August 1987, the transition started in earnest, when I had a meeting with Dave Neir, who had come down from Redmond to get me started.

I formulated "action items" I needed to do personally, as Dave Neir brought up issue after issue. Within an hour or so, I had a list of 47 tasks, mostly complex ones. Then we met with Glenn Hobin, who took down a list of sales-related action items, and then with the bookkeeping group, who got a long list of action items for closing up business.

The task lists were daunting, but this transition felt like entering heaven, because Dave's advice on every item was to do the sensible thing. At Forethought, we had always had to conserve cash by doing things in roundabout and time-consuming ways, the way startups do. We picked new landlords by how many months of free rent they would offer, and whether they were willing to accept warrants for stock in lieu of some cash, rather than for the convenience of location or the quality of facilities. We never bought equipment like copiers or fax machines, but always leased—that cost us more and was an extra bookkeeping task every month, but it conserved cash. Now my direction was either to return the leased equipment and buy better, or else to pay off the leases and forget them. We often hadn't bought needed computer equipment, while we tried to find a dealer willing to trade for our products, but now, as part of Microsoft, we were to get every developer moved up to standard equipment immediately; just place the purchase orders. Everything was to be done in the smartest and most efficient way.

Some of my action items were unbelievably good. I was to start immediately looking for a larger building, to be ready for occupancy in nine months, and it was to be a building appropriate for Microsoft. I was to order a 9600 bps leased line to Redmond, so that our networks could be bridged to the Redmond networks, and so that a new Xenix email server could be installed. I was to get an enterprise-level Ethernet LAN installed to link every workstation, and a parallel net for Macs.

A multitude of inquiries and claims from distributors and dealers had to be individually discussed and approved or disapproved. By the end of October, I negotiated a mutually satisfactory final settlement with Nashoba. The only constraint I had was to do the right thing.

Many of my action items involved contacting people at Redmond (*e.g.*, to get payroll set up, to get American Express cards for everyone, to get health insurance claim forms for everyone, to get business cards printed), and everyone at HQ was more than happy to help, but hardly anyone wanted to meddle. Microsoft was a rapidly growing business with only about 1,200 people worldwide, and ran very lean.

Two days later, on 5 August 1987, I met Aniko Somogyi. Aniko had worked for Microsoft in Redmond, but had just resigned and moved with her husband to Silicon Valley, where she planned to work for Apple in their international operations. Fortunately, someone in Redmond had mentioned to her that Microsoft had a new acquisition in Sunnyvale, and put us in touch. Aniko was extremely smart, had excellent judgment, and could accomplish anything (a typical Microsoft person), and we arranged for her to start coming in right away.

Just a few minutes after Aniko left our initial meeting, I got a telephone call from Frank Gaudette, Microsoft's CFO, who wanted to tell me—in a perfectly helpful way—that Aniko was a valuable Microsoft resource, that I should try my best to retain her for the company, and that I should be sure that she was given opportunities for recognition and promotion. It struck me as a good portent that one of the top three executives at Microsoft would take the time to set an example for a brand-new manager (me) of how Microsoft treated its people.

I succeeded in convincing Aniko to join us rather than Apple, at least for a while, and she was invaluable in getting the acquisition off to a successful start by importing knowledge of Microsoft culture and attitudes to Sunnyvale. Since she knew everyone in Redmond, she could find the way around any problem that came up. Much of the success of the whole Microsoft acquisition depended on the accident of timing that brought Aniko to Sunnyvale just as the deal was done.

Aniko did stay on permanently, got all our administrative operations ticking over, and soon went on to become the head of the GBU's international group, handling our localizations worldwide and our dealings with every Microsoft subsidiary outside of the U.S.—half of our revenue and profits. Gaining her abilities was a very major factor in our success.

120 "We Charge Those People to Talk to Them"

Another indication of how life was going to be better as part of Microsoft was when I realized that I would no longer have to spend time on negotiations that were useless except for raising money.

For much of Forethought's last year, we had spent hours and days meeting with multiple levels of Xerox and traveling all over to their various locations. We early on lost confidence in their ability to execute, but we could never totally ignore the offers of up to something above $18 million, when we needed money so desperately. At these marathon sessions, they would periodically surprise us with utterly crazy ideas that convinced us that they were unsuitable partners, such as asking us to develop Windows drivers for their old non-graphical typewriter-style printers, or urging us to develop PowerPoint on Digital Research's GEM platform, which they "liked better" than they liked Microsoft Windows.

After the acquisition by Microsoft, I found out why Xerox preferred GEM to Windows. I was talking to Jon Shirley, Microsoft's President, about his new business unit (us), and I mentioned the possibility of selling lots of PowerPoint to Xerox. "Those Xerox guys," he snorted. "We charge those people to talk to them." I realized that being part of Microsoft now, rather than a struggling startup, meant that I wouldn't have to talk to people like that endlessly. I could politely tell them I was busy, and concentrate on doing the right thing.

121 We Avoid Becoming Woroftics

Until I could find us a new building, the Graphics Business Unit of Microsoft would remain where Forethought had been.

Microsoft's first presence in Silicon Valley was surely one of the least-imposing buildings ever to bear the Microsoft name. It was in old industrial Sunnyvale, and was one of the very early post-war "tilt-up" buildings. The name refers to the construction technique: the concrete walls were poured flat on the site, and after each wall hardened, it was tilted up into place by cranes. In the early days, compromises had to be made to assure stability. The earliest tilt-ups, such as ours, had walls cast with almost no windows, just narrow slits left every few yards. We joked that they were arrow slits, through which we could shoot our defensive crossbows against attackers.

Microsoft GBU first location, 250 Sobrante Way, Sunnyvale.

The last year or so of work on PowerPoint 1.0 had been done in this building, and we would be here for more than another year, through the shipment of PowerPoint 2.0 for Mac, so this is perhaps the cradle of PowerPoint. (The building still exists, and Tom Rudkin (Rudkin 2012) has suggested that a commemorative plaque should be installed.)

As we grew, we built out the former sales and support areas into additional individual offices, uniform with the offices we already had. We also found our landlord suddenly more eager to maintain our facilities.

By the end of October, after three months, all of our operations were running much more smoothly than they ever did before. Rather than introducing bureaucracy, being part of Microsoft actually made it easier to get everything done—all the people at headquarters just tried to help us do what we wanted, in the simplest and most efficient way.

Everything with the old name on it was replaced immediately with Microsoft material. Signs were ordered from Redmond, and local companies contracted to mount them. A department at HQ sent down the big plastic letters we would need to make the Microsoft logo with its characteristic script. Some of the letters in the logo were connected, so we got seven separate pieces (including the dot over the "i"):

Left to Right: Bob Gaskins, Kathi Baker, Dennis Austin, Tom Rudkin, Aniko Somogyi, Harris Meyers, Robert Lotz, Keith Sturdivant. (From a mid-1980s fax—the location of the original photograph is unknown.)

We took a picture of ourselves holding the pieces outside the building before the sign was professionally mounted; there were so few of us that even with Aniko to hold the dot over the "i" there were hardly enough of us to hold up all the pieces. But we shuffled people around, and noticed that the M could be held upside down and the other letters reordered, to spell out

W o ro ft ic s

This magic word meant nothing, so we decided to mount the parts of the sign as specified in the corporate instructions, rather than exercising startup creativity.

122 Starting as I Meant to Go On

Early in September, we had a couple of very senior Human Relations people come down from Redmond to explain recruiting to us and answer any other HR questions in an all-hands meeting. Someone from the GBU asked about signing authorities, and one of the Microsoft HR people explained to our group that "BillG is the ultimate authority for everything in Redmond, and in the same way, BobGa [me—Microsoft people often talked in email aliases] is the ultimate authority for everything in Silicon Valley."

When I heard that, I realized that I should take exactly that attitude, about everything, until I was challenged on something. I already understood that how much authority you have in any business largely depends on how much authority you assume you have. I had started out by being a bit tentative, while finding out how Microsoft worked, but no one in Redmond seemed to be trying to tell me what to do—at all. I should start immediately to assume all the authority I could, however unreasonable it might seem.

I relied partly on my "General Manager" title, very unusual at Microsoft at that time, which inspired confidence in counterparties to contracts. I made large commitments without ever seeking approval, and never had any problems. No one internal ever questioned my authority, and no one external ever doubted my ability to commit Microsoft.

I made all offers of salary, stock options, signing bonuses, extra payments for relocation or closing of a consulting business, and the like, with no approval from anyone, as long as I was there (this was not at all like Redmond). This meant that if we interviewed someone we wanted badly, after an end-of-day conference among all the interviewers (if there were no blackballs), I could telephone before dinner and extend a binding offer the same day! This worked; anyone who has spent all day in exhausting interviews appreciates the compliment (and the relief) of an immediate offer, rather than having to re-live the interviews over a few days of wondering. Also, a good candidate would reasonably worry whether we were merely "a branch office," with all decisions made in Redmond; making an offer within an hour or two of the candidate's interviews demonstrated that we retained independence to act speedily.

If anyone seemed hesitant to join, I could send email to Bill Gates, giving him the name and phone number of the candidate, with a sentence or two of background, and Bill would call the candidate to say how eager we all were to work with the candidate, never asking me what were the terms of the offer. This also had a powerful effect.

I would sign all contracts for all amounts, with no additional approvals needed. Occasionally, someone in the legal department would muse to me that in Redmond such contracts needed further approvals, but it must be different at the GBU. I did the same for strategic agreements. I signed the "Joint Development and Marketing Agreement" with Genigraphics with no approvals; I had sent the text to a lawyer in the Legal department and gotten back an email with a few points, but it was all informally written. If something like this had gone wrong, the financial cost could have been large—though not nearly as large as the cost if our product developed with Genigraphics had not been successful. I signed facilities rental agreements with no approvals.

All of this assumption of authority paid off richly in efficiency, and over the whole time I remained at the GBU, I increasingly had reason to be glad that I'd started off down the right road. Having a free hand made a lot of difference in being able to produce good results.

123 *The Ultimate Resource*

Hiring at the new GBU was in a separate world from that of Microsoft in Redmond, for several reasons.

For one thing, both Bill Gates and Jon Shirley were initially worried about losing good people from Redmond who wanted to transfer to sunny California, so there was a very high bar for such transfers and certainly no eagerness to publicize in Redmond the fact of our having many openings. That suited me; I didn't want a group of transplants.

For another thing, the HR recruiters in Redmond didn't have any contacts in California, and they were heavily oriented toward new college hires; I had good contacts with local recruiters, and we wanted to hire people with more experience, so I continued to work directly with outside recruiters and pay them standard fees.

Another difference was that the salary scale was somewhat higher in California than in Redmond. This was true at the time of the acquisition, and every year after that. So every year, I would buy the industry salary survey volumes (at that time from the AEA, the American Electronics Association) and write a memo to my boss documenting the salary premium that was appropriate. Managers in business units in Redmond always disagreed, but my bosses always agreed with me.

This was connected to another fear in Redmond, which was that Microsoft employees in Menlo Park would turn out to be job-hoppers. Bill and Jon were used to the situation in Redmond at that time, when Microsoft was the dominant employer, and they didn't welcome a world where every boulevard was lined with attractive campuses of exciting businesses, every one looking for people, and where all an employee had to do to make a job change was to turn in at a different driveway one morning. They had relied on employee non-compete agreements, which were legal in Washington State, but which were unenforceable in California. In fact all of our engineers would cross out the non-compete clauses in the Microsoft employment agreements they were given to sign, and Microsoft accepted them that way. The provisions would have had no effect in California, and everyone knew it.

I told Bill and Jon prior to the acquisition that if we suffered turnover, they should blame me and replace me—it would be an easy judgment, because the fluid employment situation in Silicon Valley meant that poor management was revealed more quickly than in Redmond (fortunately, we had essentially no turnover). But we had to pay salaries on the scale of Silicon Valley, not Redmond, so I had to be able to control my own recruiting, and offer the terms and salary levels needed to hire the best people.

I did succeed in maintaining the AEA salary differentials for people at all ladder levels until the end of my five years, but it got more difficult as Microsoft developed a bigger HR department and more bureaucrats. The initial sensible pragmatism at senior levels that realized we had to compete at local salaries tended to be replaced by low-level bureaucracy—people would say that it was difficult to administer a salary program with different scales in different locations; or that, if it became known that you could get a raise by transferring from drizzly Seattle to sunny California, all hell would break loose; or that salary scales should be made by internal HR people and not based on external AEA sources (the attitude in Redmond where Microsoft controlled the market, versus Silicon Valley where we were very small fish in a very large pond), and on and on.

Since I decided on all the offers and made them without approvals, I could get people hired at the proper salaries with no problem. After that, to deal with annual reviews and raises, I managed to keep the progression satisfactory through all my number-crunching with the salary surveys. But by the end of the five years, it was becoming clear that my persuasiveness was ultimately going to be overcome someday by HR bureaucrats.

For the whole period until I left, the GBU did all its own sourcing of candidates and handled all hiring (including all communications to candidates and terms of offers) locally. This took a lot of everyone's time, though I think we maximized our productivity by hiring higher-quality people than would have been possible using corporate methods.

Bill's standing instructions to me were to use judgment rather than any plan: never to fail to hire a great person, whether I had budgeted headcount or not, and never to hire a less-than-great person, no matter how many slots were open and no matter how desperate we were.

124 *"Planning" for All Applications at the Same Time*

In the early months after the acquisition, I usually attended "resource planning" meetings of the whole Applications Division in Redmond; I wasn't centrally involved, but I hoped to learn about the other people in my division, and often division-wide announcements were made there.

These meetings dealt with allocating the shared resources of the Applications Division among a dozen or so applications. This involved decisions such as to take a developer off of scheduled database work for two weeks to re-do a feature for Excel that had proved to have design errors; or to allocate three writers from the Word manual to computer-based training for Works for a month and reduce the scope of the Word manual; or to have a test manager and a dozen people take another three days to test new features in Word that had been unexpectedly buggy, although that would delay their availability to test bug fixes in other products; or to allocate scarce manufacturing resources to produce upgrades for Europe, at the opportunity cost of new products needed for the U.S.

Such meetings terrified me, since I didn't see how decisions like these could be made sensibly. Every product was constantly being delayed by resource conflicts produced by problems in other products, which couldn't possibly be anticipated. I resolved to try to keep as much distance as possible. This made our first year a bit lonely, since I deliberately kept the internal workings of the GBU opaque and avoided cultivating "disciplinary" ties, so as to avoid constant comparisons of how we were different. We were "odd man out" on everything.

I didn't have a lot of business experience, especially in managing large organizations, but, in some cases, I had more experience than the people who were trying to make this system function. I just thought that their way was completely unworkable. The next fall, at the end of a long year, we got Mike Maples as our new VP of Applications, and he very soon reorganized the whole division into self-contained Business Units parallel to us, and after that things worked much better.

Contrary to the wisdom of the old joke, maybe it was really true that everyone had been out of step but us.

125 Don't Hire Anyone without a Career Path

I had always felt strongly that it was both wrong and unwise to hire people into dead-end jobs within a company, jobs that had no significant career path internally. Thus, in principle, any developer or program manager I hired might be eventually promoted upwards to become a General Manager of a business unit (and in fact, that did happen), or even higher.

But that was not true of various other jobs; for example, if I had hired a technician to duplicate disks, there would have been no career path, not even to be a manager of duplication technicians. So the proper course was to outsource a contract to a disk duplication company, a company in which such a technician did have a career path, and would also receive better management. The same principle applied widely: we didn't hire custodians, we hired building maintenance contractors.

This was my policy at the GBU, even as to receptionists (which at that time were a necessity); rather than hiring someone appropriate to that job, we hired much smarter people with an offer: if they would play receptionist for one year, then we would promote them elsewhere and replace them. This worked out fine.

I think that I once heard Bill Gates say something along these same lines about only hiring employees who had a career path, and Microsoft did also "outsource" almost all of its services, but this had been a principle of mine since long before joining Microsoft.

At the GBU, I followed this principle with zeal. We hired outside services to stock our kitchens with food and drink and keep things neat. Rather than have computer techs, we kept a room full of inventory of new computers and parts; if your keyboard broke, you put it on a table in the center and took a new keyboard off a shelf—importantly, with no paperwork or other notification. We contracted with the retail chain from whom we bought computers to come in regularly, take all the broken stuff off the table, and either repair it, or junk it and replace it in our inventory. This also meant that everyone we did hire had to be able to maintain a personal computer, since we hired no one to hold their hands.

The area where my policy contrasted most sharply with Redmond's was in what was called "User Education," the production of manuals and training materials to accompany software products. This function had become established in the earliest days of Microsoft, and was hard to get rid of. It was a standard part of software companies in those days, though I had always outsourced this function at Forethought.

User Ed was by far the most uncooperative group in Redmond. They were writers and artists and editors, who mostly didn't understand our products or technology (with a few exceptions). They took forever to produce the "documentation," slowing down product development and delaying shipment, particularly of international versions. They were endlessly complaining about working too hard and not getting enough respect or enough pay; they were indeed paid a lot less than developers, but obviously at market levels for their positions. Since this one group produced the documentation for all of the applications, they could cause big problems.

Some of their managers loved building empires, and setting up elaborate rules and procedures for how they would accept work, and establishing hierarchies of internal personnel distinctions and minimum staffing levels with high overheads. These people found lots of excuses to come down to visit me, repeatedly, expecting to extend their empires to sunny California.

I would have none of it, and decided that we just would continue without any User Ed people on staff. I thought that writers and artists had very limited career paths within Microsoft, and that was much of the reason why they focused on rituals and internal status rather than on results. Again, my decision to do something different was possible only because we were a separate Business Unit and were not required to take part in the collective User Ed function shared among all other applications.

We continued like a startup. I hired the outside company Publishing Power, headed by Judith and Michael Maurier, to do all our work—the same people who had produced manuals for us at Forethought. They worked at their own offices, and eventually we also set up a large room full of equipment in our building for them to use as needed. Their principals and people were respected members of our teams. They had Microsoft "vendor" badges and email aliases, attended our most confidential meetings, got their assignments, made commitments, and delivered as agreed—all self-managed. I was relieved of almost all concern. Occasionally, a difficult choice would arise, and then Judith and I could decide what to do in a few minutes, but normally, Publishing Power just managed everything so as to meet their agreed deadlines.

Production of manuals and training is very episodic, demanding large numbers of people for crunch periods, and then many fewer people. Since Publishing Power did similar work for other companies, and had lots of freelancers on call, they could more easily respond to these varying levels, in a way that would have been impossible had we hired Microsoft employees who were on the payroll all the time.

We contracted with individual authors of computer books to write our manuals, paying good money (tens of thousands of dollars) to hire someone intellectually capable of writing a whole book, rather than trying to use a committee of a thousand drones, each one writing a paragraph, which appeared to be the method used in Redmond. This meant that our manuals actually made sense. Rather than printing the manuals as ring binders with loose pages, we printed them as slim hardbound books; the format was clear notice that we didn't intend to have to issue revised pages. We hired R. R. Donnelley to handle our printing, and Publishing Power handled the press checks for us.

The result was that we produced far better printed material than Redmond, on tightly compressed schedules that were never allowed to delay our products, and at a fraction (about one-half) the cost of the same function for our sister products in Redmond. As long as this was true, thanks to Publishing Power, my arrangements couldn't be successfully challenged.

The User Ed people in Redmond complained repeatedly to all the executives about my "failing to build up a professional User Ed group internally." The executives would say emollient things to the User Ed managers; then the same executives would say to me that they wished they could operate in Redmond the same way I did, and would urge me to keep up my policy of no User Ed in California.

There were no User Ed people as employees in the GBU when I left five years later (only one position, to manage the vendors).

126 Our First Microsoft Company Meeting

At the announcement of the acquisition to Forethought people, Jeff Raikes had said that everyone would go to the "all-hands" Microsoft company meeting in the fall, just like employees in Redmond.

That happened on 9 October 1987. I was already in Redmond (for a huge Apple presentation to Microsoft the preceding day), but everyone else flew up, and everyone stayed overnight.

Microsoft was still a young company, and an important part of the show was putting up slides (35mm slides, very possibly made by Genigraphics, or at least on Genigraphics equipment) containing the names of employees with three years of service, then five years of service, then ten years of service (Microsoft had been founded as a partnership in 1975). I was extremely impressed to see my own name among the three-year employees. Of course, I knew that all Forethought employees were to have bridged start dates with Microsoft, but it still seemed like an achievement to have gotten that message from accounting down to whoever was tasked to make the slides for the company meeting in time for my name to appear. Again, a small detail really impressed me.

Each division got some time in the meeting. In the Apps part of the show, I gave a talk about the GBU to introduce us to the rest of the company, showing photographs of our tiny building, our offices without doors (totally bizarre at Microsoft, provoking much laughter), and our recently acquired MS-standard drink dispensers.

Toward the end of the meeting, various company-wide awards were announced. Aniko Somogyi from our group received one, and we took her recognition as proving that we all were really part of Microsoft.

127 Our Silicon Valley Holidays Survive

A few months after the acquisition, I got a chance to employ ingenuity to harmonize Silicon Valley customs with Microsoft's accounting.

For as long as I could remember, all of Silicon Valley had traditionally closed down between Christmas and New Year. It wasn't possible to contact anyone on business during that period, and family members of employees were off work and planning vacations. Forethought had always closed during that week, but Microsoft had not.

There really was no chance of having people come in that week; our building was going to be empty in any case, and so I had to find some way to fit into the Microsoft payroll system.

I arranged the following scheme: Each year I counted the number of work days we wanted to close over that week that were not Microsoft holidays. The total number of hours in those days was then divided by the number of working days in November and December, giving a number like "0.543," which meant that the year-end holidays could be offset by adding a little more than half an hour to each of the other work days in the last two months of the year.

I would issue a memo to all staff saying that each employee had the choice to work a little longer (specifying half an hour, or whatever) in November and December and not come in the last week of the year, or to keep standard hours and come in that last week. This had no practical effect on salaried employees, who kept their own schedules anyway. The whole arrangement made no difference.

It had to be a real choice for hourly employees, but they were rare in our organization. They could choose to receive overtime pay for the extra few minutes a day in November and December, or to work the standard hours only; and then separately choose to also work the holiday week (and get paid), or not (and not get paid), as they wished.

My memo and arrangements covered us with the bureaucracy, at least at the lowest level of accounting, but some HR types were uncomfortable that Microsoft employees in California got a week of holidays between Christmas and New Year while Microsoft employees in Redmond did not. I thought it was no different from every international subsidiary having its own holiday schedule.

Still, I never had to get any approval for this, never had to justify it, and my practice was never questioned.

PART VII: POWERPOINT 2.0

128 First PowerPoint Review with Bill Gates

Even with all the transition activities, we didn't slow down on Color PowerPoint for Mac or on Windows PowerPoint. We had begun holding meetings about the future PowerPoint versions on the very day that we shipped version 1.0, and momentum continued through the transition.

Dennis Austin could now give full time and undivided attention to designing how color should work in PowerPoint and how 35mm slides should be supported. Tom Rudkin could do the same for the design of how PowerPoint should appear on Windows. Tom issued the first complete appearance spec on 5 October 1987—all done in Mac PowerPoint (Rudkin, Windows Appearance 1987).

It's interesting to look at now, when we've forgotten that for a long time (until 3.0), Windows used only a mono-spaced system font. Tom was also dealing with the vexing issues of how to get a Mac application written in Pascal ported to Windows, where Pascal as a development language was poorly supported. There were frequent interactions between Dennis and Tom, because the going-in assumption was now that the first Windows version would be equal to the second Mac version, so the color and 35mm designs had to work on Windows as well, and be implementable.

At the beginning, we knew that the market strategy of the next PowerPoint would be to extend our capabilities from overheads to include color 35mm slides, but no one knew exactly what that would entail—Apple had not even released the color palette manager code, for example.

We held our first real Microsoft product review in Sunnyvale on 20 October 1987, and Bill Gates came down for the half-day review.

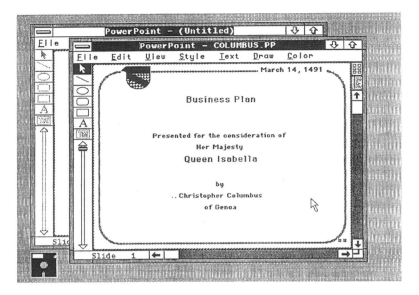

Slides in multiple document windows from first appearance specification for PowerPoint on Windows, 5 October 1987.

The extended personal review by Bill was an important event at Microsoft, because it could influence the direction of a project substantially. The next year, after Mike Maples arrived, he would hold the same kind of reviews, and much later he recalled why they were so important:

> By design, we didn't centrally control many things. We let each product team pretty much run alone. And the way that worked was that they would have phases and would report where they stood against that, but we didn't have management sign-off or fixed reviews. The deal was that Bill or I could review any product any time. We could change it or do whatever we wanted with it, but if we didn't choose to review it, they didn't stop and wait. So there would be products that for whatever reason we didn't have time to deal with, that would go from conception to shipping without ever having a management review.
>
> ... instead of having to get everybody signed off before you could go forward, at Microsoft it was that you could go forward until somebody asked you to stop. (Maples 2004)

Having Bill personally conduct a product review was traditionally thought at Microsoft to be valuable but threatening, but to us it was all value. We demonstrated the impressive amount of work that had been done since April, got Bill's feedback on it, and quizzed Bill about strategy and even about programming details.

For instance, we got a clear direction from Bill to concentrate 100% on Windows and ignore OS/2 Presentation Manager for the moment—"do that later" he said—despite the fact that much of the world was making the opposite choice. Bill thought that Presentation Manager was going to be very complex and very late, and very hard to develop for. All of that turned out to be true of Windows too, but Bill was right about the strategy. This kind of advice was hard to get.

Bill professed to think that we could ship a Windows 2.0 version of PowerPoint by October 1988, a year away. He badly wanted PowerPoint on Windows, as a demonstration of Windows capabilities and as a powerful reason to buy a new Windows PC.

Bill had talked with some senior developers working on Windows, as had we, and he'd gotten the same recommendation: that we not use Pascal on Windows. So we took a firm decision that day to recode all of PowerPoint into the C language to run on Windows, and then later port that C version back to Macintosh, to be the base of a common code version. That's what in fact happened, over the next several years, and it was good to get Bill's buy-in so early. A less-technical executive, pressed to get a Windows version shipped within a year, might easily have been tempted to take what sounded like a quicker route to try to ship first in Pascal, thinking to only later pay the tariff for conversion to C, but poor Pascal support would have torpedoed the plan.

We asked Bill about technical issues having to do with the multi-document interface in Windows, and he discussed it seriously, and then asked us to write a position paper on what we needed in Windows and send it to Tandy Trower, copy to Bill.

By the end of the day, we had agreed with Bill on what the spec for the new version should be, on Mac and on Windows.

After so many years of having PowerPoint regarded as a stepchild of doubtful worth, it was wonderful to have Bill Gates himself debating design decisions with us, gathering information we needed, advising on strategy, and urging us to get a product shipped quickly because it was so important. This was a pleasant outcome of the acquisition.

As it later turned out, we navigated a tricky course to PowerPoint 2.0, but a correct one. PowerPoint 2.0 shipped on Mac in only a year, and when it came out it kept us ahead on Mac. The very same product—an important consideration—shipped on Windows two years after that, but it was still advanced enough to put us ahead on Windows. On that base, we could produce PowerPoint 3.0 for Windows and Mac after another two years, early enough to be well ahead of all our competitors on Windows. This strategy got PowerPoint 2.0 for Mac shipped early (1988), when Mac was the battlefield, and got PowerPoint 2.0 and 3.0 for Windows shipped in 1990 and 1992, when Windows was the battlefield. A side effect was that PowerPoint on Mac was unchanged from mid-1988 to late 1992, about four years; that did undoubtedly harm the Mac product (particularly within Apple), but it was more important to dominate the vastly larger market on Windows, and that required not having our Windows version appear to lag behind our Mac version.

129 Design of Color PowerPoint 2.0 for Mac

Dennis Austin's notes on the design of PowerPoint 2.0:

> During the acquisition period, I was occupied primarily with the design of PowerPoint 2.0. We had cut a number of features to meet our schedule on the first version, and those could now be completed. The most important new feature, though, was color.
>
> A lot had happened to the Macintosh since my original spec was written. The Macintosh Plus and the Macintosh SE models were big improvements in speed and memory. More important, perhaps, they brought hard disks (SCSI interface) to the Mac world.
>
> In early 1987 the Macintosh II was announced. This was a whole new kind of Macintosh with open hardware. It had a bus architecture called NuBus and six slots to add cards. It had the 16 MHz Motorola 68020 that brought performance to equal the new Intel 386 standard. For PowerPoint, though, the key new feature was color. There were color and grayscale monitors, and the video card could display 256 colors simultaneously.
>
> The Mac II presented a big opportunity for PowerPoint because we were in a position to really showcase its color capabilities. The video card could display only 256 colors at one time (eight bits per pixel), but the card's color table could be loaded with any 256 colors. By loading the table with, say, 50 slight shades of a single color, that allowed us to display color shadings. This was unprecedented in personal computing.
>
> I started design by picking up a few art books about color. It quickly became clear to me that ordinary users, *i.e.* non-artists, would have a difficult time choosing colors for a presentation. To

help such users, I designed the color system around the use of color "schemes." The product would ship with a set of pre-configured color schemes so you could just pick a scheme instead of starting from scratch. You could still pick arbitrary colors for anything, but the schemes were a big help getting started.

... To give our color schemes the marketing sheen of artistic quality, we had them designed by Genigraphics artists and we advertised them as such. We also had background designs created as a further aid. PowerPoint 2.0 did not ship until a year after the Macintosh II, but it was the first application to take full advantage of its color capability. (Austin, Beginnings 2009)

130 Including 35mm Style in PowerPoint

Color in PowerPoint was inevitably associated with 35mm slides, an entirely different presentation format from the overhead transparencies produced by PowerPoint 1.0. This venerable format went back a long way, and had flourished with the invention of Kodachrome color film in the mid-1930s. I wrote in my analysis of 1986:

Slides in 35mm size go back to the invention of cameras for this format in the 1920's. It was discovered early that an artist's posters or drawings could be photographed in a copy stand, and the resulting slide projected for visibility by large groups. Even the slow color films available in the 1930's could be used in this way for full-color presentations. The small image size (24 x 36 mm) permitted projection optics to be much smaller and lighter than the larger "lantern slide" format previously produced directly. A variety of cartridge and tray systems were used for projection, but the 2-inch square format was standard.

In the early 1960's, Eastman Kodak introduced the "Carousel" projectors which featured a round tray with gravity feed from the top of the projector. This system displaced all others, with the result that today, 25 years later, a presenter can carry slides in a carousel anywhere in the world and be certain of finding a compatible projector at the destination. (Gaskins, PowerPoint Marketing 1986)

Now, with color, we had to decide how to create a single product that could produce presentations in both "overhead style" and "35mm style." Most of the differences that I had identified earlier seemed to be well-observed. To repeat, here was the core of the distinction:

> Whatever the historical source, today the markets and uses for overheads and 35mm slides are completely different. Video for presentations, as it begins to be used, seems to be splitting the same way into "video replacements for overheads" and "video replacements for 35mm." A computer program to make overheads should be different from a computer program to make 35mm slides in ways that go far beyond the output device drivers.

• Light Room *vs.* Darkened Room

Overheads are typically designed for presentation in a lighted room, whereas 35mm slides are typically designed for showing in a darkened room. This observation is more important than it may at first appear. In a lighted room using overheads, the human presenter is visible. There is opportunity for two-way discussion and interaction, since faces and expressions can be seen and reacted to. Documents (drawings, financial statements, site maps, contracts, ...) can be handed out for consultation and discussion. Overheads permit most of the activities of a regular business meeting to go on, with the transparencies as a device to focus attention. But in a darkened room using 35mm slides, the human presenter is very likely invisible (very few setups have light on the presenter at a podium). It is not possible to see audience reactions or requests to be recognized, so the session tends to be one-way with the audience passively listening. It is not easy to take notes or to consult documents. All eyes are on the screen, because there is nothing much else visible.

• Low *vs.* High Entertainment Value

This difference means that overheads should have a very subdued "entertainment value," and should not attract so much attention that they overshadow all else. Overheads use dark letters on a light background, visible in lighted rooms. They do not have fancy transitions (being changed by hand). The screen can be left light (without a transparency) for discussion of an extraneous point easily. The presenter will point with a hand or a pencil, casually, to points of interest. Overheads, a surprising part of the time, consist simply of word charts. Overheads have very abstract diagrams, usually schematic with simple labeled boxes and lines. Charts and graphs are as plain as will do the job. There is never a synchronized sound track, since the overheads do not constitute a performance by themselves; they accompany a meeting.

35mm slides, in contrast, need a much higher "entertainment value" so they can carry interest all by themselves—as they must, since nothing else is visible and they must be a performance on their own. They have light letters on dark backgrounds, so as not to be dazzling in a darkened room. They may have fancy transitions or fades. It is very difficult to leave the screen dark (without a slide) since then the audience is in total darkness, so extraneous points are discussed with a useless slide visible (another reason to discourage them). The presenter needs a lighted arrow pointer to point, and so usually no pointing is done. Word charts arc avoided if at all possible. Diagrams are fancier, and realistic photography will help to maintain interest. Charts and graphs are as fancy as possible—shading, three dimensions, etc.; these refinements do not add more information to the charts, but make them graphically more interesting to look at. Synchronized sound effects or narration are sometimes used.

• Meeting Size and Formality

There are other differences connected with these. Overheads are used in small group meetings, where discussion is possible. Indeed, overheads are frequently used in a one-on-one meeting, where they are not projected at all but just turned over in sequence for discussion. Thus, the overhead merges with the flip chart for single-person sales presentations.

As a group gets too large to support discussion, then using 35mm slides in a darkened room serves to control audience interference—slide show first, questions or discussion later. Overheads are not sufficiently formal for a really large group, whereas 35mm slides are pretentious shown to a single person (unless photography is required for information value).

In sum, overheads are usually used in situations where the audience is asked to concentrate on the information, and not to be awed by artistry. 35mm slides are usually used in situations where the audience should appreciate the artistic sophistication of the presentation as well as its content.

(There are, of course, exceptions to the generalizations made above, but upon close inspection these often support the distinction. "Overhead" material will sometimes be reshot onto 35mm slides for better visibility in a moderately large company meeting, without changing its essential character. "35mm" material will sometimes be reproduced onto overhead foils for presentation in a small conference room without 35mm projection equipment, or where a lighted room is required. The distinction between the two styles of use is not exactly coextensive with the distinction between the transparency sizes, but it is surprisingly close.) (Gaskins, PowerPoint Marketing 1986)

131 How Can 35mm Slides Be Made by Amateurs?

I had set aside 35mm slides in my planning for PowerPoint 1.0; this was partly on the grounds that they were prepared by professional producers, far from the content originator, using expensive equipment not suitable for offices, and that the content originator would continue to need professional assistance.

Now, I had to reconsider those ideas. Was there a way to increase the graphic sophistication of PowerPoint so that non-artists could produce adequate results? That would be necessary if PowerPoint were to be extended to 35mm slides. Otherwise, it would make more sense to produce two products: one product for the content originator, which could be used to "sketch out" the content for a presentation (much like PowerPoint 1.0, in fact), and a second product for professional producers, which they could use to "finish" the sketch received, for final presentation. I actually had some consulting analysis done, and the resulting report recommended splitting into two products: PowerPoint for business people, and a new "PowerPoint Pro" for corporate producers and service bureau producers such as Genigraphics.

But I didn't want to limit PowerPoint to be a product for amateurs making mostly overheads for "informal" presentations, and create a new second product for professionals to finish 35mm slides for "formal" presentations, because of some very simple observations. There are many more "informal" presentations made, but much less money is spent on them. There is much more money spent on "formal" presentations, but there are considerably fewer of them. So an "informal-only" product would address a much smaller market in terms of dollars, and a "formal-only" product would address a much smaller market in terms of users. A better product would do both; once it had been learned, it could be used to make both the very common informal presentations and the very valuable formal presentations. Better still, we could try to allow users to "re-purpose" presentations from one format to the other, so that material originally prepared for overheads could be easily re-used when a formal occasion demanding 35mm color slides arose.

With that decision taken, I had to solve the problems of adding 35mm slides.

The production of 35mm slides would remain expensive and difficult. Every other week, we were being visited by startups working on "desktop film recorders," which were computer peripherals, costing a few thousand dollars, that could be loaded with a roll of 35mm film (the same film as went in a 35mm camera), and then addressed like a printer to expose up to 36 frames of presentation visuals. This process was typically fairly slow, but the real problem came when the film was removed from the film recorder; now the exposed roll of film had to be taken to a processing lab and developed, using wet chemicals with very tight tolerances for temperature and contamination (tighter than generally used for processing consumer snapshots), and then the individual frames had to be cut up and mounted in 2-inch mounts. Even large companies seldom had such labs. All this struck me as implausible for PowerPoint customers.

But I had identified one good way around this: finding a way to transmit presentation files to a remote service bureau, where all the exposing and processing and mounting of film could be handled remotely on high-volume equipment. That hint turned out to be the solution to the "film recorder" problem.

Here's the starting point, from the 1986 analysis, that presented the problems to be solved:

> Overheads are almost always prepared by the person who will give the presentation or by an immediate staff member in the same department. It is extremely uncommon for overheads to be prepared by a centralized corporate graphics service department. And, even if a centralized service were willing, they would almost always be too slow; most overheads are made hurriedly, within a day of their being used, and copied to transparency film on office copiers. Color would be useful, but is seldom used since copiers do not copy in color. Thus, the layout and artistic quality of overheads is almost always in the hands of amateurs who have little knowledge of effective presentation styles, no graphics training, and very poor tools.
>
> 35mm slides are more often prepared by a corporate- or division-level graphics service department. It will take some time to make them and process them anyway, so there is more advance

planning. As befits a larger event at which they will be the center of attention, the slides are very frequently designed by professional artists and illustrators working from rough ideas submitted by the presenter. Color is mandatory. These people have very good (often expensive) equipment, and their work takes time. So 35mm slides must be planned well in advance, and cannot be easily changed at the last minute.

Implications of the Differences

For marketing purposes, the vital distinction seems to be that 35mm slides are produced by graphics arts specialists (corporate departments or independent producers) for clients, whereas overheads are produced by the clients themselves. Moreover, because 35mm slides are used for large audiences, where the slides will be the center of attention, the presenter will continue to need the help of professionals who know about graphics.

This means that for personal computer systems to prepare 35mm slides, the customer is a graphic arts department or production company. For personal computer systems to prepare overhead transparencies, the customer is the department or company which originates the content and makes the presentation.

The graphics department has artists who know a lot about graphics, but not much about personal computers. Quality is often more important to them than speed or flexibility. They will redraw everything (probably in fancy shaded three-dimensional perspective) anyway, so compatibility with other programs is unimportant.

Personal computer products for the graphics department to use are the lower-cost relatives of the software and hardware used to make animated video sequences (like Super Bowl introductions). They give the artist good control, but are relatively hard to use. They are often sold as expensive dedicated hardware and software workstations, sometimes by the same people (*e.g.*, Genigraphics) who sell complete production services themselves. This is really a vertical niche application.

A personal computer system designed for use by the content originator to directly prepare overheads obviously has very different qualities. For instance, compatibility with standard personal computer hardware and environments is crucial. The content originator already knows how to use any other programs from which data may come, and does not want to re-enter it. The graphic sophistication of charts and graphs generated by personal computer programs is appropriate to overheads. Saving time, making last-minute changes, and retaining control are most important.

Laser printers for overheads can be used for many other purposes as well (word processing, page layout, forms, ...) so chances are good that such a printer either exists in the department already or can be justified for these multiple purposes. In any case, a PostScript/Interpress laser printer costs about $6,000, heading rapidly for $2,000-$3,000.

(For imaging 35mm slides, the cost of devices will continue to be a problem: an adequate film recorder is about $8,000 plus $2,000 for a PostScript/Interpress interface. This $10,000 peripheral can be used only for making 35mm slides, an amount very hard to justify except for the graphic arts department. One way around this difficulty would be service bureaus which would receive presentation files on disk or via communications lines and return finished slides.)

A program intended to be used by a manager or a secretary as a replacement for a typewriter as a way to make overheads should not require very much artistic ability. These people do very little with graphics now, and do not have the time nor the training to do much more. They will want to begin, at least, by doing a neater and easier job of what they have done before. (Gaskins, PowerPoint Marketing 1986)

132 Looking for Genigraphics, and Vice Versa

In the earlier analysis quoted just above, I had written:

35mm slides are usually used in situations where the audience should appreciate the artistic sophistication of the presentation as well as its content.

and:

... because 35mm slides are used for large audiences, where the slides will be the center of attention, the presenter will continue to need the help of professionals who know about graphics.

and:

For imaging 35mm slides, the cost of devices will continue to be a problem ... . One way around this difficulty would be service bureaus which would receive presentation files on disk or via communications lines and return finished slides. (Gaskins, PowerPoint Marketing 1986)

As I thought about this situation, I concluded that we needed to find a source for professional graphics expertise needed for 35mm slides. Perhaps some of this knowledge could be built into PowerPoint, increasing the range of graphics sophistication that we could produce. But the "help of professionals" and the physical production of slides would require a partner who could provide services to our customers to complement the PowerPoint product.

It didn't take much thought to identify such a partner. There was a national company called Genigraphics, whose name was a household word (or at least a "business-office word") for stunning 35mm slide presentations, and surely, they would be the place to begin looking. Genigraphics wouldn't have been interested in a tiny startup, but now—I realized—we had emerged from our chrysalis and had become Microsoft. Microsoft should be able to interest Genigraphics in some kind of cooperation in which we would produce the software products, and Genigraphics would provide complementary services needed by PowerPoint customers. The combination of our products and their services would solve the problem that 35mm slides needed artistic knowledge and sophistication, and also needed expensive equipment and caustic chemicals.

As soon as the acquisition occurred, I had begun using more consulting from Darrell Boyle, once Forethought's first VP of Marketing, and now an independent consultant on "desktop presentations." So I very early asked Darrell to carry out an informal "due diligence" to establish that Genigraphics really was the market leader, really did have the organization we thought they had, and really did produce high customer satisfaction. Darrell contacted their large customers and some competing producers and reported that it was all true, Genigraphics was the obvious choice, and there wasn't a good second choice.

So I began to try to figure out this partnership and how to interest Genigraphics in joining it.

Unknown to me, at the same time Genigraphics was looking for me. Michael Beetner, who was Director of Marketing Planning for the Genigraphics headquarters in Syracuse, New York, had been spending a lot of time in Silicon Valley, looking for a business partner. He had made progress with both Apple and Adobe, but neither of those companies saw Genigraphics as really central to their strategies, and neither wanted to commit to a serious partnership.

Michael recalls that on 5 October 1987, he attended a Microsoft press conference in Silicon Valley. At the end, he went up to Jeff Raikes and asked who he should talk to about partnering with Microsoft for presentations; Jeff gave Michael my name and phone number.

Michael wrote to me much later:

> I called, and I was surprised to get through on the first call. When I suggested a meeting, you said yes, and we agreed to meet later that day. For the first time in Silicon Valley, I had found the right person and he wanted to talk. I couldn't believe my luck. I had second thoughts when I showed up at the Sunnyvale location. This did not look like a Microsoft building where the person in charge of presentation graphics would be housed. I was also amazed that you were developing on the Mac. But that all faded as we began to talk. I was very impressed by the knowledge of presentation graphics you displayed.

When we met that afternoon, Michael gave me some basic background. Genigraphics, he said, had been a spin-out from General Electric's Aerospace Electronic Systems Division, the group that had developed flight view simulations for NASA astronauts. They used their own equipment to make slides to pitch their services to other government agencies, and then decided to go into the business of making pitches in the early 1970s. There had been a leveraged buy-out in 1982. In the preceding year, 1986, Genigraphics had done about $75 million in revenue: 50% from service bureaus, 25 of them, in all major cities of the U.S., with headquarters in Manhattan; and 50% from selling computer-based workstations and film recorders, developed and manufactured in Syracuse, New York. They had about 140 full-time artists on staff, plus freelancers for peak periods. They had developed some difficult high-end capabilities, such as the ability to match Pantone PMS colors exactly, with a license from Pantone; I could appreciate the importance of this for meeting corporate identity standards.

Genigraphics thought that it was probably the only profitable competitor in its industry. The years 1986 and 1987 had seen a storm of acquisitions and consolidations among everyone in the industry. Life wasn't easy for anyone.

For that reason, Genigraphics was already interested in figuring out how to work with personal computers. They were building cards to connect their film recorders to DEC Vaxes, to IBM PC AT's, and to Mac NuBus machines, but the recorders were far too expensive to sell as peripherals in large quantities. They would like to have a way to accept work for creation or enhancement from personal computers over dial-in modems, but were short of software know-how.

I hadn't prepared anything for our unexpected meeting, but Michael and I got along so well that afternoon that we quickly sketched out ways to cooperate on the spot. Genigraphics certainly could produce slides from PowerPoint presentations, if I could help them to get software developed. Apple was promising a CD-ROM drive for Macintosh, and when they shipped it, we could develop a collection of Genigraphics' symbols (clip art) on a CD. Whatever we decided to do, we could announce our plan at the MacWorld conference in January, just three months away. It was a lot of progress for an initial conversation. I invited Michael to come back for another meeting very soon.

133 Genigraphics: First Contact

My first premeditated meeting with Genigraphics was two weeks later, 17 November 1987. As Michael had astutely noticed, the Graphics Business Unit didn't cut much of a figure in the old Forethought offices in Sunnyvale, all ten people of us. I realized that lack, and I thought a proposal would have more appeal if presented with a backdrop of the sprawling Microsoft campus in Redmond. So I reserved a nice conference room in Redmond and invited Michael to visit the Microsoft HQ for a meeting there.

I had decided to close the deal, because the longer I looked around, the more I became convinced that Genigraphics was the only possible partner. It turned out that Genigraphics' customer list included just about every Fortune 500 company, every federal government agency (including the military), every large foundation or thinktank, and every university in the country. The name "Genigraphics" was widely recognized as a synonym for high-quality presentations and many corporations actually had a "Genigraphics Department," where their own employees made executive presentations using consoles and film recorders bought from and serviced by Genigraphics.

I had prepared an extraordinarily detailed 24-slide overhead presentation for Michael, and I went through it at high intensity. I covered Microsoft's commitment to the presentation market and strategies for

Apple future hardware, with Microsoft Windows clearly waiting to come on stage next.

I proposed a detailed partnership based on what I then believed (this is from the presentation I made that day):

Shared Vision of the Future

- **PCs originate most presentations**

- **PCs communicate with workstations and producers**

- **PCs do not replace professional people or equipment**

I retained for a year or so this opinion that content originators would use PCs to begin a very formal presentation for a large audience, then turn the PowerPoint file over to professionals to finish it up. Presumably, I thought this because it was the way 35mm slide shows had been made in the past, using paper for the rough input. The Power-Point-to-Genigraphics connection was designed purposely to make it easy for artists at Genigraphics to provide improvements and final polish. It took a while before it became clear that PowerPoint could provide all the polish that most presenters wanted to pay for.

I declared that Microsoft's strategy was to completely ignore the emerging "desktop film recorder" manufacturers, who were seen as a major threat by Genigraphics, and instead to recommend to our PowerPoint customers "one or more" national service bureaus. I had already connected Tom Evslin, of Solutions, Inc. in Vermont, with the engineers at Genigraphics' organization nearby in upstate New York, and I had in my hand a concrete proposal from Tom to write the driver software and communications software that Genigraphics would need—software to be owned by Genigraphics, and open to work with any application, not just PowerPoint.

Then, I had three specific proposals:

1. Immediate arrangements to permit existing PowerPoint 1.0 users to submit presentation files as input for Genigraphics' manual preparation of visuals;

2. Careful arrangements to insure that the new PowerPoint 2.0 and new Genigraphics services would work together flawlessly, for enhancement and for imaging, and then extensive marketing of the combined result;

3. Improvement of the Microsoft/Genigraphics connection by providing a way for PowerPoint users to access and visualize the Geni-

graphics symbol libraries while composing presentations [this was the "clip art collection on CD-ROM" idea].

Proposal 1 was merely to give users of (black and white) PowerPoint 1.0 a template which resembled the paper "layout sheets" that Genigraphics gave its customers, on which their customers would hand-draw a rough sketch of a slide and write below it the Genigraphics colors and "symbols" (clip art) and type spec to be used, along with the text for the slide. Users would fill out copies of this template, one page per slide (like a notes page), and fax or send the sheets to Genigraphics. So PowerPoint would be used just to simplify and improve the existing process of submitting rough drafts for creation of slides by artists operating Genigraphics workstations.

Proposal 2 was a plan that, when color PowerPoint 2.0 shipped six months later (May 1988), we would incorporate Genigraphics colors into PowerPoint, and insert a command to send a completed Power-Point presentation to Genigraphics over a modem for further enhancement and/or imaging. At that point, we still all imagined that what could be done in PowerPoint on a Mac would be a subset of the "professional" effects that could be produced using Genigraphics' own high-end workstations. So it would "always" be true that Genigraphics' native product would be a big step above what could be achieved by direct imaging from PowerPoint. But because PowerPoint 2.0 would use exactly the same colors as the Genigraphics palette, and much else in common, slides imaged from PowerPoint could be mixed in a single presentation alongside slides from Genigraphics consoles.

Finally, proposal 3 was my plan to leverage the great collection of clip art (called "symbols") that had been built up in the two dozen service centers by the hundreds of artists who had produced tens of thousands of presentations. This collection was re-used casually inside Genigraphics, but I proposed to gather it all, arrange it in neat categories, and sell it as a jointly labeled Microsoft product on CD-ROM (taking advantage of a CD drive to be added to Mac soon). Users could insert Genigraphics' art within PowerPoint, with the revenue from selling the CD-ROM to be split between Genigraphics and Microsoft.

I suggested that Microsoft could feature Genigraphics in our advertising, both consumer and industry; could feature Genigraphics in our PR for the release of PowerPoint 2.0; could identify Genigraphics specifically on the PowerPoint box (a real first); could provide Genigraphics with demo stations at computer trade shows; could promote Genigraphics services in direct mail to our user base and to dealers; could feature Genigraphics in our user newsletters; could hold joint training seminars for leading computer dealers; and could make joint sales calls on corporate accounts.

This would be "a partnership of joint interests." The PowerPoint software interfaces would be documented and available for use by other services. Genigraphics drivers would be owned by Genigraphics, would observe Apple or Microsoft standards, and would work equally with any competitor's software. There would be no technical "lock-in" in either direction. Exclusivity would last only as long as it benefitted both parties. Each party would pay for developing its own capabilities, which it would solely own, with no other payments in either direction.

I said all that and more, pretty much in one single breath. At the end, I asked Michael what he thought of the idea. His response was, "I'm hyperventilating." He asked for a copy of my overheads.

Much later, Michael explained to me about how long he had been searching unsuccessfully for a real partnership in Silicon Valley, with repeated disappointments until then:

> I had talked to people at Harvard Graphics and others who regarded me as someone who could offer them more kick-back money for each slide imaged with our film recorders. They showed no interest in doing anything for the user, but rather how to make another buck for themselves. This is why I was hyperventilating after the meeting in Redmond. I knew that what people back in Syracuse expected, at most, was an imaging agreement that was too costly. After our meeting, I was afraid that no one would believe me, so I asked for your presentation slides, which I took back to Syracuse where I reproduced your presentation as closely as I could. They still thought that I must be exaggerating.

Although I didn't know it, Genigraphics as a company had already become convinced that PCs were essential to their future business and were prepared to move, and this was just what they were looking for.

A week later, Michael called me in California. He had made a presentation to the President and the VPs of Genigraphics, and the result had been a decision to elevate this project to the corporate #1 priority. Genigraphics' VP of Engineering had been tasked to lead the project on their side. They would like to host our next meeting on 10 December 1987, at the headquarters of their Network Services (the service bureau division), in Manhattan, Third Avenue at 47th Street.

I said I'd be there.

134 Immediate Agreement with Genigraphics

I went to New York City with Dennis Austin for the second Genigraphics meeting on 10 December 1987. I also had Tom Evslin there, ready to take immediate decisions on the software he could develop for Genigraphics. Genigraphics had fielded a complete team of marketing and engineering people from Syracuse, and for the first time, I met the President of Genigraphics' Network Services Division, Sandy (Sandra) Beetner. (Genigraphics had two divisions, each with a President; the other division was in Syracuse and handled the hardware production and sales. Sandy Beetner and Michael Beetner were/are married.) Sandy was extremely smart and knew everything about her business, from the smallest details of operations to the largest strategy issues; she rapidly became my main resource.

Sandy Beetner explained very concretely why she was convinced that Genigraphics needed to get involved with presentations on personal computers. Previously, most Genigraphics sales had been made by working with a central communications group in a large corporation, to whom the presenter gave the rough input. But now, "well over half" of the sales of her division were made by working directly with someone in an end-user department in a corporation—such as finance, legal, or sales—rather than with someone in the corporate communications group. It seemed clear that individual presenters were gaining control over the presentation function. This was a profound insight, and, needless to say, was music to my ears. I had no way to know about that change before Sandy told me, but it accurately signaled the rise of PowerPoint.

We rapidly agreed to formally sign an agreement to cooperate immediately, and agreed on the outlines of what to do for PowerPoint 1.0 and PowerPoint 2.0. We agreed to evangelize Apple on the importance of the deal, and to announce at MacWorld in the middle of January, just a month later (and a month with both Christmas and New Year in it!).

After the meeting, we negotiated the "Joint Marketing and Development Agreement" by faxing drafts back and forth and discussing them on telephone conference calls. I sent a draft to Microsoft legal to get help and advice, and got good feedback, but not a replacement document full of legalese; Genigraphics was equally flexible. We exchanged signed contracts late on Christmas Eve, 24 December 1987, and we all went home for the holidays. As usual, I signed for Microsoft with my "Director and General Manager" title.

The basic terms of the agreement provided that Microsoft would supply guidance in the design of drivers and imaging software, and that Genigraphics would develop and own this software. Microsoft agreed to bundle the Genigraphics driver with PowerPoint, and Genigraphics agreed to permit us to do so at no charge. This was an exclusive arrangement, which we would not extend to any other presentation services company and Genigraphics would not extend to any other microcomputer software company. Genigraphics could distribute its driver through other channels, but not bundled in other people's boxes; Microsoft could inform customers of other services, but not bundle their drivers in our boxes. Microsoft and Genigraphics would each promote the other as the vendor of choice, and would cooperate on sales calls in the many large accounts which we had in common. All of this covered Macintosh, Windows, and Presentation Manager on the same basis.

We got everything done for the announcement, and held our PR conference alongside MacWorld in San Francisco on 14 January 1988. Genigraphics was represented in force, including Sandy Beetner in person. That evening, I entertained the Genigraphics folks at Cafe Majestic in San Francisco, in those days a gracious traditional Victorian dining room with trendy food, returning the favor of a good dinner they'd given me in Manhattan in December at The Box Tree restaurant. The formal announcement was 15 January, and our public partnership with Genigraphics had begun.

In these early steps, before we knew each other well, I think that both parties had the same motivation: to create the impression that the combination of Microsoft, the leader in PC software, and Genigraphics, the leader in presentations, had created the most powerful force in presentations on personal computers, and that our partnership would dominate. That impression would be useful, even if nothing else could be achieved. This was a realistic attitude to begin with, but the partnership would turn out to be far more important than even I, and I think they, appreciated at the announcement.

135 Real Work Begins with Genigraphics

During early 1988, we continued to meet with Genigraphics people, but now more often with people working in the Santa Clara service bureau location. These people really knew a lot about presentations and the people who made them. I had thought that I knew about presentations, but Genigraphics' experience was on a scale I'd never imagined: they told us about one recent presentation they'd made for an aerospace company, not at all unusual, for which they had billed $249,000 over six weeks for the one presentation, and which had involved over 3,000 revisions. I believed them, even though I couldn't imagine such revisions (it was probably a logged count of total file changes to many slides, involving a lot of trial and error because there was no way to work visually, rather than entirely customer alterations).

Moreover, Genigraphics turned out to have lots of really smart people, who fit well into working with Microsoft. Genigraphics was used to working under pressure. They ran their service bureaus around the clock, 365 days a year, and were used to working overnight for an early morning deadline. They were used to having CEOs stumble in on Christmas Eve needing a presentation for three days later, and they always delivered.

Genigraphics had worked with thousands of high-level presentation users, in essentially all the large corporations, all the government agencies, all the universities and influential non-profits, and had learned from them what the market demanded—experience that we lacked.

Genigraphics had their hardware business that sold very expensive equipment and software to buyers who had serious presentation requirements, and so got detailed feedback on desired product features. They also had their service bureaus, in which account executives dealt with ad agencies, publishers, PR agencies, and the like, as well as with the business people who were the ultimate presenters. This business was a back-and-forth, in which Genigraphics learned a lot about presentation style from thousands of designers, and then proposed variants of what they had learned to thousands of clients. A lot of the knowledge about presentations stuck with Genigraphics people, both the account executives and the artists.

I had initially pushed for the Genigraphics partnership based on their reputation and name recognition among customers, thinking that each of us could gain in perceived importance from the other's stature. Very soon, though, I started to realize that we both had a lot of substance that we could learn from each other.

For instance, Genigraphics had a tradition of totally custom work for hire, based on using a high-level account executive to elicit the requirements of each individual engagement, then using experienced artists who could draw on a broad background of ideas. They had no experience in the marketing of standardized products. They could perhaps learn from Microsoft's experience with devising standard packages with no custom options, to be sold to "retail" customers in large volumes at lower prices. They also had very limited engineering knowledge of the personal computer world, so we could help them with strategic decisions, and we could help find consultants to provide the software they needed and to educate their own engineers.

In the other direction, the influence of Genigraphics on PowerPoint has been largely under-appreciated. Microsoft had a lot to learn from Genigraphics about presentations and presenters, at the level of the higher production values associated with Genigraphics. As we realized this, we moved fast to polish up our design for Color PowerPoint.

Time was very short before we intended to ship PowerPoint 2.0 (it shipped in May 1988). But even in the short time available, a very few weeks, we managed to learn enough to incorporate the standard "palette" of colors that had evolved on Genigraphics workstations, and backgrounds based on successful Genigraphics designs, and "spaced color backgrounds"—where a color appears to shade continuously lighter or darker, or from one color to another, a very distinctive feature of Genigraphics style. Some details, such as assuring that the titles and bullet points had harmonizing colors and that they contrasted properly with the new color backgrounds, would be handled automatically, using the semantics built into the color "schemes" devised by Dennis Austin. We also shipped sample presentations made by Genigraphics. Genigraphics artists at the service bureau generated most of this for us, but we also talked to engineering people back in Syracuse about technical details for our software, such as exactly how to specify colors to get the best results from Genigraphics' own film recorders.

We spent a lot of additional effort on delivering what we'd announced for PowerPoint 1.0, which was basically a way to send black and white PowerPoint files as roughs to a Genigraphics service bureau, where the slides would be manually re-created on Genigraphics' workstations, imaged, and returned—a large amount of work. Customers were enthusiastic, but leaped ahead of us and wanted more. PowerPoint customers began showing up at Genigraphics service bureaus with black-and-white PowerPoint 1.0 files on diskettes, expecting what we were working on for PowerPoint 2.0—some sort of computer magic that would turn those files into professional color 35mm slides while they waited. What they really wanted was 35mm slides directly from PowerPoint.

136 A Blind Spot in My Understanding of Genigraphics

While both Microsoft and Genigraphics were learning a lot by working together, there was one curious blind spot that we shared. This would not become apparent for a couple of years, but it was definitely there from the beginning.

In that initial presentation in Redmond to Michael Beetner, I had put up a diagram showing with a fat arrow how PowerPoint would expand from "Desktop Laser Overheads" upward to include "Desktop Color 35mm Slides," but I had a thick line separating off a still-higher level of "Professional Producers," such as Genigraphics.

I believed that PowerPoint would be able to make presentations of very good quality, but I had a superstitious belief that Genigraphics would always be able to produce a higher quality, the ultimate. It wasn't only me; when I debriefed the Microsoft product manager who had been working on an internal product spec prior to the acquisition, she explained to me how "desktop presentations" would occupy a lower quality level than "Genigraphics," which she also used as the name for the top quality possible (this was well before I had opened negotiations with Genigraphics, a development she never knew about).

I certainly thought that the Genigraphics folks had the same deep belief, that amateurs at personal computers could never compete with professional artists at custom workstations, and that large corporations would always want top-tier quality from Genigraphics. So we had the twin ideas that we would send the complete PowerPoint native files to Genigraphics so that an artist could improve them in PowerPoint, and that we would have such high compatibility that slides imaged from PowerPoint could be projected alongside other slides made entirely on Genigraphics consoles—actually, a very stringent requirement.

Indeed, the belief that Genigraphics would always represent ultimate quality was part of the motivation for our partnership, to associate the dominant companies in the two different realms.

There was plenty of excuse for Genigraphics people to believe this, but I should have seen the future more clearly.

The Genigraphics professional workstations were examples of the "indirect" creation methods which I had been denouncing for years as ready to be carried out to the ash heap of history. An "operator" entered various parameters and content, and then there was a separate "render" step before the operator saw any result. If anyone should have known that this model wouldn't last, it was I.

Here's what a Genigraphics workstation looked like. This is an early model 100, from 1976. The first photo and its description come from a SIGGRAPH paper written by an engineer from "Computed Image Systems and Services" of General Electric in Syracuse, New York. The two subsequent photos show the evolved workstation model 100B.

The Basic Genigraphics System Configuration [1976].

The basic system is composed of three elements: the Artist's Console, the Graphics Processor, and the High Resolution Recorder. See [above].

The Artist's Console consists of a full-color CRT monitor, solid-state raster display hardware, and a wide variety of input devices: an alphanumeric keyboard, two joysticks, five rate knobs, and an array of lighted and unlighted pushbuttons and switches arranged to facilitate the intuitive manipulation of graphic design elements. The Graphics Processor is a 16-bit minicomputer with a 28 kiloword core memory, a high-density, movable head disk for program storage and two magnetic tapes or diskettes for artwork storage. The High Resolution Recorder consists of a 4,000 line monochromatic CRT, a 6-sector color wheel, a 35mm camera, and the camera and image control circuitry. (Morland 1976)

Two Genigraphics 100B Interactive Workstations, operated at Genigraphics Service Centers by (top) DeAnna Foran in Oakbrook, IL, and (bottom) Preston Stuart in New York, NY. Photos courtesy of (top) DeAnna Foran, 2009, and (bottom) Abby Weissman, 1982. Copyright 2012 by The Genigraphics Arts Society, used by permission.

Here's a description of the process of "operating" a Genigraphics work-station:

> To produce 35mm slides on the Genigraphics system, the opera-tor created the slide information (bar chart, line graph, pie chart or graphics and background artwork) without actually viewing this on the screen. The slide would be created in full and then the screen was "regenerated." *It took about a minute for the screen to regenerate and produce the visual representation of the slide.* The textual and other non-graphic input was sent to the processor with a set of commands (x,y coordinates etc.). Vector artwork was generated by dropping a set of vertices on the screen using a pen, tablet and "puck" (a three button box operated with the free hand). Whilst drawing your graphic by dropping the vertices on the screen, a pink wireframe with the vertices as small squares would show you where each plotted point would be. Fill colors and borders were then plotted to the finished vector. The back-ground could be gradated from one color to a second color ... to reproduce a very smooth graduation effect.
>
> Once finished and saved to the floppy, a slide was then "im-aged" onto 35mm transparency via an electronic rostrum camera. A batch file on the VAX minicomputer would then send the imag-es to the camera one at a time. It took about 2 minutes to produce a 2000 line resolution slide. It was also possible to mix traditional media (slide text photographed on a manual rostrum via litho film negatives) and the background "double-exposed" over the text via the Genigraphics system. This saved time when slide presentations were in a hurry (as they usually were!). (Wikipedia 2011, s.v. Genigraphics, emphasis supplied)

I had a view of future PowerPoint capabilities that was clear enough to be absolutely certain that PowerPoint was going to be a better way to work, I had understood it for several years, and I explained it to every-one, including our Genigraphics partners.

So I should have been super-clear on the fact that there would never be another generation of the Genigraphics hardware workstations—that they would be surpassed by personal computers, just as I had been predicting would happen to all kinds of special-purpose computer-based workstations. If Genigraphics had believed that, then they could have foreseen that such a step would leave their service bureaus without a source of internal hardware, forcing them to adopt personal comput-ers for their artists to use. When both these steps later happened—

when first the workstation division went out of business, and then the service bureau division adopted Mac and Windows machines running PowerPoint—I wasn't surprised. But I should have been able to predict them both from the very beginning.

I should have seen clearly that PowerPoint would be able, eventually, to equal or exceed the quality produced by the Genigraphics artists, especially if some of their own design knowledge could be incorporated into styles and templates and clip art. There might well be good reasons still to employ artists (in-house or consultants) for design and creativity, but, just for the mechanics of making slides, there was no reason to expect there would be a quality level higher than that of PowerPoint.

But for some reason, we didn't understand the implications of this so clearly at the time. Apart from all our day-to-day execution work together, people from the GBU (always including me) and from Genigraphics got together every quarter or so for strategy sessions. We did notice from the beginning that we were having trouble in clearly defining what high-value services Genigraphics was going to provide alongside PowerPoint, but we all assumed that we would come up with the answers given more time.

137 Reflections from the Apps Division Staff Retreat

On 4–7 March 1988, I attended my first Applications Division Staff Retreat, apparently an annual custom. This was the senior people from the division, about a dozen people out of a total headcount of 150 or so, plus Bill Gates and Jon Shirley. Everybody traveled to an old Victorian house on the rainy Washington coast, and spent the entire weekend there, with dormitory accommodations in the bedrooms. Almost every hour was scheduled with presentations followed by discussions.

The weekend began with long presentations about each of our major competitors: IBM, Lotus, Ashton-Tate, WordPerfect, Borland, plus shorter takes on Aldus, Symantec, and Claris, for which the designated speaker had done some research to document each competitor's product line and product strategy. Microsoft encouraged an attitude of paranoia toward competitors, and in many cases this was fully justified, because competitors were outselling our applications on the MS-DOS platform.

A basic observation was that all the competitors were doing Mac products, as we were, and all were then planning to do OS/2 Presentation Manager ("PM") next. The Microsoft strategy was to address Windows on 386s next, based on Bill's view that PM would be late and difficult and would drag competitors down with it, at least for a while—there was time to address that later, as necessary. Not everyone agreed there would be time, but everyone agreed on Windows first. Bill agreed it was important to be early on PM, but still thought we'd have time. "Over the next eighteen months, our uniqueness in the marketplace will hinge on Windows." This debate, at every application software company, was the central mystery of the age. Prior to the later overwhelming success of Windows and Windows applications, and the demise of OS/2 PM, it wasn't at all obvious to decide. Even with Bill coordinating both Systems and Apps, it was not easy to achieve a unified strategy. Bill mentioned a future new version of Windows (possibly to be called Windows 3.0?), with a projected ship in early 1989. At this same meeting, Jon Shirley observed that there was not enough support for Windows in the Systems Division, and not enough support for PM in the Apps Division.

There were overviews of the Division's business. Apps then constituted about 40% of Microsoft's total revenue, including "OEM" sales to manufacturers for bundling with computers, which were small for Apps. In the U.S., 50% of the revenue was Mac products (worldwide, about 30%). Apps total sales were up 80% over the previous year.

Jon Shirley was, as always, a breath of fresh air. He sharply criticized the frantic marketing programs and plans, and recommended doing less marketing, especially suggesting that we should cut down on "margin-funded marketing." Specifically, Jon pointed out that it was better to "not sell the extra units and miss forecasts than to put in the marketing effort to just break even." He added "Shirley's Theorem": "There is no way to succeed with a bad product; it is okay to screw up a lot with a good product." He suggested the alternative strategy of shipping better products, pointing out that "WordPerfect established leadership when Word was really poor."

Much of this group was from Apps marketing, so there wasn't universal agreement. But I had already seen the same thing: endless complex and often poorly executed marketing programs, which dragged down profitability without much other effect, because of all the compromises in product quality among our other applications. But I doubted that Jon's advice would have much effect.

Bill tossed in the tidbit that mice might at that time be selling with as many as 20% of current personal computer sales, not counting the huge installed base. "Eighty-four percent of PC Excel users have mice." It's hard now to recall a world in which we were trying to sell graphical UI applications, and yet 80% of personal computers were being sold with no pointing device at all.

One group went off to brainstorm strategies for success, and came back with a list, on which the first item was "Establish a new category," and the second was "Be first when the platform changes." That sounded encouraging for PowerPoint.

In discussing another strategy report, Bill underscored that he supported an Apps strategy of "superior solutions"; "we have to be the best in each individual category," so we had to continue to invest in every one. Jon Shirley objected that, while that was a good strategy, it made a poor plan, because we didn't have the resources to achieve it. Bill agreed that the strategy wasn't realistic, because Apps development was understaffed by at least a factor of two; if we couldn't do better, we'd have to change the strategy. He suggested increasing R&D expense to 18% of sales (at the time it was about 14% for the Apps Division).

I came away from this immersion in the Apps Division internals with an intensified feeling that our Graphics Business Unit didn't work in the same way as Apps expected, but I liked our practices better.

138 Permanent Home for the Graphics Business Unit

At the internal announcement of the acquisition on 9 July 1987, Jon Shirley had said to the group that a year from then, there would be more people in the GBU than were in all of Forethought at the acquisition, and so within a year, we would need to move to a larger building in our area.

I took that seriously. Our old building was about 6,000 square feet, and our recruiting goals for the first year would more than fill it. I also thought that the poor quality of our facilities, especially the lack of truly private offices with effective sound isolation, had caused inefficiency, so it was important to do much better.

I actually started meeting with our local real estate agents on 20 August 1987, just a month or so later, to get the search underway. Rather than relying on the facilities group in Redmond, however good they might be, I planned to continue to use the same local agents who had helped us under the economic constraints of a startup, Rod Gilles and Jack Troedson of Cornish and Carey, and they came through for me. We kept in touch with the facilities group in Redmond, and we found it to be extremely easy to involve them a little bit without actually surrendering any control to them, so long as we took all the initiative and did all the work ourselves.

Beginning in November, we searched the local real estate market systematically for a suitable location. Our problem was simple, but difficult to solve: we were small now, but we wanted expansion room to grow substantially. We wanted to establish a Microsoft presence, and not have to move repeatedly as we grew. Yet, it was impossible to economically justify holding and paying for large amounts of unused space in an expensive market like ours.

We looked at a number of sites around the Palo Alto area; I ruled out moving to new areas farther away, since all our critical senior people lived close to the traditional areas along the hills on the west side of Silicon Valley. Many of the buildings just didn't seem adequate for Microsoft. After a number of field trips, toward the end of the year, I took Rod Gilles and Jack Troedson up to Seattle for a tour of the Redmond campus, to get an idea of what I was looking for, to see the Microsoft style of doing facilities and Microsoft standards, plus corporate requirements for furniture, network cabling, and such. We really did want private offices with doors and windows for everyone in the building, and weren't going to compromise on that.

We prepared requirements documents, and in January 1988, a list of 21 local sites was drawn up. I visited them all, and we evaluated them all against our requirements (location, traffic, access, aesthetics, availability dates), and a Redmond facilities group came down and did likewise, coming to a unanimous first choice by them and by us: we should aim to locate at the Quadrus complex on Sand Hill Road in Menlo Park. We chose this by the end of January 1988, and we were in serious negotiations about it by the end of February 1988.

The complex was located at 2400–2498 Sand Hill Road in Menlo Park, on a quiet knoll overlooking the Stanford campus, studded with massive rock outcroppings and over 800 mature natural trees, many of them the live oaks so characteristic of those particular hills. The effect of a few buildings nestled among many natural trees was actually very much like the Microsoft campus in Redmond. Standing on the site, you could look out over the permanently undeveloped Stanford land reserves that run up into the hills, with oaks and cows providing a high bucolic quotient. Looking the other way, you could see the Hoover

Tower on the Stanford campus, five minutes away, and on out over San Francisco Bay.

The location was out of the downtown Palo Alto traffic congestion, but 5 minutes from the Stanford Quad. Along with nearby Page Mill Road, where Xerox PARC was, Sand Hill Road is just about the only developed spot anywhere near the midway point of the length of the valley along Interstate 280. (Sand Hill Road is 45 minutes south of San Francisco, 20 minutes north of Saratoga, and directly reached by a bridge from the East Bay.) It was quick to reach the San Francisco airport along Interstate 280. We would be as close to Apple as we were in Sunnyvale, just about 10 minutes away. Our nearest neighbors would be IBM Research, Olivetti Research, the Linus Pauling Institute, Addison-Wesley publishers, and the well-known venture capital complex at 3000 Sand Hill Road. There could not be a better location for accessibility, coupled with privacy and natural beauty, so this would be a decisive recruiting enhancement. The location was absolutely appropriate for a top-tier company like Microsoft in Silicon Valley.

The location had a particular additional attraction for me: it was by far the easiest spot in Silicon Valley to reach from San Francisco. You could slip out of San Francisco, use Interstate 280, which back then was practically deserted, and from which trucks were banned, and when you reached the Sand Hill Road off-ramp, you were at the new GBU building. In those days, all the venture capital investors lived in San Francisco, and the reason why they all had offices at 3000 Sand Hill Road, next door, was that it could be reached so easily with no need to drive on choked Highway 101, or through the traffic on the valley floor. I had just given myself the same problem, since my wife and I had bought an 1882 Victorian house in the Upper Fillmore neighborhood of San Francisco that we were restoring, and soon I would be facing the VC's commute every day.

This spot had been the headquarters of Saga Foods, an institutional food service company. Its executives had intended to spend their working lives there, so they lovingly built four classic buildings into the site, designed by architect Cliff May. Harry ("Hunk") Anderson, one of the founders of Saga, included details designed especially to showcase a part of his and his wife's world-renowned personal collection of contemporary art throughout all the buildings.

Then, unexpectedly, Saga became the target of a hostile takeover bid from Marriott, and, by mid-1986, Marriott succeeded in gaining control. That eliminated the need for the campus, so it was sold off by

Marriott. It was taken over by the Henry J. Kaiser Family Foundation as an investment, and re-cast as "Quadrus Conference Center." One of the four buildings contained large indoor/outdoor meeting areas available for us to use; these would make great places to have customer events and even press announcements, close by our own support systems. It also contained two excellent restaurants, so we could stroll over on footpaths through the woods for lunch with visitors. Another building contained a fitness center. The Anderson Art Collection was still on the walls of all the buildings, partly because there was no place else to display it, with a full-time curator to look after it. There was ample parking terraced into the hillsides.

The Kaiser Family Foundation had taken over the property at a low point in the Silicon Valley commercial real estate cycle. They were very eager to sign a long lease with at least one big tenant with a very strong balance sheet, so as to improve the property's eligibility for favorable re-financing terms. When they put the property on the lease market, I was near the front of the line. This spot was just what I was looking for. Luckily, Microsoft was just the tenant (with just the balance sheet) that they wanted, a trophy tenant in their eyes.

One of the empty buildings, Building 4, somewhat apart from the others, was perfect for us. It was some 32,000 square feet, and was a long, narrow building along a ridge, so it was just right for rebuilding into Microsoft private offices: we could put a wide central hall in each wing, lined with offices along both sides of the whole length, every office with an outside window and a view. There were three floors connected by a dominating broad staircase that tied the levels together. Quadrus was perfectly happy to rebuild the building for us in exactly the way we wanted, especially since I wanted to include even more niches and alcoves and places for Hunk Anderson's art collection, which was an ideal amenity for a Graphics Business Unit. The problem was that it would take a year or so to gut and rebuild the whole building, and before then, we would have outgrown our old space in Sunnyvale.

Fortunately, Quadrus was willing to negotiate an offer that solved every problem. We could move into existing space in another building, Building 3, which could be built into offices and wired with networks to Microsoft specifications more quickly. We could have options to progressively take over more and more space in Building 3 as we grew, from 6,000 square feet up to 18,000 square feet, retaining the same entry lobby. We could begin using our permanent street address and telephone numbers immediately. While we were in the temporary building, for about a year, we would pay no rent at all, only expenses.

When it had been rebuilt, we could move into 20,000 square feet of our adjacent permanent building, at one-half rent for the first 14 months (this was in addition to the first year of free rent). We would have a one-year option after that to expand into the remaining 12,000 square feet (the third floor) of that same building, thus taking it all. Finally, we would have an option to take half or all of an un-built fifth building (18,000 square feet), which had a valid building permit and could be started in a couple of years or so. In this way, we would be able to step up our commitments gradually over four or five years, while absolutely controlling at least a total of 50,000 square feet of space.

By May 1988, that deal was done; it was handled by our local agents, with just an observer from Redmond sitting in occasionally.

Our average net cost in the first 5 years under the lease I signed, working out how much space we would occupy for how long at what price, was $2.02 a square foot. For comparison, the net cost of our then-current building in Sunnyvale, a much less attractive area, was $1.31 per square foot under our existing lease. The going rate in Palo Alto and Menlo Park was over $3.00 a square foot, with an additional premium for larger spaces, which were rare. So, our rather complex deal was quite a bargain. Expenses were fixed and capped during our lease term at a reasonable rate, and we had options to extend the lease, locking in our below-market rate.

The spot was more than merely good; in late 2011, a national survey revealed that office space along that very part of Sand Hill Road had become the most expensive in the entire country, well ahead of Fifth Avenue in New York City or Greenwich, Connecticut. But that wasn't yet true in 1988. I had used the strength of Microsoft's balance sheet to lease magnificent space at very low cost.

We started soon thereafter putting headlines on our recruiting advertisements reading "Microsoft in Menlo Park," and got lots of replies from people who, like me, wanted to work for Microsoft but didn't want to move to Seattle.

139 PowerPoint 2.0 for Mac Ships

By early 1988, PowerPoint 2.0, or "Color PowerPoint," was fairly well specified and well along. Extensive reviews were scheduled with people from Redmond, and they gradually became comfortable that we were doing the right thing.

After implementing most of what we had agreed upon with Bill Gates back in October 1987, we decided in January 1988 to extend the color features still further, based in part on things we had begun to learn from Genigraphics in the meantime.

Curiously enough, we were the only developer to commit to using Apple's Palette Manager early, and so we were the only product able to do on-screen such high-end effects as shaded color backgrounds—a stunning visual *tour de force* on a personal computer. We pioneered color menus, including users' ability to change the colors on menus and context-sensitive varying of color backgrounds on submenus.

PowerPoint 2.0 became the only package to ship with the Genigraphics color palette, a selection of colors which was small enough to look at and choose from but which covered the whole color space pretty well from light to dark for each color. We designed and included in the product over 5,000 color schemes chosen by Genigraphics' artists, based on the palette colors, and also a new approach to remapping some colors (but not all colors) throughout a presentation based on their usage. Jim Seymour later wrote in *MacUser* magazine that our 2.0 product " ... virtually reinvents how color ought to be used in software."

Testing some color features was difficult, since we were shipping before any of the desktop film recorders was complete and debugged and before Genigraphics was able to image from Mac files. We got Genigraphics to simulate our shading algorithms on their equipment and expose hundreds of frames using our colors, to be as sure as possible that "banding" in the shaded backgrounds would not be a problem. It was almost two months after our release before we saw for the first time an actual example of a difficult shaded background sent by PowerPoint to a Genigraphics film recorder. Fortunately for everyone, it looked perfect.

We had a number of demanding beta sites, plus a much larger set of undemanding sites—really seeding sites, and kept in regular contact with them to elicit problem reports. Nevertheless, an analysis after shipment showed that no bug was first reported by a beta site, which gave us confidence in our testing.

The interaction with Genigraphics inspired a lot of last-minute improvements, but all were done judiciously, to avoid future problems. Most Genigraphics issues were isolated from our code, because we had adopted an "integration" strategy which was actually more of a "segregation" strategy, whereby we added a menu item "Send to Geni-graphics... ." (It was certainly unprecedented to put another company's name on a menu in the product code—that demonstrated credible commitment.) That menu item would bring up a special sort of printer driver, to be written by Genigraphics or their consultants, which would collect the information about what output was wanted and in what quantity, the shipment address for completed slides, and so forth, and then would format that information and grab a copy of the entire native PowerPoint file. The driver would either write everything on a floppy diskette to be sent to Genigraphics, or else (eventually) would use a modem to dial a Genigraphics 800 number and transmit the same data. This took the development of the Genigraphics part out of the critical path for PowerPoint 2.0. We wanted to ship the driver in the box, as soon as possible, but first it had to be finished and tested. Even then, all the difficulty of imaging the slides was entirely separate, and the Geni-graphics driver could be updated separately, on a schedule independent of PowerPoint.

The biggest schedule crunch with Genigraphics prior to ship was all the schemes, backgrounds, sample presentations, and clip art that would ship in the PowerPoint box. These had to be completed by Geni-graphics artists early enough to be used in the manuals, in advertising, on the boxes, and in collateral. These were all Macintosh files that had to be prepared using early versions of PowerPoint on Macintosh com-puters, not on Genigraphics consoles. Getting these done involved working very intensively with Genigraphics, and we began to see the "effective exclusivity" of our partnership agreement—neither of us had any spare time to work with anyone else.

We started the introduction of PowerPoint 2.0 early, because the on-screen effect of color schemes and shaded backgrounds was so impressive. We wheeled color Macs on carts all around Microsoft Red-mond, giving demos to executives and managers in their offices and conference rooms all over the company, and did the same within Apple in Cupertino. Later, on introduction day, we reserved a large auditorium in Redmond and gave continuous demos all day long to all Microsoft employees—an idea we would repeat for future releases.

In the same way, we relied on personal visits to editors, rather than on a press event of some kind. Separate East Coast and West Coast tours, plus a special trip to Texas, were staged late in April 1988. To assure best results, we hand-carried color Mac II's with the correct displays and fonts to all the appointments, ready to go with no installation required. Somewhat to our surprise, in virtually every case, editors sat still for two hours or more of demonstration. In retrospect, this was not so surprising—they were seeing by far the most impressive color they had ever seen on a Mac II, and much more impressive than on any other personal computer.

We took the time to review the category and its advantages, as well as the new features. This was a good idea because the category of desktop presentations was vastly better known this spring than it had been the year before. We got great coverage, with color pictures of our slides or our screens in prominent places in most of the weeklies. The personal response on the press tour was extremely positive, along the lines of "looks like Microsoft has been great for you, you're still out front." Jim Seymour, a prominent columnist, published just such a remark in *MacUser* for July 1988: "Say what you will about Microsoft, they did right by PowerPoint" (p.72).

It was a visit on this tour which also prompted Jim Seymour to report in the same article that "PowerPoint 2.0 is, simply put, the most impressive combination of power, elegance, and ease of use, I've ever seen in a piece of business software." We felt that this made the trip to Texas to see him worthwhile.

There were lots of improvements in PowerPoint 2.0, but "35mm slides" became the defining feature. At the launch, we sent out thousands of small slide viewers with a "Microsoft PowerPoint" monogram painted on them, pre-loaded with ten ravishing slides that had been created on PowerPoint 2.0, mocked up and imaged by Genigraphics and mounted in cardboard mounts with the standard prominent Genigraphics logo. There was no doubt what the news was—it was 35mm slides.

We did an introduction event in San Francisco on 31 May 1988, with Sandy Beetner again there in person to present for Genigraphics, Bill Gates presenting for Microsoft, and with a guest appearance by John Sculley presenting for Apple—certainly an all-star cast.

Michael Beetner wrote to me recently, recalling that just before the event, he was reviewing all the Genigraphics slides for all the presentations (certainly no video in those days!):

> As a final step in preparation, I asked to go through the slides just to be sure none were upside down or backwards to spoil the presentation. In this exercise we came upon a slide with a beautiful red Coca-Cola logo. All I could see in my mind were press pho-

tographs showing Sculley in front of a Coke logo. I stopped the show and showed it to Sandy.

It was only two hours before the event would begin. Sandy asked a fellow from her San Francisco service bureau to re-make the slide with a Pepsi logo and have the new slide back in an hour. As the young man ran to the door, you said in amazement that you didn't know that you could get slides back in an hour. Sandy replied "You can't. I can."

A corrected slide with a Pepsi logo was produced, imaged, processed and mounted, and delivered back to our event hotel within an hour flat.

"Everyone was amazed," Sandy said later, "at which point I appealed to them to forget they ever saw it, as I was frantic that it would become the new customer service expectation!" Even if that was extreme, it was typical of how Genigraphics' services consistently stretched to meet customers' needs, even when they were unreasonable.

After the event, for some reason, Microsoft's PR people had scheduled an outing to a local baseball game, to be hosted by Bill Gates. Sandy and I decided to skip it, and instead took a driving tour of San Francisco together. My wife and I had almost completed renovations on the Victorian house we had bought in the city, so I was full of enthusiasm for my new home town.

140 Print Production for PowerPoint 2.0

We had to overcome many unexpected problems caused by the fact that all of our materials—manuals, collateral, dealer kits, sales training, reviewer's kits, and all the rest—had to be in full "process" color, perhaps for the first time in personal computer history. There was no experience with capturing full-color screens, and no established procedure in Microsoft for printing process color. I was determined that we would use color "naturally" throughout, not segregated onto separately printed inserts. This required planning all the paper specifications to support this, and clever tricks to control cost unobtrusively.

Eventually, we succeeded in finding a local supplier who, with our help, could take a screen dump on disk and return color-separated film already screened and sized to be stripped in. This made full-color illustrations no more trouble than black and white, though for the first few months, they appeared to be highly mysterious. It's hard to believe now that process color was ever an exotic and novel innovation.

All writing and editing of the manuals for PowerPoint 2.0 was done in Sunnyvale, by Publishing Power. Manuals were written in Microsoft Word, put through multiple review cycles in our office (including development and QA people, as well as marketing), then put into Aldus PageMaker on the Macintosh. Final pages were proofed on a LaserWriter and imaged on a Linotronic typesetter.

Of course, we used the case binding (like a hardbound book) we pioneered with PowerPoint 1.0, and which our customers liked so much, with its special gluing technique that made the pages lie flat. With the bigger book this time (nearly 400 pages), this worked even better than before. The comparatively low cost of goods for PowerPoint was largely attributable to this binding method—it was cheaper than either cased wire-O or ring binders, could be done on high-speed equipment, and looked much more expensive than paperback binding, though it was not. It was true that we had to make schedules and keep to them, and it was true that we had to go to Donnelley in Indiana for a press check. I believed the results were worth it.

Besides the main manual, we did the same for the Quick Reference Guide, Templates Guide, Genigraphics Phase I booklet, and SmartScrap booklet (all saddle stitched). All our product components were completed, printed in full color, bound in case binding or stitched, and shipped to be in inventory at Redmond by 6 May 1988, two weeks before the final software was released.

We received lots of positive response to the manuals again, both their appearance and their usability. "Nearly flawless," said Bill Coggshall, who was also responsible for the remark that providing software manuals in hardcover books gives the impression that "Microsoft is really sure about what it's doing, like somebody who works the *New York Times* crossword puzzle in ink." *InfoWorld* reported that "PowerPoint's manual is a beautiful, hardcover volume ... containing many helpful color and black-and-white illustrations" (12 September 1988, page S12).

141 PowerPoint 2.0 Mac Ship Party

Rather than using a conventional venue, we held our shipping party for Mac PowerPoint 2.0, for employees and for our suppliers, vendors, and contractors, at our unfinished new site for a permanent home on Sand

Hill Road on 15 July 1988. This was the first time everyone in the company had had a chance to see the site. It met with general approval.

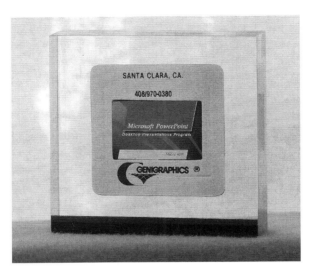

We always had a "ship award"—a memento, often involving something in Lucite, created to commemorate a success, made in limited quantities, and handed out to all the people involved. For this one, I ordered a small block of Lucite encasing a 35mm slide with a design about Microsoft PowerPoint, mounted in a Genigraphics mount with the name and phone number of the Santa Clara service bureau (it was a real Genigraphics slide mount). I thought this was a simple idea, but it turned out that, unfortunately, the melting temperature of Ektachrome film is lower than the temperature of molten Lucite. Elaborate workarounds were needed to print the color slide on a transparent plastic sheet with a much higher melting temperature. Again, the result communicated strongly the partnership of Microsoft and Genigraphics.

142 Post-Mortem for the Mac PowerPoint 2.0 Schedule

One of the perpetual problems of the Applications Division in Redmond was slipping schedules. The reasons were not simple, and were different from the reasons why most software slipped.

Most development organizations lacked insight into the real rate of progress, so some arbitrary date stayed on a manager's slides while a multitude of small, unseen delays happened until, at some point, the total of the small delays became impossible to ignore. Not so at Microsoft. Microsoft had an admirable system, by which every developer had a standard Excel spreadsheet with all his agreed tasks, broken down to the level of a few hours per task, and he entered next to each task his own estimate of how long it would take in total and how much time remained to complete it; as each task was completed, it got an estimate of zero time remaining. The Excel spreadsheet calculated the completion date for all the unfinished tasks. A set of these spreadsheets could then be rolled up automatically in another Excel spreadsheet to give a completion date for a group, and this could be iterated. The result was that it was always possible to know, to the day, when the development tasks currently agreed to be in the spec were estimated to be completed, according to the actual people signed up to do every task, hence taking into account each developer's knowledge and experience. These cascading estimates went up to Bill Gates every two weeks unchanged, so no manager could ignore or conceal a slip.

But still, there were schedule slips. At a Resource Planning Meeting in Redmond in December 1987, the leaders of various groups had discussed why most of their projects shipped four or five months later than planned. As an example, one well-understood MS-DOS application had been predicted to ship in June 1987 until as late as three months before the predicted ship date, but then slipped an additional five months, and, in the end, didn't ship until November 1987. Bill Gates had recalled a "model project, not clear we can do any better," which even so had unexpectedly slipped two months at the end—a slip of one month followed by four smaller slips of one week each.

These very common last-minute slips of two-to-five months meant that everything else involved in introducing a new product was disrupted, including sales, advertising, PR, and especially manufacturing. They weren't caused by poor visibility or estimating; they were caused by lack of knowledge of where the spec was unworkably wrong or incomplete, and lack of knowledge of bugs that were only found late. (This whole problem did get solved a bit later, under Mike Maples' guidance, and soon Apps schedules were really excellent. We really did learn how to avoid last-minute slips almost entirely, by periodic earlier consolidations, much to everyone's surprise.)

By the then-current standards in Apps, the schedule for PowerPoint 2.0 for Mac had been really very good.

The Mac version of PowerPoint 2.0 was released to manufacturing on 23 May 1988. It had been completed by the previous Friday, May 20,

but manufacturing would only accept new jobs on Monday mornings—
one more example of the shortcomings of internal services that are
exempt from market competition.

The predicted dates of release to manufacturing during development, taken from status reports filed every two weeks during this period, are as follows:

Date of Status Report	Predicted Release Date	Tolerance
—up to 26 October 1987:	15 Feb 1988	-0 /+8 weeks
—beginning 26 October 1987:	11 Apr 1988	-0 /+4 weeks
—beginning 29 January 1988:	2 May 1988	-0 /+2 weeks
—on 25 April 1988:	9 May 1988	-0 /+1 weeks
—on 6 May 1988:	13 May 1988	-0 /+1 weeks
—on 20 May 1988:	RELEASED	— weeks

The first date ever proposed as a target was 15 February, -0/+8
weeks. Following the spec finalization with Bill on 20 October, we
calculated a schedule for the newly redefined product, and in the status
report for 26 October gave a new release date of 11 April 1988, -0/+4
weeks. (Hence, in October the date of 11 April +4 weeks would have
been 9 May, or just two weeks earlier than what was achieved seven
months later.)

This release date was carried until 29 January, following the decision
to include more color features, when the date for the enlarged spec was
revised to 2 May -0/+2 weeks. (Hence, in January the date of 2 May +2
weeks would have been 16 May, or just one week earlier than what was
achieved four months later.) The final unexpected slip of one week was
caused by Apple's having falsely assured us that some of their own fatal
bugs in the new system 6.0 would be fixed before its final release. We
found out in the last week that these had not been fixed by Apple, and
workarounds for those problems added a full calendar week of work
that previously had not been thought necessary, and so was not in the
spec.

At the end of October, as soon as we had agreement for the first
time on exactly what to do, we knew within two weeks when everything
had to be done the following May. This means that all related activities
could go forward without major uncertainties caused by schedule slip.

The final Golden Masters for PowerPoint 2.0 for Mac were completed at 10:00 p.m. on 20 May 1988, ready to be hand-carried up to Redmond over the weekend, to be handed to manufacturing on 23 May 1988, at 9:00 a.m. sharp, when their window opened.

At the time, there had been wasted effort when groups would give disks to manufacturing, then continue unfinished testing and come back a few days later to substitute newer disks, sometimes repeating the substitution. This sloppy practice provided one excuse for the Monday morning rule, so as to limit new disks to once a week. We didn't do that; we released disks exactly once.

It was an extremely vexing problem that we couldn't convince manufacturing or corporate communications to work to our schedules. These "service groups" were utterly convinced that we would slip substantially on our dates, based on their experiences of two-to-five months with other projects. Despite our assurances, they thought they could generalize about software projects and knew better than we did.

As it turned out, corporate communications was almost a month late in completing some of our introduction material—some "service"!

Manufacturing, despite the fact that *all* components except disks had been in inventory by 6 May, and despite constant and accurate communications from us about when the disks would arrive, was unable to work our manufacturing into their schedule until almost a month after our release—truly unpardonable. We could have done so much better by buying manufacturing on the open market.

When the centralized groups failed us, we worked around them, like a startup. We had requisitioned 100 copies of the boxes, manuals, disk labels, and all the other components out of inventory when the parts arrived in early May, with no particular reason in mind. When we learned that manufacturing would slip, we ordered discs duplicated locally to make 100 sets of unassembled parts, and shipped them from Sunnyvale to our beta sites, field sales offices, influential commentators, and large customers. This saved the day, and it was lucky that we could do it, since we hadn't expected it to be necessary.

One indication of development quality was speed of internationalization. The "Z" version (International English version) of PowerPoint 2.0 shipped from Dublin, which was Microsoft's manufacturing site for Europe, on 15 July. The rest of the schedule was as follows—these are ship dates, with all product components as well as software translated and localized, including color printing:

Mac PowerPoint 2.0 Z (Intn'l Eng.) ships from Dublin 15 Jul 88
Mac PowerPoint 2.0 French ships from Dublin 10 Nov 88
Mac PowerPoint 2.0 French Canada ships from Dublin 28 Nov 88
Mac PowerPoint 2.0 Swedish ships from Dublin 1 Dec 88
Mac PowerPoint 2.0 German ships from Dublin 8 Dec 88
Mac PowerPoint 2.0 Italian ships from Dublin 8 Dec 88
Mac PowerPoint 2.0 Dutch ships from Dublin 15 Dec 88

These were very aggressive dates, for the time, and great news, because PowerPoint was truly an international product, and the sooner we could it get out, the better our sales.

143 Genigraphics Expands to Europe

Since Macintosh PowerPoint 2.0 was being localized for the European subsidiaries, and Windows PowerPoint 2.0 would quickly follow (so we thought), we needed an imaging service for 35mm slides in Europe. My preference was to have Genigraphics organize and manage such an operation, and Sandy Beetner agreed that she would also prefer that approach, rather than having us work with somebody else.

They hired a European manager in Switzerland and set off on a plan to execute agreements with existing independently owned service bureaus in major cities. The target was to have a dozen bureaus in place for Mac, and perhaps two dozen bureaus by the time Windows arrived. Genigraphics would act as the unified marketing agent for the whole network, and would verify quality standards. Microsoft would recommend Genigraphics affiliates exclusively, so the bulk of the business would come through that route.

Our vision was perhaps skewed; European service bureaus tended to still think of the opportunity as being large corporate sales, not the future of millions of small individual customers, as was beginning to emerge in the U.S. So an early plan was that Microsoft and Genigraphics would jointly sell large accounts on using PowerPoint and Genigraphics services, and Genigraphics would funnel the actual work to its network of confederated service bureaus. That wasn't where the business was, it was merely what the service-bureau affiliates wished were true.

This whole venture was surrounded by problems. The Microsoft subsidiaries in Europe badly wanted the Genigraphics service to be in place, and sent lots of email about it. Unfortunately, the Genigraphics

Europe manager didn't use email and complained about unresponsiveness from Microsoft. Testing was an unfamiliar discipline, and eventually had to be repeated in the U.S., where we had difficulty getting European components, such as French modems, some of which in consequence didn't work for a long time. Revenue was slow to develop, and I agreed to subsidize about 25% of the expenses for an initial limited period, by paying a monthly stipend for "market development," so as to be able to offer some level of 35mm slide imaging for PowerPoint in Europe. But this was one project that didn't work out as we had hoped.

144 *PowerPoint First Year Sales*

Sales of PowerPoint in the first year as part of Microsoft were judged to be disappointing. I thought that this was true but not completely fair. The period of poor sales had been the first six months after the acquisition. For that whole period, Microsoft had temporarily handled all our marketing and all initial contact with the sales force from Redmond, to "make sure it got off to a good start." During those six months, the Microsoft sales force didn't know we existed, and there were several problems caused by lack of attention. In the next six months, when the GBU returned to doing our own marketing and contact with the sales force, sales had met expectations.

I attempted to describe this, choosing my words judiciously, in my report on the first year. I can't do any better now:

> Year-end FY88 worldwide numbers show total sales of $4,536,915 for all the versions of Macintosh PowerPoint, 1.01 and 2.0. This is equivalent to about 23,500 units worldwide in the eleven months ending June 88. July sales (U.S.) were over 2,800 units, or $549,000, making a total of over 26,000 units for the first full year, and a total of over $5,000,000 in sales for the first 12 months. But the sales profile for the year is far from uniform.
>
> Only 5,600 domestic units were sold as Microsoft in the six months August-January. This is really incomprehensibly bad— the product was only three months old, had a great previous sales record, had no competition, had good Apple backing, good PR, and was steadily receiving excellent reviews. A new ad was hastily put together, and run to little effect. A promotion with 3M was organized, but delayed by lack of resources in getting out to dealers until late. Training for the sales force seemed to be very diffi-

cult to get done. (N.B.: this was during the period when marketing was being done in Redmond.)

Sales improved with the training of the sales force (December) and the selection of PowerPoint as a buy-in product. Sales picked up for the buy-in months of February, March, and April. With a target of between 5,000 and 6,000 units for the period, we actually shipped about 6,700 domestic units in these three months, and booked 700 more units. Sales were about 2500 units in February, 2250 in March, and about 2,000 in April—when we ran out of the 1.01 product, with a shippable backlog of 700 units at the end of April. (In each of these three months, PowerPoint was one of the Microsoft top 10 revenue products.) The backlog continued to build in May, and built still further in June—we shipped 8,271 domestic units of version 2.0 in June. (We shipped about 2,800 domestic units during July.)

The real story, I think, is fewer than 6,000 total units in the six months of August-January, as against more than 20,000 total units for the six months February-July. There is of course a demand for the new version, but sales of the product were growing substantially long before the new version was announced or shipped.

Focusing on the year-end number, we can wish that the sales performance of the Graphics Business Unit had been better—there were hopes that we would sell 40,000 units of PowerPoint during the first year. But at least we can be pleased that during the last six months we have in fact achieved the rate we were looking for.

During the six-month period August-January, sales went forward at an annual rate of about 12,000 units per year (about 1,000 units per month worldwide). This was the period when responsibility for marketing, advertising, PR, and communications to the sales force was being executed by hand-picked Apps marketing people in Redmond (a Macintosh Group Product Manager part-time, a nearly-full-time experienced Product Manager, and a nearly-full-time Associate Product Manager). This shows how hard it was to get the sales effort under way. These Redmond folks expected to succeed, and were surprised when they did not. It is almost certain that they did better than we could have done at that time.

But since responsibility for all those marketing tasks returned to the GBU, for the six-month period February-July, sales have gone forward at an annual rate of slightly over 40,000 units per year (about 3,350 units a month worldwide). This is slightly greater than the rate we hoped for. The period includes the introduction of the 2.0 product, but even before that, sales had improved to a rate of almost 30,000 units per year for the months of February, March, and April, while we were selling the same old 1.01 version.

I certainly believe that this must be considered a success on the part of the people in the Graphics Business Unit—and even more noteworthy in view of the low level to which sales had fallen during the first six months. (Gaskins, First Year Report 1988)

145 Mike Maples Arrives

A momentous event for PowerPoint was that Bill Gates replaced himself as VP of Applications by hiring Mike Maples. I heard the news on 8 June 1988. Mike was described as coming from IBM, where he had been head of system software for the Entry Systems Division, the personal computer folks. He'd been an IBM employee for 25 years, and was a product enthusiast who had a Mac II and an IBM PC at home. He was very well known and liked by the press, partly because, as Jeff Raikes described him, he was "straight-shooting and pragmatic."

(For a revealing account by Mike about his time at Microsoft, see an oral history interview that he did in 2004 (Maples 2004).)

I was very hopeful, because I thought that nobody in Microsoft knew how to manage organizations of the size of its major divisions (such as Applications). Mike Maples had managed thousands of people at IBM, so he should have an advantage there. Many people at Microsoft were wary because of his IBM background, but I thought that, if Bill Gates hired him, he had to be somewhat outside the standard IBM mold. Two years later, Jon Shirley, in an interview given when Jon retired, said that, from the end of 1985, "for the next four years, the only person we hired into this company at the officer position was Mike Maples, and we spent literally 2 1/2 years finding someone who could move into that job. And I think Mike very early on proved he was not some molded IBM-type person at all" (Shirley 1990).

Mike started quietly, learning the lay of the land. He sent out a copy of his own résumé to every person in the Division (it included his early Yo-Yo championship) and requested a résumé back from each individual. This was an effective way to put everybody on notice that a new VP would affect them personally; people spent significant time revising their résumés to send back to him. He began attending all the Apps Division meetings that he could and all the reviews or brainstorming sessions that Bill scheduled, but he said little at first.

He attended all the "Resource Planning Meetings" of his new division. I also attended them, although I wasn't centrally involved, because they involved allocating resources among all our other applications, who shared everything, whereas our "business unit" had dedicated resources. I've described my early impressions of these meetings:

> These meetings dealt with allocating the shared resources of the Applications Division among a dozen or so applications. This involved decisions such as to take a developer off of scheduled database work for two weeks to re-do a feature for Excel that had proved to have design errors; or to allocate three writers from the Word manual to computer-based training for Works for a month and reduce the scope of the Word manual; or to have a test manager and a dozen people take another three days to test new features in Word that had been unexpectedly buggy, although that would delay their availability to test bug fixes in other products; or to allocate scarce manufacturing resources to produce upgrades for Europe, at the opportunity cost of new products needed for the U.S.
>
> Such meetings terrified me, since I didn't see how decisions like these could be made sensibly. Every product was constantly being delayed by resource conflicts produced by problems in other products, which couldn't possibly be anticipated. I resolved to try to keep as much distance as possible. This made our first year a bit lonely, since I deliberately kept the internal workings of the GBU opaque and avoided cultivating "disciplinary" ties, so as to avoid constant comparisons of how we were different. We were "odd man out" on everything.
>
> I didn't have a lot of business experience, especially in managing large organizations, but, in some cases, I had more experience than the people who were trying to make this system function. I just thought that their way was completely unworkable. (From the section on " 'Planning' for All Applications at the Same Time," above.)

In the intervening year, I thought, the whole process had only gotten worse. Lots of Applications releases had suffered significant schedule slips and delays from poor management. I imagined that Mike Maples might well agree with me.

Mike soon asked me (on 25 July 1988) to prepare a briefing for him, to include my view of the presentation category and its evolution on PC and Mac, the background of Forethought prior to the acquisition, the Graphics Business Unit organization and how it had worked out, an overview of our FY88 business, expectations for our FY89 business, and my views of the longer term. Thanks to PowerPoint, I gave Mike this briefing four days later, on 29 July 1988, using more overheads than perhaps even he had ever seen before.

146 My Memo on GBU First Year Results

A week after my presentation to Mike Maples, I circulated a formal memo on "Results of Microsoft's Graphics Business Unit after Our First Year." (Gaskins, First Year Report 1988) This memo was addressed to each of the people within the GBU, by name (alphabetized by email alias)—there were now 16 people in addition to me. Their accomplishments had exceeded even my brightest hopes. Copies went to Bill Gates, Jon Shirley, Mike Maples, and Jeff Raikes. It began like this:

8 August 1988
To: Aniko Somogyi, Bob Lagier, Bob Safir, Dennis Abbe, Dennis Austin, Harris Meyers, Judy Caserta, Kathi Baker, Keith Sturdivant, Lewis Levin, Pam Miller, Rick Hawes, Robert Lotz, Sharon Meyers, Tom Rudkin, Tuan Nguyen
From: Bob Gaskins
Subject: Results of Microsoft's Graphics Business Unit after Our First Year
Copies: Bill Gates, Jon Shirley, Mike Maples, Jeff Raikes

It is now just slightly more than one year since the beginning (last July 31st) of the new Graphics Business Unit of Microsoft in Silicon Valley. This overview of the first year's results provides a convenient summary of what we have all, together, accomplished in that period of time. Of course, everything mentioned here was really accomplished by some individual GBU person, and in reading over this history you'll be able to identify who accomplished what; but for this purpose, I have deliberately suppressed all the individual names, using "we" collectively throughout, so that we can get a view of the performance of the Business Unit as a whole, the way it might appear to an outsider who didn't know us.

As will be clear, I think that we as a group have a lot to be proud of in our first year's results. We have laid the foundation to continue to grow as an important part of Microsoft, and to create innovative and exciting products during our succeeding years.

Over the past year, we have:

— Retained 100% of our PowerPoint people
— Closed down all of our old business affairs
— Created a new operations and administrative framework for the unit
— Hired 11 new people (plus 1 offer outstanding, to make a total of 19)
— Created the definition of the PowerPoint 2.0 color product
— Established working relationships with many device manufacturers
— Negotiated the development and marketing agreement with Genigraphics
— Completed development of the Mac version of PowerPoint 2.0
— Written and done the print production on all manuals for Mac PP 2.0
— Tested the Mac PowerPoint 2.0 product (software, templates, and manuals)
— Accomplished substantial development on a Windows version of PP 2.0
— Prepared full marketing materials for the Mac PP 2.0 introduction
— Accomplished a successful PR tour and launch of the Mac PP 2.0 product
— Located, negotiated for, and leased a first-class facility for our expansion
— Shipped $5M in Macintosh PowerPoint in 12 months through July 88.

Less tangibly, we have also retained much of the goodwill enjoyed by PowerPoint as a "hot" product and transferred it to the Microsoft GBU. Repeatedly on the press tour introducing Mac PP 2.0 we heard comments along the lines of "looks like Microsoft has been great for you, you're still out front." Jim Seymour published his similar remark in the July 88 *MacUser*: "Say what you will about Microsoft, they did right by PowerPoint" (p. 72).

It is always possible to imagine aspects which could have gone even better, but it is much easier to see any number of very real disasters which have been avoided. Like any new enterprise, the GBU was vulnerable to mishaps or mis-timings which could cripple or destroy an entire undertaking, but these we have successfully escaped. The Microsoft Graphics Business Unit is now successfully started along its path as part of the Microsoft organization. (Gaskins, First Year Report 1988)

(Then there follow twenty single-spaced pages expanding in detail on each area listed.) The memo ends this way:

The decision to structure us as a Business Unit with a clear mission was an essential ingredient of the success—long lines of authority up to the giant departments of Applications in Redmond would have certainly failed. Another vital ingredient was the very strong results-oriented culture at Redmond—we have spent a full year being pleasantly astonished at the willingness of every group we work with at headquarters to go far out of its way to get things done for us. With a less responsive headquarters group, it would have been very easy to fail.

But far and away the most important ingredient of our success was the people in the Graphics Business Unit. I believe that they set a standard of achievement, even within a company so strong as Microsoft. Every person in the Graphics Business Unit can take satisfaction in substantial personal accomplishment, along with pride in our results together as a business unit. (Gaskins, First Year Report 1988)

147 *Excruciatingly Slow Progress at Genigraphics*

After the PowerPoint 2.0 for Mac product shipped in May of 1988, Genigraphics was in theory supposed to be ready to receive presentations sent by customers from any copy of the software, and to image them onto 35mm slides, with or without improvement by Genigraphics artists. Accomplishing this turned out to be extremely difficult.

As early as 22 April 1988, in the middle of the press rollout for PowerPoint 2.0 Mac, I had gone back to Syracuse, New York to meet the executives of the engineering group and to get work kicked off on the project of the "Genigraphics driver." In fact, the Mac driver that would go in the PowerPoint box was a small part of the problem; all that it had to do was to grab the file, add the job order data (format, quantity, delivery address, payment information), and send it over a telephone line or write it on a diskette. By far the bigger part of the job was what happened at the other end of the phone line: how the file would be received and validated, where it would be stored, how it would be improved by artists, and then—crucially—how it would get imaged by Genigraphics' proprietary film recorders. Beyond all this software, there were the operational considerations of dealing with customers and shipping orders, but those could be solved more easily by Genigraphics.

Our first-cut schedule envisioned a system working by August, after PowerPoint would have shipped in May. Since all the steps after a user transmitted a file were internal to Genigraphics, and running on servers at Genigraphics locations, we thought we could start offering service on stable but incomplete software and correct problems as they were encountered. Three months delay would be uncomfortable, but perhaps workable.

The Genigraphics engineering organization in Syracuse was willing, but without experience in Macintosh or any other mass-market consumer software. They had always produced systems for use by at most a few thousand customers—and they had the names and phone numbers of every customer, so they could supply a fix quickly and cheaply in case of problems. To supplement this group, Genigraphics accepted my suggestion to hire Tom Evslin of Solutions, Inc. to do the in-box driver and communications, so we had high confidence in that part of the work, and to have him also provide consulting on the rest of the project.

By 22 June 1988, the "project management" at Genigraphics was formalized; responsibility was dispersed to a marketing guy in Manhattan; to a service-bureau manager in Santa Clara for contact with the GBU (the service would be offered first from Santa Clara); and to a person in Syracuse for contact with the engineers, who at Microsoft would have been called a "program manager." This was Rosemary Abowd (Schwendler), my first contact with her. The organization sounded very distributed, but Genigraphics was used to working across multiple locations. I was back in Syracuse again for a progress meeting on 13 July 1988.

By the end of July, there was some progress (800 numbers installed) along with problems. It had been decided to begin with a "demonstration capability" utilizing a standard commercial film recorder rather than Genigraphics' own device, but even so, schedules were slipping.

I was in Syracuse again on 19 August 1988; the opportunity for frequent travel to Syracuse was certainly *not* one of the benefits of the Genigraphics partnership. Tom Evslin was there again as well, and we all worked on addressing the problems.

On 1 September 1988, I had a conference call with Sandy Beetner in Manhattan, the engineering group in Syracuse, and Tom Evslin in Vermont. The Genigraphics folks had thought through some of the operational difficulties, and they had lots of changes that would mean further work. One complication was that users wanted to send presentations to a specific service bureau, one of the 25 or so around the country, so they could pick up the slides there. The driver needed to be able to select either a particular location or a generic "Genigraphics Central" that would get the slides done anywhere and returned by overnight courier. But all this implied a sophisticated network among the centers, which far exceeded what Genigraphics had in place. Also, it was beyond the absolute deadline to finalize all the details of what would be the standard offering to users—exactly what services, what prices, and what guarantees. This was very difficult for an organization which had always done custom work.

Tom pointed out that all the new considerations would have a big schedule impact, and we set a design meeting for a week or so later at his offices near Burlington, Vermont.

We met near Burlington on 8 September 1988. Tom had worked very hard over that week eliciting information from, and giving guidance to, the Genigraphics engineers, and had a pretty good handle on the work. His best estimate now of the earliest date for live service from Genigraphics was December 1988, and he was pessimistic, since he thought there were still large unknowns.

Shipping PowerPoint 2.0 in May, we had thought that the original date of August for Genigraphics' imaging was ugly but barely passable. Now the prospect of an eight-month delay seemed like very bad news. Customers were beginning to get restive. Sometimes, they would show up at Genigraphics centers with diskettes, and the Genigraphics artists would look at the presentation on a Mac and manually recreate it on a Genigraphics workstation—an incredible amount of work compared to what the customer expected.

In the end, it finally worked out. Rosemary Abowd increasingly took over control from the engineering organization, mastered all the issues, and started making smart judgments. She hired additional consulting expertise and managed it intelligently, insisting on PowerPoint and

Genigraphics standards without compromise. I participated in weekly and often daily telephone meetings with Rosemary on bugs and problems. The Genigraphics service rolled out in early February 1989, with a new PowerPoint update release to match—which finally included the Genigraphics driver in the PowerPoint box, as originally intended.

The cost of imaging 35mm slides was low in comparison with traditional Genigraphics full-service presentations, but still high enough to worry about. Genigraphics boldly decided to offer a simple guarantee that the slides they produced would look exactly like PowerPoint's screens or they would refund the total cost of the imaging job. This encouraged customers to try the imaging service, and virtually every single one was happy.

The customer acceptance of Genigraphics was high, and we had certainly monopolized all of Genigraphics' time for a year—no chance of competitors getting a look in. I had invested a great deal of my time, consistent with the importance I placed on the project. The nine-month delay in delivering Genigraphics slides had been very bad, but we survived it; it did take most of our customers a while to be ready. We were lucky that no competitive team of software plus imaging service had managed to come to market earlier.

148 Bill Gates's Review of PowerPoint 2.0 for Windows

Even with everything else, we had continued to make progress on PowerPoint 2.0 for Windows. Tom Rudkin and his group had been able to concentrate on this challenging set of puzzles. Many of the early Windows applications that were beginning to appear were very poorly done—very slow, very clunky, and very ugly compared with those on Macintosh. We knew we had to figure out how to avoid that.

Tom Rudkin's group had taken the PowerPoint code (by now, the completed 2.0 Mac code, in Pascal), and were rewriting it all in C for Windows. The idea was that this code would itself then be back-ported to Macintosh, to form the basis of a "core engine" for future versions on both platforms.

A substantial part of the code was working, including almost all the drawing. Text was not working, and was obviously going to be one of the last things completed, since Dennis Abbe of necessity was writing a completely new rich text module. On Mac, to make time savings in preparing version 1.0, we had used the fast CoreEdit code (Motorola

68000 assembler) licensed from Apple. We continued to use that in Mac version 2.0, but we had problems extending it for color, which caused some delays, and it also could not handle Far Eastern character sets. Dennis Abbe's new text module in C would be used in both Windows and Mac and would include the ability to use 16-bit characters. We had been offered code from Word, but judged it inadequately designed (for our environment) and refused it. Dennis Abbe's design was much cleaner, though it was a challenge to implement in Windows owing to the weak platform support for fonts. Our code for handling text was absolutely performance-critical; many early Windows programs suffered from sluggish and jerky text on screen, and we didn't intend to make that mistake. Text and fonts in the early days of Windows would be a constant struggle, and would lead us not to ship PowerPoint 2.0 prior to Windows 3.0 and not to ship PowerPoint 3.0 prior to Windows 3.1, because each of these Windows releases improved our ability to handle fonts.

Color on Windows had seemed completely inadequate. On Mac, we had been the first major application to use Apple's Palette Manager, the code that gave us the ability to dynamically load the 256 colors used on screen from a choice of 16 million colors; this was what allowed us to load up 100 or 200 closely related shades of blue and draw slim rectangles in all of the colors to give a smoothly shaded background. At about the same time as the color Mac appeared, IBM had introduced an option on its PS/2 computers called "8514/A display controller," which supported 640 x 480 resolution with 256 colors, but had a very different programming interface. By midsummer 1988, Tom's group had just produced a demo program with a module which fielded the Palette Manager calls from the Mac version and set the correct escape sequences for the 8514/A (using the standard 8514 driver, not a new one) to provide the same great full-color shaded backgrounds, and with automatic dithering on EGA displays. This finally gave us, for the first time, a high degree of confidence that we could use almost all of our Mac color techniques on Windows for a comparable high-end effect.

On 22 July 1988, we held a major review of Windows PowerPoint 2.0. Bill Gates came down from Redmond with Mike Maples and a number of other important people, and I invited every person in the GBU to attend the review, so that everyone would hear first-hand what Bill had to say about our work. Bill really wanted PowerPoint for Windows, so I thought everyone in the building should know exactly how we were doing.

A fortunate development was that Bill had earlier given to Tandy Trower the job of settling on user interface standards for all of our Windows applications. Tandy had experimented extensively with applying these to Windows PowerPoint, because we were at the stage of development where we could immediately adopt his suggestions, and in long meetings with him, we had settled on and agreed all the changes needed to meet these new standards—we would be the first.

This meant that we didn't need to debate details of user interface compatibility with other Microsoft apps for Windows, because that contentious topic had already been settled. This was not only a help for the review, but also a big help to development. We distributed at the review a new spec, which already included all the agreed changes in the user interface, and a new schedule that had those changes factored in. The new schedule showed that it would be possible to ship Windows PowerPoint 2.0 as early as 15 March 1989, eight months away.

We gave a demo of PowerPoint 2.0 running on Windows. Presentations could be created, saved, and re-opened. Multiple presentations could be opened at one time. Multiple slides could be created and viewed (the slider custom control worked). Cut, Copy, Paste and Undo worked within a slide and between slides. Metafiles from other applications could be pasted from the clipboard. Items could be drawn or pasted on the master slide, and appeared correctly (and selectively) on the other slides in the presentation. Drawing tools (line, rectangle, round rectangle, circle, oval) worked, as did framed, filled, drop shadows, patterns, and line styles, and all of these worked with snap-to grids, snap-to guides, and constraints, at multiple scales. File dialogs worked, and files behaved correctly over networks. Metafiles could be read, most of the other standard formats could be read, and there was support for the Aldus dynamic readers to give access to CGM, DFX, and other specialized file formats. We could print to printers of varying resolution and aspect ratio. Many other functional areas were partially completed.

The review went very well, and we all seemed to be on the same page. Bill summed up the remaining open issues as being "who has a clever idea, not issues of philosophy." One open issue was how Windows PowerPoint would incorporate a separate data-charting component. Bill stressed that we would have to look at the problem as the general case of linking and embedding objects from many different sources. He proposed that the GBU "should take on the task of architecture and design" for how such components would work among all Microsoft's applications.

A week after this review, I got feedback at a Resource Planning Meeting that Bill had reported a "good program review" for Windows PowerPoint. The demo disk we handed out that day had been used by Dave Moore for several hours, who pronounced it "stable." With all the difficulties of Windows, things were going well.

149 From Resource Planning Meeting to Re-Org

After biding his time and learning all about the people in his new organization, Mike Maples took decisive steps to change the Applications Division on 6 September 1988. That day, he reorganized everyone into new business units, just like the Graphics Business Unit had been for more than a year. Each new business unit included permanent dedicated people for departments of Marketing, Program Management, Development, QA, and User Ed; in the GBU, I had a department number assigned for this last function, but I didn't have to use it, since I wouldn't hire those people.

The reorganization affected everyone else in Apps profoundly, but affected us at the Graphics Business Unit so little that Mike didn't even have me fly up to Seattle to hear it; he just called me and we discussed it over the telephone. This gave me even more hope that the new arrangement would do nothing to disrupt the GBU.

The new business units were: Analysis Business Unit (ABU) handling Excel, Project, and Multiplan; Office Business Unit (OBU) handling Word and Mail; Graphics Business Unit (GBU) handling PowerPoint; Data Access Business Unit (DABU) handling a new database product and Basic; and Entry Business Unit (EBU) handling Works, Flight Simulator, Personal Finance, Learning DOS, and some entertainment titles. The head of each new unit was to be styled a "Business Unit Manager" (BUM) at the Director level; I don't know whether each of the others got a "General Manager" title like mine. Each BUM was responsible for the success of his own products.

Every person in the whole Apps Division was now in one and only one business unit, working only on one particular set of products, and was responsible to no one but, through his functional manager, to his BUM. This meant that almost everyone had a new boss, so the change was extremely disruptive.

Early discussion of the reorganization among senior people awakened all kinds of fears. One was that some functions were going to be downgraded, since they would be the peons in every business unit, subservient to the developers and program managers and even marketers, with no united presence to stand up for their "discipline." To combat this fear, Mike appointed one manager who had a QA background, and one manager with a User Ed background, in addition to those from Marketing, Program Management, and Development. The message was that everyone had a career path in this organization.

All the new BUMs were apprehensive about having to manage functions they had never managed before; the marketing people had never managed developers, for example, because all developers had reported up to the VP of Apps through their Director of Development. The developers had never managed anyone but other developers, because all marketers had likewise reported up to the VP of Apps through their own Director of Marketing.

Mike balanced assignments carefully so as to be sure that each business unit had a senior person in each functional area; if the BUM was a developer, he was given one of the most senior marketing people to head his marketing group, and if the BUM was a marketing type, he was given one of the leaders from the old development organization.

This was an open divergence from the old Microsoft rule that everyone should report to a manager "more technical" than himself; for the first time, it wasn't possible to claim with any plausibility at all that that rule was being observed. Perhaps the rule would have had to go eventually, but it had been a good one. I think I would have tried to maintain it; the original Microsoft might have lasted longer.

Mike also retained some resources in staff units: "Development Support" for the shared tools (the private Apps p-code compilers), and "User Interface Architecture," including Tandy Trower's cross-apps standardization work, to give him resources to provide coordination.

Mike used the occasion of the re-org to change everything. The new business units were made P&L units (like the GBU had been), so there had to be new monthly reports. Mike systemized all the reporting and reviews and announced his staff meetings for the next six months (a great help to me who, having to fly up to Redmond for each meeting, could juggle all my other travel around fixed points). He scheduled special classes on topics such as "how to read an income statement" and "how to give reviews and evaluations to people in different disciplines." He formalized a process for each business unit to give notice to the other business units of product release schedules and of changes. He instituted a new format for "contracts" between the business units, where one unit might agree to provide something to another unit, and the receiving unit was a real customer, with rights to set the spec and to demand quality delivery.

After announcing all this very clearly and distributing everything needed by the new BUMs, Mike then left for three weeks during which he would be unavailable, thereby leaving the new business units to work out their destinies. Each business unit (other than the GBU) began by writing new job descriptions for everyone.

Microsoft Applications Division senior management after reorganization into business units, 1989. Seated from left: Jeff Raikes (OBU), Bob Gaskins (GBU), Pete Higgins (ABU), Mike Maples (VP Apps), Susan Boeschen (EBU), Tandy Trower; standing from left: Charles Stevens (DABU), Peter Morse.

This change was extremely helpful to us at the GBU. I no longer had to attend the dreaded Resource Planning Meetings as an outsider, because each business unit did its own internal resource planning. The activities I couldn't participate in all went away, and new activities for all the business units were instituted. We were still a small part of the organization, though. The headcounts by December were: ABU, 103; OBU, 155; GBU, 30; DABU, 135; EBU, 95; staff, 64; total, 582. Power-Point was 5% of Apps total, and one-fifth the size of OBU.

Afterward, when the excitement died down, I congratulated Mike on the success of the re-org, but he rather downplayed its importance, saying (at least half joking, I thought) that, when you come into an organization, you just change it to shake things up—if it is organized in product units, you re-org into functional units, and if in functional units, you create product business units. Either way the change forces all the procedures to be re-invented and breaks up the people who have been working together into new groups, to be reevaluated.

Maybe that's right—Mike knew a lot about techniques for managing large groups of people—but I thought his re-org into business units with specific product responsibilities was a huge step forward.

Jon Shirley apparently agreed. When he retired two years later, Jon cited the re-org as one important factor in retaining the Microsoft culture as long as it could be preserved:

> I think that setting up the small business units, breaking applications up, breaking systems up, continuing to come up with small entrepreneurial groups that can have their own charter—I think all of that has helped a lot. (Shirley 1990)

150 Genigraphics Sheds its Hardware Business

We got the Genigraphics service offering for PowerPoint 2.0 rolled out by mid-February 1989, and shortly thereafter, developments at Genigraphics—the ones that I should have foreseen—began to happen. The first part of the year had been busy, since Genigraphics was beginning to set up the European service bureau operation with a European manager and affiliate arrangements with service bureaus who had previously been independent vendors using Genigraphics hardware. In early April, I'd been back to Manhattan to meet with Rosemary Abowd as she continued to get her hands around the Genigraphics software work.

Then in mid-April 1989, I got a call to tell me that Genigraphics had concluded a deal to sell off its hardware division in Syracuse. The division had been sold to Pansophic Systems, which had been amassing acquisitions in computer graphics, among other areas. Pansophic paid about $25 million; eighteen months later, Pansophic sold the ex-Genigraphics operation to a competitor, Autografix, for about $5 million; and a year after that, Pansophic itself fell into the clutches of Computer Associates. There really wasn't much future in this business.

So the end of the Genigraphics workstation had come much sooner than even I had expected. The immediate result was confusion, as almost all of the engineering resources left the company. It wasn't clear who would take over engineering for the remaining Genigraphics, or where it would be located. The headquarters staff also disappeared.

This left Genigraphics as now being really only the Network Services division, headquartered in Manhattan and headed by Sandy Beetner. I went back to Manhattan for a two-day meeting to re-group on 18–19 May 1989.

Sandy was left with substantial operations to be maintained. She had at the time 22 service bureaus in 22 cities, altogether about 350 people, of whom 150 were the artists, the critical producers. She had another 20 people or so in marketing, network operations, and the new international group in Europe. She had another 20 people from the Syracuse group to maintain finance and administration, and half a dozen engineers. A lot of mouths to feed, it seemed to me, compared with our small group of about twenty-five people at the GBU.

Rosemary Abowd was appointed "Marketing Manager for Imaging Services," with a charter to manage everything involving content created by anyone other than Genigraphics console operators. That put her firmly in charge of everything connected with PowerPoint and further enhanced our exceptionally close and productive working relationship.

Another person was assigned to start—already—on considering whether a Macintosh running PowerPoint (or possibly new software to be written by themselves) could be used internally as a replacement for Genigraphics consoles. It was expected that the new owners of the Syracuse hardware division would like to continue to sell Genigraphics consoles to the Network Services division, but suddenly the price seemed very high and the consoles less attractive, an effect that got stronger when the former Genigraphics hardware was sold on to a competitor.

The analysis of the market by Sandy's marketing group was that their prime "custom slide" business had been flat for three years. They were seeing more interest in personal computers to originate slides. Their initial experience with imaging from PowerPoint was that sales were on forecast, and profit was higher than expected, but there seemed to be high danger of eroding the custom slide business on which they relied. Clearly, this group saw exactly how things were going—they were not deluding themselves.

After three and a half months, imaging slides from PowerPoint was 10% of Genigraphics revenue, and up to 30% at some centers! They calculated that about 30% of all PowerPoint users wanted 35mm slides, and, of those, a quarter had already tried Genigraphics (7.5% of total users—we shared our shipment numbers with Genigraphics, to help them project demand for their services). The average order was running over $400, representing 25 or more slides. More than 40% of the total PowerPoint imaging business was done at higher "rush" pricing. About half the business was diskettes carried into centers ("walk-in"); the other half was received by modem.

This all sounded like a great success, to me.

To take advantage of the local centers, they hoped to push more business toward walk-in service which would give best turnaround and availability (people were there running the E6 line locally), and less toward communications over modems, for which they now had fewer heads. The issue was whether customers would go along.

The new strategy for the reorganized business was going to be primarily based on personal computers. In sequence, they would focus on: (1) imaging slides from Macs and IBM PCs; (2) a new service, short-run color printing, as a superior alternative to color photocopying, which was still not common; (3) custom templates and clip art created by their artists for use on Macs and PCs, sold directly to customers or at retail; (4) enhancement by their artists of presentations originated by customers on Macs and PCs, which would merge into the business of making full-custom presentations, as before. Further out in time, they planned to add video and print creative services.

I thought that category (3), selling templates and clip art, would be a reach, and said so. Someone used the name "chauffeur-driven presentations" to describe the new category (4), the services to enhance customer-originated presentations. I liked that name a lot, and even believed in it, but I remained unclear about exactly how such an enhancement service might actually work.

In pursuit of this program, Sandy proposed to work with PowerPoint competitors, entirely within the spirit of our original partnership agreement. As we had always insisted, their driver software was open to working with any product; but we would maintain our preferential marketing with each other. This had always been what I envisioned, so I had no problem at all. As it worked out, since PowerPoint remained the dominant software, we also always remained the dominating part of Genigraphics' imaging business.

The biggest problem Genigraphics had with the situation was that PowerPoint for Windows and all the business it would generate was going to be later than we all wished. That was the Microsoft problem, as well; PowerPoint for Windows wouldn't ship for another year.

One source of revenue for Genigraphics that we identified for them was Microsoft's paying for clip art and templates to be included in PowerPoint 2.0 (for Windows, and added to Mac). We said we would now look seriously into the old possibility of making a CD-ROM of clip art for use with PowerPoint and with other Microsoft applications.

151 Bathing in Fountains of Champagne

One of the oddest points of contention about the GBU having different practices from those of Redmond was about company parties. I never really understood why this topic was worth any attention, even before there was serious bureaucratic meddling—it wasn't as if we had parties very often.

A couple of times a year, usually for the holiday season and for another major event, we had rather elaborate parties in the evening for employees along with dates or significant others.

This tradition began with the first Christmas party, held in December 1987, six months after the acquisition. There were so few of us, fewer than a dozen employees and therefore fewer than two dozen people, that a conventional party was a challenge. What we did was to rent a large and gracious old home in Palo Alto for an evening, fully furnished like a movie set, and have a family-style holiday dinner with us all sitting around a single long polished table in the dining room. After dinner, we moved into the living room of the home where there was a piano and a pianist playing Christmas carols for group singing (or listening). Santa appeared with small gifts for everybody.

It wasn't that the GBU parties were elaborate in the sense of expensive—I don't believe that the cost per head of GBU parties was really any higher than in Redmond. Rather, our parties were elaborate in the sense of carefully planned and with lots of attention to details.

For example, I recall one party held at the Quadrus Conference Center. Everyone arrived around dusk, and we were standing around on the carriage drive in the dry warm evening (already a difference from parties in Redmond) sipping wine from an outdoor bar and chatting. There were performers, such as close-up magicians and musicians, moving through the crowd, entertaining small groups. Aniko Somogyi was there with a prominent Hungarian mathematician who was visiting at Stanford and who spoke with a heavy Hungarian accent. A group in the center of the crowd was talking with him about his work when suddenly a shot rang out, and the mathematician slumped to the ground, bleeding from a chest wound.

People ran inside to dial 911, and, very quickly, a real Menlo Park ambulance arrived with full red lights and sirens; uniformed paramedics attempted to staunch the mathematician's bleeding and hustled him off to Stanford Hospital, again with red lights and sirens. Almost immediately, a real Menlo Park police cruiser arrived, and both uniformed officers and plain clothes detectives got out to investigate the shooting. They questioned those of us standing near the mathematician and took careful notes, but then it was time for the sit-down dinner. We were allowed to proceed with our event.

Dinner was in one large room, with several courses. There was nightclub-style entertainment during dinner—musicians, a comedian, acrobats, whatever—and in the gaps, the detectives showed up to ask more questions; as their investigation proceeded, they questioned quite a number of individual GBU employees closely about recent "suspicious" actions, to the amusement of everyone else (reflecting a great deal of detailed script preparation). After dessert, they were able to unravel the plot behind the shooting, and led Kathi Baker away in (real) handcuffs. Following that there was a band for dancing into the night.

This sort of thing was very different from a party in the cafeteria organized by a catering company. We were lucky enough to have Kathi Baker, with a background in theater, who was able to plan and staff such occasions. Our magicians and acrobats and string quartets and comedians and harpists and such were not world-famous; they were often underemployed, but they were good. Venues included art galleries, theaters, and stylish downtown San Francisco hotels, and there were sometimes themes such as "a renaissance feast," with costumes encouraged. We always included roving entertainers and sometimes multiple rooms with different attractions to provide multiple centers of interest, so that even someone who hated small talk had lots to do at our parties.

Reports of these occasions made their way back to Redmond, where rumor had it that the drunken sailors down in Shangri-La-by-the-Bay were bathing in champagne fountains again.

I always believed that our budget for employee parties was actually lower than the same line item for groups in Redmond, partly because we had fewer employees; since we outsourced much more low-level work, including all the User Ed work, we had a lower headcount per dollar of revenue, and party costs are pretty much a function of the number of heads. In any case, I never got any complaints from my bosses in Redmond; from other functionaries, I gradually heard more about the "GBU party differentials" than I did about the GBU salary differentials.

152 PowerPoint for Windows 2.0, Then for OS/2 PM

It was a long and winding road which led to PowerPoint's first version for Windows being shipped simultaneously with Windows 3.0, and being unable to run on any earlier version of Windows or on OS/2. The story is instructive; it illustrates the confusion of the applications software markets in 1987 to 1990, right up to the moment of shipment of Windows 3.0, at which point things suddenly became very clear.

Anyone who thinks that, inside Microsoft, it was clear whether to develop for Windows or for OS/2 is mistaken. I spent three years trying to figure out what to do, with conflicting advice (but only advice) back and forth from the rest of Microsoft.

Windows PowerPoint 2.0 was begun in May 1987, even before the Microsoft acquisition, and then progressed in earnest after that (from August 1987), because getting PowerPoint onto the Windows platform was always one of Bill Gates's highest priorities, as well as our own. But we didn't ship it until 22 May 1990, which was an astonishing three full years after work began.

When Windows PowerPoint work began, Windows had been announced and "demonstrated" almost four years earlier, in late 1983. But after four years, it was still at its primitive version 1.0, the one with "tiled" windows that could not overlap. Windows 2.0 was released in December 1987, and we all along assumed it would be our eventual target. Windows 2.0 was better than 1.0, but it was still extremely primitive, a harsh and impoverished environment for applications. This was mostly because it was so incomplete, used as a sort of add-on task-switcher for MS-DOS. Compared with Macintosh in late 1987, it was hardly in the same class.

The first visual spec and accompanying document showing how PowerPoint would appear on Windows 2.0 was released as early as 5 October 1987 (Rudkin, Windows Appearance 1987), about two and a half years before it shipped. There were open issues, but the desired appearance and operation were very clearly defined. Macintosh Power-Point 2.0 was also well along by this time (shipped May 1988), and a firm design requirement was that PowerPoint should be near-identical on the two platforms, "modulo platform conventions," implying that the specification for Windows PowerPoint 2.0 was never in confusion. The long delay in getting it shipped was not caused by any vagueness or instability in the spec; that was always firm. It was the platform that moved under us.

On 23 December 1987, at an Apps Resource Planning Meeting, Bill Gates announced that we were getting close to serious work on versions of our apps for OS/2 Presentation Manager ("PM" we called it). The Software Development Kit (SDK) for PM would be released in February 1988, just a couple of months away. Excel would ship on PM in 1988 (it actually shipped in the closing weeks of 1989), and all the rest of the apps in the first quarter of calendar 1989, just about a year away (Word actually shipped in 1992, PowerPoint never). Bill added that it was still right to target Windows versions first and get them out there (presumably in the first half of 1988), then the PM versions would follow. I asked Bill specifically about PowerPoint, and he gave me the advice that our first target should be Windows, then PM.

At that date, according to Bill, Microsoft had sold about one million copies of Windows and about 20,000 copies of OS/2. The big Windows sales advantage was because customers were using it as a task switcher among MS-DOS applications, so our Windows apps needed to run in "real mode" (consistent with earlier Intel processors); he added that, by 1990, our applications might run only on "protected mode" (a later Intel processor mode that required more physical memory but offered applications easy access to much larger virtual memory) and only on OS/2-386. The "protected mode" prediction was accurate; when Windows PowerPoint shipped in 1990, it did run only on protected mode, but in Windows, not OS/2.

In the first part of 1988, the Windows PowerPoint project solved the problems of getting the code base moved from Pascal to C, and separately started on the immense task of creating all-new code to handle text formatting (replacing Apple's 68000-assembler CoreEdit code that we were using on Mac). By this time, all the final details of Macintosh

PowerPoint 2.0 were buttoned up, and the Windows version specs could be updated to match and matching schedules made. All the other Microsoft apps being developed for Windows, supposedly about to ship, were experiencing problems, and we tried to find out as much about those as possible. Most of the news increased our estimates of the work that we would have to do. "The ship on the beach is a lighthouse to the sea," as the old software maxim goes.

153 Bill Seeks Tools to Make "Windows 3.0" a Big Hit

In March of 1988, I had attended for the first time the annual Apps Retreat, designed to get all the Apps Division senior managers on the same page with Bill Gates. The message wasn't completely clear to me, though it seemed to be clear to Bill.

My notes say that some new version of Windows ("3.0?") would appear in early 1989. Our plan was to be the dominant applications vendor on Windows, along with "lots of second-tier apps," while our major competitors (Lotus, WordPerfect, Ashton-Tate) went "down the path of OS/2, which is wrong for a while." After that, it was "important to be early on PM," but "PM is so big, it will ship full of bugs and will be very difficult to develop for." So Bill's advice was to aim for Windows-386 for "88–89," and then OS/2-386 PM for "90–91–92." This was consistent with the advice that Bill had given me in December. Jon Shirley mildly protested the lack of a "clean strategy for PM" for apps, but there was little information. At the GBU, we wrote about the "Windows/PM version" in our documents, but in practice we studied only Windows and worked only with Windows code.

As the Windows PowerPoint group progressed, we discovered that we had to use IBM's "8514/A" graphics to be able to show any arbitrary 256 colors out of 24-bit color space (as we were doing on the Mac using Apple's Palette Manager). To do that, we would need more memory, which would involve complexity; the "protected mode only" projected by Bill for 1990 would solve that problem more easily, but was beyond our time horizon. There were many other similar technical issues.

By early July 1988, we had a new spec and schedule showing Windows PowerPoint shipping by June 1989. This was the basis for the review and demonstration to Bill Gates on 22 July 1988, which resulted in Bill's agreement that we were doing the right thing, and his follow-up report of general satisfaction, even though it would take us another year to ship. This ship date for Windows PowerPoint was later than our supposed ship date for PM PowerPoint, which was supposed to follow. Over this six-month period, everyone's ideas of schedules had slipped.

But then in early August 1988, just a couple of weeks later, at a Resource Planning Meeting, Bill told us that there would be a spec within two weeks for the new "Windows 3.0." The Systems guys wanted one bit of feedback from all Microsoft apps immediately: if Windows 3.0 were to have proportionally spaced system fonts, would that break our apps, because they had assumed they had only mono-spaced fonts? This was an intoxicating whiff of the future—the continued use of mono-spaced system fonts in Windows was to me one of its glaringly ugly features. Bill was suddenly extremely enthusiastic about this new Windows 3.0. He announced that Windows 3.0 was "going to make GUI mainstream, regardless of short-term profit considerations." He was "going to make Windows 3.0 the hottest, sexiest system software we've ever shipped." Moreover, he was "not going to make Windows [3.0] unattractive in any way," and would keep a small Windows Paint app and a small Windows Write app bundled, so "people can buy Windows for $99 and play around with the graphics user interface." Bill solicited everyone's ideas about how to make Windows 3.0 a big hit—"this could really help me." He estimated that we needed to sell a new Windows package at four to five times the then-current rate to make it mainstream.

This was extremely frustrating for Windows PowerPoint. Here was a new Windows on the horizon, potentially a huge help to us, but still thought to be too far in the future. Then a few days later, I had a "PowerPoint 3.0 Brainstorming Session" with Bill Gates and Mike Maples. Macintosh PowerPoint 2.0 was getting great reviews, so they wanted to chuck in some ideas for the next version before we got too far along. In the course of this, Bill told me that the target for Windows 3.0 was to freeze the spec in September 1988, just a month away, and to ship in June 1989, ten months away. It would have proportional system fonts, memory management, and a real user shell, and would use 386-only instructions, would be smaller, would have a new install (a big problem with Windows 2.0) and a new 8514/A driver for the graphics we needed, as well as other great things.

This was too much to resist. We were scheduled to ship Windows PowerPoint 2.0 in June 1989, with Bill's agreement. The perfect new Windows 3.0 was targeted to ship at exactly the same time. We would have a spec for it in a month. If we were to aim our work at Windows

3.0, we could make a much better PowerPoint product and give Bill something to make Windows 3.0 a big hit, the thing he had asked for.

154 PowerPoint Should Skip Windows, Go to OS/2 PM

There were interruptions to re-org the Apps Division and deal with Genigraphics and Macintosh PowerPoint 2.0. We didn't hear much about the new Windows 3.0, and, by October, Tom Rudkin was telling me that problems with Windows 2.0 were causing us to fall behind our schedule.

Part of the reason for our not continuing to hear about Windows 3.0 may have been high-level debates within Microsoft about Windows versus PM. Bill Gates had just been saying that he intended to make the future Windows 3.0 a big hit, but others may have had doubts about whether Windows could really overcome the immense lead of OS/2 Presentation Manager.

Mike Maples was an exceptionally clear-sighted fellow, and he had managed software strategy (including OS/2) for IBM's personal computer group, so he knew the strengths of OS/2 first-hand, whereas most of us in Microsoft Applications hardly knew OS/2 or PM at all. Mike also knew the strengths and weaknesses of both Microsoft and IBM in writing software. Fifteen years later, in an oral history interview, he recalled the time that he himself had been managing OS/2 development, when an audit was done comparing the parts of the OS/2 code written by IBM and the parts of the OS/2 code written by Microsoft:

> There was a very large audit done, led by an IBM fellow ... to look at the quality of the code. And I suppose, not to Microsoft's surprise but to IBM's surprise, the IBM auditor came back and said the quality of the Microsoft code was a lot better and it was a lot tighter. And Microsoft really was focused on a small number of really bright people while IBM was focused on a larger number of process-driven people. Not that they weren't bright—it's just that they were living up to a set of standards and a set of conventions that were probably overpowering for the software.
>
> ... It was a very difficult project because of the far-flung nature of the development organizations. You've got development organizations that don't know each other very well, that have different kinds of objectives and that are in different time zones, in differ-

ent worlds. It's a really hard thing to make any kind of development work. And OS/2 suffered from that.

... Most of the management group, the architects and the managers, were experienced IBM developers from different places. We did hire a number of young, college graduates. But the young people were trained more in the IBM way than they were in the Microsoft way. (Maples 2004)

But even knowing all that, many people thought that OS/2 PM was so far ahead that Windows could never catch up as a serious operating system product.

In October 1988, soon after his reorganization of Applications, Mike Maples devoted one of his Applications senior staff meetings to the topic of OS/2 Presentation Manager, to expose the new Business Unit Managers to more information.

At Mike's meeting, Cameron Myhrvold and Steve Ballmer from Systems predicted there would be 30 to 40 major PM applications in the first half of 1989; they were over-subscribed for ISV support. In online forums, Lotus and Ashton-Tate had posted the most questions. Software Publishing Corp. had four product groups working on PM apps. Aldus, Zenographics, Lotus, Digital Research, Micrografx, and a lot more ISVs were going to demonstrate PM apps with IBM on 31 October 1988 (just ten days away), and there would be more at Fall Comdex.

Mike pointed out that most of our competitors were doing PM first, then going back to port their apps to Windows. Major apps would begin appearing in fourth quarter 1988 (the same time as he was talking to us), with the peak in introductions about nine months later, in third quarter 1989. That peak would coincide with the Windows PowerPoint shipment. For me, in particular, Mike had the information that Zenographics would ship a PM version of a new presentation app called Pixie in first quarter 1989, Cricket (makers of Cricket Presents for Macintosh) would ship two PM graphics apps in second quarter 1989, and Silicon Beach would ship a PM graphics app at the same time. Most of these apps were said to be aiming at very high functionality to justify the cost of a platform upgrade, and were hoping to price their apps at $100 above Windows versions.

It was true that Windows was going to run in two megabytes less memory than PM, but somewhere, Mike had gotten a rumor that IBM had stockpiled 100,000 megabytes of DRAM boards, which would allow it to run special promotions based on selling OS/2 PM and plug-in memory cheaply together.

Mike's information did not end with any strong advice to consider prioritizing applications for PM over Windows, but it was hard to understand in any other way. Who wanted to be shipping a new Windows app in nine months, when all our strong competitors were shipping apps on a superior platform?

The confusing information continued during the rest of 1988. In November, we had another review of Windows PowerPoint 2.0, concluding that we would now release to manufacturing 5 June 1989, which meant a slip of about a month in the previous four months. In early December, Mike Maples spoke again at his staff meeting about our failure to be aggressive on the "winning environments of the future," such as PM.

A couple of days later, Mike visited me at the GBU, and after a demo and schedule review of Windows PowerPoint 2.0, he told me that "if Windows PowerPoint 2.0 were to slip to September 1989, it would be worth scrapping Windows for PM." Given the relatively small slip mentioned—less than three months from our then-current schedule—this was pretty strong advice to re-target for PM. Any software manager worth his salt can find a way to slip three months.

Early 1989 continued with conflicting messages. Mike's first staff meeting in January identified the confusion between Windows and PM as a continuing strategy problem. His next staff meeting at mid-month featured a report that Systems Division had reviewed OS/2 and PM, concluding that the success of PM depended on great applications. Bill Gates was reported to have asked what it would take to get our applications on PM.

155 Tentative Feelers about Windows 3.0

In late February 1989, we were holding to the Windows PowerPoint 2.0 schedule, but we got direct feelers from Systems people—perhaps prompted by Bill Gates or Mike Maples, or perhaps because they understood how PowerPoint was a match for what they were doing. After all, the success of Windows would depend on great applications, too. They wanted us to cooperate with them on Windows 3.0. They thought that PowerPoint was a strong reason to buy Windows 3.0, and could justify adoption of Windows, just as PowerPoint was already a justification to buy Macs. Later in the month, we got some Windows 3.0 code, did some testing, and reported some problems back to them.

In March 1989, I began meeting with Dennis Austin, Tom Rudkin, and Dennis Abbe about font problems. We called ourselves the "Font Special Interest Group." We had learned some things about fonts on Macintosh during the course of the Genigraphics imaging project, just then barely completed. We were having lots of problems with fonts in Windows 2.0, and they appeared to be very hard to fix. We got further details on font handling in Windows 3.0 from that group, and we started testing our code strenuously in early Windows 3.0 builds. Tom re-estimated the work to complete Windows PowerPoint 2.0 assuming we stayed on Windows 2.0, and found that there was a significant slip owing to all the new work for fonts that would be needed (and other discoveries), and that we could likely finish more quickly on Windows 3.0, even accommodating all its differences, than on Windows 2.0.

Every time I had my staff meeting at the GBU, I came away with a request from my people to escalate enquiries to the Windows 3.0 group about new features and small changes. Some of what we wanted was actually incorporated into Windows 3.0, at a cost to their own schedule. By the beginning of April 1989, I had a plan to talk to Mike Maples and Steve Ballmer about changing our strategy, to make Windows Power-Point 2.0 the first program which would run *only* on Windows 3.0. It appeared that we could make a much better product and that we might actually save time, because we would have to build so much less in our own code to compensate for what was missing from Windows 2.0.

156 Bill for Windows vs. Steve for OS/2 PM

Before I could talk to Mike Maples and Steve Ballmer about Windows 3.0, there came the next annual Applications Division Executive Staff Retreat. On 7 April 1989, Bill Gates gave an upbeat summary of progress on Windows 3.0. All the new features promised before were going well, and a number of ISVs (mostly the minor companies, per plan) had signed up. All the large OEM PC manufacturers had signed up to ship it. He thought that ship would slip a bit, to August 1989. Bill now, for the first time, recommended to the entire division that new apps for Windows should be "Windows 3.0 only."

I made a note that perhaps we should slip Windows PowerPoint to match—it would be only two months, from June 1989 to August 1989. We'd have a better chance of making that, since we would be better able to estimate what we needed to do.

Then, the next day, Steve Ballmer gave the official Systems Division pitch. In Steve's view, Windows 3.0 was going to be better: smaller, more UI appeal, protected mode on both 286s and 386s. But it suffered because it was "part of the present DOS environment."

By contrast, Steve put up a slide saying "OS/2: The Most Powerful Graphical User Interface System." Every equipment manufacturer was signed up to ship it. All the major application competitors were developing for it (the same story as before). It was true that OS/2 PM required a couple of megabytes more memory, but OEMs would help subsidize that at first. OS/2 and PM had so many technical strengths that they would surely prevail. Whereas Windows 3.0 claimed it would ship in quarter 3 of calendar 1989, OS/2 for 386s would ship an SDK at the same time and deliver in the first half of 1990. The only danger he could see to OS/2's chances to dominate was that applications for it might be delayed until there was a good graphical user interface for Unix, which could be a challenger to OS/2.

Bill interjected that he'd told Jim Cannavino at IBM, who was the brand-new head of the Personal Systems Division overseeing OS/2 development, that he needed half the people working on OS/2—the good half! Cannavino had reportedly agreed.

I thought at the time that Bill foresaw that OS/2 was becoming a disaster under the big-company development practices required by IBM, and that Windows could very well evolve faster in the hands of Microsoft alone, even coming from behind, and take the market first.

In my personal evaluation, Steve's talk sounded like so many big-company presentations in which grandiose plans are expounded by staff guys with typeset foils, but then nothing ever happens. By contrast, Bill's talk sounded like someone who personally understood all the factors needed to make the project happen, and who knew how to get it done and the names of all the people needed to do it.

157 PowerPoint for Windows 3.0, not for OS/2 PM

After seeing Bill and Steve debate Windows 3.0, even though I couldn't get any better guidance, I decided two weeks later, on 20 April 1989, that we would commit PowerPoint to use Windows 3.0, and do all the work necessary to make that happen, ignoring OS/2. We set up closer communications with the Windows 3.0 group, both in development and in marketing. We committed not to ship until after Windows 3.0

was shipping, supposed to be only four months away in August. At my next meeting with Mike Maples, five days later, I confirmed this decision with him and went over the newly revised plan. This was a decision never to run on Windows 2.0—it was not a decision to cut out an eventual (unscheduled) PM version. Mike didn't disagree.

This decision in April 1989 set us off on one of the longest years in development history, during which Windows 3.0 would be delayed by nearly a year, and we would be delayed along with it.

On 1 May 1989, we got word that the final Windows 3.0 SDK would ship that week, or the next. On 4 May 1989, we decided to rewrite our spec throughout for the new Windows 3.0 appearance and to do our testing on Windows 3.0 only. On 22 May 1989, we began a thorough re-planning of the Windows PowerPoint schedule, cutting out all work needed to run on Windows 2.0 and adding tasks to run on Windows 3.0. We were becoming deeply committed.

The following day, 23 May 1989, I was attending Mike Maples' staff meeting in Redmond, and he reported that, in a recent conversation, Steve Ballmer had predicted that Windows 3.0 would "slip to May 1990." Since Windows 3.0 was then planned for August 1989, that would be a nine-month slip. Bill Gates had immediately rejoined "No way!" Jon Shirley had worried that, if Windows 3.0 should slip to May 1990, the slip would have a big impact on revenue. (I may not have liked Steve's talk about OS/2 PM at the Apps Retreat, but he turned out to be a very accurate forecaster of Windows.)

By 19 June 1989, the release date for Windows 3.0 had slipped out to 4 December 1989, a major slip; but "code complete" was expected for early September, so that still seemed close. Late in the month, Bill Gates and Mike Maples jointly issued a new prediction for relative penetration of Windows and OS/2, for the business units to use in Applications planning. Their new estimate was

	MS-DOS	Windows	OS/2 PM
1989	75%	25%	0%
1990	50%	40%	10%
1991	25%	50%	25%
1992	0%	60%	40%

This represented a much larger penetration of Windows, and lower penetration of OS/2, in the later years than we had seen before. Shortly thereafter I got word of a project codenamed "Porthole," staffed by three people from Apps and four people from Systems. This would be a DLL (Dynamic Link Library) for OS/2 which would emulate Windows system calls, and thus would allow any Windows 3.0 application to run on OS/2 PM unchanged. This further reduced any incentive to develop for PM; you could develop for Windows and get PM for free.

In July, Excel decided, for their new version, not to follow us onto Windows 3.0; they would finish and ship a "compatibility app," which would run on Windows 2.0 but could use the proportional fonts and protected mode if available, and not much more. Word made the same decision for their very first version of Word for Windows 1.0, which shipped less than six months ahead of PowerPoint for Windows. This would give Word and Excel an outdated appearance on Windows 3.0 that would not match their appearance on PM. But neither of them was graphically demanding, and neither was going to sell Windows 3.0.

On 12 September 1989, Mike Maples told me that Windows 3.0 would still release on 5 December 1989, so no slip since June. That meant that we had to be ready to ship at the same time. A month later, on 11 October 1989, Windows 3.0 had slipped to mid-January 1990. We continued to ready all of our manuals and product components and introduction materials for our own ship.

In early November 1989, Mike Maples reported that Bill Gates and Jim Cannavino had met to discuss a proposal that, at Fall Comdex 1989 (13–17 November in Las Vegas), they should jointly announce new versions of Windows and OS/2, with the positioning that Windows was for smaller-memory machines, OS/2 for larger-memory machines.

They would also announce that, after mid-1990, Microsoft applications would ship first or concurrently on PM, not first on Windows. But Bill clarified this to us internally: "our Systems guys swore Porthole [the Microsoft project to emulate Windows on PM] would work, so we said OK—ties [that is, we'll ship concurrently by using Porthole with the Windows version]. If Porthole doesn't work, then too bad. We'll have Windows versions first." Porthole was reported to be going well, expected to be done by March or April 1990. In any case, Windows PowerPoint was to ship well before the effective date for the agreement, so I didn't factor this high-level strategizing into my plans.

The announcement suggests that Bill still thought that Windows 3.0 could release to manufacturing sometime close to its early December date. At about the same time, we completed the copy for the Windows PowerPoint 2.0 box, ready to print. The schedule called for us to have product components done and to build internal distribution product prior to the end-of-year holidays, and to ship them internationally before the holidays, and to the U.S. field sales offices after the holidays. We started to prepare disks of pre-release versions of Windows 3.0 and PowerPoint 2.0 to distribute.

158 The GBU Building Is Completed

On 10 November 1989, only a month or so later than planned, the GBU moved to our magnificent new building at 2460 Sand Hill Road.

The building had been built to Microsoft's Redmond standards, with a private office (exactly 9'×12') for every person, virtually every one with a large outside window with a view of the hills above Stanford. Every office had space and furniture to hold multiple computers (most people had three or four, unusual then), and for a couple of people to work together. There were ample conference rooms of all sizes, up to a space big enough for everyone in the building. We had large test labs with proper lab benches and enough power and network cabling for very dense populations of test machines. We had work space for people from Publishing Power and from Genigraphics, with ample computers.

Main entrance to the Microsoft GBU building, 2460 Sand Hill Road, Menlo Park, California.

Lobby of Microsoft GBU Building, 2460 Sand Hill Road.

Picnic table outside 2460 Sand Hill Road, looking out over the Stanford land reserves in the western hills.

The building was long and narrow, arranged on three floors, with two wings on each floor. A huge central staircase linked the three floors, together with smaller staircases at both ends, as well as a newly installed elevator. Our lobby and reception area were on the top floor by a visitors' parking lot under live oak trees. Each floor had a central kitchen, with the standard Microsoft free drinks and selection of snacks. The lowest floor had a larger kitchen, and tables and chairs to make a dining hall large enough for 75 people—it was here that we held our "all hands" meeting every Monday morning. This area spilled out onto a patio next to the building, where we had some round tables with parasols and chairs.

The most striking feature of the building was part of Hunk and Moo Anderson's collection of contemporary art. This art had been on the walls of Saga and had been stored during the renovation of our building. The architects of our renovation had taken particular care to provide places designed to show off the art, so we got many of the best pieces. Several times a month, curators from the Anderson Collection would lead public tours of the art, so anyone could sign up and tour the Microsoft building. I never noticed any of our competitors.

Our lobby and many large wall areas off it contained large-scale constructions and canvases from different periods by Frank Stella. The wing where I had my office contained a whole long wall of works by Richard Diebenkorn, and the small conference room by my office had collages by Robert Motherwell. (We did not put Anderson Art in any individual offices, but we did hang it in all the shared areas.) The lobby contained a juxtaposition of large-scale sculptures, and the hallways were punctuated with niches for sculptural pieces.

When we interviewed candidates, they often were people with backgrounds in both computer science and studio art, or with an interest in art, and the experience of seeing such famous pieces casually spread all around the building never failed to make a favorable impression. This was a beautiful place to work.

Altogether, there were hundreds of works from the Anderson Collection. It's impossible to put a value on such a collection of unique works, but annually I would get a piece of paper to sign on which I agreed to pay the separate insurance for the pieces located in our building (this was our only cost to host the collection). I was buying insurance to cover an appraised value of well over $100 million for the art, even then.

We could stroll out the front door and walk to the fitness center, or to one of the two restaurants in another building, through the naturally forested hills. (The restaurants featured large canvases by Sam Francis.) One of the restaurants baked fresh pastries early every morning and delivered them hot to our kitchens for everyone. There were a couple of isolated picnic tables near our building, with the best views of the undeveloped Stanford reserve land.

After Building 4 was ready and we moved in, Bill Gates would frequently say when he visited us that the GBU building was the most attractive Microsoft facility anywhere in the world. He never asked me how much we were paying for the building (I had the answer, "$2.02 a square foot," all ready). Bill would quiz me closely about the smallest details of our product development, our competitors, and our business, and knew the cost of our hardbound manuals down to the penny, but he never asked me why there was $100 million worth of art on the walls, and I never explained it to him.

There is a PowerPoint slide show online with one hundred photographs taken in the Sand Hill Road building in 1992, including many pictures of the Wizards at work. (Gaskins, GBU Photos 1992)

159 Windows 3.0 Eclipses OS/2 PM at Microsoft

On 28 November 1989, I was in Redmond to hear the latest update on Windows 3.0, and there were some big last-minute changes. There was to be a dramatic simplification of versions: the old "Windows/286" and "Windows/386" were to be merged into one product as Windows 3.0. A single retail box would now run on any processor from 8088 up, in any memory from 640KB up. An older processor and 640KB would run in real mode; an older processor and 1MB would run in standard mode (old 286); a 386 processor and 2 MB would run in enhanced mode.

There were lots of other advantages. Windows 3.0 would manage the color palette and support device-independent color bitmaps, features we had been working on with them. The new dialog and menu formats had further improvements. There would be a new file manager. There was a solid saving of 2 MB in the memory requirements of Windows 3.0 versus OS/2, representing a much larger population of eligible machines for Windows 3.0. All of this was fantastically good news.

A beta (for 1200 ISVs and 300 sites) was being built that same day. They still had 220 open bugs. They now aimed to release to manufacturing around mid-February, which would be an additional slip of nine weeks, and would perhaps ship in late February or in March 1990.

The very next day, 29 November 1989, we started prioritizing features we had cut from Windows PowerPoint 2.0 but now could add back in the extra time we would have available from the additional slip, mostly refinements in font handling and font installation.

On 12 December 1989, at an Apps Product Strategy meeting in Redmond, Bill Gates told me that Windows 3.0 had slipped to release 28 February 1990, a further two-week slip.

After the first of the year, on 8 January 1990, we set our release to manufacturing for Windows PowerPoint 2.0 for 12 March 1990, and aligned all prior milestones to that release date. On 15 January 1990, Systems announced a slip of Windows 3.0 to 15 March 1990 release, again about two weeks, and now later than our own date. We couldn't release before them, since we had to test on the final released Windows disk, but decided not to change again right away.

On 22 January 1990, we received the first real Genigraphics slides imaged from Windows PowerPoint 2.0. The interminable delays in Windows 3.0 had been extremely beneficial in one way: it allowed Genigraphics to get its new engineering group organized and functioning. We would have faced great difficulty about the non-availability of Genigraphics slides for customers if we had shipped earlier, not to mention that we would not have been able to test our own software.

On 12 February 1990, further word came from Bill Gates on Windows and OS/2. The new advice was contradictory to the "OS/2 first or concurrently" directive we had received three months before; OS/2 was firmly downgraded. Now the word was to "focus on Windows, not OS/2." "We will not do OS/2-only apps." We only do OS/2 at all for three reasons: "to beat Unix, because we said we would, [and] good to have a two-tier strategy." OS/2 should be positioned as "Corporate Windows" or "Enterprise Windows." Bill also added that "IBM must shape up soon or divorce is inevitable."

With this revision of strategy came a new and (again) much later date for Windows 3.0: we would now announce it on 1 May 1990— exactly the prediction that Steve Ballmer had made back in May of 1989, a year before. This final last-minute slip of three months was extremely costly; eight venues around the world with all their infrastructure had already been reserved for the announcement, with satellite video feeds to and from them scheduled, and all of this had to be re-booked at great expense. But Bill was the great master of detecting exactly what was or was not the minimum adequate product to ship—I always consulted him on such decisions about PowerPoint.

Ten days later, the Systems group announced internally a "new OS/2 strategy" that they had decided at their retreat on 1 February 1990: it was to "Refocus around Windows." The aim was to "sell 10 million units of Windows 3.0 fast." This would be good for two or three years and would build protection of dominant scale against any Unix incursion; longer term, it could be good for OS/2 since "OS/2 can run Windows apps but Unix can't" (Porthole again). The "only danger is OS/2's death," a good call. Windows would now be extended upwards without any limitation. "Windows must succeed; OS/2 has to leverage Windows' success."

Also, this would change the Joint Development Agreement with IBM. Working with IBM had prevented "late changes, polishing, and market-centered products which are Microsoft strengths." IBM's declining share of the PC market also reduced their value. IBM has a "negative value in development," and their "value in marketing [is] inhibited because building the wrong product." Bottom line: "Microsoft must go it alone."

This appeared to be the final resolution of the "Windows or OS/2" question for Microsoft applications. We never again while I was there even considered doing a version of PowerPoint for OS/2 PM.

Back in August of 1988, almost three years before, Bill had solicited everyone's ideas about how to make Windows 3.0 a big hit—"this could really help me." I thought we had given him what he asked for. Bill just hadn't realized how long it would take.

160 *PowerPoint 2.0 Sells Windows 3.0*

Two weeks after his definite announcement that we would pursue Windows 3.0 at the expense of OS/2 PM, on 27 February 1990, Bill Gates held a big reception for ISVs; he successfully used an early development version of Windows PowerPoint 2.0 for his slides, because he needed a way to impress the other developers with what great apps Windows 3.0 would be able to support. Later, before the Windows 3.0 introduction, Mike Maples used Windows PowerPoint 2.0 for a presentation to the Microsoft Board of Directors; PowerPoint performed flawlessly, and the color wowed them with how great Windows 3.0 was going to be.

On 5 March 1990 we pinned down the final dates: Windows 3.0 would release to manufacturing before 1 May (actually happened on 22 April). We would release two weeks later, 15 May, to give us time to test thoroughly with the released Windows disk (this happened, though at 4:00 a.m. the following morning). Windows 3.0 would announce on 22 May 1990; we would announce the same day, at the same locations. We also did a separate press introduction for PowerPoint a few days earlier, on 18 May 1990, at Cowell Theater at Fort Mason in San Francisco, with Mike Maples in person as compere, before he flew out to his assigned city to host the Windows 3.0 announcement.

The Windows 3.0 announcement was front-page news in all the major newspapers. Bill Gates did a press tour, sent video press releases to 150 TV stations, and did two dozen live TV interviews. The event was in New York and seven other world cities, with a Microsoft executive hosting in each city. Bill did a live demo and got a standing ovation. Every time Windows 3.0 was demonstrated, Windows PowerPoint 2.0 was demonstrated. I asked to get a picture of PowerPoint and a caption mentioning PowerPoint into every business-press story on Windows 3.0; Pam Edstrom's answer to me was "Can do." (One advantage of tying our introduction to that of Windows was that we got the personal attention of Microsoft's most accomplished PR genius, who understood everything about the products and was a joy to work with.)

By 19 July 1990, only two months after the announcement of Windows PowerPoint 2.0, Genigraphics had its first day when there were more Windows imaging jobs than Mac imaging jobs. People were already using the Windows version heavily. By the same time, Windows 3.0 had already sold almost half a million copies. A month later, by mid-August, Windows 3.0 had sold a million copies. By the end of calendar 1990, Windows 3.0 had sold three million copies. The projection was for 5 million copies of Windows 3.0 in its first year, compared to total sales of 15 million PCs.

I have always believed that the simultaneous shipment of Windows PowerPoint 2.0 was a big spur to the great increase in Windows sales that began with Windows 3.0. As on Mac, the people who could sign purchase orders for new personal computers wanted PowerPoint more than any other application. The extremely photogenic shaded backgrounds and rich color schemes of PowerPoint, which did get pictured in all the press coverage, provided an easily observed mark of the huge step forward that Windows 3.0 represented. The very real availability of Genigraphics 35mm slides from the day of shipment made a Windows

3.0 machine a substitute for a workstation costing twenty times as much. The complete interworking with Macintosh PowerPoint made it possible to buy a machine that met corporate standards, and yet could interchange presentations with the Macs in the corporate art department. Even if you didn't buy PowerPoint right away, it was clear that you wanted Windows 3.0.

This had been a perilous passage for PowerPoint. PowerPoint required so much from Windows that it would really have been impossibly bad on Windows 1.0 or Windows 2.0; a competitor who waited for Windows 3.0 could have beaten us out. OS/2 and PM turned out to be a dead end for every competitor who followed the common wisdom and invested there first. The fact that we were on Windows 3.0 first and nearly alone, while all of our competitors were elsewhere, gave us a clear field (Lotus Freelance didn't ship on Windows for almost a year, Harvard Graphics didn't ship on Windows for almost two years). Microsoft was betting the company on Windows 3.0, and we were the app that showed clearly why it was worthwhile.

This saga illustrates the wisdom of leaving business units to make business judgments. At the Apps Executive Staff Retreat in early April 1989, there was a discussion of the outcome of the reorganization into business units the preceding September. There were still some authoritarians who thought it was too messy to have all these independent units doing different things in different ways. Bill Gates had the right comeback, immediately: "We don't lack the power to enforce our decisions; we lack the information about what we should require." The Microsoft system of the time allowed our group to make all those many course corrections and get to the right final result for our product, while other products made different calls.

Somehow, against all the conflicting advice to concentrate on OS/2 and PM or to bash something out on Windows 2.0, I had managed to steer PowerPoint onto the version of Windows which could make it great, the version of Windows which would get Microsoft's marketing and sales push as never before.

The shipment of Windows PowerPoint 2.0 was right at the end of the fiscal year in which it had been forecast to ship much earlier, so inevitably I got some flak about "missing the forecast." But all these complaints came from lower-level people whose vision was strictly compartmentalized into fiscal years; I got no complaints about the results from the senior executives.

PART VIII: POWERPOINT 3.0

161 Bill Gates's Early Input on PowerPoint 3.0

Bill Gates never missed an opportunity to get early input into new products. As one example, he scheduled a "PowerPoint 3.0 Brainstorming" session with me and Mike Maples as early as 8 August 1988, two months after Mac PowerPoint 2.0 had shipped and more than a year and a half before Windows PowerPoint 2.0 would ship. PowerPoint 3.0 was going to benefit from a long development time, allowing a real step forward in new function, and was going to be cross-platform from the beginning.

Bill's feedback was that, in the Mac 2.0 product, people had really liked the innovative handling of true full color, the logical color schemes, and especially the shaded backgrounds—all this was unprecedented in personal computer products. People also liked the way text worked, and reviewers had all praised the overall ease of use. More of the same please.

The wishes that Bill discerned when he talked to people were for more functions that at least appeared to be integrated into the product rather than imported, including a lot more drawing and "graphing" (bar charts and pie charts)—both were already planned. He thought people would want animated transitions between slides for video (which I had planned since 1985). He also queried whether we should include outlining of some sort (already on the table for us), and perhaps some kind of project-planning connection (half-hearted, never came to anything).

Bill's main focus was on the idea of "components" to be shared by Microsoft applications. He wanted PowerPoint to incorporate links to external or embedded chart objects from Excel and wanted Word to incorporate links to external or embedded drawing objects from PowerPoint. He had a lot of advice about how this should be done, both large ideas and small technical points, and again tasked the GBU to define the standards for accomplishing this.

Such an "object linking and embedding" protocol would:

1. allow one application to literally call on code in other applications;
2. solve efficiency issues, so it could be used intensively;
3. allow us to add functions to products separately, even after shipment;
4. potentially allow us to enlist third parties to add components.

This technical vision was underpinned by Mike Maples' organizational ideas about how the Business Units could organize to reliably supply components to one another.

162 Beginning on PowerPoint 3.0

During the whole of the two years that we worked on Windows Power-Point 2.0 to produce a version equivalent to the shipped Macintosh PowerPoint 2.0, work was already going ahead on PowerPoint 3.0. After Mac PowerPoint 2.0 shipped in May 1988, the design meetings for 3.0 began in June.

Much of the early planning was done by Dennis Austin with a small group of people, while we recruited more developers. Even though Tom Rudkin was managing all the complexity of PowerPoint on Windows, he still participated in the planning meetings, so the early work benefitted from first-hand experience on both platforms. As Windows Power-Point 2.0 became more and more consuming, it took the great bulk of his time.

As early as 9 February 1989, Dennis was showing me a developed plan for breaking PowerPoint into three parts:

1. The PowerPoint "core engine," all the functions that defined the PowerPoint application but were platform-independent: text, drawing, slides, presentations, graphs, and so forth.
2. A Virtual Platform, all the functions that are actually independent of PowerPoint but depend on the platform: handling memory, graphics primitives, utilities, and so forth. This would be implemented three times, on the three platforms (Mac, Windows, and OS/2—still nominally alive at this date).

3. Product Code, all the functions particular to PowerPoint which could differ on a specific platform: commands, window appearance, menus, user interface, dialogs, and so forth. This code would exist in three versions—for Mac, for Windows, and for Presentation Manager.

By June of 1989, there was a formal PowerPoint 3.0 spec which could be reviewed outside of development. By this time, specific people were being assigned to parts of the "core engine" code and to the virtual platform code.

Later in the year, updates to Mac PowerPoint 2.0 and complexities of Windows PowerPoint 2.0 were major interruptions to work on 3.0. (There was some overlap, since Windows PowerPoint 2.0 and Power-Point 3.0 were both being developed using the same tools and in C.)

We continued to take everyone's time for recruiting, so as to staff up, the essential foundation; in the year from July 1990 to June 1991, we managed to hire more than two dozen people, doubling our numbers, with extremely good quality.

163 PowerPoint 3.0 Drawing

One of Bill Gates's interests all through the beginning of work on PowerPoint 3.0 was drawing. He worried that there wasn't enough drawing "built in" to the product, and brought up the issue repeatedly. I think that his main source of concern was that Microsoft didn't have a generic "Draw" application, and he hoped that PowerPoint could serve that function, as well as its focus on presentations. One of Bill's techniques to stimulate thought was to ask for a report on why we shouldn't acquire another company to gain a product foothold and some smart people in the area, so he asked for a couple of such assessments; we explained why buying existing drawing packages would not improve our drawing.

I agreed with Bill's desire for somewhat more drawing in the product, but I thought that there were many special kinds of complex or technical drawing that would be best served by separate applications, from us or from other companies, with their results easily imported. We needed to concentrate on the drawing actually used in general business documents, including presentations, and on inventing new ways to make that drawing easy and intuitive. We didn't want the equivalent of a general drawing application that could do anything, tediously.

Eventually, the GBU came up with a spec for the specific drawing that would be incorporated into PowerPoint 3.0, and a plan to modularize it (name "Draw") so that it could be incorporated into other Microsoft applications, using Bill's preferred "object linking and embedding" technique. It would have modular user documentation for the package, to be written by the GBU and supplied along with the code. This found a good reception, and by 24 March 1990, at the next Applications Annual Retreat, Bill announced that "I think the spec for drawing in PowerPoint 3.0 is really pretty good."

164 The First Promise of Moving from Diskettes

At that Apps Retreat, 22–25 March 1990, Bill Gates raised an interesting topic: every application product should think about, "If you shipped on 540 MB, what else would you be able to include?"

His announcement was that Microsoft hoped to start shipping CD-ROM media in its applications in 12–18 months, freeing us from the high cost of materials for the many small-capacity diskettes we had to ship, and freeing users from the tedium of feeding them for each install.

It's hard to remember now that this constraint applied to all kinds of software, but people's PCs had no way to read anything else. To get momentum within the company, Microsoft had just bought 500 add-on CD-ROM drives for the U.S. sales force and would begin sending out a monthly CD with all kinds of things.

This, of course, was perfect for PowerPoint 3.0. We had our huge fonts, our plans for clip art, template libraries, sample presentations, maps of all parts of the world—so much data that could make it easier to create presentations. If we could ship a CD-ROM, then we could include all that material for just the one-time cost of acquiring it, with zero increase in our per-unit cost of goods. The fly that could already be seen in the ointment was the worry that, if we included a lot of English-language material on CD-ROM, it would all have to be localized; of course, this didn't turn out to be a real problem.

CDs didn't arrive in time for PowerPoint 3.0's first shipment, but the slightly later Office 3.0 was indeed shipped in a CD-ROM version.

165 Even More Travel Is Recommended

Gradually, my own travel had been increasing. Mike Maples had established a firm schedule for his staff meetings in Redmond on alternate weeks; so, every other week, I flew up to Seattle and spent at least two days on the headquarters campus, keeping in touch. After a while, I started staying in the very nice Olympic Hotel, as it was then named, in downtown Seattle, but when I handed in my expense reports, I always asked reimbursement only for a lower amount corresponding to the price of motels near the Microsoft campus; no one ever commented either way on the discrepancy between my bills and my reimbursement requests. In alternate weeks, when I was not in Seattle, I usually had another longer trip, often to New York to see Genigraphics or to a sales meeting somewhere.

I was in New York to see Genigraphics often, and stayed at the Plaza Hotel, which was the "Microsoft hotel" in those days. I always booked a standard room, but they began giving me suites overlooking Central Park because I was there so frequently.

In fact, I traveled so often that I never unpacked. A duplicate for everything I needed for travel remained permanently in my suitcases, ready to go. When we had the closets in our house rebuilt, mine featured places for my permanently packed bags. I booked so many airline tickets that our travel agent started sending me free tickets to expensive sporting events. I sent them back and called up the head of the travel agency to denounce him for giving kickbacks to travelers rather than reducing our costs (I should also have mentioned his vulgar taste in bribes), then transferred all our business to a new travel agency.

In May 1990, Mike Maples decided that there wasn't enough contact between the Business Units and the international subsidiaries. The solution was for Business Unit managers to try to make two trips a year to Europe to tour all the major subs there, plus one international trip per year somewhere else, depending on product plans (Australia, Japan, South America, ...). Added to all the domestic travel I was already doing, I spent more and more time away from Menlo Park. This worked out okay, since we were staffing up through intensive recruiting, and everyone was still working at a startup pitch.

I thought that the new international travel standard was good, especially since I could also see the Genigraphics staff in Europe, and make visits to their locations, as well as to our subsidiaries. I worked out a standard program of flying from San Francisco or Seattle to London, catching up there on the eight time zones difference with a personal day or two, then touring the subsidiaries on the continent, then back to London for a day or two of personal time to decompress, and then home. I never had time to take a proper vacation, so I had ample accrued vacation days for these few personal days around my European trips.

These personal days in London were a silver lining to the exhausting travel. They were extremely enjoyable for a former English major, and I was reminded of the time when I'd worked in London for Northern Telecom Systems Corporation. On these trips, I became so well known to the Savoy Hotel in the Strand that they knew to open and decant a bottle of vintage port from their cellars for my room before I arrived, and to have the theater desk book a single ticket to some well-received play for each night of my stay. They usually gave me an upgrade to a suite with a magnificent view looking up and down the Thames. Gradually, I decided to buy a home in London. I bought books about neighborhoods and tracked central London residential property prices in the *Financial Times* (at that time, falling steadily—to a generational low). On every trip, I'd inspect and rate different neighborhoods for their potential. This research paid off: shortly after I retired from Microsoft, my wife and I bought a home in central London and lived there most of the time for the following ten years.

Another technique recommended by Mike to gain better knowledge of the subsidiaries' needs was to appoint an International Manager in each Business Unit to handle all international issues, to know all local requirements, to be an evangelist to the country subsidiaries, and to represent the international requirements internally to development. This was new to the other Business Units who had only recently been created, but reflected what the GBU had long before already done with our Aniko Somogyi. Aniko also increased her international travel.

In December of 1990, a poll of the international subsidiaries reported that the Graphics Business Unit was doing the best job of exchanging information with the subs, despite our being so much smaller than any of the others. All the credit for this went to Aniko's intelligent and creative effort in inventing her role and carrying it out.

Closer contact with the subsidiaries was helpful in details of content that we included with PowerPoint (clip art, maps, and so forth, plus the obvious date and currency formats), but there were very few details of how the PowerPoint application worked that were the subject of distinct international requirements (one was vertical text, for Far Eastern languages). This tended to confirm my original observation, long be-fore PowerPoint, that presentations were the same all over the world.

166 Reorganizing For PowerPoint 3.0

Following the shipment of Windows PowerPoint 2.0, it was time to reorganize development again to find ways to bring everyone's efforts to bear on PowerPoint 3.0. We'd never before had more than one devel-opment manager in charge of a specific release.

In early June of 1990, Dennis Austin and Tom Rudkin settled on a way to break up the work. Dennis would continue on the central plat-form-independent features of PowerPoint, including the new text work by Dennis Abbe. Along with this, he would monitor the "Microsoft apps standards" activities (around user interface standards, and linking and embedding), and the supporting tools activities. Tom would take over our drawing for PowerPoint and the creation of the "embeddable drawing" code for other apps, on which a lot of work was needed. He would also handle all the competitive responses and updates to the 2.0 version that he had just released, including the transition to using Windows' own fonts, plus a number of multimedia and Core Power-Point issues.

By the end of July 1990, we put on a full program review for Mike Maples, complete with a newly revised spec and schedule for Power-Point 3.0. Bill Gates had read the new spec and schedule and sent his feedback via Mike. Bill himself came down for a visit two weeks later, on 16 August 1990, and got a reprise; he was approving, with lots of spe-cific suggestions, large and small.

We continued to hire as aggressively as possible, to prepare for the big push on PowerPoint 3.0. We retained more local recruiters who knew the quality of people we needed, and set up a standing weekly meeting to review résumés and decide on screening interviews. Even after live screening interviews, which rejected most potential candi-dates after they had talked to just one or two of us, and even after talk-ing to references, we still put in a full day of interviews for every candidate, and we still rejected most of them (we read hundreds of résumés, even after knowledgeable pre-screenings had rejected thou-sands more, for every offer extended). Hiring mistakes can be so ex-tremely damaging that it was worth exceptional effort to avoid making such mistakes.

167 Genigraphics Development in Silicon Valley

A vital move forward for Genigraphics had been their decision to re-duce dependence on the rump of engineering that remained in Syra-cuse, New York after the sale of the hardware division to Pansophic, supplemented by consultants. Despite facing the difficulty of "how do you hire the first engineering manager," and despite our rather limited ability to help in that, they hired a very good and experienced engineer-ing manager to start a new development group for Genigraphics in Silicon Valley. He had begun on 13 September 1989 and had started recruiting programmers immediately.

That same day, we held a joint program review with Genigraphics to kick off the new group. Rosemary Abowd continued to act as what Microsoft would have called the Program Manager, so the transition was smooth. At the meeting, it was stressed that 50% of Genigraphics' PowerPoint customers sent in slides using modems, a percentage that had not decreased despite marketing efforts to promote the centers for walk-in business. Hence it would be critical to include better network-ing and better reception of electronic files in the new work.

We thought that the Genigraphics group would not have time to get anything going prior to the ship of Windows PowerPoint 2.0. As it turned out, with the dramatic slip of Windows 3.0 and hence Power-Point 2.0 to May 1990, they managed, in those eight months, to get their first services working, and working very well, in time to benefit from the huge introduction.

Especially over the following two years, as we worked on PowerPoint 3.0, and with the move to Windows 3.1 which would include TrueType fonts for the first time (changing the coupling between applications and drivers), the GBU and Genigraphics developers worked closely together. They were working on hardware that no one else had tried to use, and their ultra-high resolution revealed any mistakes in Power-Point. PowerPoint developers explained to them precisely what we were doing and the ins and outs of the changing Windows graphics. We went over bugs and imaging problems in regular joint meetings. We were also able to supplement their QA effort as part of our own testing. By the time PowerPoint 3.0 shipped, Genigraphics had evolved to really perfect imaging that never disappointed users.

168 A Prototype Conference Room of the Future

After we moved into our permanent building on Sand Hill Road and shipped PowerPoint 2.0, we went on to do a lot of work to turn one of the large conference rooms off the lobby into a venue for video presentations. We wanted to show what the future might hold, even though it was unrealistic for ordinary customers.

In 1991, we commissioned a room full of furniture designed specifically for us by a local designer. The conference table was modular so that an end could be removed to turn an oval into a "U"-shape with an open end toward the screen wall, and underneath were concealed connections for power, network data, and voice telephony. Blackout shades on the windows were vital, because large projection displays were dim.

We built a custom-made podium, with room for a keyboard/mouse, and a large CRT set down almost horizontally into the podium, with hidden wiring to connect to a desktop ("tower") computer in a connected rear cabinet, with a network connection there.

For a display, we used a large rear-projection monitor set into a hole in the wall. This required building a false wall in the conference room with a six-foot space behind it, reached by a corridor door giving access to the rear-projection device set behind the wall, for adjustments and maintenance. The display was a huge and heavy Barco "Retrodata 600" unit with three CRTs (one each for red, green, and blue) in a projector base, shooting up into a mirror and from there reflected onto the back of a translucent screen, all built into one floor-standing case; it was made by a specialized company called "BARCO," standing for "Belgian American Radio Corporation."

We also built matching custom projection tables to hold an overhead projector and a 35mm projector, and we installed an electronically controlled screen that descended to cover the hole-in-the-wall monitor.

It was obvious from the beginning that our demo setup would never become common. The display behind the wall was delicate and required specialized maintenance, the computer in the conference room required regular updating, and to get a presentation onto it required that the conference-room computer be on the network, or else that we carry some sort of media to load the conference-room machine. At Microsoft, we had all of our computers including all of our conference rooms networked, but our customers mostly didn't have network ports in conference rooms.

333

What you wanted was a laptop with true full color for the podium and with video out, plugged into a video projector installed in the conference room. But laptops like that didn't exist until *just* before my presentation in Paris in 1992, a year later, and really practical video projectors didn't exist until several years later than that.

It was clear to us that both the CRT buried in the podium and the huge projection CRTs hidden behind the false wall were prototypes—someday there would be color laptops for use on the podium and color flat panel displays or color LCD projectors for the wall-sized image. We were consciously demonstrating the future, not trying to be practical. (The figure at the podium is Robert Safir, Wizard #14, who managed the design and installation for the GBU.)

169 Stand By to Repel Boarders

I thought it was vitally important to keep our location on Sand Hill Road defined as "the PowerPoint building," or "the GBU building," and definitely not let it become "the Microsoft Bay Area building." I managed to do this with complete success, and it contributed to our continuing independence.

Partly, it was accomplished by not having too many empty offices. The plan I worked out with our landlords, the Kaiser Family Foundation, contained terms under which we began completely rebuilding a large building as our eventual home, and during the eighteen months or so of construction, we occupied an area of progressively increasing size in another building, with the space growing larger on a schedule tied to my hiring plan. This was mostly motivated by cost, so as not to pay for unused space, while having guaranteed and scheduled options to expand. But another advantage was that it avoided having large amounts of obviously unused space early on, which would have attracted raids by other parts of the company. If I had allowed other groups to move in, even "temporarily," our facility would have been mentally reclassified as a "company resource," and control would have passed out of my hands into staff groups responsible for the Redmond campus.

A particular danger was that groups in drizzling gray Redmond were extremely creative in finding reasons why they should have a sub-group located on sunny Sand Hill Road in Menlo Park. Every group in Redmond had to come down to the Bay Area frequently to meet with other companies in Silicon Valley, so practically every organization in Redmond wanted to have at least an office or two under their permanent control in our building (as, in the other direction, there was a "GBU office" in one of the buildings in Redmond, where I or anyone else from the GBU could store materials, make phone calls, and schedule meetings). But I always rejected such requests. We kept one single vacant office just off the lobby where visitors, from Redmond or from other companies, could make private phone calls or read email at a Xenix terminal, but it lacked amenities, and nothing could be left in it.

The most persistent group was Microsoft Consulting Services (MCS), which was just getting started and wanted to hire individual salaried "consultants" to work with enterprise clients, and to put them into my building, one at a time, to avoid having to pay to build up any local infrastructure. I concentrated on rejecting the presence of consultants very firmly, and I made the case to the head of the consulting group in Redmond (during our periodic conversations on the subject) that our building was too far out in the suburbs; his pricy consultants deserved no less than to spend their billable hours in downtown San Francisco, forty miles away, on a high floor of some new skyscraper with expansive Bay views, where they would be much closer to expensive restaurants with good wine lists, in which to do their vital work with their enterprise clients. The logic of this was obviously unarguable, and MCS soon opened its own offices in just such a location in San Francisco's financial district, and never bothered me again.

I got help from my boss, Mike Maples, who understood this issue; even after we moved into our final large building, he always rejected other groups' appeals of my rejections. Indeed, one time Mike called to ask me if possibly his own son, who attended Stanford but was going away for the summer, might store a few boxes in our building for a couple of months! (I easily made that work.)

Having a physical location entirely under the exclusive control of the GBU was an important ingredient in retaining the startup spirit of the business unit for five years.

170 *Melinda French Discovers a PowerPoint Feature*

In early 1990, there was a study of customers' preferences in packaging, conducted by a product manager named Melinda French (now Melinda Gates).

Melinda studied the industry-standard ring binders with punched pages, versus the case-bound hardback books that I had introduced for PowerPoint 1.0, which we were still using for PowerPoint.

Her research showed that customers slightly preferred the loose-leaf binders over my case-bound books; the "biggest reason for preferring binders over case was so loose sheets could be fed to the auto-feeder of a copy machine to make illegal pirate copies for friends or colleagues." (Microsoft did not copy-protect diskettes, so higher-quality documentation was one good reason to buy the product rather than copy it.) This aspect of customer preferences was not one that Microsoft could share. Apart from that, the case-bound books were preferred.

When I introduced case-bound manuals, I hadn't understood that they were also an anti-piracy measure, but apparently that was true. In addition, of course, case-bound was cheaper, lighter, and more usable. Despite all that, the conclusions of the study were not supportive of introducing more case-bound books, for reasons unclear to me.

171 *PowerPoint Improved the Fonts in Windows 3.1*

I had always been interested in type fonts and typesetting. When I was in college, I had a job as proofreader in an "advertising production agency" in Los Angeles. My cubbyhole was back in the filthy typesetting area, where I stood around while compositors set metal type from California job cases and locked it into forms on imposing stones for printing, and I watched them distribute type back into the cases after use—essentially as it had been done for four hundred years. I stood next to the Linotype machines while operators assembled brass matrices and shot hot lead into them to cast whole lines of body type, and I brushed the extra bits of lead off the slugs before pulling myself a proof to read. I was responsible for the correctness of everything we produced, so I had to be able to detect a single wrong-font character (which could happen very easily then, when physical metal types or matrices could get into the wrong case). I studied fonts and books about them, and continued that study for years. For the rest of my working days, I carried a magnifying loupe in my jacket pocket, so I could examine closely any type I ran across.

The fact that PowerPoint on Mac and Windows would produce overhead transparencies using properly spaced typeset text in real fonts was a big part of its appeal. While raising money for PowerPoint, after the LaserWriter had shipped in 1985, I used to prepare my pitch using MacDraw or something, and print it in lovely fonts on the LaserWriter. Then I would make a second copy of my opening slide by hand using an Orator typeball on an IBM Selectric typewriter. When I stood up to talk, I'd put the typewriter slide on the overhead projector, containing my topic, name, position, company, date, occasion, and so forth. I'd talk for a couple of minutes about what I was going to say, and then I'd look at the screen, feign surprise, say "well, that doesn't look right!" and pull the typewriter slide off the stage of the projector and replace it with the slide containing the same content, but in multiple proportional type styles, sizes, and weights. That always looked a lot better to me, but I'm not sure that potential investors always understood—they saw typewriter slides every day.

The very early versions of Windows started out in a world where Word dominated, and Word (like all its competitors of the time) had a particularly old-fashioned way of dealing with fonts. Word had been designed to work with character-oriented "letter-quality" printers, such as daisy-wheel mechanisms. Since the printer was completely inflexible, Word had to import that inflexibility into its screen display, so it consulted a "driver" for the printer before making decisions about where to place characters on screen—the screen was no more than a preview of the printed output on a specific printer. All the font information came from the driver for the currently selected printer. Change your printer, and Word would, unasked, silently reformat your whole document, "re-flowing" the text, breaking lines and pages at new points, to reflect how the new printer would print your document, using its own different fonts and font metrics.

Of course, this was incomprehensibly wrong for PowerPoint and totally wrong for the emerging graphical world of Windows. PowerPoint couldn't tolerate changing the user's decisions about line breaks and page breaks—those were user design decisions. PowerPoint on Mac (and nowadays all graphical programs) worked by putting characters and images in theoretically perfect positions and then making a realization of that ideal as closely as possible on any screen and on any printer or other device. This meant that non-graphical printers (the whole installed base, in those days) could not be well supported, but we looked forward to a day when nobody would care; people who bought graphical personal computers would buy graphical printers.

Since there was a PowerPoint version on Mac also, we needed to "round-trip" documents between the two platforms; this meant you could begin a presentation on either Mac or Windows, close it and move the file to the other platform, edit the same presentation file there, then close it and move it back to the original platform, where it would open and display correctly, with all line breaks and page breaks where they had always been. This alone was enough to rule out the archaic idea of formatting for a specific printer on a specific computer.

These considerations meant that we needed the same fonts on Windows as already existed on Mac, down to a one-to-one mapping of font names. Further, to keep the line breaks the same, it meant that we needed precisely the same font metrics on Windows as already existed on Mac (which were the Adobe font metrics from the PostScript-based LaserWriter). Every character in every font had to look pretty much the same (same glyph) and be the same width and height with the same offsets and kerning and such (same metrics) as its corresponding character in the font on the opposite platform. We also needed for Windows to know about the small errors in character placement on screen caused by the relatively coarse screen resolution, and to provide information to manage the accumulated errors so that extra space was inserted between words, not between random characters mid-word—this took a while to explain and work out.

Up through Windows 3.0, on which we shipped Windows Power-Point 2.0, the Windows platform didn't handle fonts well and didn't ship with a complete set of fonts. So for our first PowerPoint on Windows, we licensed 22 third-party fonts to match the Apple/Adobe standard fonts (which also matched the fonts installed at Genigraphics) and shipped them with PowerPoint, on a number of additional diskettes. A user needed screen fonts and printer fonts.

Then after Windows 3.0, in preparation for the big jump to Windows 3.1 (which, despite the modest version bump, took two years), the Windows folks decided to get into the typography business and to add standard fonts to Windows in a new format. That was great—but only if the new fonts were designed to match the corresponding fonts on Macintosh. The new format could have real advantages (say, better rendering at small sizes on coarse screens by superior "hinting"), but there had to be equivalent fonts to the Mac fonts, and they had to have the same glyph assignments and basic font metrics as the Macintosh and as other devices (such as film recorders) that had matched that standard—for that matter, they had to match the third-party fonts that we had licensed and shipped with PowerPoint 2.0 and that our customers had already used in presentation files.

This requirement was non-negotiable for any decent world, but it was extremely hard to convince the Windows folks to adopt, because they thought they were making slightly better fonts than Mac, with some better characters included, and they didn't want to do anything to help Adobe or PostScript. I finally had to push the issue up to Mike Maples and Bill Gates, but it took many months for the Windows folks to bow and agree to adopt the Adobe font metrics, mistakes and all.

What they ended up doing was licensing the TrueType format from Apple. As I recall, it was a swap, whereby Microsoft adopted Apple's TrueType font format, and Apple pretended to adopt Microsoft's TrueImage page description language that was advertised to replace PostScript. In this way, both Microsoft and Apple gained decisive leverage against Adobe's hopes to exact ruinous license terms for use of PostScript and its "Type 1" outline fonts. Then Microsoft made new fonts that matched the Macintosh fonts exactly.

This was a big win for the world at large, and PowerPoint should get some credit for making it happen. I know that at the time many people besides me understood the vital importance of matching font metrics, but they weren't talking to the Microsoft Windows developers as often, and they didn't all have Bill Gates's ear to tell him that, unless the Windows folks changed, they would break his favorite program to demonstrate Windows. If we hadn't succeeded in forcing this point, I really don't know what we would have done.

Word's old model, where the program found out from the installed printer's driver what was the font and size and style repertoire of the printer and designed the document for that printer, was for the case in which the printer was connected with a parallel cable a few feet long.

PowerPoint, in contrast, wanted to send presentation documents across the country to an imaging bureau, where the file would be imaged on an ultra-high-resolution device connected to another computer, a device totally unknown to the computer that made the presentation. Of course, when opened on this remote computer, all the line breaks and juxtapositions of pictures and text had to be perfect, just as the user designed it. This created problems when a user used a font which was not one of the standard Windows or Mac fonts, if the font (glyphs and metrics) was installed on the user's computer but not on the imaging computer.

An equally important variant of the same problem occurred when a user carried a presentation on a floppy disk from one location to another, and then was unable to display it or print it properly, because the destination computer didn't have the same fonts installed as the originating computer; recall that at this time we didn't yet have laptops, so the whole computer system couldn't usually be carried. I was always being asked to help Microsoft executives in Redmond solve this problem. For the PowerPoint 2.0 introductions, on both the Mac and the Windows press tours, we ourselves had hand-carried to every appointment our own computers with the proper fonts already installed, to work around this difficulty.

To deal with this whole class of problems, we asked the font people in the Windows group to create embeddable fonts, so that an application could embed the whole font file inside an application document file. They actually did this, creating various levels of permission bits, and the option either to embed the entire font (all the glyphs and metrics) so that the text later could be edited to include any character, or to embed only the subset currently in use, which meant that no new characters could be added. This latter option was convenient for something like a logo set in a special corporate font (we had such a font in which the upper-case M "character" was the whole Microsoft logo), where there would never be a need for any other characters in that same font, permitting some space for the font to be saved.

Embedded fonts received only partial use, because type foundries were suspicious that such an idea would lead to font piracy and so tended at first to set their fonts to be non-embeddable. But most people used fonts that shipped with Windows, which were and are embeddable, and the ability to embed fonts is now widely used by many programs, though it has been particularly valuable to PowerPoint users.

All these considerations about fonts came up first in connection with PowerPoint, because we were one of the very early programs on Windows to be truly graphically demanding. Earlier programs for Windows had compromised so much that they were often very poor, and as long as that was the only choice, the makers of good Mac programs didn't move to Windows.

There was frustration that more and better programs were not moving from Mac to Windows. Microsoft evangelists worked closely with Mac developers to try to understand the issues, but Mac developers tended to give up on Windows pretty quickly, because it lacked so much, and to just wait for better versions of Windows to come along, or to put their faith in OS/2 Presentation Manager.

PowerPoint had no option—our whole charter was to move to Windows, so we had to explain to Windows' developers the facilities needed to do a good job. Because we were within Microsoft, we could more easily keep looking until we located the right people in Windows to whom to explain the issues. Sometimes we were able to get schedules extended to do the extra work we were requesting—not just for ourselves, but for all Windows developers.

The PowerPoint group was a set of developers who knew intimately the problems of Windows and were motivated to explain to the Windows developers in Systems exactly what was wrong. I had to explain to Bill Gates why PowerPoint was taking so long, and Bill could go to the Windows group and reinforce what we said.

It took five years of GBU work before Windows 3.1 and PowerPoint 3.0 shipped on the same day, with most of the font problems solved. By this time, Windows had become a platform which was just about competitive with Mac, leading to its great success. PowerPoint had contributed to that successful evolution.

172 Refocusing with Genigraphics

As all the connections with Genigraphics deepened, we had a major meeting on 10 October 1990 at the new Genigraphics headquarters in Shelton, Connecticut.

I had seen Sandy Beetner frequently during this whole time. A year earlier, in October 1989, I'd visited the headquarters of the service bureau business in Manhattan, and, on the same trip, I'd met with some of their new private equity investors, to reassure them that Microsoft had honorable intentions in working with Genigraphics. One such meeting was on a very high floor of the World Trade Center, looking out at the magnificent view; another, even more memorable, was in a tiny private dining room on a high floor of Rockefeller Center, looking out at a miniature lawn and garden on a roof high in the open air.

In January 1990, I'd gone back for several days to attend Genigraphics' national convention of people from all the service bureaus, giving a talk about the future of PowerPoint and meeting a lot of the people there.

Then during 1990, there had been major changes. The headquarters was relocated from 757 Third Avenue to Shelton, Connecticut. Late in the year, a layer of management was trimmed. So in October, I went back to Shelton, along with the Genigraphics people we were working with in Silicon Valley.

The main issue was what it always was: the business of automated imaging of slides from PowerPoint, at fairly low prices, was growing nicely. It was running as much as 25% of Genigraphics' total revenue, up from 15% last year. And it was growing fast: imaging in October totaled four times as much as in July.

In the summer of 1990, in fact, in a creative and clever move, Genigraphics had opened a new imaging center in Memphis, Tennessee, right next to the super-hub of Federal Express. This location was not expensive downtown real estate like all the other Genigraphics centers; this was in an industrial neighborhood. It had network connections to receive large numbers of PowerPoint presentations for imaging and a production line of computers and cameras to get the imaging done. It had the usual E6 processing line, maintained at Genigraphics' narrow tolerances, and facilities for rapid mounting and packaging. By being next to the FedEx hub, the Memphis center could image slides into the wee hours of the morning, and still get them to the FedEx hub next door just in time to make the last planes out, so as to arrive by the beginning of business hours the next day, thereby increasing their effective capacity for overnight imaging.

But custom business in the local service bureaus was down, partly because it was being displaced by PowerPoint imaging. At the meeting, we discussed the fact that PowerPoint was not (yet, as it turned out) being used by professional "producers" but was, as intended, being used by business presenters. Those presenters, it appeared, were not on the whole seeking to work closely with Genigraphics' professionals, but only wanted quick and cheap imaging.

Of most concern was our failure, during some three years of our partnership, to think of any successful Genigraphics products for business presenters other than 35mm slides. Customers didn't want to buy color overheads or short-run color printing, and they didn't want help on finishing presentations; they just wanted 35mm slides, mostly by modem and FedEx. This product was supplied most cost-effectively by the Memphis location, not by the existing service bureaus. It's hard to be clearer about the problem than this; it was understood.

In this situation, it was hard for Genigraphics to afford to keep up with the pace of the developing new business, and particularly in international markets, where adoption was slow—it was time to transition out of the European arrangement. Over the next few months, Genigraphics wound down its international network, we terminated our contract outside the U.S. and Canada, and we updated PowerPoint's international versions to support any local imaging source.

We thought about a number of ways to better promote Genigraphics services to PowerPoint customers in the U.S., but with no particular confidence of success. For the immediate future, though, we agreed on a number of areas where Genigraphics could provide its high-level design services to Microsoft, for which I was eager to pay at commercial prices. In effect, this was a large design contract whereby we would outsource a lot of design work for PowerPoint 3.0 to Genigraphics' artists.

By the beginning of November 1990, less than a month later, Genigraphics had good news: a round of over $1 million in new equity investment, which, coupled with ending the drain of the international business, gave them some breathing room. There also was a set of proposals for new Genigraphics services, trying to develop something in addition to imaging slides, but the ideas were acknowledged to be weak; what could be flat-priced wasn't very interesting (scan and insert a photo $50, colorize a black-and-white presentation, $5 a slide), and what was more interesting (draw a new logo, design a custom template) couldn't be quoted at a flat price, because it was still a custom business. It's much harder to sell a custom service than a standardized product.

173 Another Bill Gates Review of PowerPoint 3.0

By late October 1990, we had reached Milestone 1 of the PowerPoint 3.0 development, so we could check the accuracy of our scheduling.

The work so far had taken about twice as long as expected (about three-quarters of that difference because of underestimating known work, about one-quarter because of unexpected new work added). This would extrapolate to a release to manufacturing more than a year away, in November 1991 (actually happened in May 1992).

With that information, we could make a revised spec and schedule and host another review by Bill Gates, which took place about a month later, 27 November 1990.

Bill confirmed for us that Windows 3.1 would include TrueType fonts, and it was expected to ship by mid-1991. This raised an issue we were all too familiar with: should PowerPoint 3.0 require Windows 3.1, as PowerPoint 2.0 had tied itself to Windows 3.0? We had become hostages to the fortunes of Windows development and suffered, but, in the end, it had worked out very well. I was strongly inclined to make us hostages again. In addition to TrueType, Windows 3.1 would incorporate "multimedia" features that would let us include video and audio in slide shows more easily.

We reviewed all our competitors for Bill, offering the surmise that everyone else was struggling to ship on Windows at all, and concluding that the situation could leave us in a strong position; this turned out to be right. The first to ship, we guessed, would be Software Publishing Corporation's Harvard Graphics for Windows; that guess was wrong, and they wouldn't ship for more than another year. Whenever they were able to ship, we had a response prepared. We had already written a translator to convert old Harvard Graphics MS-DOS presentations into Windows PowerPoint 2.0 format and had tested it with several large companies who had libraries of Harvard Graphics files. Using this, we would be in a position to mount a "competitive upgrade" offer in which we would match SPC's price for an upgrade to their first Windows version with a similarly low price for our Windows PowerPoint 2.0 and throw in our translator, at least for specific customers. Bill thought that the translator was well done, "the interface is nice—good job."

On features, Bill was still on board with the improvements to drawing. We had designed a way to incorporate "outlining" by turning the old "Title Sorter" into an outline view of a presentation, in which the slide titles would be top-level items, and all the other text on the slide (which was naturally in outline format—every text box was a multi-level outline) would be subordinate to that. In "outline view," you could see all the text in the whole presentation in one scrollable list, which was often convenient for editing. If you wanted to, you could begin a new presentation in "outline view" and enter all the slide titles and text, then switch to "slide view" and edit the appearance, or you could begin the other way. Bill liked this, and thought it was worth slipping our release-to-manufacturing date to include it.

174 Genigraphics' Enlarged Role in PowerPoint

The incorporation of knowledge from Genigraphics into PowerPoint 2.0 had been limited by the short time available prior to the initial Macintosh shipment, but during the next four years leading up to PowerPoint 3.0, we had ample time and were working closely with the Genigraphics people in Silicon Valley on a daily basis, so the influences of Genigraphics on PowerPoint 3.0 were larger.

By the time PowerPoint 3.0 shipped, it used the same basic default palette of RGB colors that Genigraphics had evolved for its work-stations; it contained 5,000 color schemes (logical sets of colors from the default palette) chosen by Genigraphics , with an easy graphical way to select one; it boasted a set of 160 templates designed by Geni-graphics and based on successful templates used in the service bureaus; and it shipped with a library of 500 pieces of newly redrawn clip art based on the Genigraphics symbol library used in the service bureaus. Genigraphics artists also made all the sample presentations we shipped, including our "signature" presentation (Columbus's pitch to Queen Isabella for funding to discover America), which was used in the manual, on the product box, in all the collateral, and in all advertising. Much of the appearance of PowerPoint 3.0 was influenced by Genigraphics' experience, because we outsourced it to Genigraphics.

One of the advantages of outsourcing all these visual decisions was to take them out of the hands of multiple groups in Microsoft. We had plenty of people at the GBU who had opinions about visual appearance, both developers and marketing people, neither always based on much experience. Other parts of Microsoft were also ready to offer advice, particularly various levels of "corporate communications" people, who helped very little but had strong, uninformed prejudices. Because of the reputation enjoyed by Genigraphics, all I had to say was "this was de-signed by Genigraphics artists" in order to end all discussion. I also believed that our customers (not necessarily the art critics, nor even our own marketing people) preferred the appearance of presentations made in PowerPoint over those of our competitors partly because our appearance echoed elements of the Genigraphics style which was already widely familiar.

Less visibly, working closely with the Genigraphics engineers on their imaging had enabled us to tune various parts of PowerPoint, such as the number of slim rectangles of closely related colors used to create "shaded backgrounds" and the precise way the colors changed, to minimize faults such as banding when imaged. Aiming now at Windows 3.1, which would contain new fonts and the ability to embed the fonts inside PowerPoint files so they were available for imaging, we were able (through a lot of work by Genigraphics as well as ourselves) to solve all the nagging problems that had complicated the lives of users. We were able to improve the formatting and the compression of the files that PowerPoint transmitted to Genigraphics for imaging in order to save time and trouble on their end, and we even incorporated this into maintenance upgrades of previously shipped product.

As elements of Genigraphics style appeared in PowerPoint, it became more and more interesting to their own artists. Here was an emerging system that produced output similar to that of a Genigraphics workstation and imaged the very same high-quality 35mm slides, but worked much more easily ("direct-drive" rather than typing in parameters) and much more quickly (no more waiting to render a single slide visual). The artists would occasionally point out advantages of the way some small graphic detail was handled in the workstation software, and often we agreed that it was better and would improve to match. Equally often, of course, they preferred the small details of PowerPoint.

To get all this done, we had constant interaction. We frequently hosted Genigraphics people in our building to use equipment and testing facilities, and we hired them to augment critical testing on the graphics in PowerPoint. Working groups met constantly, and we had frequent management contact. Eventually, Rosemary Abowd half-moved to Silicon Valley, at least for much of the time, so we had excellent communication and interaction.

175 The Temporarily Successful Story of 3-D Charts

There's a good example of how subtle and powerful were the influences of Genigraphics on PowerPoint. When we worked on bar charts and column charts, I adopted a specific Genigraphics approach appropriate for presentations. Genigraphics' style did not render a bar chart as truly three-dimensional in perspective. Instead, it started with a flat two-dimensional bar chart and its labeled square axes, all in the same plane; it then added apparent thickness to the bars in such a way as to make them recede back from the axes. This made it much easier for a viewer to compare the heights of the front faces of the bars, and to estimate their values from the axis ticks and labels. I learned this way of doing charts from Genigraphics and incorporated it into our PowerPoint spec. The handling of pie charts was analogous.

Note that we are not talking about actual three-dimensional data here; this is a way to enhance ordinary two-dimensional data, without compromising its usefulness.

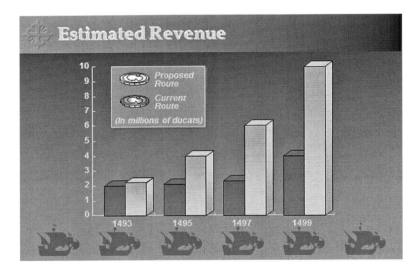

POWERPOINT 3.0 CHART

This superior design, with the front faces of the bars rectangular and directly readable from the axis in the same plane, was different from the less informative way that Excel did such charts "with true perspective," and so there was a lot of resistance for me to overcome. The creation of the charting component for all Microsoft applications had fallen into the hands of the Excel people, and we thought their work was very far below the standards needed for PowerPoint.

Finally, I had to escalate the question to Mike Maples, a rare occurrence, and I got a binding commitment to do the charts our way and to make our way the default (this was signed in blood on 2 April 1991). Our way, the Genigraphics way, really was obviously a superior technique to add visual interest without destroying the information value of the charts.

Unfortunately, understanding of this refinement was lost very soon after I left, and the behavior of charting in PowerPoint deteriorated to match that of Excel in later versions. Complaints about PowerPoint's 3-D charts as "chart junk" afterward became a common theme of critics.

(The sample below, one of the current defaults, illustrates what the problem has been. I don't know in detail what the situation is these days; amidst much greater complexity, different menu choices lead to varying defaults, and there are many options—there may be a combination that gives the right arrangement of front faces, axes, and gridlines, while keeping an illusion of depth. If so, it's not easy to find.)

Series 1

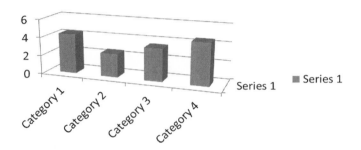

POWERPOINT 2010 CHART

176 Genigraphics Symbol Library in PowerPoint 3.0

Way back in 1987, at the first meetings with Genigraphics, I had proposed to leverage their collection of clip art (internally known as "symbols") that had been built up in the two dozen service centers by the hundreds of artists who had produced tens of thousands of presentations. This collection was circulated and re-used casually inside Genigraphics, but I had proposed to gather it all, arrange it in labeled categories, and sell it as a product on CD-ROM (taking advantage of a CD drive for Mac supposed to be shipped by Apple soon), so that users could insert Genigraphics' art into PowerPoint files. Microsoft would do the manufacturing and distribution, with the revenue from selling the CD-ROM to be split in some ratio between Genigraphics and Microsoft. I thought that this would be an easy way for Genigraphics to realize the value of the clip art library that it had built up over many years.

We didn't announce that plan at the January 1988 press conference, and in fact, it never happened.

We did try to gather up the whole collection to turn it into a product cheaply. But upon examination, it turned out that the clip art "symbols" had been created across all the distributed service bureaus, for many different specialized presentations, without any standards other than appearance. There were lots of near-duplicates. Many symbols had a specific background color built into them; an early proposal from Genigraphics was to provide each symbol with multiple background colors, whereas what we really wanted was clip art independent of the background of the slide (which, in PowerPoint, might be changed at any time, either manually or by choosing a new template design), with transparent areas, rather than swatches of a background incorporated. Most had been drawn purely for a specific effect, with strokes and polygons in any arrangement that looked perfect on the workstations; we wanted to be able to "disassemble" the clip art in PowerPoint hierarchically (a standard feature for compound objects), so that a user could edit the clip art sensibly. This meant that things shown in the clip art should be unitary groupings of primitives, and hidden parts of things shown in the clip art needed to be drawn and then covered up with whatever was in front of them. The summary was that the symbols had been designed and used by artists in a custom business, and now we needed something different for a retail off-the-rack business.

Hence, the entire symbol library would need to be redrawn—a lot of artists' time that would need to be paid for. There wasn't any product that could be made almost for free. If that was true, then the choice of a format had to be made, and it wouldn't be Genigraphics' proprietary format, particularly since the consoles were no longer being bought. That meant that the work wouldn't be done on Genigraphics consoles at all. What could be re-used were the ideas; it wouldn't be necessary to figure out which symbols to draw all over again, and the artists could use the conventions of Genigraphics' style (some of them influenced by limitations of the old consoles), which were widely recognizable as "presentation style."

In the end, we decided to have Microsoft pay Genigraphics to redraw the entire collection in Windows metafiles, scalable and editable (not bitmaps). The result would be the property of both Microsoft and Genigraphics, with a short-term contractual limitation on the ability of either to transfer rights to direct competitors, but otherwise, both parties had unlimited rights. Some of the Genigraphics artists redrew the same symbols they had themselves created previously. The artists used a simple graphics editor on Windows machines—in fact, it was the one we ourselves at the GBU had written for use in other Microsoft applications.

By the end of January 1991, we had the ground rules. The artists would observe a set of strict conventions to assure that the art could be disassembled into its primitives and edited by PowerPoint or by the drawing code we supplied for other applications. We had conventions to minimize the use of drawing primitives that had a different visual appearance on Mac and Windows. All art should print well in black-and-white and grayscale, for use in word processing documents, as well as in its original full color. The results were formally tested to verify that all the conventions had been followed. Such metafiles could be arbitrarily resized and recolored, and users could make any edits de-sired, such as inserting a logo on an object shown in the clip art.

When the project was done, we had over 500 "symbols," each a complex editable drawing. The cost had been about $250,000, or on the order of $500 for each piece of clip art, an amount representing a couple of hours of work.

The resulting symbol library, or clip art collection, could be used in any Windows program, all Microsoft apps and all those of our competitors, and we shipped the whole collection free with PowerPoint 3.0. We, of course, had created translators (in fact, very complex and sophisticated programs, which we also built into PowerPoint) to faithfully convert Windows metafiles to Macintosh formats, so the collection was equally available on Macintosh PowerPoint.

We also extended the symbol library to include a small amount of new clip art suggested by international subsidiaries, and licensed the whole collection for worldwide distribution. We had one single collection for all Microsoft applications, worldwide, on both Mac and Windows. (For internal use at Microsoft, an additional clip art library was assembled including such items as small images of the boxes of all our products, pictures of typical Microsoft employees at work, maps of the campuses with approaches shown, diagrams of company buildings, and so forth.)

For PowerPoint 3.0, both Windows and Mac, we added a built-in facility to "insert clipart," which enabled a user to easily browse the collection and select any drawing to insert. In later versions, this was extended to other collections and web-based collections.

There was no way to sell the collection in 1992, as we had envisioned in 1987, because everyone with a Mac or Windows machine who could draw had decided to get into the clip art business, and the prices that could be charged for clip art were falling toward zero; even though the quality of the Genigraphics clip art was very high, our best marketing intelligence said that almost no one would pay for it.

The Original Classic Handshake Symbol, circa 1984. This symbol went through a number of incarnations. This version was drawn by Abby Weissman at the NYC Center. It was later reproduced for the Microsoft Clip Art Library in 1989, again drawn by Abby Weissman. Artwork copyright 2012 by The Genigraphics Arts Society, used by permission.

Part of the value to PowerPoint 3.0 was the ease and convenience of the mechanism for finding and inserting clip art. Another value factor, which made it worth working with Genigraphics for their collection, was that their clip art consisted of symbols that had surfaced over and over again in real business presentations made by Genigraphics for real customers, so it tended to be much more usable than random pictures drawn by freelance artists who had no business clients and who were just doing blue-sky clip art out of their heads ("14 mushrooms of North America, $1.99"). This "enhanced usefulness" eventually became its own problem, when PowerPoint users found some of the Genigraphics symbols so compelling that they used them over and over, until they became presentation clichés and started to cause groans.

The whole project provided a way for Genigraphics to get paid for the task of rolling its symbol library forward onto personal computers, while continuing to own it; and since the situation was that Genigraphics would eventually be forced to move to using PC-based or Mac-based replacements for its old proprietary workstations, this enabled them to keep using their symbol library in an even more flexible form. The project provided billable work for Genigraphics' artists during slack periods and successfully preserved a whole heritage of clip art long used in business presentations. But it didn't turn out to be a huge asset of Genigraphics just waiting to be monetized, as we had hoped.

177 Real Templates in PowerPoint 3.0

The formal feature of templates (and libraries of templates) was introduced in PowerPoint 3.0. Before that, in the two earlier versions of PowerPoint, there had been a simpler idea of a "default" presentation format. Even from the very first, however, it was trivial for any user to make a new default format (using the product itself), and to install the new format so that every new presentation started out with the personalized version.

Templates were much different, designed to be a "make this presentation pretty" feature, or "make this presentation look like that one." There was no special template file format: any presentation could be used as a template with no preparation, and any template could be "applied" to any existing presentation. That action would substitute the master slide; substitute the slide setup (size, shape); substitute text styles with the same names; change the color scheme, title style, and body text style (for slides that followed the master); recolor embedded graphs to match the new color scheme; and change notes and handouts similarly. No slides would be inserted from the template presentation. This meant that any existing presentation could be converted to match the style of any other, or to match a standard, and a user could easily visualize an entire presentation in as many template styles as desired. The same functionality underlay the ability of users to cut slides from any presentation and paste them into another one, upon which the slides transferred would automatically assume the look of the destination presentation (or not, under user control).

This ability to take an existing presentation and apply so much design retrospectively from a template was characterized internally as "bash it out now, tart it up later," a description of a way of working attributed to British musician Nick Lowe.

With the template system, it was also trivial for individual users or groups to design or re-design presentations to be their own templates (including default layouts and typographic arrangements) using PowerPoint itself, and to set their own template libraries to be their automatic defaults. The introduction of templates and template libraries in PowerPoint 3.0 also attracted independent designers. Eventually, many thousands of independent companies would produce and sell PowerPoint templates for particular uses, and many corporations adopted their own internal standard templates; but nothing prevented any individual user from adapting a template or using different personalized templates.

The new libraries of template presentations for PowerPoint 3.0 were made by Genigraphics, under a contract from Microsoft. With the new template features, Genigraphics could supply separate libraries of templates for different media—for black and white overheads, color overheads (made on new color printers and color copiers), color 35mm slides, and color video. All of these shipped with the product. As with other Genigraphics contributions, their templates incorporated years of practical experience built up by working with knowledgeable clients.

178 Not Chiefly ...

Among all the changes and improvements in PowerPoint 3.0, it was inevitable that many people would suggest new features that would force someone else's idea of "good presentation style" onto our users.

The range of suggestions was amazing. Perhaps users should be prevented from using type smaller than some font size, or type smaller than some fraction of the slide height, or type too small for the typical use of the format (*e.g.*, bigger type for 35mm slides). Or perhaps users should be forbidden from using more than seven bullet points on a single slide, or more than two levels of bullets. Or perhaps users should be prevented from putting more than a dozen boxes on a slide. Or ... there was no limit to the ideas of "slide Nazis" for enforcing their own perceptions of good presentation style. "No mortal but is narrow enough to delight in educating others into counterparts of himself."

I always rejected not only such ideas, but even any discussion of them. I would cut off debate by repeating Thoreau: "I came into this world, not chiefly to make this a good place to live in, but to live in it, be it good or bad" (from his *Resistance to Civil Government*). I thought it was not our business to tell every user what we thought was good style. We had gained success by trying to find out what our users wanted to do, and then making it as easy as possible for them to do exactly that; it was poor strategy to change to dictating and limiting formats.

I remembered how one of my friends at Bell-Northern Research, John Ahlstrom, had been using some program or other one day when he received an error message brusquely rejecting his input, to which he immediately replied: "It's a poor tool that blames its workman."

Besides, any rules we could devise would permit some kinds of badness; there really was no fix for bad presentations except education of the users. And any rules we could devise would prevent some standard and legitimate uses of PowerPoint, not to mention all kinds of nonstandard uses (*e.g.*, for supertitles in opera houses). To this day, I use PowerPoint to fill in printed forms, since I no longer own a typewriter: just drop the form into an auto-scanner, insert the scan on the slide master of a new presentation, then return to normal view and fill in the content in text boxes over the background form, and print the result. It would be a pity to cripple PowerPoint so as to make it unable to do such special tasks.

Reviewers for the computer press were frequently recruited from among "designers" who thought that the unwashed masses of presenters should be prevented from making ugly slides and that the reviewer knew which slides were ugly, but I was sure they were wrong.

We occasionally got requests from large corporations (or, at least, from Microsoft sales people looking for features they thought might help to sell large corporate adoptions) to introduce limitations into the product, typically not as "hard" rules, but rather a way for corporate standard-setters to create a corporate "policy" that would be enforced against all individual users of PowerPoint within that corporation. Specifics were ways to enforce use of only specified templates, and to remove commands from the menus, in addition to the usual limits on font sizes or bullet counts. I thought it was wrong to make the product less flexible and attractive for the actual users; if they liked it less, that might actually reduce large corporate sales. Corporations could easily set defaults in the product to be what they wanted for internal installs, and that, along with education for users, was best for everyone.

179 Incentives to Fix a Problem with Support

In January 1991, I observed at one of Mike Maples' staff meetings an interesting example of using economic principles to fix a business problem. The problem was that telephone calls to Microsoft's Product Support Services were growing too fast, indicating that users were having too many difficulties with our products. In fact, as a company, Microsoft was spending more on product support than on product development! Support then was answering over 7,500 calls per day, and still failing to answer them all, while hiring as fast as possible. The average call duration was over 10 minutes, up a third from a year before.

Most of the volume was dealing with early Windows problems, not with our applications. But so far as it did involve Applications, Mike analyzed the problem as being one of incentives. Up until then, the cost of support was socialized; the Applications Division got a monthly bill from Support for all the costs of calls about all products, and that bill was allocated among the Business Units by headcount.

Now, each month the actual Support costs for each Business Unit's products would be charged to that Business Unit directly. Moreover, each Business Unit could negotiate its own terms with Support, such as directing it not to spend more than a certain fraction of revenue (leaving the Business Unit to deal with any customer dissatisfaction).

No changes would be made in the way that Support worked in an attempt to control costs. Instead, "ultimately the Business Units will fix the situation by making support calls unnecessary."

Soon, Product Support started tallying the top 10 questions or problems that it dealt with for every product, and fed these back to the Business Units. It was an obvious move for the Business Unit Manager to do whatever was necessary to deal with those most-common support issues in each new release, by changing the product or adding better help, or whatever. That did, indeed, reduce support calls and their cost substantially.

180 Microsoft Office Rears Its Head

While we were working on PowerPoint 3.0, there was a development that seemed to be possibly good for PowerPoint and for Microsoft, but that I thought might well lead to unwelcome changes. That was the beginnings of Microsoft Office.

The earliest Office product I knew about was put together in 1989, by simply shrink-wrapping Mac Word, Mac Excel, and Mac PowerPoint 2.01 together to make a limited-time bundle, with a special discounted price—about half the usual retail. Standard product boxes were literally taken out of inventory and shrink-wrapped with no attempt at creating greater uniformity among the components.

Something similar was repeated the next year, 1990, on Windows, after PowerPoint 2.0 had shipped—again we just packaged the three separate products together.

Early reaction to the Office product was interesting. Microsoft had completely moved its attention to graphical user interfaces on Mac and Windows, but many customers were still focused on MS-DOS and didn't take Mac or Windows seriously. To such people, Office looked like merely a promotion—"buy the two applications you need (Word and Excel), and get a frivolous add-on for free (PowerPoint)." MS-DOS users used word processors and spreadsheets, but not many used presentation software (because the experience was necessarily so poor on character-oriented systems).

Some MS-DOS-based competitors, such as Harvard Graphics, also thought like the MS-DOS customers. Harvard, a product of Software Publishing Corporation, had shipped its initial product for MS-DOS in March of 1986, only about a year before PowerPoint 1.0 on Mac. PowerPoint had shipped on Windows in early 1990, simultaneously with the ship of Windows 3.0, but Harvard Graphics failed to ship a Windows version of its product until nearly two years after that, in early 1992—just before we shipped PowerPoint 3.0! Even then, they failed to take much advantage of Windows, hewing closely to the design of their long-successful MS-DOS version. This was a striking example of how success in the prior generation of character-oriented products could be a crippling handicap in the new generation of graphics-oriented products.

That two-year delay, after the breakthrough success of Windows 3.0 had spotlighted PowerPoint, would seem to adequately explain how Harvard Graphics was displaced by PowerPoint; but to the Harvard folks, it appeared that the Microsoft Office bundle had taken all the money out of the presentation graphics market. Tess Reynolds, Business Unit Director for Graphics, who headed the Harvard Graphics group, offered this view of how her product came to a bad end (in an email written 18 August 2006):

At its peak around 1990–91, Harvard Graphics had over $150M in worldwide revenues and 65% market share. We were the most profitable product at SPC, earning 35–40% profit before taxes. We developed Harvard Graphics for OS/2 and Windows. We built a product for the Macintosh but never released it. ... The business unit took up 13 buildings on SPC's campus on Rengstorff, plus one more R&D facility in Madison, Wisconsin. The original team of 6 grew to a business unit of 200 R&D, marketing, support and documentation professionals. Many more jobs were created throughout SPC's centralized sales, manufacturing and administrative teams. Above all, we had a blast! *Until the day Microsoft created the Office bundle, and essentially included graphics for free."* (Reynolds 2006, emphasis supplied)

People who understood Mac and Windows, which of course included Bill Gates above all, saw Office quite differently, as a way to get into the hands of Word and Excel users better versions of those products plus the one application which would demonstrate the value of Windows by enabling users to create any kind of graphical material. Word was, as it is mostly still to this day, a one-dimensional text editor; it's hard to even make a "WET PAINT" sign in Word. Excel could create a fixed repertoire of "graphs" (bar charts and pie charts and such) from numerical tables, but otherwise was also completely textual. Word and Excel were both better and easier to use on Windows than their counterpart versions on MS-DOS, but PowerPoint was the application which would seal the deal to move to Windows.

After those Office packaging experiments, Bill Gates wrote a memo in February 1991, in which he said he thought we should move to an "Office" product:

Another important question is what portion of our application sales over time will be a set of applications versus a single product. The marginal cost to us of users using a higher number of applications is zero and if we can make it easy enough to use applications casually so that it is a benefit to have multiple applications then users will pay for this privilege and the industry as a whole will benefit. It appears that only Microsoft and Lotus will have complete quality families of applications and we are somewhat ahead. Please assume that we stay ahead in integrating our family together in evaluating our future strategies—the product teams WILL deliver on this. Our understanding of system software and our early investment in integration and having all of our applications development on one site with a uniform culture including more focus on technology will allow us to lead. We will be open with what we are doing but our skills will distinguish us.

I believe that we should position the "OFFICE" as our most important application. The simplicity a company can get by having all of these applications available to all of its users is very high—an employee can use another person's machine, you can enclose files in mail knowing people will be able to not only look at them but also edit them, there is no requisition overhead in trying to figure out what people should get, there is one vendor to ask for integration from or reasonable licensing policies. (Gates 1991)

All that made good sense to me. But I could also see immediately that the new Office strategy would lead inexorably to a legitimate demand on the part of customers for greater uniformity in the details of how the applications worked. PowerPoint had many small design advantages for its common functions which, I thought strongly, were superior to the corresponding functions in Word or Excel. I'd hoped that, over time, customer pressure would induce improvements in Word and Excel; but the Office bundle might accelerate unification, so that decisions had to be made sooner, by political logrolling.

At first, when an Office bundle was sold, only 12% of the revenue was allocated to PowerPoint; 44% went to each of Word and Excel, supposedly based on some calculation of the historical sales of the individual components. I always believed that those calculations had been influenced more by the fact that both Word and Excel had much larger headcounts, were at headquarters where they could negotiate better, and were much more vociferous about being unwilling to take any cut in revenue per copy—essentially political considerations.

Heedless of that, I was enthusiastic from the beginning to be sure that PowerPoint would be included in Office, even at the 12% share. The share would be temporary, of course; much later, in 2010, Jeff Raikes remarked that PowerPoint was frequently the most-used application in the Office product, ahead of Word and Excel (Raikes 2010).

The important consideration to me was that the Office bundle would be extremely popular, and could only help to popularize Power-Point, although I retained my forebodings about its effect on product quality. If product quality decisions were going to be made through politics in the future, then the big battalions located at headquarters were going to have an advantage.

That process began to be visible during 1992, which was my last year with Microsoft. After PowerPoint 3.0 appeared on Windows (and later Mac), it was put into another Office bundle, called Office 3.0 on each platform. By now, after three years, there were some superficial efforts to make Office look like a single product; there was, for instance, a single install (which pretty much just invoked the three separate installs for the products), and that was undeniably an improvement. But the way even these small points got introduced was extremely political.

Bill's memo from early 1991 came back to me:

> Please assume that we stay ahead in integrating our family to-gether in evaluating our future strategies—the product teams WILL deliver on this. Our ... having all of our applications devel-opment on one site with a uniform culture ... will allow us to lead. (Gates 1991)

I could see the logic of a single Microsoft Office super-product, and I thought it made sense; it was actually inescapable. But I could also see that it would put an end to competition among the individual compo-nents to design the best solutions for users, probably prematurely. And it would ultimately also put an end to the Business Unit structure.

While you are fighting individual local battles, you want to leave ini-tiative to the individual guerrilla groups in the business units to figure out what to do. Once it becomes a general war, you may decide you need a "unified command" across the whole theater. This development is unlikely to be welcomed by the entrepreneurial guerrilla command-ers, even if it means that the war is being waged more successfully and that victory draws nearer.

Mike Maples stayed with Microsoft for three years longer than I did, so he saw the same problems as they developed further. In his oral history, he was asked about Office, and he explained some of the prob-lems with separate management:

> The collection of products was less expensive than the individual prices of the products. So now you had a revenue allocation issue. You sell one Office for $500 – who gets how much? And each of the product guys said. "Well, I'd rather sell full product than sell Office." Then you had a consistency issue: "I like the way my file menu works versus the way your file menu works." And then you had a schedule issue: "Mine's going to be ready in November..." "Mine's going to be ready in September." (Maples 2004)

This last issue of schedule inconsistency was particularly interesting. Even with only three components, you had to scrap inventory and build new product every time one of the products had an upgrade (remember, there was no Internet upgrading), and it was very difficult to find a window to launch a new Office version when all three product versions were reasonably fresh. With just a few more components, timed independently, you could hardly build or launch Office at all. But each component product had its own logical schedules, and its own problems that caused its schedules to change unexpectedly, and it was hard to imagine how to arbitrarily synchronize the components.

I could foresee all these new problems, and I could foresee that they would inevitably be solved by re-consolidating the business units and re-instituting a new form of the old political wrangling of the mono-lithic Apps Division. I knew that I wouldn't be able to gracefully tolerate the change to being part of a larger Office organization.

Sure enough, that's what happened after I was gone. Mike again:

> So it was the tradeoff between what does the Word [or Power-Point or Excel] customer want and what fits into the Office scheme. So we organized. Essentially we took the business units and organized an Office Business Unit—we upscaled the organi-zation. But that changed things because the Excel development team was 10–15 people and now the Office development team was 100 or so people. People are making trade-offs. (Maples 2004)

I didn't disagree with the wisdom of moving to an integrated Office product, and I thought it would be very successful (as it was). Office helped to make PowerPoint popular, and PowerPoint helped to make Office such a great success. Fortunately, for me, I would be gone before the organizational effects materialized.

181 Video in PowerPoint 3.0, Despite the Consultant

In February 1991, we hired a leading PC software industry pundit to come out and talk to us for a day, for $10,000 plus expenses, plus first-class air transportation. This sort of money induced some effort to tell us useful information.

His information wasn't really very useful, and I was particularly struck by the pundit's skepticism about video. His opinion was that "there is no big move to video," and he discouraged our paying attention to video features.

My intuition was exactly the opposite. I'd been writing about the eventual move to video projection of presentations since 1984, and I thought I could see the change on the horizon. Agreed, the projectors were not yet great (or even tolerable), but I knew from my audio-visual industry contacts that many manufacturers were working to make better video projectors. I had studied the technologies in depth, and couldn't see any reason why they wouldn't succeed.

So PowerPoint 3.0 invested heavily in video features. We designed an elaborate "slide show" feature, which took over the whole screen and—if the PC had the hardware—pumped video out to a large monitor or projector. In addition to the remote control features, we implemented a large inventory of animated transitions (wipes, fades, and so forth), which only were visible in video presentations.

We added special animation features, such as "progressive disclosure"—the effect that Steve Jobs got by sliding a sheet of opaque paper down his overhead. If you made a five-item bullet list with this feature, you wrote one slide, and when you printed your presentation, you got six sheets of output—one with no bullet points, then one with the first bullet point alone, then a third sheet with bullet points one and two, and on up to five (this saved typing extra slides). But in a slide show, each click to advance caused one more bullet point to materialize on the same slide on screen. We also added "flying bullets," which animated each new bullet point to fly in to its place from any edge of the screen. This was really attention-grabbing, and (predictably) over-used.

We added the feature of saving a presentation as a slide show, using an extension of ".pps" (rather than the usual ".ppt"). It was really exactly the same file format, but a file with the extension ".pps" opened directly into full-screen slide show mode. Any slide show could advance automatically with timings for each slide, to be a self-running demo station or kiosk. Such a file, like any other, could embed the fonts it used, to show properly on any computer. We made a free "viewer" program, which could be distributed freely with PowerPoint slide shows.

All this was almost useless when we shipped, because the video projectors could not yet be bought. In fact, it was a full year after this encounter with the consultant before I was able to give the world's first public video presentation from a laptop (described later). But not long after the shipment of PowerPoint 3.0, users began to want to use video, and after a few years, it became the only common projection format.

182 PowerPoint 3.0 Will Be Hostage to Windows 3.1

Through the first half of 1991, PowerPoint 3.0 gradually became more and more committed to requiring Windows 3.1, a topic which had become live in the program review with Bill Gates back in October 1990.

Like Windows 3.0 before it, though, Windows 3.1 was a target always slipping off toward the future, though by now, we were not surprised. Back in late November of 1990, Windows 3.1 had been expected to ship by "mid-1991." By late February 1991, it had slipped to "release to manufacturing 15 November 1991," which pushed it really into 1992. Even so, we had identified some specific places where Windows PowerPoint was much slower than Macintosh PowerPoint and where small improvements to Windows could really increase PowerPoint's performance (along with that of all other applications); the Windows folks were intending to make those improvements in version 3.1, so that was one powerful reason to require it.

By early April 1991, Windows 3.1 had slipped to a "pre-beta" in late April, with the biggest risk factor identified as TrueType fonts (our biggest attraction). In mid-May 1991, the report was that Windows 3.1 was "moving into 1992 to add features."

Windows 3.1 accumulated enough new features and improvements that it soon became highly desirable to have all Microsoft's customers upgrade from 3.0. On 24 July 1991, we held a PowerPoint 3.0 program review with Mike Maples, who said that Microsoft now intended to make it hard for anyone to resist the upgrade to Windows 3.1, and that he thought it would be perfectly in order for PowerPoint 3.0 to require Windows 3.1 or Macintosh System 7.0—and to refuse to run on Windows 3.0, or with EGA graphics, or on Mac System 6.0.

One big reason for Mike's enthusiasm was that Windows 3.1 would give us built-in TrueType fonts and embedded fonts in PowerPoint presentations; a couple of days later, Mike asked me to prepare a one-page explanation for Microsoft executives on how to avoid showing up for an external presentation with a PowerPoint 2.0 presentation that looked terrible, because it used fonts installed only on the exec's office machine. If Microsoft executives had this problem, he pointed out, so did all of our customers (as I knew better than anyone!).

On 26 July 1991, Steve Ballmer told an Apps group that Windows 3.1 pre-betas would go out to 2,000 people in the next month (slipped from April), followed by a proper beta period with 10,000 copies.

On 10 September 1991, Mike Maples gave me his latest opinion update: he thought that Windows 3.1 was continuing to have great troubles over the fonts, and that even with a further slip, to release as late as February 1992, the date would still be "high-risk." Despite that, his counsel was to "slip PowerPoint 3.0 to match Windows 3.1." He was concerned enough about the state of TrueType fonts that, as a fallback, he thought I should go ahead and execute all the contracts and do all the work to be fully prepared to ship in the PowerPoint 3.0 box the same twenty-two fonts from our third-party source that we had shipped with Windows PowerPoint 2.0.

By 3 October, Mike had revised his opinion to be that Windows 3.1 would be "lucky" to ship in March 1992. Their next official release to manufacturing date issued was 9 March with a possible slip of two weeks, so we reset our own release of PowerPoint 3.0 to 23 March.

183 Complexity Grows in the PowerPoint 3.0 Project

Through the autumn of 1991, even while PowerPoint 3.0 slipped modestly in synchronization with Windows 3.1, the whole project was becoming ever more complex, testing the ability of a group as small as ours to keep up.

Much of this work was handled by our exceptionally astute program managers. A "program manager" at the Microsoft GBU was someone with the same computer science education and programming experience as a developer would have (and hired to our same standards), but someone with more interest in communications and interpersonal organization, at least for a while. A program manager would be making decisions that a developer could make, but about tasks other than the program code—that is, a program manager didn't have responsibility for any tasks listed on the code development schedule. Program managers were a group reporting independently from development, but they worked very closely with developers. Elsewhere in Microsoft, program managers had been drafted into writing all the program specs, but we were lucky enough to have that mostly done by our development leads and managers, in the original Microsoft way.

Our program managers worked with other groups, inside Microsoft (including the GBU itself) and in other companies, negotiating and managing the many technical tasks involved in creating software products. They typically had no ability to impose decisions but had to make their case and convince other groups to do the right thing. It was extraordinarily helpful to have really technical people free of development constraints who could take this responsibility. Other companies tried to use MBAs from marketing groups in such roles, consulting with busy developers from time to time, with uniformly poor results.

We were, first of all, remaking all of PowerPoint into a new single version, with as much common code as possible for Windows and Mac, and this meant simultaneous development with building and testing of both platforms (in multiple localizations) every day. We were enlarging and beefing up every set of features, and adding much more—pretty much everything we wanted, unlike PowerPoint 2.0, where some badly needed features were cut for schedule reasons.

Our close dependence on Windows 3.1, and our being the only serious initial client for its new TrueType fonts, meant that we also had to spend more time than ever monitoring its progress and traveling to Redmond to provide detailed feedback.

One of the biggest problems was the fact that I had finally agreed, on the basis of what turned out to be untrustworthy promises, to depend on the "charting" component coming from the Excel people. Their standards of quality were very low; they weren't used to producing presentation graphics, after all. This meant that the process was excruciating, because the working-level developers just didn't know how to do what was needed, and that the process frequently became political, because their bosses didn't want them to take time to learn. In the other direction, we were spending huge resources to produce a "drawing" component, initially for the Word people, but they had very different ideas about the drawing appropriate for documents (much more complicated, *e.g.,* to prepare patent applications) and didn't like what we were giving them any better than we liked Excel's charting. This whole area of shared components among business units was basically unsuccessful. Charting in Excel just wasn't the same as charting in PowerPoint, and drawing in PowerPoint just wasn't the same as drawing in Word. Commonality of function and user interfaces would be the best, wherever possible, but requiring fully identical function was usually not the right answer.

We were adding a lot of content (clip art, maps, templates, presentations), all of which had to be handled like the program code—specified in as much technical detail and then tested and managed for builds just as carefully—because it all went on the disks in the boxes, and a mistake could be very expensive.

Everything was being developed also in a language-independent way, so that all the international versions could be generated automatically (by inserting strings in any language, including English). We were doing double-byte character handling for Far Eastern languages with a developer on site loaned from MSKK Japan. We had committed dates to produce French, German, Dutch, Swedish, Italian, Spanish, Portuguese, Finnish, Norwegian, Danish, Turkish, Russian, Hungarian, Czech, and Japanese versions, with more to come. Each of these needed translation of the manuals and packaging in addition to the software and all the on-disk content.

Moreover, the work of localization was being transferred to the business units. This had already started by having a localization manager in Redmond who reported to Aniko Somogyi at the GBU, and we were expected to staff up to take on all the responsibility locally. (Interestingly, the international folks recommended that we not hire any User Ed people, but instead continue to rely on vendors such as Publishing Power for everything—their experience with employee writers and editors and artists had been as poor as everyone else's.)

We were working very closely with the Genigraphics engineering group in Santa Clara, helping them solve common problems with imaging all our new features, and the new environments of Windows 3.1 and System 7.0. This had to work, so we had no choice but to participate fully. We also did what we could to enhance their operations and business success. From time to time, we bought or loaned equipment that they needed to make progress.

There was a lot of interest in PowerPoint 3.0 within Microsoft, because Windows 3.0 had really taken off and was selling well (for the first time) along with PowerPoint 2.0 and our other Windows applications. There was a feeling that Windows 3.1 would consolidate these gains and make Windows substantially easier to use and cheaper to support, and PowerPoint 3.0 was an important component of demonstrating that. So we got enhanced opportunities to review our progress frequently with Bill Gates and Mike Maples. This was all very much to the good, since it assured that there would be no surprises on either side in such a high-profile project, but preparing for and delivering the reviews inevitably required time from the people doing the work, as well as from me. I also found myself trouble-shooting our product on the Redmond campus, preparing explanations of how fonts under Windows 3.0 had to be installed in every system individually, and getting the Audio-Visual group to upgrade the computers in every conference room to have enough memory to run Windows 3.1 and to have 256-color graphics cards; this was self-defense, to be sure that people in Redmond had good experiences with PowerPoint.

Besides the main tasks, PowerPoint 3.0 and the independent drawing editor (the one for use by Genigraphics and as a component by the other business units), we had picked up a great number of auxiliary tasks. There were several small updates to PowerPoint 2.0, both Mac and Windows, each of which needed development and testing for release. We were making the PowerPoint 3.0 "Viewer," a stand-alone free application that could open and show presentations, for free distribution with presentation files. We had created the translator to convert Harvard Graphics presentations to PowerPoint format. We had pioneered the "object linking and embedding" standard to link charting into PowerPoint, and to link our drawing into other applications. We were responsible for getting "graphics conversion filters" written and tested, to convert a couple of dozen standard and proprietary graphics formats, some only popular outside the U.S., to and from Windows metafiles. We were similarly responsible for code to convert Windows GDI to and from Mac QuickDraw with high fidelity, also for use by all applications. The task of writing setup code to install all the components of PowerPoint 3.0 on both platforms was itself a non-trivial task. Since we were not using the standard Microsoft Apps development environment, we had to provide many of our own tools. There were a variety of "corporate duties," such as adding to PowerPoint 3.0 the minimum needed for "Pen Windows" (though there was never any serious work that would have made PowerPoint really usable on such a platform) and spending time on "MultiMedia Windows" (never well defined). I could go on, and on.

One response to all this complexity was to continue to tax ourselves to recruit more people. We still held a meeting of all managers once a week to review promising résumés. We paid extra retainers and bonuses to the outside recruiters who had produced the best candidates in the past, and who could screen out résumés most efficiently. All the managers spent valuable time screening candidates, and every candidate who passed the screening got a full set of interviews by our best people, which took many hours away from other tasks. We got a lot of good people during this period, but it was expensive in time; as before, we concentrated only on experienced people who could make a net contribution within a short time. We continued this heavy investment in recruiting through calendar 1991, and then shut it down to concentrate on using the resources we had to finish PowerPoint 3.0.

In fact, we were so busy in the latter part of 1991 that we couldn't even work in a holiday party, so we had to reschedule it to 18 January 1992 at an art gallery and performance space in the South of Market district of San Francisco.

184 My Unsystematic Testing Program

Obviously, as the organizational complexity of working within Microsoft grew, my personal duties became more and more administrative. I had more and more reports to write, more and more tasks involving the larger number of people, and more and more meddling from corporate groups to deflect. I no longer got to spend as much time in product discussions as I once had, though I still did my best and still considered product questions to be the most important.

By this time, our development methods had improved to result in a daily "build" of PowerPoint 3.0 for all platforms and localizations, made late every afternoon. By the end of ordinary business hours, there was, every day, a new version of the program on the servers. As the evening drew on, there were fewer telephone calls, and there weren't many people still working and sending email from Redmond, so I had fewer interruptions.

I adopted the habit of using a couple of hours every evening to test the most recent build by using it. I'd get the latest version and just try making presentations, concentrating on the features currently being worked upon. Often I made very complex and beautiful slides, though they required unrealistically repetitive and tedious formatting (which could reveal bugs). We joked about writing a book on such techniques, to be called "PowerPoint: Secrets of the Great Tedium Masters."

This daily use of the program gave me some partial insight into what was being accomplished, and allowed me to give immediate feedback on details of features as they reached the point of first being usable. While I worked, I'd keep an email message open on my Xenix terminal, adding to it all the anomalies I found. After a couple of hours, I'd send the long email to QA, and drive an hour home for a very late dinner.

My reporting by email was self-indulgent; the following morning, someone in QA would have to go through my email and transcribe the bugs I'd reported into the official online bug-tracking system. But that allowed someone else to immediately double-check my observations, filter them or augment them, and discuss them with the developer working on the area while it was still under active development. In a very kindly gesture, the folks who did this would enter my email alias—"BobGa"—as the source of every bug resulting from my email reports, even though they did a lot more work than I did.

You wouldn't expect this way of testing to be very effective, compared with the whole QA group which was perpetually executing systematic test plans created to thoroughly cover areas of the product, and doing so on huge rooms full of a range of system configurations. But my peculiar way of relaxing at the end of the long days was allowing me to pick the low-hanging fruit, catching the easy and obvious bugs that someone else would otherwise have quickly found. (The harder and more subtle bugs were indeed caught by proper QA procedures.) Later, I was told that, in the post-mortem after shipment, it was discovered that more than 50% of all the bugs entered into the bug-tracking database were tagged with "BobGa" as the originator.

185 Continued Changes in Genigraphics' Business

On 17 September 1991, I went back to Connecticut again for a summit at Genigraphics headquarters.

Again, the news was that the imaging business was growing fast. For the most recent quarter, it was up 85%. Imaging from Mac and Windows now made up 31% of Genigraphics' business, up from only 12% for the corresponding quarter a year earlier. In a year and a half, they had produced over 700,000 35mm slides for over 7,000 customers. The Memphis location next to FedEx was doing one-third of the total business.

A typical job involved some corrections—perhaps 25 to 30 slides initially, followed by changes to 4 or 5 of the slides so that they needed to be imaged again. Many customers were using the shaded backgrounds, the templates shipped in the box, and the clip art.

Interestingly, 5% to 10% of the total Memphis imaging output was being delivered overnight to hotels. It was common for a customer to finish a presentation at the last moment, transmit it to Genigraphics, then fly to the destination and receive the slides there. This observation had given rise to related thoughts—could the local Genigraphics service bureaus offer services through hotels? Could they offer a service to "fix your slides at the last minute," which would allow you to take your received slides and a corrected version of your presentation into the local service bureau up to midnight, 7 days a week, and have the corrected slides by 7:00 a.m.? Could there be a way for the user to telephone Memphis and tell them orally what to change, then Memphis would make the change and send the corrected files to the local service bureau for local imaging and pickup by 7:00 a.m.? These were all high-cost services, but, at the time, there was almost no one who traveled with a computer, and a presenter who was away from his office to make a slide presentation, and who needed changes or more slides, might be eager to pay for help. (None of these ideas was ever tried seriously.)

We were able to set up a new contract with Genigraphics for them to develop the templates in the PowerPoint 3.0 box, and agreed that they should work on them during the Genigraphics "slow period" beginning in December. We would mock up visual samples in PowerPoint 2.0 within a month, agree on a spec by 1 December, and have the templates completed by 15 January 1992 for QA. Connected with this was further work to create the "signature presentation" (Columbus's pitch to Queen Isabella) for us to use in all our advertising, printed materials, and product boxes; it too would require mocking up, but then the appearance in PowerPoint 3.0 had to match perfectly.

As early as 30 January 1992, Sandy Beetner called me to tell me that Genigraphics was downscaling, again. More executives were gone, along with some other people in the Services group. Apart from that, support for the "older business," the consoles made by the former hardware division and still used by Sandy's remaining service bureaus, was being phased out—so the big change we'd foreseen had arrived. Gradually, Genigraphics acquired more Macs and Windows PCs, partly to work on projects for PowerPoint. After PowerPoint 3.0 shipped, a few months later, it started to become obvious that, fairly soon, Genigraphics would be using PowerPoint on personal computers to replace its old consoles.

186 Planning for the Windows 3.1 Announcement

On 10 January 1992, Steve Ballmer told me about the plans for announcing Windows 3.1, which ratcheted up the pressure on Power-Point 3.0. The announcement was planned for a big event on 6 April 1992, several thousand people, plus satellite locations.

The big idea was to have *all* the announcements related to Windows 3.1 at the same time, for maximum impact. There would be Windows 3.1, on diskettes and on CD, the new C compiler to support the new 32-bit Windows, font products related to the new fonts in Windows 3.1 (a cartridge for HP printers, extra font packs), and PowerPoint 3.0.

That's pretty much what happened. When April came, I did a quick trip to the U.K. for local PR there a couple of days before, and was back in Menlo Park the night before 6 April; we got a video downlink to our building through a truck-mounted satellite dish so the whole GBU could watch the big show. We did our release to manufacturing in May, and I was back in Europe for a tour of all the northern subsidiaries just as their localized versions of PowerPoint 3.0 were being released.

In early June 1992, another program review, taking into account all we'd learned from shipping the Windows version, gave us a release to manufacturing for the Mac version of late August, 16 weeks after Windows (a 3-week slip). This was just about the gap between Windows and Mac that had been predicted for at least six months.

187 Increasing Development Effort for PowerPoint 3.0

On 5 February 1992, Dennis Austin gave me a presentation stressing how much work was going into PowerPoint 3.0 (estimated to completion) and particularly into PowerPoint for Windows—about 300 person-months of development time, not counting the large amount of work done on the graphing component by Bear River Associates for us.

At the time, about 50% of the 275,000 lines of code in PowerPoint 3.0 was "core code" shared between Mac and Windows versions; our goal was to get that up to 70%.

	Date Shipped	Development in Person/Months
PowerPoint 1.0 (Mac)	Apr 1987	34
PowerPoint 2.0 (Mac)	May 1988	26
PowerPoint 2.0 (Win)	May 1990	185 (+ graph)
PowerPoint 3.0 (Win and Mac)	May 1992 / Sep 1992	300+ (+ graph)

For PowerPoint 1.0, much of the 34 person-months (all Dennis Austin and Tom Rudkin) was original design from a blank sheet of paper. Starting from that, it had taken only 26 additional person-months to design the color 2.0 and get it shipped on Mac, versus something like eight times as long just to ship the Windows version of the same thing. That had been a surprise to us, and to everyone up to Bill; we didn't realize how much more mature the Mac platform was. That investment had broken the back of the Windows problem for us, so for PowerPoint 3.0 more of the work had gone into extensive new functionality, but Windows and its own evolution was still exacting a price.

It was striking that only 6% of the development investment had gone into the whole of the original PowerPoint idea and a shippable version (as part of Forethought), versus 94% of the development effort that had gone into developing the idea further (as part of Microsoft).

As of that same day, the schedule was to release an Alpha 1 version for me to take to Paris on 13 February 1992. This would be followed by Alpha 2 on 13 March 1992 and Release Candidate 1 on 3 April 1992. Our announcement was still scheduled to coincide with that of Windows 3.1, so the RC1 code could be used for that event on 6 April 1992 (we were already working with the people charged with doing presentations for the Windows 3.1 announcement). We then would plan to release to manufacturing the Windows version on 27 April 1992 and the Mac version on 3 August 1992. We had decided that the Windows version simply had to make the Windows 3.1 ship; it was much safer to plan to do our final release procedures for Windows first and then for Mac, focusing the whole business unit on one platform at a time.

International versions in English would be released simultaneously, French and German a month later, French Canadian and Spanish and Italian a month after that (translations had long been underway already). This was extremely aggressive for international versions of new Windows applications, but the world was getting smaller.

It would turn out to be more than four years between the release of Mac PowerPoint 2.0 and Mac PowerPoint 3.0 (though with some minor updates). This was testing the faith of our Macintosh users severely, and might have opened us to competition if anyone else had managed to ship a much better Mac product. But the Windows platform and the Windows Office applications suite were the critical issues. People at the GBU used to ask me sometimes why we were gambling everything on Windows, at the cost of starving Macintosh and ignoring OS/2. My answer to them was that Bill was betting the entire company on the success of Windows, so tossing PowerPoint onto the pile of chips didn't really raise the stakes appreciably.

188 The World's First Laptop Video Presentation

At this point, I set off on a European tour to get PowerPoint 3.0 in front of Microsoft people early—actually before we demonstrated it widely in the U.S.

The very first public use of a laptop to project video from Power-Point took place on 25 February 1992, at the Hotel Regina, in the Place des Pyramides, Paris (across from the Tuileries gardens). With a laptop casually under my arm, I entered at the back of a ballroom filled with hundreds of Microsoft people from the European, Middle Eastern, and African subsidiaries. I walked through the audience carrying the laptop, up to a podium at the front; there I opened the laptop, and plugged in a video cable on the lectern. I began delivering a presentation to intro-duce PowerPoint 3.0 for Windows, using PowerPoint 3.0 running on the laptop, feeding video out to a hulking projector located in the mid-dle of the audience; it projected my "video slides" onto a huge screen behind me. No one had ever seen PowerPoint running on a full-color laptop computer before, let alone being used to produce a real-time video show in full rich color with animated builds and transitions. The audience, all Microsoft people who talked to customers frequently, grasped immediately what the future would bring for their own presen-tations; there was deafening applause.

Laptops at the time were thought of (accurately) as being severely underpowered compared to desktop computers. No one before had ever considered demonstrating a new Windows application on any laptop, because it would run too slowly. The fact that PowerPoint ran so fast in a live demonstration on a laptop, with the screen animations at fully acceptable speed, assured our insider audience that PowerPoint 3.0 would be super-fast on desktop computers.

The computer hardware was only barely there. I was using an early production sample of a new color notebook computer from Texas Instruments, which was the first to have a 640 x 480 256-color display and video out, with sufficient CPU to do graphics (price about $4,000). We had loaded the machine with Windows 3.1 Release Candidate 1 and PowerPoint 3.0 Alpha 1, plus a Genigraphics presentation about PowerPoint 3.0. The unreleased Windows 3.1 was required in order to use TrueType fonts and to include audio and video, as well as for many other graphics improvements that PowerPoint 3.0 relied upon.

Even being Microsoft, we could manage to get hold of only two such machines in the U.S. The two Texas Instruments laptops arrived in California just a few days before we left for Europe; they were hand-carried to Paris, on separate airplanes, since no similar machines were available anywhere in Europe. We took with us a selection of European power supplies for them and several backup sets of the diskettes for all the unreleased software, copies of which we had also sent ahead.

I spent the entire day of Monday, 24 February 1992, and late into that night, in the ballroom of the Hotel Regina with a staff of local audio-visual consultants, installing and trouble-shooting a massive video projector, the only kind that then existed.

In 1992, a video projector for more than a few people was the size of a large refrigerator, cost in excess of $100,000, and had to be attended by several technicians to keep it going. This was the "light-valve" projector, from yet another division of GE; like the early Genigraphics products, it had been produced originally for view simulation. The whole concept of the projector was implausible. It required an hour to warm up before it could be operated. It accepted NTSC video, thus beginning with unpromising quality, and converted that into cyan and magenta video, which it used as primary colors to create a full color image. Internally, for each primary color, a mechanism rotated a conductive glass disc inside a glass envelope under high vacuum. The disc passed through a heated oil bath which left a thin film of viscous oil on it. An electron beam (as in a CRT tube) scanned the oil and deposited a charge on the surface of the oil. This caused the surface of the oil to deflect and bend light rays to create the image (hence, "light-valve"). The light to project each primary color came from a xenon arc that could deliver as much as 3500 lumens. By the standards of 2012, the projected quality was dreadful, but in 1992 it looked amazing.

Testing and tweaking went on far into the night, but on Tuesday morning, I could "casually" carry my laptop through the crowd up to the front, plug in the video cable, and start up PowerPoint. The demo went off without a hitch, as did the rest of the introduction.

I continued on a tour of the European subsidiaries, giving several more, smaller demonstrations. Similar demonstrations were given in the U.S. and in other parts of the world over the next three months. Windows 3.1 was shipped in April 1992, and PowerPoint 3.0 immediately followed in May 1992. In response, many notebook computers with full color and video out were shipped later that same year.

189 A Heavy Company Tax on Shipping

One of the oddest problems of the growing complexity of Microsoft was that it imposed an expensive tax on shipping a glamorous product.

I had always restricted circulation of pre-release versions of our software to specific people who would really use it and who could knowledgeably report any problems—some "alpha" sites within Microsoft and our vendors, and some "beta" sites outside the company. Partly, this was because the cost of wide betas was high but the payoff from investing in them was small; despite targeting our betas carefully, we had never had an unknown bug (that turned out to be real) reported first from a beta site. We did too much testing ourselves to leave much for beta testers to find, so we needed "working" beta testers who would merit our attention.

I also knew that early versions released promiscuously inevitably got copied onto many machines, where they could lurk and later result in erroneous last-minute reports of bugs. Such reports could easily cause a delay in shipping, but were merely an expensive distraction because the bugs in the old versions had long before been noted and fixed.

For PowerPoint 3.0, I found that the pressure for early access to copies of the software was much stronger than for other products. I concluded that this was because it provided such dazzling demonstrations of what would be possible on Windows 3.1 that everyone in the company wanted to be an "insider" and gain prestige from showing it off to other people.

As the shipment of Windows PowerPoint 3.0 neared, I received growing demands for copies of it from other parts of Microsoft, and growing dissatisfaction with its unavailability. Impatience rolled up the company, becoming stronger—"the field and internal marketing are disaffected ... must be sure they are mobilized to get behind the product." I accommodated these demands, but always with the conviction that they were merely a mild form of extortion, which took attention away from shipping with no advantage to anyone except to satisfy the need to feel important on the part of the extortionists.

The problem was that, if we were to start making early software available to anyone, we would have to do a wholesale distribution to every part of the company; otherwise, we would be slighting all the people who were not so favored. We also had to prepare enough explanatory material so that the early distributions would be easy to appreciate, and so that we could insure that nearly everyone could use them successfully. Once we started to make wide distributions, we had to assume that copies would rapidly end up with journalists and competitors, so we needed to present everything attractively.

If there had been an Internet available to all the Microsoft people, then we could have made software and documents available easily. But this was well before the Internet age, so we had to produce physical packages and ship them.

On 23 March 1992, we used our local Silicon Valley suppliers to manufacture and assemble 275 copies of the early "A2" (second Alpha) version of the software. Each package included 5 labeled diskettes for all the software, together with a cover letter, instructions for installation, a 25-page demo script, and a 400-page photocopied book called "The Insider's Guide." This last was just the standard user manual, but we retouched it by adding a new preface so as to cast its reader in the role of an "insider" who was getting valuable early access to important information (if you took this seriously, you had failed the intelligence test). The diskettes were set up with everything needed to run through the demo script, and thus could be used by anyone to see what the product would do, and to show it off to other people.

One hundred and fifty copies were individually sent or hand-delivered in the U.S., to give recipients a sense of importance: 25 to executives, 15 to business unit managers, 30 to various groups involved in launch activities and to product support, and 80 to system engineers in all the U.S. field sales offices. Another 125 copies were sent out internationally, 100 to all the various country subsidiaries and 25 copies to the central International group where localization was managed.

Just a month later, at the end of April 1992, we had to manufacture locally and dispatch 3,000 copies of "Preview" software—a special release created just for this purpose. This time, each packet included 7 labeled diskettes, plus copies of much of the collateral, the data sheet, a copy of the demo script again, a "reviewer's guide," the "Insider's Guide" again, and other material. This made a substantial, and very heavy, package. We sent 2,000 copies of all this to Microsoft people in the U.S. and 1,000 copies to people in the international subsidiaries.

This second "Preview" distribution was a huge undertaking, but it was better motivated, if only by internal failings. Manufacturing would begin on 6 May 1992, but there were such long delays in their getting product assembled and shipped that it was self-defense for us to manufacture these 3,000 copies of the product ourselves, using suppliers in Silicon Valley, and to ship them out directly—despite the fact that the Microsoft manufacturing group should have been able to do the job much more efficiently. The fact that our "Preview" distribution went out just a couple of weeks before the Golden Masters were released to manufacturing assured that there was no possibility that any useful feedback could be received and acted upon (and, of course, there was none). It was merely the quick-turnaround product manufacturing for internal use that the corporate group should have managed to do for us overnight upon release.

In our small group, the people who had to get all of this material ready and manage its production were necessarily the same people who at the same time were trying to get the product itself shipped. It represented a new tax on shipping, imposed so that more people would feel "included" and "involved," in the hope that they would reciprocate with goodwill toward our product. It was a curious custom that other Microsoft employees required such conspicuous displays of our regard for them.

190 What to Do After PowerPoint 3.0?

As with every previous version, as soon as Windows PowerPoint 3.0 was in the last phases of release, we consciously started holding meetings about what to do next.

I made one such list of work items on 8 June 1992, a week after release. The list included releasing Mac PowerPoint 3.0 on Mac, exactly the same program, and the international versions for both Windows and Mac, but after that the possibilities went downhill:

1. PowerPoint 3.0 for Macintosh (four months to release)
2. Western-language international versions of PowerPoint 3.0
3. Kanji version of Windows PowerPoint 3.0 for Japan
4. An early upgrade release in 1993, with more slideshow features
5. A larger upgrade in 1994 for the new version of Windows, codename "Chicago"
6. Revising the Draw component to work with a new metafile format
7. More work on graphics format translators
8. More work on setup and installation
9. More clip art (for the product and for internal Microsoft use)
10. More templates
11. A release of PowerPoint 3.0 on CD-ROM

A quick look showed that this didn't amount to anything very interesting; it was all "maintenance engineering."

Three weeks later, 26 June 1992, I made a list of what had been suggested to me were the most important additions to PowerPoint that could be considered for the next major version:

1. Tables
2. Org Charts
3. "Build" sequences automated for charts and graphs
4. Navigation buttons in on-screen presentations
5. More "Shapes" (parameterized drawing primitives)
6. Read more competitors' file formats directly
7. Macros [part of a general "direction" being promoted]
8. Wizards [another "direction"—I referred to them as "lizards"]
9. Collaborative work on presentations by multiple users
10. Database of presentations and resources
11. Special-effects text [external component, by another group]
12. Conformance to new "family look" for all applications [Office]

None of this sounded very interesting to me, and yet I didn't have any better ideas for major extensions of PowerPoint. The original version 1.0 had really done a good job for black and white overheads. Version 2.0 had done a good job of adding color and 35mm slides through Genigraphics. Version 3.0, just shipped, had polished both overheads and 35mm slides and added most of what I thought would be useful for live video presentations, which wouldn't become common for a few years anyway. That was about everything I wanted to do.

I thought there was only limited advantage to adding tables, because Dennis Austin had developed such a slick way to build them rapidly using drawing primitives that worked well for the small tables found on slides. (Sometime after I left, the drawing was changed so that Dennis's neat features no longer worked as well, and Word-style tables were added to compensate.) Similarly, I thought that most org charts demanded a lot of unique tweaking, and that better features for general drawing would be of more use than a non-functional automation. Adding just "more" of anything—more shapes, more clip art, more templates, more of whatever, was repeating what had already been done. "Wizards" were specialized overlays on the standard product interface; they were used in other products to make it easier to do some common task, which I almost always thought should be handled better in the basic product design. The task of getting PowerPoint sledge-hammered into shape to match Word and Excel as part of Office was mostly political, and I certainly didn't want to participate in that.

Really, I was left with no conclusion other than that I had finished what I intended to do with PowerPoint. Doubtless there were many good ideas for the future direction, but I didn't know what they were. It was very likely time for me to withdraw.

PART IX: LEAVING POWERPOINT

191 My Longstanding Plan to Retire from Microsoft

I had always intended to leave Microsoft as soon as I had the resources to retire. This was not because life at the GBU following the acquisition was unpleasant—on the contrary, the opportunity to work with the finest people I've ever known was wonderful. And for a long time, our place in the Microsoft organization was ideal, with substantial support and little interference, so we could really accomplish big tasks. One couldn't ask for a better outcome to a startup acquisition.

But I was always longing to return to the lifestyle of a perpetual graduate student, with the freedom to concentrate on whatever subjects and projects interested me. It was impossible for me to run a startup and at the same time read several long scholarly books a week, or live for a while in a different city or country, or assemble a thoughtfully chosen wine cellar, or learn to play a new musical instrument—or much of anything else.

I don't think that my intention was suspected by my associates, for I always kept long hours, traveled constantly, and worked unreasonably hard, but I was treating it as an opportunity to achieve real "work/life balance," over a period measured in decades. I didn't want to work at a slower pace for a longer time; I knew from the beginning, from immediately after the Microsoft acquisition, that my plan was to continue to work unreasonably hard for only a while, and then to retire permanently and not work at all. That seemed very achievable, because even as early as 1987, there was press interest in "Microsoft millionaires," and I'd received enough MSFT stock options at the acquisition that, if Microsoft continued to be successful, then I would be also. At Microsoft, "we all got paid off the bottom line," through stock appreciation.

381

I was very interested to assure the future of PowerPoint, but I had no interest in being promoted up the ladder of a company, even Microsoft. I had been past the age of 40 when I began working on Power-Point in 1984; I made it a concrete goal to be retired prior to my 50th birthday, which would mean leaving by mid-1993. Seen from the vantage point of mid-1987, just after the acquisition, six years seemed like plenty of time. By late 1989, only two years later, I had begun making concrete plans—extremely concrete.

I can reconstruct when I got serious about leaving, from the evidence of my annual pocket appointment books. Starting with the book for 1990, at the end of each preceding year (hence, starting in late 1989), I used the blank pages at the end to carefully draw a handwritten chart of closing prices for MSFT stock and the value of all my to-be-vested options at that price. I marked a specific target value.

Each time I went to Redmond, at least every other week, I would hear the closing price of MSFT as I got on the plane to leave Seattle, and on the Alaska Airlines flight back to SFO, I would sit down, take out my pocket diary, and look up the price in those last pages of tables. Sometimes it seemed like the extraordinary specificity of my goal was actually bringing it into reality. As time went on, over the next three years, the numbers almost predictably climbed to exactly my goal.

So, for the five years and some I was with Microsoft, I was always planning to be able to retire permanently, and to accomplish that goal before age 50, which would mean retiring by mid-1993, just after a cliff in the vesting of my options. It's hard to execute such a contingent plan precisely, but by late 1992, MSFT stock had gone up enough to fund my plans.

Options on MSFT stock were granted to me and other PowerPoint people in August of 1987 at $0.23 per share (current 2012 shares—all values corrected for later splits), with further grants in later years. By March 1993, when I left, MSFT shares were $2.27 per share—an increase of 887%, to almost exactly ten times my starting value, in five and a half years. Despite what Forethought's investors had feared when they were offered stock, MSFT was not overpriced in 1987. By way of comparison, Google's stock price, in the corresponding period from 18 months to 84 months after the GOOG IPO, increased by only 35%. The difference between ten times the option grant value and one-and-one-third times the option grant value makes a huge difference to the recipients. Microsoft produced lots of millionaires over quite a number of years, not just at the IPO.

In later years, I've felt like Max Palevsky, the founder of Scientific Data Systems computer company (acquired by Xerox), who had been a graduate student in philosophy, at the University of Chicago, at Berkeley, and at UCLA, when, in 1949 or 1950, he heard a lecture at CalTech by John von Neumann about computers and promptly dropped out of graduate school to work in the computer business:

> "Many of us early workers in computers were philosophy majors," Mr. Palevsky told the Chicago Tribune in 1968. "You can imagine our surprise at being able to make rather comfortable livings."
> —obituary, *Wall Street Journal*, 7 May 2010 (Miller 2010)

192 Finding a Good Time to Leave

Several considerations reinforced my longstanding plan to retire by early 1993. The major thing was that we were completing the huge leap forward for PowerPoint 3.0 (on Windows 3.1, then on Macintosh, with common code). This was a major expansion of the concept of the product, and it was necessary to get a lot of things right with a single vision, so I had spent a lot of time assuring that.

It became clear to me that version 3.0 of PowerPoint would be the last one I would need to manage. It was being developed with built-in internationalization (it was "localized into English" by the same mechanism used for any other language), with plans already developed to ship in all major languages, including, for the first time, Far Eastern character sets (Japanese, Korean, and Chinese), so this would complete the worldwide product. The product was on a roll; revenue had just exceeded the $100 million per year level as version 3.0 began shipping. PowerPoint was undeniably now going to be successful.

All of our competitors had misjudged how quickly Windows would succeed, and had either stayed with MS-DOS too long, planning to move to OS/2 PM, which didn't work out for them, or stayed with being Macintosh-only too long, allowing PowerPoint to get way ahead as the Windows market dwarfed Mac, so all indications were that the success would continue.

This was the positive incentive to leave: the task was essentially done. I was still playing the role of the product visionary, the "keeper and re-iterator of the vision" for PowerPoint, as I had been from the very beginning. I might or might not still have a persuasive vision for the future, but if I were going to retire any time soon, then for the next version of PowerPoint, someone else would have to take over the duties of visionary. That would only be possible when I was gone. It wasn't a process that I could control. Best to get the process started while PowerPoint was in a posture of great success.

193 *Reasons to Be Gloomy*

In addition to its being a good time to leave for positive reasons, there were also some negatives, which were reasons to leave even if they were not my primary motivation.

A big factor was that the next task was to create a real Office product. In my very last memo written at Microsoft, on 13 September 1992, I demonstrated that I understood the plan:

> The strategy for desktop apps over the next eighteen months is to achieve great consistency, and be the leading suite of apps for Chicago [codename for the version of Windows to follow 3.1] in late 1993 and early 1994. This strategy dominates most considerations, because it leads to the greatest (and most easily defended) market share. ... Word/Excel/PowerPoint are not really thought of as separate in our future plans ... .

I not only understood, I thought it was a good idea. I just didn't want to do it myself.

Also, it had been a loss for me when my boss Mike Maples was promoted to be part of the "Office of the President" group, leaving me without his direct help. Mike had come from an organization where everything not explicitly permitted and approved was forbidden, and had seen how that worked, so he had formed exceedingly sophisticated views about how much direction from upper-management was desirable, and how to make it effective. Mike truly made it appear that he concentrated on helping his direct reports to make and achieve their own plans, and on setting up systems and providing information so they could improve those plans, along with providing diplomatically delivered advice. This was an effective way to motivate the independent business unit managers who reported to him while leaving all the responsibility with them, but it was a subtle set of skills not shared by most of the managers who had grown up inside Microsoft.

The development and shipping of PowerPoint 3.0 had been extremely difficult, and I thought the tasks had been made harder by the fact that Redmond was beginning to develop the large bureaucracies and the technical means to meddle efficiently with distant business units.

Microsoft had multiplied to have ten times as many employees as when we joined, from 1,200 to over 12,000. One straw in the wind was that we saw Bill Gates less often, and he was less able to give close consideration to PowerPoint, as his own responsibilities multiplied.

With Microsoft's growth, it was becoming far harder to get "the right thing" done. In the early days, people in Redmond had shared the vision and realized what was needed. Now, increasingly, people working on other applications and on Windows were doing wrong things, short-sighted things, self-serving things, easy things, as in all large organizations. During the development of PowerPoint 3.0, I had spent weeks campaigning in Redmond to get critical improvements into Windows 3.1 and into the standards and components shared with Word and Excel, sometimes having to enlist Mike to raise issues to the highest levels, in order to avoid making terrible decisions. This was another negative reason to leave: the company was becoming too bureaucratic and political to do the right thing.

I wasn't the only one who noticed these changes in Microsoft. The same year that I started counting down the days to when I could retire, at the 1990 Apps Retreat held 22 March 1990 at Bill Gates's summer compound on the Hood Canal, Mike Maples kicked off the year's discussions by posing the question: "What was better three years ago?" (Coincidentally, that was just about when I had joined Microsoft.) Mike provided some answers to his own question:

Now:
1. more bureaucracy, more process
2. less personal initiative
3. less communication
4. less knowledge of other functional groups
5. less ownership of results
6. less focus on products, more on process (specs, schedules)
7. ratio of "hard-core" people has declined
8. more interference, slower decisions

Mike went on to pose the question: "Where will we be in three more years?" If Mike saw all the same things I saw, then I wasn't imagining the decline. (Mike himself retired about three years after I did.)

The post-acquisition condition of Microsoft had clearly gone downhill. After benefitting so much from the ineptitude of some of our competitors, Microsoft was losing some of what distinguished us from them. During my first couple of years, I hadn't had to spend any appreciable time circumventing bureaucracy or stubbornly refusing to agree to second-best plans—we had continued to work as we did when we were a startup. But by my fifth year, I was doing far too much of such work, as Microsoft became a big company.

It's important to have perspective here. Working at Microsoft was farther each year from the initial bliss I had experienced, but it was still far better than any other company I knew about, and was full of wonderfully smart people. I didn't leave because it had become intolerable, not at all. Still, it was clearly already in decline.

194 The Mechanics of Leaving

The incredible work of the GBU people had managed to bring PowerPoint 3.0 to a very successful conclusion, in spite of all the difficulties. PowerPoint 3.0 for Windows had shipped in May 1992, and PowerPoint 3.0 for Mac was in the final hours of shipping in September 1992, so my job was done. I didn't have any particularly great new ideas for the next steps for PowerPoint, and the corporate ideas were unimaginative. At the same time, the MSFT stock price went up to past my target price, giving me all the financial resources I thought I'd need.

So I decided to accelerate my plan. Instead of waiting to resign on 22 February 1993, my previous plan, I would leave right away, on 15 September 1992, so I wouldn't be caught up in future planning beyond PowerPoint 3.0. I could do something else for five or six months, which would take me past the cliff in the vesting of my stock options.

In the reorganizations after Mike Maples was promoted to the Office of the President, I'd ended up reporting to Pete Higgins. Pete was now as eager for me to leave the GBU as I was to leave, so he strongly tried to help me make the change. Pete said to me that both Bill Gates and Mike Maples had told him that it would "not be in the interests of Microsoft for [me] to leave" the company, a curious echo of what Frank Gaudette had said to me about Aniko Somogyi in my first week as a Microsoft manager. Bill and Mike both wanted me to move to Redmond and start something new all over again. I should talk to Rick Rashid, who was just starting Microsoft Research, and to some other groups. I went up to

Redmond to talk the whole thing over with Mike Maples, who was happy with the idea that I'd need to stay on the payroll for six months, because that would give me time to find a good match in Redmond.

I expected that my leaving might well be final; others expected that I would soon find opportunities that I couldn't resist in Redmond; but everyone agreed that it was a good idea to make the transition quickly, simultaneous with the final release of PowerPoint 3.0. We set my last full-time day at the GBU to be 25 September 1992.

Ten days before that, on 14 September 1992, I called Sandy Beetner at Genigraphics to tell her that I was leaving, and then immediately after that call I walked down the hall to my staff meeting to say the same thing to my direct reports. I explained, honestly, that this was a very good time for me to leave, personally, and it was a pretty good time for the GBU and for Microsoft, since the new projects would be planned by whoever was going to be responsible for them. The formal public announcement was made to the whole GBU at an all-hands meeting the following morning.

Mike wanted me to relocate to Redmond right away, and then find a new job there; I didn't want to relocate without an irresistible opportunity. Bill and Mike had one specific group in mind for me, a group getting ready to turn a research project into a product, which they thought could use some help; but even with such sponsorship, the target group wasn't exactly welcoming. I could see that it wasn't a great fit.

I had reached the level of doing a project that took about 100 people, and I wasn't looking for a chance to learn to do projects that took 200, or 1000, or 10,000 people. I remembered Mike Maples' telling me, sometime around the time he moved up to his Office of the President job, that in his career progression from being an individual contributor to managing tens of thousands of people, just about every step up had been less fun than the preceding one. That resonated with me. If anything, I wanted to go back to doing projects that one person could do. But I didn't have a new idea that I felt strongly about, and, if I had, I would probably have thought that it was safer to do another startup outside, rather than try to operate within the large company that Microsoft had become.

Most of what I ended up doing in these final months turned out to be isolated tasks for Bill Gates or Mike Maples, typically appearing as a suitably senior technical person in meetings with other companies that were not particularly critical. Our agreement was for six months, which was intended to keep me on the payroll and preserve all my options through that vesting cliff in late February 1993; my final paperwork to leave Microsoft permanently was executed on 5 March 1993. So I ended up leaving just about two months earlier than my longstanding blue-sky plan had optimistically envisioned.

195 Circumspice

On my last day at the GBU, 25 September 1992, I put my personal things in a banker's box.

The collection of books from my bookcases had already been boxed and sent up to San Francisco. Since it was ten days after my announcement that I was leaving, I was well out of all the loops, with no further commitments and nothing in my inbox except memos to large distribution lists. I used PowerPoint to make a single slide, reading "*Si monumentum requiris, circumspice*," added a typographic ornament, and then printed a copy and taped it to the door of my office.

That was, as I knew from memory (no web to check the quote or the spelling, in those days), part of what is written on the wall above the tomb of Christopher Wren, in the crypt of his St. Paul's Cathedral in London: "*Lector, si monumentum requiris, circumspice*" (Reader, if you seek his monument, look around you).

At 3:00 p.m., there was an extremely thoughtful celebration of my leaving. Everyone in the GBU was there, including Publishing Power, as well as Sandy Beetner and Rosemary Abowd from Genigraphics. We all had a lot of laughing, and I received a number of mementoes and keepsakes (some still on my desk to this day).

Even though I was, in some sense, supposed to be glad to be retiring, I recalled my own oft-repeated *précis* of the last of Samuel Johnson's essays in *The Idler*, No. 103, for Saturday, 5 April 1760, on the topic of "the secret horror of the last": No one ever does anything for the last time, knowingly, without a feeling of regret. "... Of a place which has been frequently visited, [even] though without pleasure, the last look is taken with heaviness of heart ... ."

I took the long drive home to San Francisco for the last time. That drive had seemed reasonable while I was commuting, but in later years, whenever I passed the Sand Hill Road exit on Interstate 280, I couldn't believe that I ever drove all those miles, morning and evening, for several years.

196 The Superannuated Man

My longstanding plan to retire before age 50 was not entirely arbitrary, but had a particular literary inspiration: I had for some years been reading Charles Lamb's essay entitled "The Superannuated Man." (The essay is easily found on the web.)

In the spring of 1825, at age 50, Lamb was suddenly retired and given a pension by his City employer. He had entered service as an office clerk at the age of fourteen, and had spent 36 years there, spending eight to ten hours a day, six days a week, with a day off at Easter, a day off at Christmas, and one week of holiday in the summer. He says, "My health and my good spirits flagged. I had perpetually a dread of some crisis, to which I should be found unequal." Then one morning, the partners of the firm called him in, proposed that they give him a pension, and sent him home.

He wrote in a letter to Wordsworth a few days later:

> I came home FOR EVER on Tuesday in last week. ... I am daily steadying, and shall soon find it as natural to me to be my own master, as it has been irksome to have had a master.

In the essay he says:

> For the first day or two I felt stunned, overwhelmed. ... I was a poor Carthusian, from strict cellular discipline suddenly by some revolution returned upon the world.

But by two weeks later, he notes:

> I am now as if I had never been other than my own master. It is natural to me to go where I please, to do what I please. I find myself at eleven o'clock in the day in Bond Street, and it seems to me that I have been sauntering there at that very hour for years past. I digress into Soho, to explore a book stall. Methinks I have been thirty years a collector. There is nothing strange or new in it. I find myself before a fine picture in the morning. Was it ever otherwise? ... It is 'Change time, and I am strangely among the Elgin marbles. It was no hyperbole when I ventured to compare the change in my condition to a passing into another world.

During my last couple of years at Microsoft, studying those tables of options values while flying home from another trip to Redmond, the memory of this essay made a big impression on me. I worked hours as long as Lamb had worked—although he left school at 14 and worked for 36 years, whereas I left school at 36 and worked for 14 years (a sobering comparison). I could easily visualize what it would be like to be my own master, and resolved to try to do it at the same age as Lamb.

When I left, I found my experience much as Lamb had described his. "I have a quiet home-feeling of the blessedness of my condition. I am in no hurry." And a year or so after retiring, I was, like Lamb, living in central London, sauntering in Bond Street (where a passerby saw me through a shop window and rushed inside to ask for my autograph, saying "May I thank you for *The Godfather*?"), exploring a book stall (I found many books in London I'd long wanted, and I had another whole house full of new shelves for them), and walking among the Elgin marbles (pretty pale stuff compared to the nearby Egyptian Hall, with its Rosetta Stone). And it all seemed perfectly natural. "I have worked task-work, and have the rest of the day to myself."

197 PowerPoint Continues Its Success without Me

I was extremely pleased that there were no bad effects from my retiring, at least none that I could discern as an outsider. My leaving didn't seem to disrupt the group, and didn't interfere with the product's continuing success.

After I left, none of the other senior people followed me immediately. They stayed at their posts, and shipped yet another version, Power-Point 4.0, in the next year (February 1994).

I had no part in PowerPoint 4.0 at all, not even in its earliest planning. As I had expected, one of its primary claims to fame was better integration with the other components of Office, the "full Office look and feel." I thought that was great, but I was glad I hadn't had to do it, and hadn't had to take part in the political wrangling surrounding it. The people from our group who accomplished the transition did a much better job than I could have done. There were a number of finely crafted mechanisms from the early PowerPoint versions that were damaged, then forgotten and lost, when the chainsaws went to work to level down to a common base. But most customers appreciated the uniformity more than they missed what was lost.

Whatever its effect on the PowerPoint product, the push to Office was a correct competitive move, just as Bill had predicted. Lotus shipped a very similar Windows bundle called "SmartSuite," and Word-Perfect shipped a very similar Windows bundle called "PerfectOffice."

The suites became the focus of competition, and Microsoft's entry eventually dominated, which kept PowerPoint bobbing on top of the waves of change.

When PowerPoint 4.0 shipped in 1994, ten years after Dennis's and my beginning in 1984, at least four of the senior people at the GBU were still there from the Forethought days—Dennis Austin and Tom Rudkin were the two senior development managers, Darrell Boyle, once Forethought's VP of Marketing, was the senior marketing manager, and Glenn Hobin, the Forethought VP of Sales who gave us the numbers we had to have in 1987, was the senior sales manager directing liaison with the Microsoft sales force. Thus, a good part of the Microsoft GBU management continued to be the group who had worked on PowerPoint at Forethought. Some other Forethought people who joined the Microsoft GBU also remained, while still others from the earliest days had requested moves to Redmond and had senior positions there. To the original crew, of course, had been added scores of additional great people, who almost all stayed for years, and many of whom made major contributions.

I counted this as a very successful exit, personally. There was no drama, no disruption. Sales continued to roughly double every year.

198 Genigraphics Comes to an End

If PowerPoint went on to new successes in 1994, the news was not so good for Genigraphics, which ended its business, as I had known it, in that same year.

By the time it happened, I had no close connection at all, but the writing was on the wall before I left. The success of PowerPoint had severely eroded the lucrative custom business of Genigraphics, replacing it with the price-sensitive and impersonal business of imaging slides.

By far the cheapest way to supply slide imaging was from the new Genigraphics Memphis operation—files arrived by modem, were imaged on a production line, developed and mounted, tossed over the fence to where the airplanes were parked, and delivered the next morning by Federal Express. This left the two dozen downtown service bureaus increasingly under-utilized.

Sandy Beetner once explained to me that the service bureau locations had the potential to make Genigraphics "worth more dead than alive." The bureaus were located in high-rent downtown locations in each city, convenient for the advertising agencies, financial companies, and Fortune 500 corporate headquarters who were their prime customers. In almost all cases, shedding these leases would be expensive. Every location had an Ektachrome E6 processing line, which involved potential environmental contamination issues and remediation costs. If it ever got to the point where the service bureaus were uneconomic, it was foreseeable that a bankruptcy proceeding could be the only practical way to get rid of them. No buyer would volunteer to buy the headaches of shutting them down.

Something like this scenario probably happened. In June 1994, more than a year after I left, it was announced that Genigraphics had filed for bankruptcy, and that some assets (including the Memphis slide imaging facility) had been acquired by InFocus Systems for $1.5 million.

Many people have casually written that Genigraphics was put out of business by the move to use PowerPoint for live video presentations, eliminating the need for 35mm slides. That was doubtless on the horizon, and would have influenced the views of the future of everyone concerned, but I don't think that had happened by 1994. Video shows were still not that common then, video projectors were not very satisfactory, and 35mm slides were very widely used. The Genigraphics driver and communication software were shipped in PowerPoint boxes until PowerPoint 2003 came out, nearly ten years later. Eastman Kodak continued to manufacture new 35mm slide projectors until 2004, about the same time.

Instead, I think that the two causal factors were: (1) the trend to replacement of Genigraphics' high-margin hardware by inexpensive personal computers running PowerPoint—that led to large losses in selling off the hardware division in Syracuse (the people who designed, manufactured and supported hardware products such as the consoles and the film recorders), and (2) the end of the high-margin custom services business which had incidentally involved making slides, and its replacement by low-margin commodity slide imaging from Power-Point—that led to large losses in the illiquid downtown service bureau locations.

Both the Syracuse hardware division and the two dozen downtown service bureaus in major cities were very specialized and very expensive capital investments, designed to deliver evolved high-value products. When the need for these specialized investments went away, they lost value to all buyers. The hardware division with its factories had been sold for more, but a year later, its buyer sold it on to a competitor for less than $5 million. The post-bankruptcy services division was sold to InFocus for about $1.5 million. The total isn't much, compared to all the investment that had gone into the specialized facilities.

Once upon a time, getting the ultimate-quality Genigraphics slides could only be done by paying for time on a Genigraphics console and paying for the time of a Genigraphics artist to use it. "Genigraphics charged $240 an hour for console create time in 1988. Color computer-generated presentation output was out of reach for most small businesses and barely tolerated by the larger ones, who frequently paid rush fees of 150 to 200 percent to make their tight deadlines. It wasn't unusual for a simple title slide to cost hundreds of dollars" (Endicott 2000).

PowerPoint 3.0 and the Genigraphics imaging service made available what were seen as the same ultimate-quality slides, without needing to pay for the hardware or the artists. A personal computer with Power-Point, plus a lot of slide imaging, could be bought for no more than the cost of a single Genigraphics full-service presentation. This change also expanded the creation of professional-quality 35mm slides beyond the exclusive domain of the professionals, by empowering anyone to create effective equivalents cheaply. One term for this process is "laicization," the assumption by lay people (the laity) of the powers previously reserved to specialists.

Could that have been changed? Could Genigraphics have avoided turning excellent 35mm slides into a lower-margin business? I don't think so. Genigraphics had competitors who also made good professional film recorders (indeed, Genigraphics eventually used them), and who could write drivers to "print" from Windows and Mac machines, and write software to send presentations over modems—those were not secret technologies (indeed, Genigraphics began by buying such software from Solutions, Inc.). PowerPoint had competitors who would have worked with those film recorder manufacturers, and PowerPoint would have as well.

One way or another, the pioneering but aging Genigraphics consoles were going to be replaced by an application running on Mac and Windows. Microsoft and Genigraphics, by working so closely together and doing such a good job, may have speeded things up a bit, and gotten the quality of the replacement up faster, but the outcome was foreordained.

And Genigraphics didn't suffer from lack of knowledge of what was going to happen. I had disclosed our plans to them in late 1987, and by the early months of 1988, they could see PowerPoint 2.0 for them-selves. There were no secrets, at all. If any alternative plan had existed to make better use of Genigraphics' experience and knowledge and great people in that newly revised world, they would have figured it out. Their services were not replaced by those of any competitor; the market for their services just went away.

Genigraphics, I believe, was not disadvantaged by partnering with Microsoft. Everything was technically open, so they could (and did) work with our competitors, and the fact that PowerPoint came to dom-inate the market was actually a help (so far as it could be). Genigraphics did much better than any of its competitors—if anyone in that business had survived, it would have been Genigraphics.

The plan they adopted, to take the lead in obsoleting Genigraphics' own equipment and services, seems to me to have been the best one available. The plan just couldn't generate the profits necessary to cover the liquidation costs of previous investments, but that couldn't be predicted in advance with any accuracy. The only possibly superior plan might have been for Genigraphics to have developed very early its own consumer software, like PowerPoint, for Macintosh and Windows, and to have out-competed Microsoft and all the other software companies; but this possibility was hardly realistic, since virtually no vertical-market workstation company managed to succeed with a personal computer application. The successful word-processing software for PCs did not come from companies that had made successful word-processing workstations, the successful desktop-publishing software for PCs did not come from companies that had made successful publishing workstations, and the same was true in every other category. All the barriers to success would have been the same in this case.

Following the bankruptcy, the companies who bought the imaging assets also failed a few years later, even without the overhang of what had turned out to be malinvestments, indicating that the imaging business itself had a short lifetime. The remaining vestige of the name Genigraphics today seems to exist by making "research posters" for scientific meetings from PowerPoint, a business which depends on the fact that most people don't own printers that can print a 36-inch by 60-inch sheet and laminate it, just as they once didn't own 35mm film recorders and E6 processing lines.

Video as a replacement for 35mm slides would come, and would make 35mm slides obsolete, but that hadn't happened yet when Geni-graphics went out of business. I have absolutely no inside information, but just judging from the external forces, I think that the two developments described above—the end of the custom hardware business and the end of the custom services business—explain what happened.

199 The Strangest PowerPoint Feature Ever Shipped

PowerPoint 4.0, the next version after I left, did offer one completely new feature which was widely touted and demonstrated, called "the AutoContent Wizard." In contrast to the many excellent innovations that have been added over the years since I left, this one was different. As I described earlier, I had nothing to do with even the earliest planning for PowerPoint 4.0, so I never heard of this feature until after it was shipped, when I bought an upgrade.

The AutoContent Wizard was a set of pre-written PowerPoint presentations, with a list of general topics from which to choose—things like "selling a product or service," or "recommending a strategy," or "reporting progress," or "communicating bad news." If a user of PowerPoint 4.0 had bad news to communicate, he could select that topic, and it would open a PowerPoint presentation containing half a dozen or so slides, each one a vague and general outline of platitudes and banalities arranged in bullet points. The people who designed the presentations must have supposed that users would understand that, obviously, they should "edit" the pre-written general content to become their own specific content—for example, the user would want to mention just what *was* the bad news that was being communicated.

In practice, though, many users would open the pre-written generalities, read them over much like choosing a Hallmark sympathy card, think "yes, that captures what I want to say; I feel like it's very unfortunate, but we did our best," or whatever, and then would print off the presentation and deliver it unchanged. Someone from Genigraphics later told me that they imaged thousands of copies of the pre-written "AutoContent" presentations onto 35mm slides, verbatim.

Ian Parker described the feature in a 2001 article about PowerPoint in the *New Yorker* magazine. He thought that the feature had come about in the following way:

> AutoContent was added in the mid-nineties, when Microsoft learned that some would-be presenters were uncomfortable with a blank PowerPoint page—it was hard to get started. "We said, 'What we need is some automatic content!' " a former Microsoft

developer recalls, laughing. " 'Punch the button and you'll have a presentation.' " The idea, he thought, was "crazy." And the name was meant as a joke. But Microsoft took the idea and kept the name—a rare example of a product named in outright mockery of its target customers. (Parker 2001)

(Because the feature was added after my time, I can't corroborate Parker's account; some other details in his article seem to be based on misunderstandings, and the same may be the case here. But his version circulated widely because it seemed so plausible.)

The year before, Peter Norvig had created a celebrated parody, in which he "imagined what Abe Lincoln might have done if he had used PowerPoint rather than the power of oratory at Gettysburg." Norvig describes how he used the AutoContent Wizard to ease his task:

> I started up PowerPoint and let the "Autocontent Wizard" help me create a new presentation. I selected the "Company Meeting (Online)" template, and figured from there I'd be creative in adding bad design wherever possible. I was surprised that the Autocontent Wizard had anticipated my desires so well that I had to make very few changes. Four of the slide titles were taken directly from the template; I only had to delete a few I didn't need, and add "Not on the Agenda" after "Agenda."
>
> I wasn't a professional designer, so I thought I'd be in for a late night doing some serious research: in color science to find a truly garish color scheme; in typography to find the worst fonts; and in overall design to find a really bad layout. But fortunately for me, the labor-saving Autocontent Wizard took care of all this for me! It suggested a red-on-dark-color choice for the navigation buttons that makes them very hard to see; it chose a serif font for the date that is illegible in low-resolution web mode, and of course Excel outdid itself on the graph ... . (Norvig, The Making of the Gettysburg PowerPoint Presentation 2000)

At least, Peter used the feature "properly" by editing the generalities into Abe Lincoln's own specifics.

Despite this sort of reception, the AutoContent Wizard actually stayed in the product, with the same name, for almost fifteen years, and wasn't removed until PowerPoint 2007.

That seemed to me another example of "Shirley's Theorem," which I had heard from Jon Shirley at my first Apps Retreat at Microsoft in early 1988: "There is no way to succeed with a bad product; it is okay to screw up a lot with a good product."

200 Where Did All the Competitors Go?

After my time, not only did the Office product result in very good sales for PowerPoint, Word, and Excel (and eventually other components), but also, all of the competitors dropped out of serious competition. As Windows 3.1, then Windows 95, then Windows 98 became the standard, Microsoft's applications had accompanying success.

The reason behind this was that no one except Microsoft had been taking the Windows platform seriously enough. As the tide of DOS ebbed, it became clear that all our competitors had been in the water without their bathing suits. Windows had been hard to develop for, initially, and had demanded close attention for long periods of time— but all of our competitors were capable of such development, and could get the same information as Microsoft's own Applications Division.

I've always suspected that the real problem was that all our application competitors were guilty of wishful thinking—they wanted anyone but Microsoft to own the next standard platform (they'd had enough of that with DOS), so they fooled themselves with OS/2 and Unix and Macintosh, while ignoring the likelihood that Windows was going to be the big winner. Their self-preservation instincts led them to bet on Microsoft's failure.

And then, when Windows did clearly begin to dominate, those dilatory competitors were acquired by other companies even more hostile to the idea of Microsoft's owning the standard applications platform, and even more determined not to believe it.

Lotus Development Corporation was the subject of a hostile takeover by IBM in 1995, apparently aimed at getting its Notes "groupware" product. Jim Manzi left the following year, Ray Ozzie the year after that. Freelance and its other products became increasingly uncompetitive.

WordPerfect was bought by Novell in 1994, which sold it on to Corel in 1996. WordPerfect never managed to get competitive Windows versions out in timely fashion, including its presentation app.

Aldus was bought by Adobe in 1994, and its Persuasion and other products continued to lose ground to competitors.

Harvard Graphics was so successful on MS-DOS that it had become the dominant part of Software Publishing Corporation; by 1993, it generated up to 80% of SPC revenue. But they failed to ship their first Windows product until almost two years after PowerPoint 2.0, right before we shipped PowerPoint 3.0! In 1994, Harvard/SPC laid off half its employees; Fred Gibbons resigned, and the shell was sold on in 1996.

Borland had bought Ashton-Tate in 1991, but by 1993 was trying to combine its products with those of WordPerfect to make an Office competitor, and in 1994, after WordPerfect was sold to Novell, the Borland components went to Novell also.

So by 1994–95, all of the competitors we had obsessed over in Microsoft's Applications Division were no longer threats. None of them had been strong Windows developers. Aldus Persuasion and Lotus Freelance had both been about one year later than PowerPoint on Windows, and Harvard Graphics had been about two years later than PowerPoint on Windows—a year or two is a long time on an exploding new platform.

All of the new acquirers were even less enthusiastic about Windows development: IBM was not going to help Lotus get to Windows, Novell was not going to help WordPerfect and Borland get to Windows, Adobe was not going to help Aldus get to Windows, and Harvard/SPC had no source of help at all.

Altogether, about a dozen large companies, supposedly full of realistic managers who faced up to the facts, just didn't want to see that Windows was improving from version to version and would ultimately be the most important platform for their applications. The fact that Windows could run DOS code offered some evolution from the former dominant platform, and Microsoft's strategy of licensing assured that hardware OEMs would beat one another's brains out to make Windows the lowest-cost platform with the broadest choice of hardware. Yet all these software companies failed to take the obvious course of targeting Windows.

This seemed amazing to me, since I'd been focused on Windows from well before the release of Windows 1.0, and had never relaxed that focus over more than ten years. But perhaps my early conviction was just luck. Certainly, before Windows 3.0 in 1990, there had been room for doubt. Ray Ozzie later (in 2005) remembered that:

> In 1990, there was actually a question about whether the graphical user interface had merit. Apple amongst others valiantly tried to convince the market of the GUI's broad benefits, but the non-GUI Lotus 1–2–3 and WordPerfect had significant momentum. But Microsoft recognized the GUI's transformative potential, and committed the organization to pursuit of the dream—through investment in applications, platform and tools—based on a belief

that the GUI would dramatically expand and democratize computing. (Ozzie, Disruption 2005)

But after 1990, specifically after they examined our PowerPoint 2.0 on Windows 3.0 in May of 1990, there should have been time for all our competitors to deliver great Windows applications, if they only had applied themselves. They should have had decent products for Windows 3.1 and major upgrades for the blockbuster Windows 95 release. Instead, they temporized, and by 1994–95, when their Windows versions should have arrived, they were all going out of business.

201 A Microsoft Sand Hill Road Campus Disappears

In my report on the first year of the GBU, written in August 1988, I had written about my locating and negotiating our space on Sand Hill Road:

> "Ten years from now, we at Microsoft may well look back at this deal and say that it was the most memorable success of the first year of the Graphics Business Unit, securing the right spot for a growing Microsoft presence in Silicon Valley." (Gaskins, First Year Report 1988)

When I left, at just about the end of the five-year initial lease, in 1992, we still had options to expand much further on the site. I had options to expand our space by 6,000 to 8,000 square feet per year, so that in five years we would double our footprint from 33,000 square feet to 66,000 square feet.

But also, I had received an even better offer, to sell to Microsoft the entire Sand Hill Road campus: all four buildings (of which we occupied one), plus valid issued planning and building permits for four more buildings on the site. All development on Sand Hill Road had to be approved by both Menlo Park and Palo Alto, and there was always opposition, so having the needed permits issued was very valuable. The terms of the offer to sell to Microsoft were excellent, because it was then again, as it had been when we signed our initial lease, a slow time for Silicon Valley real estate. I left behind me a long memo recommending the purchase.

Instead, the PowerPoint group was downgraded to a "Graphics Product Unit" and was relocated to temporary accommodations down on the valley floor, in central Cupertino, as a first step to creating a Silicon Valley Campus elsewhere. A few years later, in 1998, Microsoft finally opened that campus to consolidate PowerPoint with Hotmail, WebTV, other Macintosh activities, the local sales offices, and a "Bay Area Embassy" to evangelize independent developers. They ended up on a plot of very similar size to what had been passed up five years earlier on Sand Hill Road, but located on the other side of the valley, near Highway 101, in Mountain View's Shoreline area. (Forethought had once been located there; as a struggling startup, with our windows overlooking the regional landfill, we could watch the bulldozers pushing garbage around.)

202 The Distribution of PowerPoint Returns

It happens that there is enough information to calculate roughly how the returns to the PowerPoint work were distributed among the various participants at the time that I left.

When I left the GBU in late 1992, I had a report telling me that the total net value of the stock options (at the late-1992 stock price, minus the strike prices) for everyone in the unit was over $110 million. This is for everyone (about 65 people), but not including me—my figures were aggregated into my boss's department. Most GBU employees had very handsome net option values, with the senior people (senior in contribution ranking and/or early date of option grant), of course, having quite a great deal more. The Bill Gates advice on option grants had always been to allocate the most stock to the top contributors at every level.

I had no idea, of course, how much longer people would hold their options after 1992, while Microsoft continued to rocket upward; most options vested over four years or longer, which would have substantially increased the returns further after I left. But the $110 million figure is correct over the five years 1987–1992.

At the point of selling Forethought to Microsoft, investors of $3 million received $12 million, and insiders (founders, former employees, current employees) received about $2 million, both from a period of about three years. Five years later, the employees had received $110 million. So the people who did the 1987–1992 work got collectively about fifty times as much as the people who did the 1984–1987 work, and about ten times as much as the investors of 1984–1987. The acquisition and the Microsoft option grants can be seen as a conceptual recapitalization, in which the continued participation of the dead hand of the past was bought out—on mutually agreeable terms—so that active contributors assumed the risk, and only they participated going forward.

We have some records of how much development work it took for each release of PowerPoint, which is a pretty good index of total effort. For PowerPoint Mac 1.0, the version shipped just prior to the acquisition, we invested 34 person-months of development work. Over the next five years, for Mac 2.0, for Windows 2.0, for Windows 3.0, and for Mac 3.0, we invested 561 person-months of development work. This means that out of the total effort that went into making PowerPoint a successful and dominant product, 6% was invested prior to the acquisition, and 94% was invested after the acquisition.

(Nothing in this comparison includes the twenty years since 1992. We're only talking about 6% of the work done in 1984–1987 versus 94% of the work done in 1987–1992).

Those numbers mean that about sixteen times as much work went into PowerPoint after its acquisition by Microsoft. The split of $110 million value in the Microsoft period versus $14 million for both investors and employees in the Forethought period (8:1) can be seen as related to the split of work accomplished (16:1), with an adjustment of a factor of 2 for the lower risk of the later period.

My intuitive take on this is that things worked out to be surprisingly fair. The split between investors and employees (6:1) for the first startup phase seems tilted toward the investors, but this reflects our continuing lack of success and the difficulty that results from requiring multiple rounds of investment. Fundamentally, it reflects the fact that the bulk of the expenditures at Forethought (much of what was spent on published products and the organization to distribute them) did not create wealth, but consumed it. It was primarily the much smaller expenditure on PowerPoint which created the wealth. The people who produced that outcome, particularly the founders and early employees, have to bear the penalties for very modest success.

The split between continuing employees and startup employees (50:1) seems tilted toward the continuing employees, but there were a lot more of them, and they particularly included all the PowerPoint employees from Forethought who joined Microsoft, and participated in the rewards of the next five years.

(Correcting the figures for inflation to 2010 gives very roughly a current value of $22 million to the Forethought investors, $4 million to the Forethought employees, and $168 million to the Microsoft employees between 1984 and 1992; this does not include salaries for either period, the distribution to me of MSFT stock, nor Microsoft's profits.)

So, the investors who invested early did moderately well, and the employees who worked on PowerPoint did extremely well (and Microsoft did extremely well—PowerPoint was one of the most profitable products in the company). The two apparent "tilts" both operated to reduce the payout to early Forethought employees who had contributed to the initial failed business plan, or who worked in the unsuccessful publishing group, or both. All this seems to be very roughly "the day's wages for the day's work," and rather more fair than many startup outcomes.

203 How Accurate Were PowerPoint Sales Forecasts?

Startups are proverbially known for their over-optimism in sales forecasts (there is little incentive to be cautious), so I was interested in early 1994 to go back to the last set of five-year forecasts used to raise the final round of investment in Forethought and compare that to the actual sales achieved.

I went back to the last Forethought business plan to get our five-year revenue projections from July 1986, prepared for that last round of funding, and compared those projections to the actual revenues for the following five years (plus three additional years, for which I have good data or estimates).

Of course, the actual results of Microsoft are not the same as those of Forethought would have been; but for this period, I'm not sure whether they are much larger. We had many advantages being part of Microsoft, but we also had problems, such as trying to get the attention of the sales force. Prior to 1991, before the success of Windows 3.0, the Microsoft actuals may not be very different from what Forethought could have done with Apple's help. After that, and beyond the limit of the five-year forecast, there's no doubt that Microsoft sold more than an independent software vendor could have.

I have stated the actuals in Forethought Fiscal Years to match the plan—these years end in March, so "FY1987" included nine months of calendar 1986 plus the first three months of calendar 1987, and so on; "FY1993" is mostly 1992 going through March 1993, which was the month I retired, during which we realized $112 million in PowerPoint sales. The next year, sales doubled again. (By contrast, Microsoft Fiscal Years, not used here, ended in June.)

Here are the actual PowerPoint sales results, as against our Forethought business plan:

	PowerPoint Macintosh			PowerPoint Windows		
	Forethought Plan	Microsoft Actual		Forethought Plan	Microsoft Actual	
FY1987	$ 0.5 M	$ 1.0 M	200%	—	—	—
FY1988	$ 3.2 M	$ 4.5 M	141%	$ 2.2 M	—	0%
FY1989	$ 4.2 M	$ 9.9 M	236%	$ 4.9 M	—	0%
FY1990	$ 5.5 M	$ 8.9 M	162%	$ 7.8 M	$ 1.5 M	19%
FY1991	$ 6.5 M	$ 8.9 M	137%	$ 11.6 M	$ 15.2 M	131%
FY1992	—	$ 9.9 M		—	$ 32.7 M	
FY1993E	—	$ 19.3 M		—	$ 92.7 M	
FY1994E	—	$ 23.0 M		—	$ 193.0 M	

	PowerPoint Total			PowerPoint Cumulative		
	Forethought Plan	Microsoft Actual		Forethought Plan	Microsoft Actual	
FY1987	$ 0.5 M	$ 1.0 M	200%	$ 0.5 M	$ 1.0 M	200%
FY1988	$ 5.5 M	$ 4.5 M	82%	$ 6.0 M	$ 5.5 M	92%
FY1989	$ 9.1 M	$ 9.9 M	109%	$ 15.1 M	$ 15.4 M	102%
FY1990	$ 13.3 M	$ 10.4 M	78%	$ 28.4 M	$ 25.8 M	91%
FY1991	$ 18.1 M	$ 24.1 M	133%	$ 46.5 M	$ 49.9 M	107%
FY1992	—	$ 42.6 M		—	$ 92.5 M	
FY1993E	—	$ 112.0 M		—	$ 204.5 M	
FY1994E	—	$ 216.0 M		—	$ 420.5 M	

We see that the Forethought business plan numbers were achieved; for the five years of the forecast, the actuals turned out to be 200%, 82%, 109%, 78%, and 133% of plan. For the whole five years, the cumulative actual was 107% of plan. That's just about sub-micron precision for a five-year sales forecast by a startup for an unfinished product.

But the actual totals were achieved in an unexpected way. We sold rather more Macintosh PowerPoint than predicted, and quite a lot less of Windows PowerPoint, for the first four years. The two errors just happened to cancel each other out (which is not to say that they were independent—more Macintosh and less Windows both happened because Windows was so delayed).

PART IX: LEAVING POWERPOINT

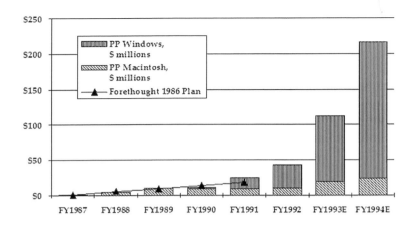

PowerPoint sales: Forethought plan against Microsoft actual (sales in $ millions, Forethought fiscal years ending March).

If we had remained Forethought, we would have been mightily disappointed with our Windows results relative to plan for several years. Microsoft was disappointed too, of course. The great advantage in being part of Microsoft during those years was that we didn't have any trouble getting the investment needed for the Windows product, which ultimately succeeded in 1990 with the shipment of Windows 3.0. It seems to have been very difficult to get this level of total commitment to an early Windows 3.0 product in other companies. It took a *lot* more investment to get Windows PowerPoint to market than anyone had expected.

By calendar 1992 (a different basis from the fiscal years discussed above), PowerPoint had grown to over 1,000,000 units sold for the year, and commanded a 63% market share of global presentation graphics software sales. For calendar 1993, this increased to over 2,000,000 units sold, and global market share of 78%. (In both years, about half of total revenue came from outside the U.S.)

204 *PowerPoint and GBU Profitability*

I received my last financial report for the PowerPoint business unit in January 1993, covering the first six months of the Microsoft Fiscal Year 1993—the last half-year period that I was responsible for. The totals shown on that sheet for the six months are:

PowerPoint Financial Results, July 1992—December 1992		
Gross Sales	$ 54,890,000	104%
Adjustments	$ 1,977,000	4%
Net Revenues	$ 52,913,000	100%
Cost of Revenues	$ 8,380,000	16%
Gross Profit	$ 44,533,000	84%
Operating Expenses	$ 12,003,000	23%
Operating Income	$ 32,530,000	61%
Allocated Expenses	$ 7,291,000	13%
Burdened Operating Income	$ 25,239,000	48%

"Burdened Operating Income" is the PowerPoint business unit's contribution to Microsoft's Operating Income line, with all expenses other than income taxes and special charges already allocated. For this period, when the PowerPoint business unit had an operating income of 48% of net revenue, Microsoft as a whole reported an operating income of 35%, and the industry average (from *Software Industry Bulletin*) was 11%.

So the PowerPoint business unit, already by the time I left, was running at revenue of over $100 million per year, and putting $50 million of that to Microsoft's bottom line. And this was despite my investing in the product as rapidly as I could.

How a business is being managed is often demonstrated in its profitability. The bureaucrats might debate whether there were too many magicians or string quartets at the holiday party, whether it's a good idea to have $100 million worth of contemporary art on the walls, whether developers should be paid more in Menlo Park than in Redmond (and whether they are worth the difference), whether people should be asked to come into the office between Christmas and New Year, and similar imponderables; there are also the important decisions about recruiting the finest people, settling on insightful product strategies, and achieving high product quality and timeliness. Relative profitability is a good measure to look at to see the combined effect of a lot of such decisions.

PART X: AFTERTHOUGHTS ABOUT POWERPOINT

205 How PowerPoint Took Advantage of "Social"

PowerPoint was able to take advantage of various network effects, which are often these days referred to as "social," based on "social needs." PowerPoint was used by groups (initially companies) to establish common purpose and direction. As more people use the product, there develops "a brisk trade and economy in slides" (Gold 2002).

The phrase "brisk trade and economy in slides" comes from the late Rich Gold, who was a PowerPoint enthusiast, constructing his presentations, including all his original illustrations, in PowerPoint. I recommend his paper "Reading PowerPoint," in *Working with Words and Images: New Steps in an Old Dance*, edited by Nancy Allen (2002). This essay was written in 1999, while a researcher at Xerox PARC, so Rich Gold was observing the early years of PowerPoint usage.

The "social" aspect of PowerPoint usage is often totally invisible to academics and consultants, who use PowerPoint all by themselves to produce material for a more effective personal performance, and for whom higher production values take on a dominating importance. Such lone-wolf presenters care a great deal about exactly how a transition into video works to awe the audience, but don't care at all about, say, how easy it is to re-use the Group VP's slide with the quarterly objectives in order to demonstrate that one is on board and can be counted on as loyal (even if the spoken words that go along with the Group VP's slide serve to overlay it with some doubts). Presenters in business very often see the audience as colleagues who need to be influenced over repeated interactions, very different from a consultant performing a single hit-and-run presentation.

Similarly, efforts to introduce new presentation formats that are more like continuous video, such as using only smooth seamless zooming and panning, without any explicit slide-to-slide transitions, may be overlooking the need for discrete slides that can be individually re-used and repurposed, through that "brisk trade and economy in slides," to express solidarity and unity.

Handing the microphone to Rich Gold:

> The driving social need leading to the rise of PowerPoint was—no surprise—corporate communications. It is simply mind-bending how many thousands of people and how many tens of companies, working together, it takes to make even the simplest object. To achieve these remarkable feats (and it is achieved over and over as the tens of thousands of objects in our world attest) requires more than just communication (the exchange of information); it requires common purpose and direction.
>
> As a result (or a necessary condition) corporate workers swim in a thick soup of communications ranging from voice mail to email, from brochures to video conferences, from annual reports to web pages, from memos to meetings, from corporate speeches to hallway gossip. Each communication form takes a different amount of time to construct (hallway conversations are constructed in real time; annual reports might take six months to produce) and a different amount of time to consume (the hallway conversation takes as long to consume as to construct). What PowerPoint brings to the table is not efficiencies in time. PowerPoint slides are actually quite time-consuming and difficult to produce.
>
> And the information (to use that compromised word) contained in a forty-five-minute PowerPoint presentation can usually be contained in a short memo. What PowerPoint dramatically inspires is unifying directional community formation, much as a war dance inspires the fighting power of a tribe about to go to war. If everyone is focused in the same direction, it is far more likely that whatever the company is manufacturing will get manufactured. When the PC made verbally glossed wall reading not just possible but easy, ubiquitous PowerPoint was the result.
>
> Because the slide in PowerPoint is so stable and formalized, and the means of PowerPoint production are so ubiquitously distributed on most PCs, and it is so easy to electronically exchange slides, and we live in an age of appropriation, annotation, and quotation within most corporations, there is a brisk trade and

economy in slides. It is not uncommon to see presentations composed primarily of slides produced for other talks by other people. While this can produce a jarringly ugly and disjointed visual experience, it does not matter as much as you would expect so long as the verbal gloss, which is the heartbeat of the presentation, flows.

Within a corporation itself, just who owns a slide—the employee or the corporation—is a slippery question. Each slide certainly is another corporate asset that can and should be used to maximize ROI (Return on Investment) in multiple ways. On the other hand, each employee within a corporation is an independent agent, with his or her own career track and elaborate set of social relations. To simply use someone else's slide in your own presentation, while not illegal, is, within this context, unethical.

What arises as the resultant vector is an elaborate gift culture in slides. "Can I use one of your slides in my presentation?" is an oft-repeated phrase in any company. The answer is almost always "yes," but it sets up, or adds to, a balance sheet of favors that over time must get reconciled. If the favor is considered large, or if the two participants are of unequal status (either way, it turns out), the phrase "I will give you credit" is appended to the request. Eventually, a network of slides and favors bonds together entire departments and can form the basis of corporate cultural identity.

It is not uncommon, for instance, for a certain slide to be used so often, by so many different people, that it completely breaks free of its original owner and is considered an "ur-text" of the company. Such texts, because they remain in PowerPoint (unlike slides produced in Illustrator, for instance), are highly malleable and can be seen to mutate over months and even years as they are cast and re-cast into different presentations. A knowing audience can read these changes, as Soviets used to read the appearance of Politburo members on the balcony, for changes in the corporate wind. (Gold 2002)

Rich Gold observed and recorded the same behavior I saw, particularly in such delicious details as "if the two participants are of unequal status (*either way, it turns out*), the phrase 'I will give you credit' is appended to the request."

Note that even when all presentations are actually delivered as video from electronic PowerPoint files, the notion of "a slide" is still a first-class concept in PowerPoint, and slides can still be "traded" by copying and pasting slides between presentations while specifying that the slides retain the formatting of the original presentation. In this way, a wholly electronic presentation can look just as miscellaneous as a "deck" put together in 1992 by trading physical overhead transparencies, with each slide retaining the identification of its source. This would not be available in a presentation software package that dispensed with the concept of a "slide."

Rich Gold's analyses are extremely insightful. I wish that he had written a lot more about PowerPoint. Many of his observations have roots in presentations before PowerPoint, but part of the interest of what he observes so carefully is that it could only come fully into existence after PowerPoint had become commonplace on desktops in businesses.

206 *When Did Video Presentations Become Common?*

When PowerPoint 3.0 shipped in 1992, video slideshows projected from a laptop computer were initially possible only for presenters in specialized venues using professional equipment, but new video projectors that were small, bright, and relatively inexpensive gradually became available over the next several years, so that video became the most popular PowerPoint presentation format for everyone, and eventually, it displaced traditional overheads and 35mm slides. Within a few years, what had been a unique demo would become commonplace worldwide in auditoriums and large corporate conference rooms, and then would become ubiquitous in small meeting rooms in businesses of all kinds during the tech boom of the very late 1990s.

I haven't found it easy to gather good evidence to establish when video presentations became commonplace, but it certainly didn't happen overnight.

In 1996, Michael Wolff was presenting at a tech-industry conference in New York where, he recorded, only the "snappy people" were doing direct video projection (which he refers to as "Power Point," with an internal space—it took a long time for the preferred orthography to become familiar):

> [In 1996] Most presentations were by the numbers. With low-tech slides or overhead transparencies or, for the snappy people, Power Point. (Wolff 1998, 176)

So as early as 1996, PowerPoint was becoming associated with video projection, though it had been designed to make the "low-tech" 35mm slides and overheads (and probably had been used to make the actual slides and overheads that Michael Wolff was seeing).

By 1999, three years later, Rich Gold was writing:

> While there are perceptual changes in equipment (from noisy overhead projectors to finicky laptops), PowerPoint is now, most amazing, directly affecting the very architecture of corporate buildings. Until recently, conference rooms were dominated by the oval table, perfectly suited for a document-based culture. Companies are now in the midst of remodel fever, replacing the ovals with "U"s, the open end of which faces a wall of white screens, perfect for a wall reading society. (Gold 2002, 269-270)

The table arrangement can facilitate either overheads or video projection; Gold's passage is evidence for his observed transition away from overhead projectors to laptops and video projectors, and perhaps for more frequent use of presentation visuals once video arrived.

On 4 April 2000, a Dilbert cartoon unmistakably portrayed direct video projection of a presentation from a computer in a conference room for the first time in the strip, being used by a consultant. The next such case in a Dilbert strip was two years later, in 2002, when Dilbert himself does a video presentation for the first time, on a more mundane topic, and, in the interim, conventional presentation visuals continue to be shown. For comments on the whole history of PowerPoint in the Dilbert strip see (Gaskins, Dilbert's History 2012).

For another bit of evidence, in *Author Unknown: On the Trail of Anonymous*, by Donald W. Foster, the author describes what he was doing one day in April of 1999:

After making up the bed, reviewing my notes, and testing my PowerPoint slides for the next day's session, I opened a large envelope containing my evening's reading material. (Foster 2001, 97)

Now, the odd thing here is the mention of "PowerPoint slides." Why not just "my slides"? Would he have written "I reviewed my Word paper that I planned to read from tomorrow"? Or, "I double-checked the assumptions in my VisiCalc spreadsheet"? I think not: "I reviewed my paper," "I double-checked my spreadsheet."

My theory is that "PowerPoint slides" means "electronic slides," as it did for Michael Wolff. The verb "testing" suggests that what he had was a file on his portable computer, not a printed and copied set of overhead transparencies.

A particularly knowledgeable view is available in Tom Evslin's novel *hackoff.com* (Evslin 2006)—this is the same Tom Evslin who had worked on the PowerPoint and Genigraphics software, so he would have been particularly aware of the change. The novel takes place between the years 1999 and 2003, and concerns a startup; PowerPoint is used a lot, particularly for paper "pitch books." When projection is needed, the novel portrays a world in which there is a transition going on, from slightly old-fashioned people who still make physical transparencies, to the newer "technically comfortable teams" who make their pitches with video projected directly from PowerPoint on laptops.

Another data point is the disappearance of the projectors used to show 35mm slides. I had written in my marketing analysis of 1986:

> In the early 1960's, Eastman Kodak introduced the "Carousel" projectors which featured a round tray with gravity feed from the top of the projector. This system displaced all others, with the result that today, 25 years later, a presenter can carry slides in a carousel anywhere in the world and be certain of finding a compatible projector at the destination. (Gaskins, PowerPoint Marketing 1986)

And today, just another 25 years after I wrote that, a presenter can be equally certain *not* to find a Carousel slide projector available—not to mention that eBay is the only source for a tray to carry the slides.

Eastman Kodak discontinued manufacturing of the line in 2004, following an unexpected crash in Carousel sales that made it impossible to continue production. There's little doubt that the cause of this was the rise of PowerPoint and digital projection, but I was still shocked by the announcement. I had confidently expected Carousel slide projectors to last out my lifetime easily, because I thought other uses of 35mm slides would keep them alive.

Some of the louder complaints about the end of 35mm slide projectors came from teachers who used them for high-quality source material (photos, paintings, maps, and the like) in classrooms, rather than for presentations, and who were not satisfied by the poor quality of early digital video.

A commenter on Edward Tufte's blog was the first place where I found out about Kodak's decision in late 2003:

> I have just received, through an email discussion list for archeologists, news that Kodak will discontinue production of the Carousel projector in 2004. Although the notice I received did not say so, it seems likely that the use of digital projectors and Powerpoint [sic], especially in business and industry, is to blame for this.
> —Mark Hineline (email), September 18, 2003 (Tufte, Bulletin Board 2003)

And Tufte replied:

> The carousel certainly had its difficulties and inconveniences— loading of slides upside down and backward (is that right?), munged edges of slides with multiple use (causing the slide to jam), too much light in the room, touchy and very hot light bulbs, some problems with archival quality of slides after repeated projection, and difficult projector/screen relationships in many rooms not originally designed for projectors. Of course a few of these problems are common to any projection method. One of the few successful uses of PP is as pure slide projector, at least for images that do not require superb resolution.
> —Edward Tufte, September 23, 2003 (Tufte, Bulletin Board 2003)

The unexpected decline of the Carousel 35mm projector allows us to roughly date when presentations that had previously used 35mm slides began to be primarily projected from personal computers: it was roughly the turn of the century, nearly 15 years after PowerPoint had been introduced.

The software to send presentations to Genigraphics to be imaged into 35mm slides was removed from the PowerPoint box beginning with PowerPoint 2003, about the same time that production of Carousel projectors ended. So by 2003–2004, video presentations had become very common. This was about twenty years after work commenced on PowerPoint, and more than ten years after the fully functional PowerPoint 3.0 had shipped.

This video evolution, in businesses, was predicted in my strategy documents from the mid-1980s; what was unexpected was that the same hardware would also extend PowerPoint use into university teaching, children's school reports and science fair projects, sermons in churches, supertitles for opera houses, and many other uses that its creators had never imagined.

207 PowerPoint and the Advancement of Science

In my personal experience, it was 1998 when I realized that PowerPoint really was everywhere.

The day I recall noticing this was in June of 1998, when I attended a conference on the recent history of cryptography organized by the British Society for the History of Mathematics. It was held in the Manor House at Bletchley Park, the celebrated site where Alan Turing and so many other experts worked on their wartime code-breaking exploits, including building early computers.

There were very interesting talks all day long, and, sometime late in the afternoon, I noticed that just about every one of the speakers had used PowerPoint for their overheads—I could tell because of the fine details of typography and graphic style. (These were real physical overheads, not video projection.) Usually, at academic conferences, I had been used to seeing a mix of some PowerPoint with a number of alternatives (word processors, drawing programs, or whatever), but this was very predominantly PowerPoint. The folks from British GCHQ had even used elaborately prepared color overheads, always uncommon. I realized that I was focusing on my personal interest in the format of the presentations rather than their content, and even remembered at the time that I was viewing them in what was "essentially the same as the spirit in which *The Tailor and Cutter* annually criticizes the portraits in the Royal Academy, interested, not in the artist, not in the subject, but in the cut of the subject's clothes" (Housman 1969).

I was digesting this observation when, at the end of the last talk, the organizer (Professor Judith Field from the History of Art Department of Birkbeck College) suddenly announced, "I've just been told that the inventor of PowerPoint used by the speakers today is in the audience. Will he please identify himself so we can recognize his contribution to the advancement of science?" I stood up laughing, as the audience responded with enthusiastic applause and laughter. The attendees consisted mostly of academics, civil servants, and military research people—all highly likely to be users of PowerPoint themselves. They got the joke, which was that sophistication in presentation technology certainly did not itself advance science, and perhaps, in particular, that the GCHQ color overheads had been a bit inappropriately fancy and over-decorated for this kind of a gathering.

I interpreted the audience's enthusiastic applause as confessing half-guilty amusement and agreement with the point that we all spend too much time on presentation formatting, not enough on advancing science and communicating it—mixed with an admission that they all, too, used PowerPoint.

208 Was PowerPoint the First Presentation Program?

A lot of people first saw presentations made on computers using PowerPoint, and so they assume that PowerPoint was the first such program. Absolutely not, not even for personal computers. What PowerPoint pioneered was making presentations on the new generation of personal computers with graphical user interfaces, the first widely used platform that was adequate to do a really good job, and hence became the first to deliver satisfaction to ordinary business users. This is what made PowerPoint the first really successful competitor.

Just about any large computer with a plotter attached had been used to make presentation materials somehow, going back into the 1960s. All this was very ad hoc, and documentation would be hard to produce. But people working around computers, in universities and research labs as well as in companies, needed to make presentations and tried to use whatever equipment they had.

Genigraphics had been delivering graphical workstations based on minicomputers (originally DEC PDP-11s) and film recorders to customers since about 1973, and also used the same equipment in its own service bureaus. For commercial presentation graphics on computers, Genigraphics was the dominant pioneering force, but it also had competitors. All of this was the "indirect drive" style of interaction, entering data and then generating a preview of the result, thriving more than ten years before we began on PowerPoint.

By 1986, just before PowerPoint was shipped, there were many new companies already making presentation graphics programs for personal computers, both Apple IIs (introduced 1978) and MS-DOS IBM PCs (introduced 1981). The 1986 PowerPoint marketing analysis listed more than *thirty* of them. IBM alone was distributing three different programs just for making overheads on an IBM PC; they were all unsuccessful, because they didn't work very well.

The PowerPoint innovation was to design a new way of working on "direct drive" graphical user interfaces, and to produce such a product sharply focused on the precise target of presentation visuals.

Though not the first, PowerPoint did immediately become the standard for presentation programs. In each of its first three major versions, PowerPoint was clearly the best product and the best-selling product; it was best received by actual customers, and generally (if not at every moment) also by reviewers, although they were often professional producers or academics. This reception was an oddity at Microsoft, where both Word and Excel had struggled for years with the customer perception that they were inferior to their competition— Word behind WordPerfect, and Excel behind Lotus 1–2–3. For this reason, it was almost in poor taste at Microsoft to frankly say that PowerPoint had always been the leader in its category, but that was the case. The reason for this was the excellent match between what Power-Point did and what customers wanted to do.

209 Is PowerPoint the Problem, or Is It the Users?

Most people think that PowerPoint is a tool that can be used well, although (as is usually true in most things) the majority of users are not as effective as they could be.

The other view is that there is something inherently corrupting about PowerPoint itself, which pollutes the thoughts of its users. This view is associated above all with Edward R. Tufte, of Yale University, and with his pamphlet entitled "The Cognitive Style of PowerPoint" (Tufte, Cognitive Style, 1st ed, 2003) (Tufte, 2nd ed, 2006).

First, though, a declaration of interest: Edward Tufte is the son of Professor Virginia Tufte, who was my major professor in the English honors program at USC when I was an undergraduate. I learned a great deal from her, and I received a great deal of assistance; as a consequence, I've always had for her son a strong presumption of intelligence, based on the heritability of IQ, as well as on the evidence of his several excellent books. So, even though Edward Tufte has described PowerPoint as "poking a finger into the eye of thought," I've been inclined to listen to what he has to say.

Tufte says, in a representative passage,

> PowerPoint ... is costly to the content and the audience. These costs arise from the *cognitive style of the standard default PP presentation* [italics in original]: foreshortening of evidence and thought, low spatial resolution, an intensely hierarchical single-path structure as the model for organizing every type of content, breaking up of narratives and data into slides and minimal fragments, rapid temporal sequencing of thin information rather than focused spatial analysis, conspicuous chartjunk and PP Phluff, branding of slides with logotypes, a preoccupation with format not content, incompetent designs for data graphics and tables, and a smirky commercialism that turns information into a sales pitch and presenters into marketeers.
>
> PowerPoint comes with a big attitude. Other than video games, not many computer programs have attitudes. Effective tools such as web browsers, Word, Excel, Photoshop, and Illustrator are not accompanied by distinctive cognitive styles that reduce the intellectual level of the content passing through the program. (Tufte, 2nd ed, 2006, 4)

It's interesting that Tufte clearly realizes, and even emphasizes with his own italics, the subtle point that many of the problems he sees are specifically with *"the standard default PP presentation."* Since the defaults can easily be changed (any presentation made in PowerPoint can be set as the default style), and a single default can be augmented with unlimited libraries of templates constructed in any style desired, I've often wondered myself why users don't change and replace the defaults more often.

It is mostly that standard default presentation which gives the impression of "smirky commercialism that turns information into a sales pitch and presenters into marketeers." There isn't much wrong with that for sales pitches and marketing presentations, which were the original targets for PowerPoint. The mystifying question is why that "presentation style," which is properly characteristic of marketing and sales presentations, has been adopted for presenting other kinds of information, such as teaching. (I'll discuss this in the two sections immediately following.)

A legitimate complaint, it seems to me, is that of "preoccupation with format not content," which is often the result of what I analyze as confusing different styles of presentations, and using inappropriate entertainment effects in presentations that should focus on information. The problem was greatly intensified when the older differentiated formats of overheads and 35mm slides and "multimedia" all collapsed to a single format of projected video:

> This meant that every presentation could now mix the features of all three styles, so gradually the three styles became less distinct. With no constraints from physical media, presenters had no limitation and increasingly no firm intuition as to what was appropriate. Most presentations had previously been done using overheads, and most presenters had used nothing else. Presenters now began to experiment by adding features formerly used only with 35mm slides (such as vaguely related clip art, or subtly shaded backgrounds). They tried adding elements from multimedia shows (such as sound effects, attention-grabbing transitions between slides, moving text, and bullet points that "flew" to their places from somewhere off screen).

> Much of this was novel and interesting the first few times, but virtually none of the extraneous decoration or entertainment had any purpose or benefit in the kinds of meetings where overheads had been used. Successive versions of PowerPoint made these elaborate features easier and more tempting to use, leading to more complaints about bad presentations. PowerPoint could still make very straightforward "overhead-style" presentations, but they were not seen as often as they should be. (Quoted from Part I, "How Different Presentation Formats Were Used," above.)

It's certainly legitimate also to complain that the defaults for data graphics and tables are incompetently chosen and are "chartjunk," at least in more recent versions of PowerPoint—as I have myself complained (see my own remarks about 3-D chart styles, above).

It's interesting that there are many credible people who don't think that Tufte has the analysis just right; these people usually think that the problem is more with the users of PowerPoint than with the product itself. Several of them were quoted by David Feith in a *Wall Street Journal* article in 2009 about Tufte and his critics:

"Any general opposition to PowerPoint is just dumb," argued Harvard psychologist Steven Pinker in an email. "It's like denouncing lectures—before there were awful PowerPoint presentations, there were awful scripted lectures, unscripted lectures, slide shows, chalk talks, and so on."

Computer programming pioneer Larry Wall [creator of the Perl programming language] has argued similarly, stating: "I do quarrel with logic that says 'Stupid people are associated with X, therefore X is stupid.' Stupid people are associated with everything." (Feith 2009)

Steven Pinker is the well-known author and professor of psychology, first at MIT and then at Harvard. Ten years earlier, in another newspaper interview, he had gone even further:

Mr. Pinker argues that human minds have a structure that is not easily reprogrammed by media. "If anything, Powerpoint, if used well, would ideally reflect the way we think," he said. (Zuckerman 1999)

Stephen M. Kosslyn, formerly Chair of Harvard's Department of Psychology, and now Director of the Center for Advanced Study in the Behavioral Sciences at Stanford University, has a recent book entitled *Clear and to the Point: 8 Psychological Principles for Compelling PowerPoint Presentations* (Oxford University Press: 2007), in which he observes:

Rather than the program's being fundamentally flawed, the problem is that some users, like kids in a candy store, become gluttonous consumers of the options presented by the PowerPoint program—and forget to focus on nutrition. (Kosslyn 2007, 3)

Kosslyn also makes the comparison:

Just as you wouldn't blame Microsoft Word for every bad article you've read, you shouldn't blame the PowerPoint program for every bad presentation you've seen. (Kosslyn 2007, 3)

That's probably the correct conclusion, further reinforced by the observation that a lot of people who do make poor presentations also write so poorly that they never even attempt the long-form technical reports which Edward Tufte would often prefer to presentations.

All this is not to detract from Tufte's criticism of bad presentations, and his insightful analyses of some of the particular sources of their low information quality; I agree with him most of the time. All those presentations really are bad, and can be improved.

210 Did PowerPoint Invent "PowerPoint Style"?

The "style" of PowerPoint presentations has been experienced by very many people for the first time in PowerPoint, in the default presentation and in the templates shipped with the product.

This experience has led many of those people to assume that "presentation style" or "PowerPoint style" was invented and imposed by PowerPoint, and further to think that any other style, different and perhaps better, could have been imposed by PowerPoint, if only its creators had been better designers.

Actually, as I've described, the style of PowerPoint's defaults and templates was shaped by analyzing a corpus of manually produced overheads that I had gathered, and by adopting some features of the Genigraphics style for 35mm slides. Both of these sources went back decades before PowerPoint, and they were much alike. PowerPoint was designed to make it as easy as possible to continue to make marketing and sales presentations in the exact style already in common use, out of a conviction that business presenters would not be successfully induced to change.

Other people often casually attribute to Edward Tufte the idea that PowerPoint invented its style of presentations, but that's not accurate. His pamphlet begins:

> In corporate and government bureaucracies, the standard method for making a presentation is to talk about a list of points organized onto slides projected up on the wall. For many years, overhead projectors lit up transparencies, and slide projectors showed high-resolution 35mm slides. Now "slideware" computer programs for presentations are nearly everywhere. Early in the 21st century, several hundred million copies of Microsoft PowerPoint were turning out trillions of slides each year. (Tufte, Cognitive Style, 1st ed, 2003, 3)

And later,

> Years before today's slideware, presentations at companies such as IBM and in the military used bullet lists shown by overhead projectors. Then, in 1984, a software house developed a presenta-

tion package, "Presenter," which was eventually acquired by Microsoft and turned into PowerPoint. (Tufte, Cognitive Style, 1st ed, 2003, 11)

The first passage is shortened and the second omitted in the 2nd edition of Tufte's pamphlet, which may have led others who know less about the history to jump to the conclusion that the style of PowerPoint was newly invented, when really it was copied from existing models used widely in businesses.

211 Why Have So Many Adopted "PowerPoint Style"?

The real mystery to me is why PowerPoint—including its default presentation style based on traditional business presentations—has been adopted so widely in other contexts. I think that this is also a major concern of Edward Tufte in his pamphlet "The Cognitive Style of PowerPoint" (Tufte, 2nd ed, 2006).

Why do medical researchers use PowerPoint style at academic conferences and press briefings? Why did Secretary of State Colin Powell use it at the United Nations? Why do clergymen deliver sermons accompanied by slides in PowerPoint style? Why do military officers give briefings to commanders in PowerPoint style? Why do lawyers in courtrooms frame their arguments in PowerPoint style? Why do engineers use PowerPoint style for technical discussions? Why do teachers use PowerPoint style in classrooms, and, even more, why do teachers require elementary students to compose book reports and such in PowerPoint style?

I could easily imagine that all these non-business presenters might adopt a different style. Perhaps more complete sentences, fewer bullet points. Perhaps more full-slide images, fewer frames and borders, or simpler borders without the date and the occasion on each slide. Perhaps something else entirely.

Tufte characterizes the style of business presentations themselves unfavorably:

> ... *marketing* (advocacy not analysis, more style than substance, misdirection, slogan thinking, fast pace, branding, exaggerated claims, marketplace ethics). (Tufte, 2nd ed, 2006, 7)

Whether or not that's an accurate general description of presentations in business contexts, it certainly isn't what school children should be practicing when they make book reports. Tufte characterizes teaching as being much the opposite:

> The core ideas of teaching—explanation, reasoning, finding things out, questioning, content, evidence, credible authority not patronizing authoritarianism—are contrary to the cognitive style of PowerPoint.
>
> Especially disturbing is the introduction of PowerPoint into schools. Instead of writing a report using sentences, children learn how to decorate client pitches and infomercials, which is better than encouraging children to smoke. ... Rather than being trained as mini-bureaucrats in the pitch culture, students would be better off if schools closed down on PP days and everyone went to The Exploratorium. Or wrote an illustrated essay explaining something. (Tufte, 2nd ed, 2006, 7)

I have enthusiastic agreement with this final point of Tufte's, and I also remain puzzled why so many teachers obviously feel the other way: why they think that PowerPoint, straight out of the box, is what they want to use themselves in their classrooms, and what they want their pupils to learn to use.

The use of PowerPoint to make school book reports in the style of sales pitches is not worldwide, by the way. Along the Western Pacific Rim, PowerPoint is used by young people to make creative animated videos and computer games, in styles which are completely different from the defaults (Greenberg 2010). Google Trends these days lists the regions that lead in searches for "PowerPoint" (normalized for total search volume in the region) as the Philippines, Singapore, Viet Nam, Thailand, India, Malaysia, Portugal, Indonesia, and—in ninth place—the United States; the leading languages for searches (similarly normalized) are Tagalog, Vietnamese, Thai, Indonesian, and—in fifth place—English.

PowerPoint, as I've said, makes it extremely easy to use other formats and to install a different default. Why don't all teachers adopt templates in some other style? I've looked at a number of websites offering PowerPoint presentations for classroom teachers, and I'm surprised at how closely they hew to "presentation style" and how bad most of them are. The unthinking use of bullet points to list the personal pronouns in Spanish or the characters in *Romeo and Juliet* does seem very strange. I can only conclude that the world has changed, and that standards of taste are not the same as they once were.

I learned about the conventions of business presentations in order to duplicate them at a time when most presentations were about business (I never saw early military briefings). So I still associate business with those stylistic conventions. I don't have the negative associations that Tufte has, but I definitely feel the business-like appearance. It looks strange to me to see doctrinal articles of faith or literary analyses presented in the same way.

Tufte's (and my) association of "presentation style" with strictly business presentations must not be universally shared by those of younger generations. The first people outside business who wanted to use PowerPoint as a tool to display words and images on screens probably used the program's defaults unthinkingly. Others saw this and—not being affected by prior negative associations, because they had no experience of business presentations—took up the style. Within fifteen or twenty years, we have produced a population for whom PowerPoint style is no longer perceived only as "pushy," "a pitch," "smirky commercialism," or "trivial" (as Tufte reacts to it).

The particular business connotations of "presentation style" are probably an extraneous consideration, which can put off some people who belong to the generation of Edward Tufte (and me).

212 Showing One Thing and Saying Another

Back in the days before PowerPoint, it was (I claim, based on my experiences) well understood that the presenter did not just put up slides and then read them aloud. The message to be presented already existed in some longer form—sometimes a text document, sometimes a set of annotations, sometimes just in extensive speaking notes worked out on cards or in the presenter's head—and the slides were intended to provide a focus for the talk and for discussion.

These days, the common complaint about presenters "just reading the slides" indicates that this has been lost. Both in business presentations, and in all the other realms where PowerPoint is now used, some presenters have the misunderstanding that they are supposed to put "everything" on the slides, then show up and read them, fairly slowly. Some people do this on purpose, so the presentation will be complete for an audience reading only the slides later—particularly if there is no long-form document or other material underlying the presentation.

Rich Gold explained very well how it is supposed to be done:

As in most verbally glossed wall writing, the presenter is expected to explain the artifacts on the wall, often pointing and gesturing at them, as the talk progresses. Because they are wall writings, the audience has already reviewed much of the writing, but has not fully comprehended it. The role of the presenter is to explain these artifacts, to fill them out, to make them appear comprehensible. The presenter is also supposed to give the images and words appearing on the screen a truth value by reprocessing and explaining them in real time. ... [Notes] exist only to remind the presenter of what he or she should think about, and then comment upon, in real performance time.

Presenting PowerPoint slides is, then, much like playing a sax in a jazz band. The slides (and notes) provide the bass, rhythm, and chord changes over which the melody is improvised. Clearly the chops required to do this have been practiced and studied, but they are laid down afresh for each presentation.

... The audience reads, synchronously, the PowerPoint presentation while reading with both eyes and ears. With all facing the presenter and his or her slides, the audience enters into a deep reading reverie. Audience members' eyes read the slides and decode the images. While the slide makes sense on one level, it is only by listening to the gloss, provided by the presenter, that the deeper levels are revealed. ... wholly new thoughts arise in the listener's mind, improvising one octave up from the speaker, like a clarinet over the sax. (Gold 2002, 263-265)

I fear that many users of PowerPoint have never seen it done right, so they don't know how far short they are falling.

Sometimes it's even worse, when the speaker does *not* read. A very sad story was recounted in an article in the *New York Times* in 2001, about school children who were being taught how to use PowerPoint. There were a number of promising examples, but the last example revealed a style of presenting even worse than "just reading the slides":

... a few floors below, in a computer class of eighth graders who were presenting PowerPoint projects, the spirit was less willing.

The teacher, Anna Rubio, had asked the students to use PowerPoint to create an electronic portfolio, describing and linking to digital projects that they had done during the year.

One by one, students lumbered up to a computer at the front of the dimly lighted room and opened their slides, which appeared on a screen behind them. They did not say a word or even look at their audience, but simply clicked the mouse button, drilling through their presentations in silence. Wild graphics, garish colors and bold titles flashed by. Their classmates paid almost no attention and, like bored employees stuck in a late-day board meeting, looked at their own computer screens instead.

"I asked them if they wanted to read it or show it," Ms. Rubio said. "I guess no one wanted to read it." (Guernsey 2001)

"To read it or show it"! The teacher herself must never have seen a presentation, let alone a good one, like Rich Gold described.

213 The Transition Away from "Long-Form" Writing

At the time PowerPoint was invented, the world contained a lot of "long-form" writing—that is, documents of many pages arranged logically into sections and sub-sections, with connected paragraphs and sentences. It was expected that a serious business proposal or plan would take that form. A set of PowerPoint slides could be used to give a talk about such a plan, or could even be written to be a quick summary of the high points, but could not possibly substitute for the underlying document.

In the ensuing twenty-five years, some people claim, there has been a gradual decline of long-form writing of all kinds—long books, long articles and essays, long business plans, have all tended to fall out of favor. This is often connected to a supposed decline in the attention spans of people over the years. The argument goes that electronic media have brought a lot of quick-cut formats, including television commercials, music videos, computer games, email and text messages, blog posts, Facebook updates, tweets, web pages in general, and online journalism in particular. Supposedly, increasing exposure to such communication has eroded interest in and tolerance for long-form writing of all kinds.

I don't know whether or not there is anything to this, but it is certainly true that, over PowerPoint's lifespan so far, there has been a change whereby a presentation has substantially lost its role as an accessory to a written document and assumed more and more the role of primary document, with no long-form backup available. Anyone who grew up reading long-form documents can't help feeling that a good deal of subtlety of understanding is being lost.

214 *PowerPoint for Startups*

To me, one of the most surprising areas where PowerPoint presentations have come to substitute for "real" long-form documents is in business plans for startups.

Back in the mid-1980s, when PowerPoint was seeking funding, you gave a pitch, but you also presented the potential investors with a proper business plan. This took the form of a long document in Word or WordPerfect, plus a set of projections in Multiplan, or VisiCalc, or SuperCalc. Whether the potential investors ever read these documents is another question, but they had to be provided.

I have a set of these documents for PowerPoint itself, dated mid-1986. The text document ("Business Plan") is 54 pages. There are two spreadsheets, "Sales Forecasts, Budgets, and Cash Flow" in 15 pages, and "*Pro Forma* Income Statement with Cash Flow, FY1987–FY1991") in another 15 pages, making a total of 85 pages. The accompanying presentation used to pitch this business plan consists of ten slides total, eight word slides and two charts for the forecasts.

Once PowerPoint shipped, other startups were some of the most enthusiastic users, of course, since it gave them excellent quality presentations at very low cost. But initially, I'm sure, they also prepared full business plans, as I had done.

This convention started to erode in the great "dot-com bubble" of 1995–2000. In the frenzy to get deals done, there was thought not to be time to write 85-page business plans any more. Since profitability had become less predictable, it was also less important to prepare detailed five-year guesses of when it might arrive. And what plans did exist for sales and profits often were not very attractive, compared to a snazzy PowerPoint presentation of the concept. Tom Evslin's novel *hackoff.com* (Evslin 2006) is set in "the Internet bubble and rubble" of those years, and documents a world in which PowerPoint presentations rule and "technically comfortable teams" make their pitches with video projected directly from PowerPoint on laptops, without even printing out the slides. In the real world, many people began to suspect that there was little detailed planning behind all the PowerPoint slides. Tom, who himself contributed much to PowerPoint, later commented to me, about the bubble years:

> [I saw] how crucial PowerPoint was in the last frenzied round of money-raising. It has indubitably been used to raise more money

than any other tool in history. In many cases, it not only represents but substitutes for reality. You must be both proud and amused. (Email, Tom Evslin to Robert Gaskins, 26 May 2001)

I continued to think that pitching startups without complete and thoughtful written business plans was faintly disreputable, and that any fundable founder would have a complete set of five-year projections. It's true that, at Microsoft, I'd gotten used to a system in which we made detailed projections for one year and general plans out to three years, realizing that it was futile to try to plan beyond that horizon. But the lessons of the copybook headings stay with you.

I found out how much I was out of date when I read a blog posting for 25 June 2007 by Marc Andreessen, browser-writer and investor, in his series "The Pmarca Guide to Startups":

> Don't bother with a long detailed written business plan. Most VCs will either fund a startup based on a fleshed out PowerPoint presentation of about 20 slides, or they won't fund it at all. Corollary: any VC who requires a long detailed written business plan is probably not the right VC to be working with. (Andreessen 2007)

As further evidence, there was a request for startup ideas from Sequoia Capital, one of the top venture capital investment firms (their request remains the same today). They say:

> We like business plans that present a lot of information in as few words as possible. The following business plan format, within 15–20 slides, is all that's needed: ... (Sequoia Capital 2011)

To help students prepare for this world, the University of Chicago's Graduate School of Business started requiring prospective students to submit PowerPoint presentations as part of their applications for admission. For the fall 2008 application, they said:

> In four slides or less, please provide readers with content that captures who you are. ... You are limited to text and static images to convey your points.

The current version of their page for 2011–2012 has changed this only a little:

> In a maximum of four slides, tell us about yourself. ... There is no right, or even preferred, approach to this presentation. ... Acceptable formats for upload in the online application system are

PowerPoint or PDF. (University of Chicago, Booth School of Business 2012)

PowerPoint was the tool that I wanted for a startup, so it isn't surprising that it has become a standard tool for all new startups. But what still amazes me is that the 54 pages of prose and 30 pages of spreadsheets should no longer be worth thinking and writing.

215 PowerPoint and the Military

PowerPoint got off to a very slow start in infiltrating the military forces of the world, but ultimately prevailed and conquered.

At first, of course, PowerPoint was only available for Macintosh, and the U.S. military were not big users of Macs. In fact, like other large bureaucratic organizations with centralized purchasing decisions, the military were slow to adopt personal computers, and then even slower to move on to the new graphics-oriented PCs. But the military had a long tradition of making overhead presentations, so it was reasonable to expect that someday they would be important customers.

When PowerPoint finally got onto Windows (1990), military groups were the home of many specialized military-specification graphic output devices for which no Windows drivers existed. There was also a tendency for military groups to have outdated graphics plotters and non-graphic printers, which Windows would never support properly. This slowed the adoption of Windows.

Between 1990 and 1992, there was a major DOD procurement of personal computer software, which might set a standard that would last for years. Some Microsoft sales people were trying to sell Windows and PowerPoint in response to this request, and one of the contract conditions was that output had to be produced on existing devices, such as pen plotters, which were incredibly slow devices that mechanically moved a pen over a sheet of paper, either stationary or mounted on a drum, at inches per second—drawing out a PowerPoint slide with an ordinary amount of text would have been impossibly slow. I refused the request from Sales to write or to fund the writing of an advanced Windows driver for pen plotters (sufficient to render PowerPoint output), and, in response, the sales group denounced me directly to Bill Gates as the wrecker who was preventing Windows from being adopted by the military. But Bill didn't fire me as they had hoped (he didn't even mention it to me), and over time, the military did acquire modern graphical output devices and modern computers and became big users of Windows and of PowerPoint.

If my plan really had been to keep PowerPoint out of the military, then I certainly failed miserably. Ten years after that, the complaint was that the military already relied so heavily on PowerPoint that defense readiness was compromised. Greg Jaffe wrote on the front page of the *Wall Street Journal,* on 26 April 2000:

> Old-fashioned slide briefings, designed to update generals on troop movements, have been a staple of the military since World War II. But in only a few short years PowerPoint has altered the landscape. Just as word processing made it easier to produce long, meandering memos, the spread of PowerPoint has unleashed a blizzard of jazzy but often incoherent visuals. Instead of drawing up a dozen slides on a legal pad and running them over to the graphics department, captains and colonels now can create hundreds of slides in a few hours without ever leaving their desks. If the spirit moves them they can build in gunfire sound effects and images that explode like land mines.
>
> "There is an arms-race dimension to it," says Peter Feaver, a military expert at Duke University and frequent PowerPoint briefer at various war colleges. "If there are three briefings in a row, and you are the one with the lowest production values, you look really lame."
>
> PowerPoint has become such an ingrained part of the defense culture that it has seeped into the military lexicon. "PowerPoint Ranger" is a derogatory term for a desk-bound bureaucrat more adept at making slides than tossing grenades.
>
> [*Paragraphs omitted*]
>
> Despite such countermeasures, PowerPoint is showing no signs of retreat. Indeed, it seems to be spreading. James A. Calpin, an officer in the Naval Reserves, just returned home from duty in Operation Northern Watch in Turkey, where PowerPoint has just begun to surface in officer presentations. "I was able to come in and spruce up their briefings, and they were just wowed. People over there just loved it," he says.
>
> Foreign armed services also are beginning to get in on the act. "You can't speak with the U.S. military without knowing Power-Point," says Margaret Hayes, an instructor at National Defense University in Washington D.C., who teaches Latin American military officers how to use the software.

Unfortunately, Ms. Hayes admits many foreign officers, including those fluent in PowerPoint visuals, still struggle to understand their U.S. counterparts' complicated slide presentations. "We've gotten away from inviting our colleagues from the Department of Defense to brief our visiting officers. Some of their presentations are a little bit too complex and too inhibiting," she says.

All of which makes Duke University's Mr. Feaver wonder if the U.S. military is misusing the technology. "If we really wanted to accomplish something we shouldn't be teaching our allies how to use PowerPoint," he says. "We should give it to the Iraqis. We'd never have to worry about them again." (Jaffe 2000)

Another ten years on, and the attack on overuse of PowerPoint in the military had become a frequent source of headlines. It seemed that the military in 2010 was primarily focused on making and viewing PowerPoint slides. PowerPoint had become the underlying reason for unsatisfactory results in the Afghan War. Elisabeth Bumiller covered the story for the *New York Times:*

> ... "death by PowerPoint," the phrase used to described the numbing sensation that accompanies a 30-slide briefing, seems here to stay. The program, which first went on sale in 1987 and was acquired by Microsoft soon afterward, is deeply embedded in a military culture that has come to rely on PowerPoint's hierarchical ordering of a confused world.
>
> "There's a lot of PowerPoint backlash, but I don't see it going away anytime soon," said Capt. Crispin Burke, an Army operations officer at Fort Drum, N.Y., who under the name Starbuck wrote an essay about PowerPoint on the Web site "Small Wars Journal" ... . In a daytime telephone conversation, he estimated that he spent an hour each day making PowerPoint slides. In an initial email message responding to the request for an interview, he wrote, "I would be free tonight, but unfortunately, I work kind of late (sadly enough, making PowerPoint slides)."
>
> Defense Secretary Robert M. Gates reviews printed-out PowerPoint slides at his morning staff meeting, although he insists on getting them the night before so he can read ahead and cut back the briefing time.
>
> Gen. David H. Petraeus, who oversees the wars in Iraq and Afghanistan and says that sitting through some PowerPoint briefings is "just agony," nonetheless likes the program for the

display of maps and statistics showing trends. He has also conducted more than a few PowerPoint presentations himself.

General McChrystal gets two PowerPoint briefings in Kabul per day, plus three more during the week. General Mattis, despite his dim view of the program, said a third of his briefings are by PowerPoint.

Richard C. Holbrooke, the Obama administration's special representative for Afghanistan and Pakistan, was given PowerPoint briefings during a trip to Afghanistan last summer at each of three stops—Kandahar, Mazar-i-Sharif and Bagram Air Base. At a fourth stop, Herat, the Italian forces there not only provided Mr. Holbrooke with a PowerPoint briefing, but accompanied it with swelling orchestral music.

President Obama was shown PowerPoint slides, mostly maps and charts, in the White House Situation Room during the Afghan strategy review last fall.

No one is suggesting that PowerPoint is to blame for mistakes in the current wars, but the program did become notorious during the prelude to the invasion of Iraq. As recounted in the book "Fiasco" by Thomas E. Ricks (Penguin Press, 2006), Lt. Gen. David D. McKiernan, who led the allied ground forces in the 2003 invasion of Iraq, grew frustrated when he could not get Gen. Tommy R. Franks, the commander at the time of American forces in the Persian Gulf region, to issue orders that stated explicitly how he wanted the invasion conducted, and why. Instead, General Franks just passed on to General McKiernan the vague PowerPoint slides that he had already shown to Donald H. Rumsfeld, the defense secretary at the time.

Senior officers say the program does come in handy when the goal is not imparting information, as in briefings for reporters.

The news media sessions often last 25 minutes, with 5 minutes left at the end for questions from anyone still awake. Those types of PowerPoint presentations, Dr. Hammes said, are known as "hypnotizing chickens." (Bumiller 2010)

The implication in these stories that the problems were somehow caused by PowerPoint was countered with a letter to the editor of the *Times* by no less than Peter Norvig (Director of Research at Google, and himself author of the brilliant parody "The PowerPoint Gettysburg Address") and Stephen M. Kosslyn (the Director of the Center for Advanced Study in the Behavioral Sciences at Stanford, previously Chair of the Department of Psychology at Harvard):

Letters to the Editor: A Tool Only as Good as the User

To the Editor:

"We Have Met the Enemy and He Is PowerPoint" (front page, April 27) describes how many military personnel bemoan the overuse and misuse of PowerPoint. They could just as easily have bemoaned bad written reports and summaries, and blamed Microsoft Word.

Don't blame the messenger: The problem is not in the tool itself, but in the way that people use it—which is partly a result of how institutions promote misuse. ...

—Peter Norvig and Stephen M. Kosslyn (Norvig and Kosslyn, Tool 2010)

One aspect of the misuse detailed in the Bumiller article was reinforced by an answering comment published online in *The Tank* the next day, April 28, 2010, by Michael Gordon (Senior Fellow, Institute for the Study of War, and a *New York Times* correspondent), reinforcing the loss of trackable documentation and its replacement by "an oral tradition":

With PowerPoint, the military has been moving toward an oral tradition and away from the written word, with all the demands for precision, nuance and serious exposition that writing requires. And it's not just a problem for the military. The procedure has become quite common in other areas of government, among contractors and in think tanks.

Sometimes PowerPoint presentations are used as a kind of bureaucratic filibuster: they can be a way to eat up time and restrict the opportunity for hard questions. But even when that is not the intent they are generally not the best means of communication. Clear and concise writing requires that issues be thought through and that is not always necessary if all that is required is to slap a few bullets on a slide. (Gordon 2010)

It is now possible to buy actual uniform tabs and patches for "PowerPoint Rangers," recognizing various levels of "achievement." From the webpage:

The U.S. Army uniform board has just released a new patch for those trapped in staff positions and who have served above and beyond the call of duty in making time-consuming PowerPoint presentations day after day, week after week, month after month without recognition.

The new "PPT1000" patch, shown above, is authorized to those who have put in at least 1,000 hours on PPT presentations. Subsequent awards for 2,500 hours, 5,000 hours, and 10,000 hours are to follow. Posthumous awards for those putting in over 25,000 hours will be presented to the next of kin, upon request.

The patch may be sewn on the right shoulder of the battle dress uniform or affixed to the flight suit/ACU with Velcro. A special pin version will be developed for the Army Class A uniform. Subdued versions are not authorized at this time.

Similar patches have been authorized in the past for serving in combat, but since our real mission today is to beat the other services out of $$$ by creating spectacular PPT slides, the Board deemed this was absolutely appropriate at this time.

Please submit your request to your commander or servicing MILPO for issue.

A similar patch and pin is under development for qualified Excel operators. Microsoft Word operators will not be recognized because the Army chooses to avoid the preparation of written products, particularly with signatures. (Placke 2011)

I have the 5,000-hour patch myself (similar to the picture, but with "5000 HOURS.PPT" in red), the most advanced level currently available, which I wear on a vintage jean jacket. My request for the 25,000-hour patch, which I have certainly earned, is pending; but if it is only awarded posthumously, then I'm not ready for it yet.

216 Famous CEOs Who Banned PowerPoint

I don't have a systematic collection of companies or executives who have banned the use of PowerPoint in their organizations, but there are a lot of such stories. Every year or so brings a call to ban PowerPoint from some large company, or from business and life in general, or even from a whole country (Switzerland).

Edward Tufte repeats one such story, about Louis Gerstner at IBM:

> When Louis Gerstner became president of IBM, he encountered a big company caught up in ritualistic slideware-style presentations:
>
>> One of the first meetings I asked for was briefing on the state of the [mainframe computer] business. I remember at least two things about that first meeting with Nick Donofrio, who was then running the System/390 business....
>>
>> At that time, the standard format of any important IBM meeting was a presentation using overhead projectors and graphics that IBMers called "foils" [projected transparencies]. Nick was on his second foil when I stepped to the table and, as politely as I could in front of his team, switched off the projector. After a long moment of awkward silence, I simply said "Let's just talk about your business."
>>
>> I mention this episode because it had an unintended, but terribly powerful ripple effect. By that afternoon an email about my hitting the Off button on the overhead projector was criss-crossing the world. Talk about consternation! It was as if the President of the United States had banned the use of English at White House meetings. (Gerstner, Jr. 2002, 43)
>
> (Tufte, 2nd ed, 2006)

Interestingly, one of the people who taught me a lot about how presentations are used in some big companies was my old friend Fred Lampe, who was on the six-month global strategy task force with me at Northern Telecom, and who had joined NT from IBM Boca Raton. Fred taught me about, and performed with me, an IBM technique in which he and I worked together, one of us speaking at a podium, and the other sitting with a file case full of folders of all possible backup overhead transparencies. When someone in the audience asked a question, the speaker would begin to give an initial sentence or two of answer, while the other quickly located the foil directly addressing the question and handed it up; the speaker would put it on the stage of the projector without looking and smoothly go on answering, indicating where on the slide the numbers or other requested data were located. Such refinements convinced me that IBM had been a serious company for presentations (as was Northern Telecom).

Another example is a story about Steve Jobs at Apple, concerning refocusing reviews in mid-1997. The final direct quotation from Steve is memorable: "People who know what they're talking about don't need PowerPoint."

> One of the first things Jobs did during the product review process was ban PowerPoints. "I hate the way people use slide presentations instead of thinking," Jobs later recalled. "People would confront a problem by creating a presentation. I wanted them to engage, to hash things out at the table, rather than show a bunch of slides. People who know what they're talking about don't need PowerPoint." (Isaacson 2011, 337)

This is interesting, because Steve Jobs is remembered as much as anything for the effectiveness of his own (properly-used) presentations and their visuals, and a whole book has been written about his presentations. (Note also that Walter Isaacson uses "PowerPoints" in the plural to mean "slides" or "presentations"; I doubt Steve would have used the word that way.)

A third famous example is Scott McNealy at Sun Microsystems. In 1997, McNealy told the *San Jose Mercury-News*:

> "We had 12.9 gigabytes of PowerPoint slides on our network. And I thought, 'What a huge waste of corporate productivity'. So we banned it. And we've had three unbelievable record-breaking fiscal quarters since we banned PowerPoint. Now I would argue that every company in the world, if it would just ban PowerPoint, would see its earnings skyrocket. Employees would stand around going: 'What do I do? Guess I've got to go to work.' " (Bostic 1997)

(How quickly hardware progresses. I probably have 12.9 gigabytes of personal PowerPoint slides on my own laptop right now, on a solid-state disk, taking up more space than McNealy's number for all of Sun fifteen years ago in 1997, when Sun had over 20,000 employees.)

There are claims that McNealy's ban was not enforced (Zuckerman 1999). In 2001 though, perhaps keeping up the joke, Scott McNealy confirmed that his PowerPoint ban was still in place:

"Look at our stock chart in the last four years since we've banned PowerPoint. Our productivity has skyrocketed!" (Hillesley 2007)

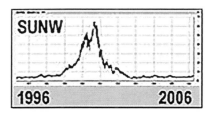

Shortly thereafter, inexplicably, the stock chart went the other way, despite the strategic banning of PowerPoint. The causation had apparently failed to continue to operate. By 2009, Sun was out of business, in a particularly ugly way.

In 2001, I went to a party where I was able to do some research about the banning of PowerPoint at Sun. One of the people at the party was a woman from Sun, so I asked her about whether Scott had really banned PowerPoint. Her answer was that Scott liked to talk about banning PowerPoint, but what he had actually done mostly was to discourage buying PCs (which ran Microsoft software), and to encourage buying workstations which ran Sun's own operating system and Unix applications—which meant that there was not a version of PowerPoint that could run on Sun workstations. "But," she said, "everyone brings in their laptops so they can use PowerPoint to get their presentations done."

The actions of all these CEOs seem to center on the problem of getting people to pay attention to reality, and to stop manipulating PowerPoint slides as ritual objects. The problem has been parodied insightfully by Scott Adams in Dilbert strips, like this one from 24 December 2005:

(See (Gaskins, Dilbert's History 2012).)

217 Why Didn't Xerox PARC Invent PowerPoint First?

If the secret of PowerPoint is that the specific application is an exceptionally good match to personal computers with graphical user interfaces, why wasn't that noticed at Xerox PARC (Palo Alto Research Center), where such computers were pioneered? Didn't the people at PARC want to make presentations, like everyone else? And if business people were eager to buy a Mac and a LaserWriter to use PowerPoint (as they demonstrably were), wouldn't a similar application have sold Xerox products? After all, both the Mac and the LaserWriter were copied from earlier work done at PARC.

I wondered about these questions at the time while I was initially working on PowerPoint. Not only did I have a lot of friends working at PARC, but when I was leaving Berkeley, I interviewed extensively at Xerox, in four widely separated cities, and ended up with a job offer to work at PARC for a year or two, then move to Dallas and join the ill-fated Office Systems Division (OSD) there, to work on commercial products with connections to the Systems Development Division (SDD) that was developing the Star as a commercialization of the Alto. I ended up working for Bell-Northern Research, just across the street from PARC in Palo Alto, and continued to know a fair amount of what was going on at Xerox. Xerox announced its Star product in 1981, the same year in which IBM shipped the PC.

It really seems that Xerox failed because of two rather simple mistakes. First, the applications for Star were designed by researchers who didn't know enough about the interests of the customers, and no one in marketing could correct the mismatch. Second, the systems were closed to outside developers. If the systems had been open to independently developed software, as Mac and Windows were, the first mistake need not have been fatal. But Xerox had developed Star in the same way as its copiers, with everything proprietary, including the computer processors and all their development systems, so there was no way for anyone else to create software for the Star.

M. Mitchell Waldrop, in his book *The Dream Machine*, observes:

> However, if being closed meant that Xerox could lock in its customers, it also meant that it had to guess right about what those customers wanted; it had no way to tap into the creativity of the wider community. And in at least one instance, the Star's software designers spectacularly failed to guess right: the Star had no spreadsheet program. Nobody at PARC had ever thought to write

one because nobody in a research lab ever needed one. What they did need was a good way to write technical papers—"so we got all caught up with WYSIWYG word processing and printing," says [Jerry] Elkind [former head of CSL at PARC, who was responsible for setting up early beta-test sites for Altos]. It was precisely the inverse of priorities in the business world. In the executive suites of 1981, word processing was widely considered to be low-level stenographers' work, whereas a spreadsheet was just the kind of application a manager might use. And the result was another sale for Apple, not for Xerox. (Waldrop 2001, 447-448)

The Star was designed deliberately *not* to be sold for use by secretaries and clerks, and it was priced to match—it was roughly ten times the price of a personal computer. Instead, it was designed for use by executives and professionals, the "information workers" who were all the rage in those days. "A Xerox promotional brochure would state in 1981 that the Star was 'designed specifically for professional business people with little or no typing skills.' " (Hiltzik 1999, 247) Yet, through simple misunderstanding, applications to do what the executives and professionals personally wanted to do—one example was spreadsheets, and I would say that another was presentations—were not included. What was included was really excellent word processing and long document preparation, which was considered by many business executives to be beneath their dignity.

In fact, Xerox's ignoring presentations was arguably more disastrous than ignoring spreadsheets. Spreadsheets could, demonstrably, be done on conventional character-oriented personal computers such as Apple IIs and IBM PCs, which sold for a tenth the price of a Star; many customers knew they wanted spreadsheets, but also knew they didn't have to pay for a Star's screen to have them. A program like PowerPoint would have been so obviously superior on the Star, compared to anything available on an IBM PC with DOS, that the customers would have had a reason to buy Xerox's graphical user interface. Better control of presentations would have justified purchases of Star systems. We saw this later, when PowerPoint sold Macintoshes and then sold Windows.

David Liddle, leading the group developing the Star, complained about the lack of marketing information:

All the while that I was running SDD I couldn't get an operating division to agree to market and sell the product. We had to build it based on what we could see in terms of the use of the Alto within Xerox. And how we could best extrapolate that to the marketplace. We weren't getting professional marketing and professional planning feedback during that whole period of time. So we were mostly driven by what we had learned in research. (Smith and Alexander 1999, 236)

PARC got many things precisely right, including the whole concept of networked personal computers with graphical user interfaces. But the failure to understand what senior business people did outside of research establishments was a fatal flaw, and one which could not be easily repaired within a closed system. By 1984, Xerox had decided to add an option to Star to run IBM-PC software (DOS, not Windows), which would have included lots of old-fashioned, non-graphical presentation applications, and to put a VisiCalc clone on its machine. But by 1984, also, Apple had started shipping Macintosh, and Microsoft had demonstrated Windows, and PowerPoint was already being developed for those open environments, as were products from thousands of other independent software developers.

But even if PARC did miss the importance of applications such as spreadsheets, how did they in particular miss the presentation application? Didn't the people at PARC make presentations?

I've never studied closely the presentations given at academic meetings and conferences (as I did business presentations), but I saw a lot of them during the years 1968–1984, including many transparencies made on Xerox Altos, by people from PARC as well as by academics from the numerous universities that had received Altos and graphical printers from Xerox.

My memory of presentations at academic and scholarly meetings, back then, is that it was not fashionable to show a lot of care in preparing visuals, when they were even used. Every academic meeting room had an overhead projector, and sometimes speakers would use very sparse slides, either hand-drawn or typed on a typewriter and copied, or would even write on blank slides in real time while they talked, but with nothing like fussy rounded-corner borders or putting the date and the occasion and the institution name on every page, and usually (as I recall) in portrait page orientation, rather than the landscape orientation common in business presentations (many impact printers could only produce portrait-oriented pages). I think that I find a sort of confirmation of these memories in some of Edward Tufte's criticisms of PowerPoint from an academic viewpoint, such as his complaint that PowerPoint "uses only about 40% to 60% of the space available on a slide to show unique content, with all remaining space devoted to

Phluff, bullets, frames, and branding" (Tufte, 2nd ed, 2006, 15), and his advice to issue the corporate directive "From now on your presentation software is Microsoft Word not PowerPoint. Get used to it" (Tufte, 2nd ed, 2006, 30).

I recall the academic transparencies prepared from Altos and Xerox printers as looking better because they appeared "typeset," but otherwise much the same—portrait orientation, looking like they had come from a "typesetting typewriter." It's likely that these had been produced using some version of the Bravo line of word processing editors.

But presentation graphics was a peripheral use for Altos; when the users at Xerox PARC needed to make presentations, they would have used what they had, and I'd guess that, for them, the simplicity of the typewriter-like appearance of slides from a word processor had the proper "casual" and "thrown-together" appearance appropriate to an academic meeting, avoiding the studied striving and distasteful impression of effort evident in a sales presentation.

On the other hand, I think it's very likely that one or more people, somewhere in Xerox, did suggest a presentation application; they had as many as 1,500 Altos in use, so someone must have thought of the idea. Either the suggestion was rejected, or the suggestion was accepted but later cut from the product spec for lack of time. In either case, it would have been because of the same skepticism that I often ran into with my plans for PowerPoint—the feeling that the presentation market wasn't really important (lacking the market research I had), and/or the view that some combination of word processor and drawing program would suffice (as I was told about MacWrite and MacDraw, and like the proposal to make bullet charts a feature of Microsoft Word). Running into this rejection internally would have assured that the product would launch without such an application, since it could only be developed at Xerox.

The situation didn't last forever. Twenty years after the Alto, Rich Gold, who was at the time a researcher at PARC, wrote his article "Reading PowerPoint." This was written in 1999, and Gold says:

> ... During the last eight years, as a researcher at Xerox PARC, I have become a heavy PowerPoint user and have even become known for my presentations. I have ghost-written other people's PowerPoint slides. I could even say I have at last found my medium. *I think in PowerPoint.* ... I look at PowerPoint as a central, and powerful, form of reading in this new era. (Gold 2002, [emphasis supplied])

If anyone with Gold's interest in observing business use of presentations had been at PARC twenty years earlier, imagine how eagerly that person would have embraced the Alto and tried to get a presentation application developed for it. That might well have succeeded, and the result might have improved the reception of Xerox's Star, although it still would have been hampered—by being closed and by its cost—in the competition with personal computers running PowerPoint.

218 The "Smartest Acquisition" in 35 Years

In 2010, Preston Gralla, writing in *ComputerWorld*, could look back over Microsoft's first 35 years and characterize the acquisition of PowerPoint as Microsoft's "smartest acquisition" out of hundreds in its whole history (Gralla 2010). Judged by success of the acquired product, and even more so relative to price of the acquisition, that has to be true.

I think a very big reason why PowerPoint was the smartest acquisition was that it was the first. Everything about the success of the acquisition of Forethought hinged on the facts that we were the first product group at Microsoft outside the main campus, that we had a nascent independent culture (though everyone was also very positive about being part of Microsoft), and that Microsoft had no previous experience managing distant product groups and no precedents for what to expect.

It was also important for the PowerPoint acquisition that Microsoft in 1987 was itself like a big startup, only 1,200 people, with a strong memory of how a small company has to cut through red tape to stay alive, and how large partners can tie you up. The groups in Redmond lacked precedents and processes and procedures to control a distant subsidiary, and they also lacked a bureaucratic imperative to extend their control; they were, by and large, very happy to have someone else take responsibility and get a product shipped without increasing the load on the original overworked groups at headquarters. Back in 1987, Bill Gates's message was "Don't screw up PowerPoint." Many of the decisions that left us free to diverge from the ways of Redmond were personally made by Bill, and they paid off.

In making its first acquisition, Microsoft anticipated two "tips" that would be advised by Paul Graham many years later:

> Tip for acquirers: when a startup turns you down, consider raising your offer, because there's a good chance the outrageous price they want will later seem a bargain.

... Another tip: If you want to get all that value, don't destroy the startup after you buy it. Give the founders enough autonomy that they can grow the acquisition into what it would have become. (Graham, More Googles 2008)

By 1992, with 12,000 people, Microsoft was already beginning to forget that culture, having hired lots of people from larger companies, people who specialized in red tape, knew how to spin it out, and wanted badly to get on with the job. There were, by then, other groups outside Redmond, so rules and practices were developed to begin to manage them more tightly. Networks were slowly improving, so there was better communication. If PowerPoint had been acquired in 1992, when all the Redmond groups had their processes and procedures in place for muscling in on the new acquisition, it would have been very different.

Also, in the Microsoft of 1992, any group as small as PowerPoint would have been given non-negotiable terms to move to Redmond as part of the deal. The people with a significant chunk of the company would have agreed, done the deal, moved (or at least have begun to move) to Redmond for whatever length of time was needed to get the final holdback piece of the purchase price released (hardly ever more than one year), and then found that there was so much meddling that they might as well quit. It's not at all hard to understand why so many recent Microsoft acquisitions have been followed quickly by the exits of the talent just purchased. Mike Maples commented, talking about a later acquisition:

> I think that's the worst case scenario: you buy a product that's 70% there; the market is just developing and all the smart guys leave. (Maples 2004)

But as it was, the PowerPoint group had lots of time to continue with the entrepreneurial behavior which had given us our initial success, and which continued to drive our success over the next few years. As it made sense to create more homogenization with the rest of Microsoft, it was available. As far as an outsider can judge, it seems that Office came into being rather smoothly, with the PowerPoint senior people accomplishing the transition, and then one by one moving on or retiring, with no fatal disruption. (I was the first to leave.)

This experience suggests to me that it's probably always the case that a company's "smartest acquisition" is going to be an acquisition carried out early in the company's life, while a successful acquisition is still possible. The idea that large companies cannot help smothering their acquisitions is the conventional wisdom, and it probably is the simple truth. I can testify that, in the first days after an acquisition, the acquirers can move in with tactics of "shock and awe" and make any changes they want, while the acquired startup is still not sure what is happening. Apparently, in larger companies, the temptation to do that is irresistible.

219 PowerPoint Observed in Books

When trying to assess the cultural impact of PowerPoint, one source of information is mentions of its name in books. The diagram below is simply the results from search by Google's "Ngram Viewer," looking through Google Books holdings in English for the word "PowerPoint" (written solid, with two upper-case letters) for the years 1984–2008; it shows the changes in mentions over time.

The chart seems to show that PowerPoint had little impact before about 1991, began growing then (about the time PowerPoint 3.0 was released on Windows 3.1), and since then has had a fairly steady rise in mentions. This corresponds pretty well to what I would have expected. (The search is sensitive to case and to word division; all of "Powerpoint," "Power Point," "powerpoint," and "power point" have lines essentially flat at zero; the special typographic formatting has become standard.)

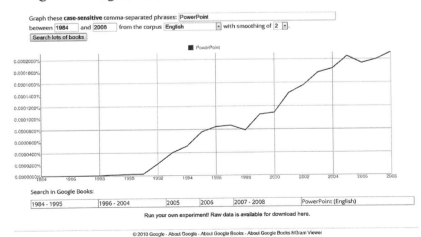

220 PowerPoint Observed in News Articles

Another way to assess the cultural impact of PowerPoint is mentions of the name in news articles. There's no perfect way to do this, but the website www.newslibrary.com can be used to get one value, for newspapers in the United States. One can search it by year for news stories containing the word "PowerPoint." A factor to keep in mind is that the site has fewer total articles from earlier years—fewer than 2 million for 1987, compared with almost 19 million for 2007. The numbers for total stories and mentions can be used together to calculate a frequency index of stories mentioning "PowerPoint" among all news stories for the year.

In 1987, there were just 5 articles out of 1,805,678 total indexed that mentioned PowerPoint. By 2007, that had grown to 14,495 articles mentioning PowerPoint out of 18,933,239 total. That growth means that articles mentioning PowerPoint were more than 250 times as frequent in 2007 as in 1987. Again, real popularity doesn't arrive until around the year 2000.

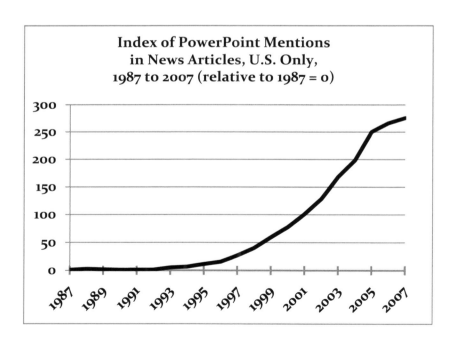

221 PowerPoint Observed in Dilbert

The archive of Scott Adams's Dilbert strips begins in 1989; since then, there have been over 8,000 strips catalogued, and another added every day. In the popular mind, Dilbert has become prominently associated with presentations, and it has given rise to several oft-repeated catchphrases about PowerPoint. It is thus surprising to discover that only about 100 strips out of the 8,000-plus deal with presentations, about 5 strips per year (but slightly more frequency in later years). Of these, 37 strips mention PowerPoint by name, the earliest in 1996 (all data through calendar 2011). In addition to the strips noted below, I've gathered all the strips dealing with presentations into a document with further commentary; see my "Comments on Dilbert's History of PowerPoint" (Gaskins, Dilbert's History 2012).

We happen to know from Adams's own testimony that he was an experienced and satisfied user of PowerPoint. He has blogged:

> My guess is that people who work long hours get a sort of charge every time they complete a discrete task. People who don't get that charge, on average, probably find jobs where they can work fewer hours.
>
> I recall my corporate days, where I would spend eight hours refining a Powerpoint [sic] presentation that, in all likelihood, would have no impact on the business. I always felt a charge of pleasure when it was done. Each time I reviewed the beauty and majesty of my graphs and bullet points, I would get a new little surge. (Adams 2007)

The portrayals of presentations in Dilbert presumably are intended by Adams to be recognized by a wide audience as "realistic," so the range of presentation technology that appears is likely to be characteristic of the period when a strip appeared. The early depiction of the usage of overhead projectors and transparencies, and of 35mm slides, is mostly surprisingly accurate and consistent with the analyses used to guide PowerPoint's development.

1989 May 14
The earliest presentation portrayed in the archive of Dilbert strips has Dilbert using a flip chart. This was nothing but a large pad of paper bound at the top, on which "slides" could be drawn in advance; when

445

needed, pages could be flipped to blank sheets at the back to use like a whiteboard (non-erasable, easy to transcribe later for participants).

1991 September 17

For the first time, Dilbert appears to use a computer in preparing for a presentation. There's no indication what program he is using.

1991 September 18

(The next day.) Dilbert examines overhead transparencies mounted in cardboard frames; the implication is that these mounted transparencies are the result of computer work shown in the preceding day's strip. The cardboard mounts invariably had rounded corners, and if an overhead had a printed border it was usually rounded at the corners to echo the mount. PowerPoint 1.0 made its default a rounded-corner border to provide this same cue. The mounts made it easier to change transparencies when standing at the projector by preventing their sticking together, and protected them for re-use (when they were harder to make manually). PowerPoint 1.0 transparencies were at first often mounted in those same cardboard frames, but decreasingly so as years went on.

1991 September 19

(The next day again.) The first portrayal of projecting transparencies of any kind. Dilbert is projecting (projector not shown) an image with the rounded corners of the lighted areas caused by the shape of the inner edge of the cardboard mounts. The "stage" (lighted platform) of an overhead projector was usually square, and transparencies and their mounts were sometimes made square to match—as seen here. After overheads changed to be mostly made on photocopiers (even prior to PowerPoint), mounts became available to match the shape of the copier transparencies (US Letter or A4) that could go through the copying machine, but overhead projectors remained square to accommodate both portrait and landscape transparencies.

1992 June 7

The first sighting of 35mm slides in the Dilbert strip. Dogbert asks for "Lights, please," reflecting the fact that 35mm presentations were made in darkened rooms (overheads were projected with room lights on, for discussion during meetings). The darkening of the room is shown by that stage direction. Dogbert also has a "clicker" remote control for the projector—common on 35mm slide projectors, but impossible for overhead projectors. The aspect ratio of the projected images is not square, as for the previous overheads, but approximately correct for 35mm slides (2:3). The inside edges of cardboard mounts for 35mm slides were very slightly rounded. Note also that a "formal" retractable high-reflectivity screen is used, as opposed to overheads shown projected onto a wall or board.

1994 November 1

The first view of an overhead projector machine in the Dilbert strip. Unlike Dogbert's unseen 35mm projector at the back of the room, requiring a remote control, the boss's overhead projector is at the front of the room, where he can manually lay overhead transparencies onto its stage. The light source (the bulb) is in the big box below the stage; the small box supported on a stalk holds a mirror at 45 degrees to reflect the image from the stage onto the screen—or, as apparently in this case, the wall, without benefit of the retractable screen used for the 35mm slides. A cautious presenter avoided looking into the mirror.

1996 June 28

The first mention of PowerPoint. It is in quotation marks, and the all-caps style of the speech balloons means that we can't tell whether the internal capital letter is present. The context is at a desk with a computer, preparing (not presenting). This is more than 9 years after PowerPoint shipped; apparently it took that long before Scott Adams believed the name would be generally recognizable. All the PowerPoint people were thrilled by this recognition, so much so that this strip mentioning PowerPoint, the only one at the time, was reproduced in the program for the GBU tenth anniversary (Belleville, Peterson and Somogyi 1997).

2000 April 30

A big breakthrough comes in early 2000: we have the very first image of direct video projection from a computer in the conference room. Dogbert is the presenter—perhaps as a consultant, which explains the fancy setup. The computer may be a bulky early laptop, or may be intended to represent a compact desktop with CRT. This was just about eight years after I'd made such a presentation for the first time. Proper wall-screens like this one were often used, rather than the wall, because early video projectors were so dim, and a reflective screen helped. Color came for free with video, very different from overheads that had to be made on black-and-white copiers and from expensive color 35mm slides.

2002 November 17

Dilbert presents for the first time using a boxy laptop on the table in the presentation room. This is two and a half years after Dogbert first did something similar, but now the computer is unmistakably a laptop, and the topic of the meeting is more pedestrian. Dilbert's use of a laptop and direct video takes place more than ten years after I had done the same thing for the first time in Paris. The projected image still is shown with a square shape and rounded corners, which could be a mistaken convention left over from portraying overhead projectors; video projectors (even transparent LCD panels laid on the stage of an actual overhead projector) were usually non-square, like monitors.

2004 February 10

The 8th mention of PowerPoint in the strip, nearly eight years after it was first mentioned, and for the first time there are no quotation marks needed—seventeen years after PowerPoint was shipped. There's no way to tell whether the projection is from video or conventional overheads (PowerPoint could produce both), but during this period the coloring of the projected images in the strips becomes more vivid, suggesting video.

450

2005 December 23

The 9th mention of PowerPoint, for the second time with no quotation marks, a couple of years after the previous mention. Again the name is used in the context of preparing in a cubicle. The only output shown is a printed paper handed to the boss for one-on-one reading, perhaps reflecting the continuing substitution of PowerPoint documents for conventional full-text documents.

2005 December 24

The 10th mention of PowerPoint is the next day, again used without quotation marks. The usage ("I am entering the PowerPoint zone") makes PowerPoint sound like a very familiar concept, nearly twenty years after it was first shipped. This strip captures very neatly the complaint of CEOs who have banned PowerPoint, that people begin concentrating on the slides rather than the reality. This is the one Dilbert strip that I chose to put on my home page many years ago. It explains a very common and insidious way to betray yourself when using Power-Point.

2006 August 2

Another eighteen months later, there are three mentions of PowerPoint in three successive days, none with quotation marks (from now on

PowerPoint is used very familiarly). The first day shows preparation on a flat-screen monitor in a cubicle.

2007 April 3

Lying is a process, if you use enough slides. As presentations become more common in the strips, the skepticism of their veracity increases.

2007 June 5

PowerPoint appears as a secret weapon for terrorists. This was seven years after Peter Feaver had said about PowerPoint, "We should give it to the Iraqis. We'd never have to worry about them again." (Quoted in the *Wall Street Journal* by Greg Jaffe, 26 April 2000.)

2009 September 17

Apart from the insightful humor of the presenter's self-esteem in this strip, it seems to possibly be an example of a very small meeting in which the PowerPoint slides are handed out as hard copy for participants to read, often with no projection and with the readers instructed to turn the pages in unison.

2010 January 18

With suitable outsourcing, the two irreducible functions in a company can be (1) preparing PowerPoint presentations, and (2) being the audience for PowerPoint presentations.

2010 June 12

PowerPoint as the Matrix, an alternative to reality.

2011 September 27
PowerPoint as a portal to a realm where fantasy and reality are reversed. The theme of presentations having become disconnected from reality is now a common theme in the strips.

222 Why Did PowerPoint Become Popular So Slowly?

Based on the mentions in books, the mentions in news articles, and the mentions in Dilbert cartoons, it seems that PowerPoint took a long time to become a cultural force, some ten or fifteen years from 1987. Then, in the last decade or so, it has had a greater presence.

I think the reason for this pattern is the gradual diffusion of Power-Point use from strictly business presentations to other areas of life. PowerPoint was adopted very rapidly in businesses to replace manual processes. By 1990, only three years after its first appearance, Power-Point had reached Windows (so it was available on the machines selling in largest volumes), and could make color 35mm slides (so it could save real money, as well as making the vastly more common overheads). Windows use in businesses exploded, and so did PowerPoint. Seen in its original context, PowerPoint was almost an overnight hit, displacing all competitors. The first phase of its growth was very rapid, among customers in the target market. At the time, there was no particular idea that PowerPoint could have a much larger audience.

But then, somehow, the idea grew that everyone should use Power-Point. Professors adopted it as a regular part of teaching and used it at academic meetings and conferences. Elementary school teachers introduced it as something children should (even must) use. Clergy adopted it for religious services. Lawyers used it in court. Politicians and government bureaucrats adopted it for public meetings. And on and on.

In this much larger market, PowerPoint use was growing slowly but steadily.

As far as I can figure out, the expansion of PowerPoint's appeal to new market segments was not caused by added new software features which fitted it to do new things. One clear exception: it seems that much more extensive animation and navigation in slide shows was what made PowerPoint appeal to those looking for an inexpensive engine to make games and short animated videos, particularly young people along the Western Pacific Rim. Perhaps someone else can identify other new capabilities that I'm missing.

It probably is true that the evolution of projection hardware played a part. As video projectors got smaller and brighter and more common, anyone who wanted to use projection from a laptop would have been steered to PowerPoint as the natural tool to use. And in particular, as video replaced overhead projectors and 35mm projectors in classrooms, often with a convenient "video in" connector at the front of the room, more instructors would have been encouraged to move from older formats to PowerPoint, and perhaps to use visuals more often, an influential example. But nothing else that I can see explains many of the groups who began to use PowerPoint.

Once many more non-business groups became interested in re-purposing business presentation technology, PowerPoint was spreading pretty much with the rise of inexpensive and high-quality personal computers, by now mostly laptops. Computer use outside of businesses grew steadily. Microsoft lowered the price of the Office bundle to unheard-of lows, and included full PowerPoint in even the cheapest versions (under $100—hardly anything compared to the original prices of $495 per individual application, almost $1,500 for Word, Excel, and PowerPoint). Increasingly, the Office suite was included pre-installed on computers. Anyone with a computer might expect to use it.

223 *You Could Look It Up*

There's a lot of reference material about PowerPoint. One number that always amazes me is Google's estimate of how many search results it could return for the vestigand "PowerPoint." That number always fluctuates considerably, doubtless an artifact of Google's calculation of it, but it currently is often more than *300 million* search result listings.

A search at Amazon.com for "PowerPoint" currently results in listings for over 10,000 products, including thousands of books and thousands of templates (some templates with the most unexpected themes).

Oxford University Press dictionaries added PowerPoint as a standard entry in the year 2010.

> PowerPoint (Pow·er·Point)
> Pronunciation: /ˈpouər͵point͵/
> noun, trademark
>
> A software package designed to create electronic presentations consisting of a series of separate pages or slides.
> "PowerPoint." Oxford Dictionaries, Oxford University Press, April 2010.
> http://oxforddictionaries.com/definition/PowerPoint
> (accessed 26 March 2011).

PowerPoint is also in the Encyclopedia Britannica (since 2008):

> Microsoft PowerPoint
> Software
> Virtual presentation software developed by Robert Gaskins and Dennis Austin for the American computer software company Forethought, Inc. The program, initially named Presenter, was released for the Apple Macintosh in 1987. In July of that year, the Microsoft Corporation, in its first significant software acquisition, purchased the rights to PowerPoint for $14 million.
>
> PowerPoint was designed to facilitate visual demonstrations for group presentations in the business environment. Presentations are arranged as a series of individually designed "slides" that contain images, text, or other objects. Version 1.0 allowed users to generate text and graphics pages for black-and-white handouts, notes, and overhead transparencies. Version 2.0, developed for both Macintosh and Microsoft's Windows operating system, was upgraded to output 35-mm colour slides. The 1992 release of PowerPoint 3.0 introduced the now-standard virtual slideshow. Subsequent versions have added more features: slide transitions, background designs, animation, graphics, movie and sound clips, and AutoContent. In 2003 the renamed Office PowerPoint reflected Microsoft's emphasis on standardizing the user interface and program functions across their suite of Office programs, which included Word (a word processor) and Excel (a spreadsheet program).

PowerPoint was developed for business use but has wide applications elsewhere such as for schools and community organizations. The program was initially packaged as a stand-alone product, but its inclusion in the best-selling Microsoft Office suite has assured its dominance in the presentation-software market.

"Microsoft PowerPoint." Encyclopædia Britannica Online, 2008. http://www.britannica.com/EBchecked/topic/1491611/Microsoft-PowerPoint
(accessed 23 December 2008).

It's interesting that both the dictionary and the encyclopedia know PowerPoint primarily (and now accurately) as a way of making digital presentations for video projection; Oxford says "designed to create electronic presentations," while the Britannica says "virtual presentation software." Both also seize on the underlying design, with Oxford saying "consisting of a series of separate pages or slides" and Britannica saying "arranged as a series of individually designed slides."

The name PowerPoint has also achieved a meaning beyond the specific Microsoft product:

> Now, of course, PowerPoint is as generic a product name as Kleenex and Xerox.
> —Henry Petroski, "From Plato's Cave to PowerPoint," in *Success through Failure: the Paradox of Design* (Princeton University Press: 2006).

You also run across the casual remark that reveals PowerPoint's generic cultural influence:

> [1]Henceforth, we use "PowerPoint" to refer to any digital slideware.
> —Footnote 1 from Ira Wagman and Michael Z. Newman, "PowerPoint and Labor in the Mediated Classroom," *International Journal of Communication* 5 (2011), 1759–1767.

224 *PowerPoint Operator*

When PowerPoint was in development, I thought that its greatest advantage would be the control that it gave to the individual presenter:

... the most important advantage of using a program like the one envisioned here is control. When successfully completed, this program will allow the content originators to directly and personally control their own presentations. For anyone who makes presentations regularly, the advantage (in time and in quality) of gaining enough leverage to directly and personally create all needed presentation materials far outweighs all other advantages. (Gaskins, PowerPoint Marketing 1986)

PowerPoint was designed for relatively low-power and relatively inexpensive personal computers, specifically for direct use by the "content originator," the business person who was *not* a graphics operator but a "knowledge worker," the person who knew what the presentation should say, and who needed to communicate about his or her job. With PowerPoint, that person could be in direct control, without having to work through the dreaded graphics department.

Bob Lucky from Bell Labs remembered the earlier environment when he wrote about PowerPoint:

In the old days, preparing these Vugraphs required much time and thought. I remember when they had to be sent to the art department, and you had to argue schedule and budget with the trolls who jealously guarded the access to the artisans who alone were empowered to create the precious foils. (Lucky 1998)

Cutting out the "trolls" and "artisans" was the message of PowerPoint. It would get rid of the "AV specialists" and all the people, both inside a corporation and outside in agencies and service bureaus, who were intermediaries in getting what the speaker needed.

This was subtly different from categories which were thought of as closely related at the time, such as "desktop publishing." Desktop publishing software was usually aimed at "publishers" of newsletters and such publications, not at each individual writer or editor (who continued to use something like Word or WordPerfect). Word processing was, in the mid-1980s, still seen as a job for typists; managers did not aspire to type their own letters (though they would soon come to do so). But PowerPoint was for the direct use of managers and executives and knowledge workers, who did want to use it.

The transitions of Genigraphics reflected this. When presenters began using PowerPoint, they sent their files over modems directly to Genigraphics for imaging and got the slides back, with no intermediaries in their own companies. Later, as video projection took over, they just connected a cable to their own laptops and put their PowerPoint slides on screen directly, with no middlemen at all. All control had passed to the presenters, just as we intended.

Some years after I left Microsoft, I was walking down the high street half a block from our home in London (this is Victoria Street, which runs from Buckingham Palace Road to Parliament Square, past Victoria Station, Scotland Yard, and Westminster Abbey). I saw in the window of an employment agency an advertisement for a "Powerpoint Operator." The artists who worked at Genigraphics consoles had been called "operators," and as I read the card in the window, I realized that the cycle had gone all the way around. The Genigraphics console operators might be gone, but it was now possible for people to make a living simply by knowing how to use PowerPoint on behalf of others.

Window of employment agency in Victoria St., London SW1.

Even though the idea of PowerPoint operators was antithetical to the premise that content originators could directly produce their own presentations, I was still very pleased. I was proud that our software had created a new possibility for employment, and that just knowing how to use PowerPoint was valuable enough to create jobs and permit people to make a living through their knowledge. The emergence of the job of "PowerPoint Operator" was a validation of the importance and utility of the software; its output was so useful that it was worth paying people to manipulate it on your behalf.

Closeup of one of the positions advertised in the window.

Actually, the job description sounded eerily close to my own former position at the GBU. "Excellent Knowledge of PowerPoint," check. "Responsible for creating lengthy presentations," check. "Knowledge of Word and Excel also necessary," check. "Must be prepared to take on admin tasks also," just the same as my previous job. It was temporary, but my previous job was temporary too. I considered going in and introducing myself as a "PowerPoint Operator," or at least telling them that the second "P" in PowerPoint is capitalized, but I let it go.

Thus grew the tale of Wonderland:
Thus slowly, one by one,
Its quaint events were hammered out—
  ...
Alice! A childish story take,
  And, with a gentle hand,
Lay it where Childhood's dreams are twined
  In Memory's mystic band,
Like pilgrim's wither'd wreath of flowers
  Pluck'd in a far-off land.

> — Lewis Carroll, *Alice's Adventures in Wonderland,*
>   "All in the golden afternoon" (opening poem)

ABOUT ROBERT GASKINS

Retired, San Francisco and London
March 1993—Present (April 2012)

Soon after I retired, my wife and I moved to London, where we fully restored an 1890 Victorian "mansion flat" in central London close by Buckingham Palace and № 10 Downing Street. I became interested in the concertina, the only native English musical instrument and the high-tech musical sensation of the Victorian age, and learned how to play antique examples of the Maccann duet concertina, a nearly forgotten late-Victorian refinement. I studied its history, did extensive research at British research libraries and museums, and published research articles.

I constructed an authoritative digital reference library about concertinas at www.concertina.com, which has gradually expanded to present the work of over a dozen leading scholars plus that of many occasional contributors, as well as collections of historical documents. At the same time, I carried out a project for the Horniman Museum in London to digitize the Wheatstone factory records from their concertina history archives, now free online at www.horniman.info. The Concertina Research Forum was founded to facilitate interaction among researchers, and I hosted an international meeting of the CRF in London (June 2002). The BBC World Service consulted me as a principal resource for the program "The Concertina Man" (September 2004), to commemorate the bicentenary of Sir Charles Wheatstone's birth. I was elected an Honorary Life Member of the International Concertina Association, London, in November 2005.

We lived most of each year in London for ten years (1994–2004), then moved back to live full-time in our 1882 Victorian house in San Francisco that we had purchased in 1987.

Current contact information is online at www.robertgaskins.com.

Microsoft Corporation, Menlo Park, California
Director and General Manager, Graphics Business Unit
July 1987—March 1993

As the creator of PowerPoint, I joined Microsoft to be the head of its newly acquired Graphics Business Unit (GBU), the first business unit outside Redmond, reporting to Bill Gates (later to the innovative manager Mike Maples). I retained full P&L responsibility, with local control of product strategy, budgets, facilities, recruiting, compensation, capital equipment, software development, development tools, quality assurance, marketing, advertising, PR, manuals, internationalization, and worldwide sales liaison. We continued working in the style of a startup and at the same intensity for as long as I was there, through the first three generations of PowerPoint.

PowerPoint 1.0 (for Mac, April 1987) produced output of black-and-white overhead transparencies (together with speaker's notes and audience handouts). PowerPoint 2.0 (for Mac, May 1988, and for Windows, May 1990) added output of professional 35mm color slides, including online transmission for overnight imaging and processing by Genigraphics. PowerPoint 3.0 (for Windows, May 1992, and for Mac, September 1992) added output of live video color slideshows, including slide transitions, builds, animations, and synchronized sound and video clips.

These first three PowerPoint versions completed the basic product functionality, which has been refined in further releases since then. They were shipped in over two dozen national languages and won scores of awards worldwide. Sales grew steadily to a 1992 market share of 63% of presentation graphics software sales on Windows and Mac worldwide against seventeen competitors, with sales of over one million copies of PowerPoint per year (1992).

PowerPoint revenues grew on my watch to well over $100 million annually (in 1992), about half from outside the U.S. We were one of the most profitable units at Microsoft, earning an operating profit margin of 48% of revenues (Microsoft's operating margin for the same period was 35%, the software industry average was 11%). After I left, others from the original team continued working and, ten years later, by 2003, PowerPoint revenues for Microsoft exceeded $1 billion annually. In 2010, Microsoft announced that PowerPoint was installed on over a billion computers worldwide.

PowerPoint was packaged and sold as a stand-alone product prior to the creation of "Microsoft Office," which began (in 1989 for Mac and in 1990 for Windows) as a transparent overwrap around the separately manufactured boxes of Word, Excel, and PowerPoint. Only after the success of the physical bundle were the three applications progressively revised to work more alike, provided with a single install program, and packaged together (as well as sold separately). Still later, the parts of Office began to be specified and developed as an integrated product, with advantages both to users and to Microsoft. It was this innovation that also required changes to the Microsoft organization, away from the loosely coupled confederation of independent application business units.

While I headed the Graphics Business Unit, we grew from 7 people to nearly 100 people (about 70 employees and 30 vendor personnel). Microsoft grew from about 1,200 people to 12,000 people during the same period. As with any startup, credit for the long-term success of PowerPoint is due to those who were there early to set the direction: the "Wizards of Menlo Park," the 119 people who worked on PowerPoint from the beginning until the end of the years on Sand Hill Road (1984 to 1994).

Forethought, Inc., Sunnyvale, California
Vice President, Product Development
July 1984—July 1987

I joined Forethought when it was a year-old startup that had stalled out and was looking to do a restart around some new business plan, the focus of which soon turned out to be my PowerPoint idea. I had responsibility for our product strategy, all development, product marketing, publications, and manufacturing. Within a month, I had written the original PowerPoint description, the first of a succession of product marketing documents refining the PowerPoint product definition.

A couple of months later, I was able to recruit Dennis Austin (from Gavilan and before that Burroughs) to head the software design and development for PowerPoint. About eighteen months after that, we attracted Tom Rudkin (from VisiOn and before that Intel) to head the work on a future Windows version of what was being designed and implemented first for Macintosh.

We raised about $3 million in new money for the restart from top-tier venture capital investors led by New Enterprise Associates (Dick Kramlich and Tom McConnell) and Lamoreaux Partners (Phil

Lamoreaux), plus Abingworth plc (U.K.), and the very first venture investment ever made by Apple Computer's Strategic Investment Group (Dan Eilers). An outside board member was Bob Metcalfe, inventor of Ethernet and chairman of 3Com.

While we developed PowerPoint, our company operations were simultaneously built up by contract publishing and selling of software belonging to other developers, so that we were ready and able to sell and ship over $1 million worth of PowerPoint on the day of its initial release—unprecedented for a Macintosh application.

Three months later, PowerPoint history was sharply changed by an offer from Bill Gates to buy PowerPoint and to turn Forethought into Microsoft's Graphics Business Unit, to be located in Silicon Valley. The offer was orchestrated by Jeff Raikes, who had convinced Bill that presentations would become a major application category, and that just adding a feature to format Word outlines on overheads (Bill's first thought, according to Jeff) would not be competitive. We accepted the offer and became Microsoft's first significant acquisition. The price was $14 million in cash, which returned $12 million to our investors in under three years. I and all the rest of the PowerPoint people, plus many of our other Forethought employees, became Microsoft employees, just a year or so after the Microsoft IPO.

The decision to be acquired, rather than to try to pursue our own IPO, already underway, was not easy at the time; after the stock market crash on "Black Monday" three months later, it appeared brilliant.

One hopeful sign in favor of joining Microsoft was that, where other potential acquirers had sent only accountants to do due diligence by reading our bank statements and interviewing our bookkeeper, Microsoft also sent Dave Moore to actually read through the text of all our program source code and to interview our developers. Fortunately, Microsoft turned out to be an excellent fit, and our group remained intact and maintained an amazing degree of organizational independence within Microsoft for as long as that made sense.

Bell-Northern Research, Inc., Palo Alto, California
Manager, Computer Science Research
May 1978—July 1984

For my first job out of school, I set up a new department at the principal U.S. R&D laboratories of Bell-Northern Research, the product development affiliate for Bell Canada and Northern Telecom, Ltd. (much later called NorTel Networks), just across the road from Xerox PARC at Stanford.

I initiated and managed research and advanced development activities in many fields of computer science and communications, with members of my department focusing on networks of personal computers (using a PDP-10 [DEC-20] on ARPAnet, plus Three Rivers PERQs and Wirth's Lilith); graphical user interfaces; digital typesetting; object-oriented systems and programming (Intel iAPX-432 systems, Smalltalk); digital voice-over-IP LANs; SGML (later XML); and extensive research on public-key cryptosystems. I headed the laboratory's university liaison program, funding a number of external university research programs, ranging from computer system architecture to extending Donald Knuth's TEX program for typesetting Arabic scripts.

Northern Telecom Systems Corporation, London, U.K.
Product Marketing Consultant, "Project Vienna"
March 1983—July 1984

At Bell-Northern Research, I had spent six months commuting to Minneapolis for meetings of a small strategy group (codename "Anpac") to decide the global Northern Telecom response to personal computers—first to the early Apple II and IBM PC, but more importantly to what we saw as the near future, networks of graphical personal computers such as my group had been experimenting with at BNR.

After that, I volunteered to join the leaders of a European subsidiary team for a crunch project to create and ship a line of networked personal computer and server products, hardware and software, designed for 9 languages. Within 14 months, we shipped the first Intel-286-based personal computers in Europe, based on Microsoft system and application software (which was how I came to know Bill Gates).

Based on my experiences traveling around the world for this project, and receiving hundreds of presentations from people who used overheads and slides and flipcharts (a few made on computers, most not), I began to think about the possibility of a new application to make presentations using the then-undelivered future graphical personal computers such as Macintosh and Windows—the idea which would later be the basis for PowerPoint.

Education, Self-Directed
1960–1964

I was expelled from high school for showing disrespect of the administration, a charge which was undeniably true. My biggest beef was that they hired a replacement teacher for honors mathematics who refused to continue using my favorite textbook, the then-new *Fundamentals of Freshman Mathematics* by Allendoerfer and Oakley (1st ed. 1959), and who switched to a much dumber math textbook.

I was happy to be expelled indefinitely, and just dropped out permanently. I never completed high school or any equivalent, never took any equivalency test, and nobody ever cared. My scores on national exams gave me admission to universities anyway, and I tried out two of them for one semester each, but I was interested in studying other things. (1960–1961)

I interrupted university for a self-directed three-year program to study libertarian economic theory and history. I began with a year's term as one of the first two residential interns at the Foundation for Economic Education (at that time headed by Leonard Read), located on an estate in Irvington-on-Hudson, New York, just north of New York City. In that first year, I mostly read in their large library the classic books, which were in those days out of print and hard to find, talked with frequent important visitors to the Foundation, and made occasional field trips to visit individualist luminaries such as Rose Wilder Lane. (1961–1962)

The second year, I lived in Manhattan and regularly went to listen to the weekly open seminars of Ludwig von Mises at New York University. More significant to me, during the same period I participated in Murray Rothbard's salon held in his Manhattan apartment, an echo of his "Circle Bastiat" group of a decade earlier. When Rothbard's contemporaneous notes from that period were published in 2007, I found to my surprise that he had mentioned me then as being one of "the nation's leading young libertarians," a comment on how few of us there were in those days. So the second year focused on Rothbard and Mises, and on reading classic books that came up in their discussions. (1962–1963)

In the third year, I attended the Phrontistery, a one-year program in libertarian economics for eighteen students, held at Rampart College in Colorado, where the visiting faculty included a number of scholars from many universities: Milton Friedman, Gordon Tullock, James J. Martin, Ludwig von Mises, Murray Rothbard, F. A. Harper, Bruno

Leoni, G. Warren Nutter, Arthur A. Ekirch, Sylvester Petro, Oscar W. Cooley, and Roger J. Williams.

Murray Rothbard later wrote about this period too, and mentions in his notes that at the Phrontistery "for the first time in public some of the group also unfurled the 'black-and-gold-flag' [one side pure black, the other side pure gold], the colors of which we [the salon in New York] had all decided best represented anarcho-capitalism." The flag belonged to the fellow-Phrontisterian who had sewn it; she and I married two years later, and now, nearly 50 years after it was made, the original historic banner stands in a corner of the library at our home in San Francisco. (1963–1964)

I might well have continued my studies if something like the current Economics Department of George Mason University had existed then, but increasingly I realized that "I came into this world, not chiefly to make this a good place to live in, but to live in it, be it good or bad" (Thoreau, in *Resistance to Civil Government*). So I adopted one of Robert LeFevre's gnomic sayings: "The one who knows what freedom is, will find a way to be free." The road was cleared, and I was going back to the world.

Los Angeles City College, Los Angeles, California
1964–1966

I re-entered conventional higher education at Los Angeles City College, a large and well-established two-year community college located on what had once been the original campus of UCLA in central Los Angeles, where I studied English literature and was selected to be the editor of the campus literary magazine.

University of Southern California, Los Angeles, California
B.A., 1968, in English Literature

I transferred to the University of Southern California as a junior, and joined the honors program in the English Department. There, one of my major advisors was Professor Virginia Tufte, who was particularly encouraging in helping me to gain admission offers from several leading graduate schools. (Her son Edward Tufte, who was about my same age, would later attract a great deal of attention for his important work on presentation of information, and incidentally also for his opinions about PowerPoint.) I was elected to Phi Beta Kappa, and received the Order of the Palm award at graduation.

University of California, Berkeley, California
M.A., 1973, in Computer Science, Linguistics, and English

I was admitted to the Ph.D. program in the English Department at UC Berkeley in 1968. My wife was admitted to the Linguistics Department for a Ph.D. at the same time, and 1968 was an excellent year to arrive in Berkeley. I entered with a Special Career Fellowship from the Ford Foundation for five years of complete support. My intention was to specialize in Shakespeare and follow an academic career teaching literature and linguistics, but before I registered for my first classes, I read in the catalogue and discovered classes in the Computer Science Department (in the College of Letters and Science, spun off from the Math Department).

My advisor, Josephine Miles, the poet, thought that some exposure to computers would be broadening, so I enrolled in a beginning programming class. I was immediately enthralled, took more classes (CDC 6400 assembly language from Butler Lampson was memorable), and soon I formally broadened my program; this was possible because the Special Career Fellowship made me independent of any department.

I was approved to undertake an "individual interdisciplinary Ph.D. program" in the College of Letters and Science, combining all of the individual degree requirements of all of the Computer Science, Linguistics, and English Departments. This was a wise step for the purpose of getting an education, but not necessarily wise for the purpose of ever completing the degree.

Pursuing a Ph.D. in three fields at the same time provided ample excuses for any shortcomings. The computer scientists thought I was reasonably smart, at least for a student whose interests were in such nebulous areas as analyzing literary language and music. The literary people thought I was a tolerable critic, at least for a student whose interests were more in linguistic structure of language and in computer analyses. The linguists thought I had some useful observations, at least for a student whose interests were more in formal languages and literary language than in collecting field data about obscure tribal languages.

Over the next ten years, I passed:

—university Ph.D. language examinations in Latin and in French

—Computer Science Department Ph.D. comprehensive written exam

—Linguistics Department Ph.D. comprehensive written exam

—English Department Ph.D. comprehensive written exam

—Ph.D. oral examination, with examiners from all three departments

—oral defense of topic for Ph.D. dissertation, with examiners from all three departments (at this period, the dissertation defense was conducted after preliminary work and before writing), with the topic "Use of Two-Level van Wijngaarden Grammars for Natural Language Analysis" (Advisor: Charles J. Fillmore).

This completed the requirements for the "Cand. Phil.," which, at the time, was the formal "all but dissertation" degree status for Ph.D. students, with an M.A. degree awarded along the way.

But by 1978, after ten years at Berkeley, I had decided I wanted to write that dissertation far less than I needed to move to Silicon Valley, where I could get the experience to do a software startup for the new single-user personal computers.

These were early days; at the time I felt I had to leave Berkeley, Bill Gates had left Harvard less than three years earlier, and he was then still in Albuquerque, writing software for the MITS Altair (Bill only relocated Microsoft to the Seattle area after I had moved to Silicon Valley). The first Apple II had just been introduced. And just as 1968 had been a great year to move to Berkeley, 1978 was a great year to move to Silicon Valley.

University of California, Berkeley, California
Computer Scientist
July 1973—May 1978

While a graduate student, I co-authored (with Laura Gould) a textbook on programming for linguistic and humanities research, used in courses at Berkeley and Stanford, and in summer sessions for college teachers in the humanities organized by the American Council of Learned Societies. I did extensive consulting with Berkeley faculty members on the use of computers to study literature, languages, arts, and music. I was graphics consultant for the Berkeley Campus Computer Center. I spent some years as chief programmer for Berkeley machine translation research (Chinese to English). I did the programming of ancient Egyptian hieroglyphic fonts and typesetting for the Berkeley Late Egyptian Dictionary. I wrote a program to generate haiku, which was embedded in the idle loop of a campus CDC6400 and became the most prolific poet up till that date, with a selection published in an anthology of computer poetry edited by Richard W. Bailey (*Computer Poems*, 1973).

One of my motivations for choosing Berkeley was Professor Bertrand Bronson in the English Department, who had pioneered the study of the traditional tunes of English and Scottish popular ballads by coding the music and transcribing it to punched cards for analysis on tabulating machines; I was able to help him with computer analyses and concordances. There were many more projects in graphics and music and natural language.

Western Institute of Computer Science, Santa Cruz, California August 1979

In 1979 (after I had joined Bell-Northern Research), I attended the International Course in Programming Methodology, an advanced course in programming taught by Edsger W. Dijkstra. It was taught in a lecture hall with an aisle behind each row of seats. Dijkstra would frequently assign an in-class programming problem, and while we all worked on it, he would walk the aisles behind the seats, looking down over our shoulders at our progress. That course was followed by another course of forty-nine lectures from Dijkstra, C. A. R. Hoare, Ole-Johan Dahl, John Backus, David Gries, and over twenty additional members of IFIP WG2.3, a four-week residential course, held on the campus of the University of California at Santa Cruz, August, 1979.

Dijkstra recorded his own thoughts about the course in his contemporaneous typescript "trip report" (EWD 714), now archived online at the University of Texas: "I found the UCSC [UC Santa Cruz] campus not an inspiring place, and the longer I stayed there, the more depressing it became. ... We had to share the food—and what was worse: also the space in which to consume it—with the participants in other 'educational' activities—such as a cheer-leaders school and a school of American football ... In short: the place breathed an atmosphere of uncivilization." "The audience was of a higher calibre than we had been led to expect ... eight people from various Bell Laboratories [he would have included "Bell-Northern Research" in that category] ... 30 to 40 per cent. could only be described as mathematical illiterates ... ." "... my overwhelming memory from this WG2.3 meeting is the very lousy impression I got from Xerox PARC ... [a place where] research in computing science is primarily viewed as gadget development, rather than as gaining insight."

Twenty-two years after this, Dijkstra was still using a pen to write his own overhead "foils" (transparencies) in his distinctive handwriting, and was thoroughly disapproving of how others had come to use PowerPoint. From another trip report (EWD 1310), this one in the same handwriting, as he prepared to receive an honorary doctorate in Athens, May 2001: "Fortunately I had discovered in time that I had left my prepared foils in Nuenen and the University had provided me with blank ones and pens. I used Wednesday's free moments to make new ones." And a month later, June 2001, after he appeared at a "Software Pioneers" conference in Bonn that featured 16 speakers: "I mention another way of looking at the whole happening, viz. regarding it as a 16-fold confirmation of the ruinous influence of PowerPoint, for the less of it you use, the better your lecture. ... The bloody electronics only encourage the next steps of the replacement of content by form ... ."

Hackers' Conference, Sausalito, California
November 1984

In 1984 (after I had joined Forethought), I was one of about 150 people chosen to spend the whole weekend of November 9–11 at the world's most beautiful repurposed 16-inch gun battery (Fort Cronkhite), on the Marin headlands just north of the Golden Gate, attending the original Hackers' Conference. This meet-up was initiated by Kevin Kelly and Stewart Brand, and designed by Lee Felsenstein, Bill Budge, Andy Hertzfeld, and Doug Carlston, timed to coincide with the publication of Steven Levy's book *Hackers: Heroes of the Computer Revolution*.

Stewart Brand claimed that the invitees were "the most interesting and effective body of intellectuals since the framers of the U.S. Constitution," a claim that escaped criticism from those attending. Invitees paid a flat $90 for the weekend, including conference, round-the-clock food and drink, and dormitory bunks. Steve Wozniak donated $5,000 for videotaping, and scraps of footage from the weekend later became a DVD. The T-shirt design was by Don Knuth's student Scott Kim.

REFERENCES

(Many documents below which are otherwise unpublished can be found online, linked from a directory located at www.robertgaskins.com/powerpoint-history/ along with the full searchable text of this book, incorporating live hyperlinks.)

Adams, Scott. 2007. "Work Pleasure." *The Dilbert Blog*. 27 December, 2007. dilbertblog.typepad.com/the_dilbert_blog/2007/12/work-pleasure.html

Andreessen, Marc. 2007. "Part 3: 'But I Don't Know Any VCs!' " *Pmarca Guide to Startups*. 25 June, 2007. Archived at www.robertgaskins.com/powerpoint-history/documents/andreessen-pmarca-guide-to-startups-2007-jun-25.pdf

Austin, Dennis. 2003. "PowerPoint: Conception, Birth, and Early Childhood." November, 2003.

Austin, Dennis. 2009. "Beginnings of PowerPoint." May, 2009.

Austin, Dennis, and Robert Gaskins. 1985. "Presenter [PowerPoint] Design." 21 August, 1985. www.robertgaskins.com/powerpoint-history/documents/austin-gaskins-powerpoint-design-1985-aug-21.pdf

Austin, Dennis, and Robert Gaskins. 1985. "Presenter [PowerPoint] Output Samples." 21 August, 1985. www.robertgaskins.com/powerpoint-history/documents/austin-gaskins-powerpoint-output-samples-1985-aug-21-1986-feb-21.pdf

Austin, Dennis, Tom Rudkin, and Robert Gaskins. 1986. "Presenter [PowerPoint] Specification." 22 May, 1986. www.robertgaskins.com/powerpoint-history/documents/austin-rudkin-gaskins-powerpoint-spec-1986-may-22.pdf

Belleville, Cathy, Lucy Peterson, and Aniko Somogyi. 1997. "PowerPoint: The First Ten Years." 20 April, 1997. www.robertgaskins.com/powerpoint-history/documents/belleville-peterson-somogyi-gbu-10-year-reunion-1997-apr.pdf

Boettinger, Henry M. 1969. *Moving Mountains: The Art of Letting Others See Things Your Way*. New York and London: Macmillan, 1969.

Bostic, Keith. 1977. "Interview with Scott McNealy." *San Jose Mercury-News*, 3 August, 1997.

Bumiller, Elisabeth. 2010. "We Have Met the Enemy and He Is PowerPoint." *New York Times*, 27 April, 2010.
www.nytimes.com/2010/04/27/world/27powerpoint.html

Dijkstra, Edsger W. 1969. "Notes on Structured Programming." August, 1969.
www.cs.utexas.edu/~EWD/ewd02xx/EWD249.PDF

Dijkstra, Edsger W. 1975. "How Do We Tell Truths That Might Hurt?" 18 June, 1975.
www.cs.utexas.edu/~EWD/ewd04xx/EWD498.PDF

Dijkstra, Edsger W. 1979. "Trip report E.W. Dijkstra, Mission Viejo, Santa Cruz, Austin." 14 September 1979.
www.cs.utexas.edu/~EWD/ewd07xx/EWD714.PDF

Dijkstra, Edsger W. 2001. "Three trip reports rolled into one." 10 September 2001.
www.cs.utexas.edu/~EWD/ewd13xx/EWD1310.PDF

Endicott, Jim. 2000. "Growing Up with PowerPoint." *Presentations*, February, 2000: 61–66.

Evslin, Tom. 2006. *hackoff.com: An Historic Murder Mystery Set in the Internet Bubble and Rubble*. dotHill Press, 2006.

Feith, David. 2009. "Speaking Truth to PowerPoint." *Wall Street Journal*, 31 July, 2009.
online.wsj.com/article/SB10001424052970204619004574318473921093400.html

Foster, Donald W. 2001. *Author Unknown: On the Trail of Anonymous*. New York: Holt, 2001.

Gaskins, Robert. 1984. "Presenter [PowerPoint] Original Proposal." 14 August, 1984.
www.robertgaskins.com/powerpoint-history/documents/gaskins-powerpoint-original-proposal-1984-aug-14.pdf

Gaskins, Robert. 1986. "Presenter [PowerPoint] Marketing Analysis." 27 June, 1986.
www.robertgaskins.com/powerpoint-history/documents/gaskins-powerpoint-marketing-analysis-1986-jun-27.pdf

Gaskins, Robert. 1986. "Presenter [PowerPoint] New Product Summary and Review." 15 July, 1986.
www.robertgaskins.com/powerpoint-history/documents/gaskins-powerpoint-summary-and-review-1986-jul-15.pdf

Gaskins, Robert. 1986. "Presenter [PowerPoint] Status Update." 14 August, 1986.
www.robertgaskins.com/powerpoint-history/documents/gaskins-powerpoint-status-1986-aug-14.pdf

Gaskins, Robert. 1987. "Forethought Future Business Strategy." 25 May, 1987.
www.robertgaskins.com/powerpoint-history/documents/gaskins-forethought-strategy-1987-may-25.pdf

Gaskins, Robert. 1987. "History of Forethought Since the Restart." 25 May, 1987.
www.robertgaskins.com/powerpoint-history/documents/gaskins-history-of-forethought-1987-may-25.pdf

Gaskins, Robert. 1987. "Lessons from the Experience of the Restart." 25 May, 1987.
www.robertgaskins.com/powerpoint-history/documents/gaskins-lessons-of-restart-1987-may-25.pdf

Gaskins, Robert. 1987. "Response to Microsoft." 1 June, 1987.
www.robertgaskins.com/powerpoint-history/documents/gaskins-response-to-microsoft-1987-jun-01.pdf

Gaskins, Robert. 1987. "Response to Microsoft, Extended." 15 June, 1987.
www.robertgaskins.com/powerpoint-history/documents/gaskins-response-2-to-microsoft-1987-jun-15.pdf

Gaskins, Robert. 1988. "Results of Microsoft's Graphics Business Unit after Our First Year." 8 August, 1988.
www.robertgaskins.com/powerpoint-history/documents/gaskins-gbu-first-year-report-to-microsoft-1988-aug-08.pdf

Gaskins, Robert. 1992. "Photos of GBU on Sand Hill Road, 1992" (PowerPoint presentation; ".pps" is a self-running slideshow, ".ppt" is a conventional PowerPoint presentation). 1992.
www.robertgaskins.com/powerpoint-history/documents/gaskins-gbu-photos-sand-hill-road-1992.pps
www.robertgaskins.com/powerpoint-history/documents/gaskins-gbu-photos-sand-hill-road-1992.ppt

Gaskins, Robert. 2002. Interview by Peter Day. "Power Mad." BBC Radio 4, London. 10 February, 2002. www.robertgaskins.com/powerpoint-history/documents/bbc-power-mad.mp3

Gaskins, Robert. 2002. Transcript of interview by Peter Day. "Power Mad Transcript." BBC Radio 4, London. 10 February, 2002. www.robertgaskins.com/powerpoint-history/documents/bbc-power-mad-transcript.pdf

Gaskins, Robert. 2007. "PowerPoint at 20: Back to Basics." *Communications of the ACM* 50, no. 12 (December 2007): 15–17. On the web at www.robertgaskins.com/powerpoint-history/documents/gaskins-powerpoint-at-20-cacm-vol50-no12-dec-2007-p15-p17.pdf

Gaskins, Robert. 2012. "Comments on Dilbert's History of PowerPoint." 2012. www.robertgaskins.com/powerpoint-history/documents/gaskins-comments-on-dilbert-history-of-powerpoint.pdf

Gaskins, Robert, and Dennis Austin. 2002. Interview by Steffan Heuer. "The Revolutionaries of the Office." *Brand Eins* (March 2002). Translated by Susan Grabau. www.robertgaskins.com/powerpoint-history/documents/brand-eins-the-revolutionaries-of-the-office-trans-susan-grabau.pdf

Gaskins, Robert, and Laura Gould. 1972. *Snobol4: A Computer Language for the Humanities.* Berkeley, CA: University of California, 1972. On the web at www.robertgaskins.com/files/gaskins-gould-cal-snobol4-1972.pdf

Gates, Bill. 1991. "Market Share of Applications in the United States." 19 February, 1991. www.robertgaskins.com/powerpoint-history/documents/gates-memo-on-office-1991-feb-19-comes-px00577.pdf

Gerstner, Jr., Louis V. 2002. *Who Says Elephants Can't Dance? Inside IBM's Historic Turnaround.* New York: Collins, 2002.

Gold, Rich. 2002. "Reading PowerPoint." In *Working with Words and Images: New Steps in an Old Dance,* edited by Nancy Allen, 256–270. Westport, Connecticut: Ablex Publishing, 2002. (Gold's chapter was written in 1999). Archived at www.robertgaskins.com/powerpoint-history/documents/gold-reading-powerpoint-1999.pdf

Gordon, Michael. 2010. "Does the Military Overuse PowerPoint?" 28 April, 2010.
www.military.com/opinion/0,15202,214244,00.html

Gould, Laura. 2007. *Cats Are Not Peas: A Calico History of Genetics.* 2nd ed. Wellesley, Massachusetts: A K Peters Ltd., 2007.

Graham, Paul. 2005. "Why Smart People Have Bad Ideas." April, 2005.
www.paulgraham.com/bronze.html

Graham, Paul. 2006. "The 18 Mistakes That Kill Startups." October, 2006.
www.paulgraham.com/startupmistakes.html

Graham, Paul. 2008. "Six Principles for Making New Things." February, 2008.
www.paulgraham.com/newthings.html

Graham, Paul. 2008. "Why There Aren't More Googles." April, 2008.
www.paulgraham.com/googles.html

Graham, Paul. 2009. "Apple's Mistake." November, 2009.
www.paulgraham.com/apple.html

Graham, Paul. 2010. "The Top Idea in Your Mind." July, 2010.
www.paulgraham.com/top.html

Gralla, Preston. 2010. "Microsoft turns 35: Best, worst and most notable moments." *ComputerWorld.* 24 March, 2010.
www.computerworld.com/s/article/print/9173238/Microsoft_turns_35_Best_worst_and_most_notable_moments

Greenberg, Andy. 2010. "The Underground Art of PowerPoint." *Forbes*, 10 May, 2010.
www.forbes.com/2010/05/10/microsoft-software-iphone-technology-powerpoint.html

Guernsey, Lisa. 2001. "Learning, One Bullet Point at a Time; Pupils Who Can't Even Spell 'PowerPoint' Can Use It as Slickly as Any C.E.O." *New York Times.* 31 May, 2001.
www.nytimes.com/2001/05/31/technology/learning-one-bullet-point-time-pupils-who-can-t-even-spell-powerpoint-can-use-it.html

Guyon, Janet. 2011. "John Sculley on Apple's Jobs and the Experience of a Lifetime." *Wall Street Journal*, 13 September, 2011.
online.wsj.com/article/SBB000142405311190328570457656604208131 21788.html

Hillesley, Richard. 2007. "PowerPoint: A pig through the python." *Tux Deluxe.* 16 March, 2007.
www.tuxdeluxe.org/node/38

Hiltzik, Michael A. 1999. *Dealers of Lightning: Xerox PARC and the Dawn of the Computer Age.* New York: HarperCollins, 1999.

Housman, A. E. 1969. "Swinburne." *American Scholar*, 1969: 59–79. (Written 1910.)

Isaacson, Walter. 2011. *Steve Jobs.* New York: Simon and Schuster, 2011.

Jaffe, Greg. 2000. "What's Your Point, Lieutenant? Please, Just Cut to the Pie Charts." *Wall Street Journal*, 26 April, 2000. online.wsj.com/article/SB956703757412556977.html

Jobs, Steve. 1985. "Steve Jobs and NeXT." *Entrepreneurs* (video). www.youtube.com/watch?v=sOlqqriBvUM#!

Kosslyn, Stephen M. 2007. *Clear and to the Point: Eight Psychological Principles for Compelling PowerPoint Presentations.* New York: Oxford University Press, 2007.

Linzmayer, Owen W. 2008. *Apple Confidential 2.0.* San Francisco: No Starch Press, 2008.

Lucky, Robert W. 1998. "The World According to PowerPoint." *IEEE Spectrum*, January 1998: 17. Archived at www.robertgaskins.com/powerpoint-history/documents/lucky-robert-w-the-world-according-to-powerpoint-ieee-spectrum-1998.pdf

Maples, Mike. 2004. "An Interview with Mike Maples (OH 387)." Edited by Nathan Ensmenger. Charles Babbage Institute, Center for the History of Information Processing, University of Minnesota, Minneapolis. 7 May, 2004. conservancy.umn.edu/bitstream/107465/1/oh387mm.pdf

McManis, Chuck. 2011. Comment on *Hacker News.* 24 March, 2011. news.ycombinator.com/item?id=2364307

Microsoft Corporation. 1987. "Microsoft Letter of Intent for Forethought." 13 May, 1987. www.robertgaskins.com/powerpoint-history/documents/microsoft-letter-of-intent-for-forethought-1987-may-13.pdf

Miller, Stephen. 2010. "Max Palevsky 1924–2010; Computer Pioneer Turned Investor, Activist." *Wall Street Journal.* 7 May, 2010. online.wsj.com/article/SB10001424052748703686304575228630504567558.html

Morland, D. Verne.1976. "Computer Generated Stereograms." *Computer Graphics* (SIGGRAPH-ACM), 14–16 July, 1976. www.roi-learning.com/dvm/pubs/articles/stereo/index.html

New York Times. 1987. "Microsoft Buys Software Unit." 31 July, 1987. www.nytimes.com/1987/07/31/business/company-news-microsoft-buys-software-unit.html

Norvig, Peter. 2000. "The Making of the Gettysburg PowerPoint Presentation." January, 2000. www.norvig.com/Gettysburg/making.html

Norvig, Peter, and Stephen M. Kosslyn. 2010. "A Tool Only As Good as the User." *New York Times, Letters to the Editor.* 30 April, 2010. www.nytimes.com/2010/04/30/opinion/l30power.html

Ornstein, Severo M. 2002. *Computing in the Middle Ages: A View From the Trenches 1955–1983.* 1st Books Library, 2002.

Ozzie, Ray. 1985. "Windows 1.0 Press Kit." 20 November, 1985. www.docs.com/8NAK

Ozzie, Ray. 2005. "The Internet Services Disruption." 28 October, 2005. www.ozzie.net/docs/the-internet-services-disruption/

Parker, Ian. 2001. "Absolute PowerPoint." *New Yorker.* 28 May, 2001: 76–87.

Peterson, W. E. ("Pete"). 1994. *Almost Perfect: How a Bunch of Regular Guys Built WordPerfect Corporation.* Rocklin, California: Prima Publishing, 1994. Extended version on the web at www.wordplace.com/ap/

Placke, Jim. 2011. "PowerPoint Pogue's Homepage." *NBC (Nuclear, Biological, and Chemical) Links.* 22 November, 2011. www.nbc-links.com/powerpoint.html

Raikes, Jeff. 2010. *The Jeff Raikes Story: Part Two.* Microsoft Developer Network Channel 9 video. 8 April 2010. channel9.msdn.com/series/history/the-history-of-microsoft-the-jeff-raikes-story-part-two

Reynolds, Tess. 2006. "The Harvard Graphics Story." Computer History Museum, Corporate Histories Collection. 18 August, 2006. corphist.computerhistory.org/corphist/view.php?s=stories&id=302&PHPSESSID=ee784131a507bea027d90c96f07b64c1

Ries, Eric. 2011. *The Lean Startup.* Crown Business, 2011.

Rudkin, Tom. 1987. "Appearance of PowerPoint under Windows and Presentation Manager." 5 October, 1987. www.robertgaskins.com/powerpoint-history/documents/rudkin-windows-powerpoint-first-spec-1987-oct-05.pdf

Rudkin, Tom. 2012. "Forethought Before PowerPoint 1.0." April, 2012.

Sequoia Capital. 2011. "Writing a Business Plan." 22 November, 2011. www.sequoiacap.com/ideas

Shirley, Jon. 1990. "Looking Back on Seven Years with Microsoft." *MicroNews* (Microsoft employee newsletter), June 1990: 4–6; July 1990:4–6.

Smith, Douglas K., and Robert C. Alexander. 1999. *Fumbling the Future: How Xerox Invented, then Ignored, the First Personal Computer.* San Jose: toExcel, 1999.

Swaine, Michael. 1991. "Calling Apple's Bluff." Interview with Dave Winer. 1 September, 1991. www.drdobbs.com/article/print?articleId=184408623

Trower, Tandy. 2010. "The Secret Origin of Windows." 8 March, 2010. www.technologizer.com/2010/03/08/the-secret-origin-of-windows

Tufte, Edward R. 2003. Bulletin Board. "The End of the Carousel Slide Projector?" 18 September, 2003. www.edwardtufte.com/bboard/q-and-a-fetch-msg?msg_id=0000n8

Tufte, Edward R. 2003. *The Cognitive Style of PowerPoint.* 1st ed. Cheshire, Connecticut: Graphics Press LLC, 2003.

Tufte, Edward R. 2006. *The Cognitive Style of PowerPoint: Pitching Out Corrupts Within.* 2nd ed. Cheshire, Connecticut: Graphics Press LLC, 2006.

University of Chicago, Booth School of Business. "Fulltime Admission, Essay Questions and Slides." 27 January, 2012. www.chicagobooth.edu/fulltime/admissions/essays_slides.aspx

Waldrop, M. Mitchell. 2001. *The Dream Machine: J. C. R. Licklider and the Revolution That Made Computing Personal.* New York: Viking, 2001.

Wikipedia. "Genigraphics." 22 November, 2011. en.wikipedia.org/wiki/Genigraphics (accessed November 22, 2011)

Winer, Dave. 1988. "Outliners and Programming." 1988. davewiner.userland.com/outlinersProgramming

Winer, Dave. 1999. "From the It Could Have Been Me Department." 28 August, 1999. www.scripting.com/1999/08.html

Winer, Dave. 2010. "Microsoft Rejection Letter, 1987." 10 April, 2010. www.scripting.com/stories/2010/04/10/microsoftRejectionLetter19.ht ml

Wolff, Michael. 1998. *Burn Rate: How I Survived the Gold Rush Years on the Internet.* New York: Simon and Schuster, 1998.

Y Combinator. 2012. "Application Form Winter 2012." www.ycombinator.com/apply.html

Zuckerman, Laurence. 1999. "Words Go Right to the Brain, but Can They Stir the Heart?" *New York Times.* 17 April, 1999. www.nytimes.com/1999/04/17/arts/words-go-right-brain-but-can-they-stir-heart-some-say-popular-software-debases.html

INDEX OF NAMES